The Riddle of Barack Obama

THE RIDDLE OF
BARACK OBAMA

A Psychobiography

Avner Falk

 PRAEGER

AN IMPRINT OF ABC-CLIO, LLC
Santa Barbara, California • Denver, Colorado • Oxford, England

Library of Congress Cataloging-in-Publication Data

Falk, Avner.
 The riddle of Barack Obama : a psychobiography / Avner Falk.
   p. cm.
 Includes bibliographical references and index.
 ISBN 978-0-313-38587-2 (hardcover : alk. paper) — ISBN 978-0-313-38588-9 (e-book)
 1. Obama, Barack—Psychology. 2. Presidents—United States—Biography. I. Title.
 E908.3.F35 2010
 973.932092—dc22
 [B]
                              2010016626

ISBN: 978-0-313-38587-2
EISBN: 978-0-313-38588-9

14   13   12   11   10   1   2   3   4   5

This book is also available on the World Wide Web as an eBook.
Visit www.abc-clio.com for details.

Praeger
An Imprint of ABC-CLIO, LLC

ABC-CLIO, LLC
130 Cremona Drive, P.O. Box 1911
Santa Barbara, California 93116-1911

This book is printed on acid-free paper ∞

Manufactured in the United States of America

CONTENTS

PREFACE

Thank you for reading this book. As you may see, I have put an inordinate amount of time, effort, thought, and emotion into writing it. As you begin to read it, you may notice that this book differs from the dozens of books already published about Barack Obama in several ways. For one thing it is, to my knowledge, the only psychological biography so far of the 44th U.S. president, and it is written by a professional clinical psychologist. *Inside Obama's Brain* by the British Jewish journalist Sasha Abramsky is an attempt at a "psychological profile writ large" of Obama (Abramsky, 2009, p. 10), but it is not a biography; it is not written by a psychologist, psychiatrist, or psychoanalyst; and its author admires his "enigmatic" subject (Abramsky, p. 253) so much that he fails to see any of his weaknesses, errors, or emotional problems. However great a leader, Obama is not a superman; he is all too human, and no human being is problem free.

For those who can read it correctly, Obama's memoir *Dreams from My Father* is a treasure trove of psychological information about its author. Not only is it a fascinating account of Obama's lifelong struggle with his image of his father and the consolidation of his identity as a result of that struggle, it also contains at least two actual dreams that the young Obama recalled having about his father. Unfortunately, the strict rules of fair-use quotation have prevented me from quoting those dreams verbatim and have allowed me only short verbatim quotations from the memoir, as well as from Obama's other book, *The Audacity of Hope*. I encourage you, my reader, to look up those two books whenever possible, especially when Obama's actual dreams are discussed.

This book is written by an Israeli Jewish psychologist who, unlike Obama, is non-American and non-Christian but who has always been keenly interested in the United States. I received my graduate education and professional training in clinical psychology in the United States and have visited it several times after returning to my home country of Israel. I seek to understand America both from the inside and from the outside. I like my subject, Barack Obama, empathize with him, and even identify with him, while at the same time also recognizing his human frailties. I am well aware that this confession may expose me to charges of a lack of objectivity, or even of unconscious projection, but in my view there is no such thing as an objective or a definitive biography. Biographers choose their subjects for a variety of personal reasons, such as the conscious quest for wealth or fame, but they are also motivated by unconscious forces, such as an identification with, idealization of, fanatical rejection of, or ambivalent attitude toward their subject. Some biographers tell their own life story vicariously by writing the biography. A good biographer strives to be aware of his personal motives for writing the biography (Baron & Pletsch, 1985).

As an Israeli, I naturally have thoughts and feelings about President Obama's handling of my country's conflict with the Palestinian Arabs. Many Israeli Jews on the left of the political spectrum are happy about the pressure that Obama has brought to bear on Israel to end its occupation of the Palestinian Arab lands, halt its settlement activity in those territories, and help create a Palestinian Arab state in these areas. They hope that Obama will finally end our tragic and interminable conflict with the Arabs and bring peace to our war-torn region. At the same time, many Israeli Jews on the political right, which controls the Israeli government at this time, are quite upset about what they see as Obama's moving America away from its traditional support of Israel to an even-handed or even pro-Arab position. As in my book on the Arab-Israeli conflict (Falk, 2004) and my other books, I do not take sides in this dispute but rather seek to understand the conscious and unconscious psychological motives behind each party's view.

Writing a biography is a hazardous occupation. In a positive or laudatory biography, the subject may serve as a vehicle through which the biographer unconsciously seeks to shore up his own self-esteem through projective identification with his subject. In a negative or derogatory biography, the subject may serve as an unconscious container for the biographer's unconscious externalizations of what he or she dislikes about himself or herself. A good psychological biography is well balanced, though not necessarily ambivalent, with the biographer trying to see his subject's psychological strengths as well as his weaknesses, and being able to read between the

lines of the subject's writings, speeches, and actions, using his psychoanalytic understanding and experience (Moraitis, 1985).

While this book is the fruit of rigorous scholarship, I have attempted to
write it in a nonscholarly fashion, using as few technical terms as possible,
and explaining those that I had to use in simple English. I hope you find
reading this book as exciting as I have found writing it.

Avner Falk
Jerusalem, Israel, June 2010

ACKNOWLEDGMENTS

This book would not have been possible but for the unwavering support of my old friend, colleague, editor, and mentor Ömer Vamık Djemal Volkan, MD, a man of many honors and titles. He is the Senior Erik H. Erikson Scholar at the Austen Riggs Center in Stockbridge, Massachusetts; the current president of the American College of Psychoanalysts; a former president of the International Society of Political Psychology; a professor emeritus of psychiatry at the University of Virginia; a training and supervising analyst emeritus at the Washington Psychoanalytic Institute; a former director of Blue Ridge Hospital in Charlottesville, Virginia, and of the Center for the Study of Mind and Human Interaction at the University of Virginia; and the author of 30 books in psychoanalysis, psychohistory, psychobiography, psychogeography, and political psychology, which are also my own fields of scholarship. Professor Volkan read an early version of the manuscript of this book and strongly encouraged me to write it.

I am also deeply indebted to my editors at Praeger, Robert Hutchinson, Valentina Tursini, and Erin Ryan, and to my copy editors and production manager at Apex CoVantage, for their invaluable comments, patience, assistance, persistence, suggestions, and guidance in the preparation of the manuscript of this book. They have helped me avoid many scholarly pitfalls and greatly improve my manuscript.

Any errors of fact or interpretation in this book, however, are mine alone, and I should be grateful to you, my reader, for correcting me. As the ancient Roman philosopher Seneca the Younger said, *Errare humanum est, sed perseverare diabolicum.*

INTRODUCTION

In the summer of 2008 a momentous and revolutionary event occurred in U.S. political history. A 47-year-old senator from Illinois, Barack Hussein Obama, the only African American member of the U.S. Senate, was elected by the U.S. Democratic National Convention as its nominee for president of the United States. This was the first time a black American had ever been nominated for this office, the highest office in the world's mightiest country. This brilliant African American was the son of a bright but self-destructive Kenyan father, who had died in a tragic Kenyan car accident in 1982 after losing his job and his legs and struggling with wife abuse, child abuse, and alcoholism, and a bright but immature white mother who had died of cancer in 1995.

Soon the young Obama was leading the public-opinion polls as the candidate most likely to become president, with a 10-point lead over his 72-year-old Republican rival, John McCain. On November 4, 2009, Obama was elected president of the United States, the first African American president in U.S. history. There had been nothing like it in U.S. history. On January 20, 2009, Obama took the oath of office as the 44th president of the United States. The young British Jewish journalist Sasha Abramsky (born 1972), who lives in the United States, thinks it a testament to his subject's extraordinary charisma that an African American named Barack Hussein Obama, whose last name rhymed with the first name of America's public enemy number one, Osama Bin Laden, and whose middle name was the same as the last name of America's public enemy number two, Saddam Hussein, could be elected to this office (Abramsky, 2009, p. 75).

While Abramsky is not a psychologist, psychiatrist, or psychoanalyst, he has psychological intuition. Webster's dictionary defines *intuition* as "quick and ready insight…the power or faculty of attaining to direct knowledge or cognition without evident rational thought and inference." (Mish, 2009). Another good definition of intuition is "when you know something but don't know how you know it." Abramsky's book *Inside Obama's Brain* was published as I was completing the manuscript of this book, and its publication presented me with a new challenge: I had to read his book and quote his psychological statements about our common subject, either agreeing with them or disputing them. Abramsky thinks that "writing a book about a figure as enigmatic as President Barack Obama is every political writer's fantasy" (2009, p. 253). I agree with him that Obama is enigmatic: This is why this book is titled *The Riddle of Barack Obama*. Whether or not Abramsky has cracked this enigma is another question. You can tell by reading both his book and mine.

Unlike this one, Abramsky's book is not a biography: it is a series of chapters, each dealing with an aspect of Obama's character or life. A list of the chapter titles will give you an idea of what Abramsky's book is about "Focus," "Looking Inward," "Reaching Outward," "Sense of History," "Self-Confidence," "Poise," "Tackling Race Head-On," "Curiosity," "Thinking Outside the Box," "The Smooth Politician," "The Iowa Caucus," "The Inspirer," "Team of Rivals Redux," "The Leader," and "A New Morning." One of the problems with Abramsky's book, however, is that it is almost totally laudatory and that he sees almost nothing but Obama's psychological strengths and almost none of his weaknesses, as if Obama were a superman with no emotional conflicts or problems. Obama is human, and, as such, he is not immune to "the heartache and the thousand natural shocks that flesh is heir too," as the great William Shakespeare put it (Shakespeare, *Hamlet*, Act 3, scene 1).

Character strength is a key issue in modern psychology. There are dozens of schools in psychology, of which I shall be concerned primarily with two: *psychoanalysis* and *positive psychology*. The term *positive psychology* could make you think that other psychological schools, and perhaps psychoanalysis in particular, are schools of "negative psychology." Nothing could be farther from the truth. The two schools are neither mutually exclusive nor contradictory. While positive psychology focuses on human strengths and virtues, psychoanalysis by no means restricts itself to the study of psychopathology, human weaknesses, human suffering, character defects, personality disorders, and emotional illness. Modern psychoanalysis also deals extensively with ego strength, reality testing, integrity, the true self, and other aspects of the healthy, well-adjusted, and well-functioning personality.

Nonetheless, while this book is primarily a psychoanalytic biography of Obama, it is also useful to examine Obama from the viewpoint of the positive-psychology school, founded by Martin E. P. Seligman (born 1942), an American psychologist who, perhaps due to his own personal development, gradually moved from studying the psychology of helplessness, depression, and death (Seligman, 1975) to studying the psychology of emotional health, optimism, and happiness (Seligman, 1991, 2002). Seligman and his colleague Christopher Peterson (born 1950) wrote the *Character Strengths and Virtues* handbook, the first serious attempt in psychology to identify and classify the healthy psychological traits of human beings (Peterson & Seligman, 2004). It is quite interesting to compare Obama's character strengths and virtues as identified by Abramsky with those of the *Character Strengths and Virtues* handbook.

Just as the *Diagnostic and Statistical Manual of Mental Disorders* of the American Psychiatric Association classifies emotional and mental disorders by their names and symptoms, the *Character Strengths and Virtues* handbook provides a theoretical framework for the practical applications of positive psychology by identifying six classes of core virtues, each made up of four character strengths, which can be assessed by psychological tests, questionnaires, and other psychological methods (Peterson & Seligman, 2004). The *Character Strengths and Virtues* handbook is the obverse, or the other side of the coin, of the *Diagnostic and Statistical Manual*: it deals with mental wellness rather than with mental illness. We cannot understand human beings without studying both their psychological strengths and their psychological weaknesses.

Some scholars think that the *Character Strengths and Virtues* handbook is culture-specific, in that it applies to U.S. culture and is not valid in others. Others think that the character strengths and virtues are valued by the vast majority of cultures throughout history and that these traits lead to increased happiness when acquired and practiced. The positive-psychology claim of universality for its character strengths and virtues means not only that positive psychology tries to broaden the scope of psychological research to include mental wellness as well as mental illness but also that the leaders of the positive-psychology movement are challenging the cultural and moral relativism of psychoanalysis and anthropological psychiatry, suggesting that human strengths and virtues are universal and may even have a biological basis.

Without necessarily agreeing with this broad claim to cultural universality on the part of the positive-psychology school, I shall use its tools to shed light on my American subject, Barack Obama. The positive-psychology list of character strengths and virtues can be summarized in six core categories:

1. *Wisdom and Knowledge:* creativity, curiosity, open-mindedness, love of learning, and perspective
2. *Courage:* bravery, persistence, integrity, and vitality

3. *Humanity:* love, kindness, and social intelligence

4. *Justice:* citizenship, fairness, and leadership

5. *Temperance:* forgiveness and mercy, humility, prudence, and self-control

6. *Transcendence:* appreciation of beauty and excellence, gratitude, hope, humor, and spirituality (Peterson & Seligman, 2004, pp. 29–30)

Abramsky thinks that Obama has many, if not all, of these character strengths and virtues.

These "character strengths and virtues" are intimately connected to what Obama himself calls his "values" (Obama, 2006a, pp. 53–84). Many of these character strengths and virtues are character traits that are valued as virtuous either by the society in which we live or by positive psychologists like Seligman and Peterson. Obama himself is so deeply concerned with values that he devoted a whole chapter to them in his book *The Audacity of Hope.* I shall try to explore in this book how he came by his values and by his virtues.

Which of these character strengths and virtues of the healthy and happy individual, then, does Obama actually have? Many psychological and political observers of the 44th president of the United States would agree with Abramsky that he has quite a few, or even most, of these character strengths and virtues. Unless you believe Obama haters and conspiracy theorists like Jerome Corsi (2008), David Freddoso (2008), Webster Tarpley (2008a, 2008b), Bernard Goldberg (2009), or Michelle Malkin (2009), Obama certainly has empathy, compassion, fairness, emotional and social intelligence, generosity, and kindness. He also has great self-confidence, incredible perseverance, and "fierce ambitions" (Obama, 2006a, p. 243).

Obama's humor is another very important character strength and virtue. His extraordinary stand-up comedy acts at the White House Correspondents Association's dinner on May 9, 2009, at the Kennedy Center Honors dinner on December 6, 2009, and again at the White House Correspondents' Association Dinner on May 1, 2010, showed a highly developed and exquisite sense of humor, in which he beautifully sublimated his anger at his subordinates and others into jabs, teases, and jokes. Indeed, it is primarily thanks to these character strengths and virtues that he became president of the United States. Despite his "reckless" mother (Ripley, 2008), his abandonment by his father, his mother's remarriage, his "boisterous" maternal grandfather whom he loved but who became unemployed and depressed when Obama was 10 years old, and his extraordinarily complicated childhood and adolescence, Obama has succeeded in building himself into a psychologically healthy, active, and happy individual, who, with his character strengths and virtues, has attained the highest political office in the country that is still considered the leading economic, military, and cultural power in our world.

At this point I should like to draw your attention to an important distinction in first names between Obama and his father. While Obama's online birth certificate (whose number is blotted out) gives his father's name as Barack Hussein Obama and his own name as Barack Hussein Obama II, his father's original first name was in fact *Barak* rather than Barack: we know this from an article that he published in the *East Africa Journal* upon his return from the United States to Kenya (Obama, 1965). In this book, I shall consistently refer to the father as Barak and to the son as Barack. None of Obama's other biographers seems to have paid any attention to this seemingly trivial matter, which, to me, is quite important psychologically, for, throughout Obama's life, his ambivalent identification with his father has been a major psychological issue.

This book is a study in applied psychoanalysis, and more specifically in psychobiography (Falk, 1985, 2007). Many conservative historians, political scientists, and biographers dislike psychoanalysis and do not want psychologists or psychiatrists dabbling in their field. Yet human action cannot be understood or explained by applying the commonsense psychology used by conventional historians. Nonetheless, applying psychoanalytic knowledge to politics, biography, or history is a tricky business. There are many scholarly pitfalls on the way: the best known of them is reductionism, the reduction of complex psychological phenomena to a single cause in a person's childhood such as an unresolved Oedipus complex. Rudolph Binion (1976), for example, reduced Hitler's genocidal madness to Freud's repetition compulsion or what Binion called traumatic reliving.

Like everything important that we do, political action is *overdetermined*—the product of many different and complex processes, social, personal, public, historical, economic, cultural, racial, familial, and psychological. These processes interact, and one cannot understand human activity without considering all of them. The method must therefore be *interdisciplinary*, and the leader's personal development must always be considered along with the leader's cultural, political, historical, and social background. While it is crucial for us to understand what happened to the leader in his family of origin, in his early-life development, in his infancy, childhood, and adolescence, it is also important to understand all the other forces that shaped his personality and gave him his strengths and virtues.

Like any other scholarly work in history, biography, and politics, this study uses all the available primary sources on Obama's personal and political development: his letters, memoirs, books, speeches, and actions, as well as published interviews with him and with people who have known him, and their letters and memoirs. It also uses well-researched secondary sources about Obama, such as David Niven's pocket biography (2009) and Abramsky's psychological portrait (2009).

While it may seem to us that the personal is divorced from the political, in fact there is an intimate relationship between the two. The political leader acts out his personal feelings, thoughts, wishes, and conflicts on the public scene, in which political entities such as the party, the city, the state, or the country may take on parental and other personal roles in his unconscious mind. At times the country that he leads may play the role of the early or idealized mother in his unconscious and even conscious feelings. At other times his nation may play the role of the extended family, or one of his mentors or preachers may play the role of the father.

While narcissism is a key psychological ingredient of political leadership, and most charismatic leaders are narcissistic, *there are different kinds of narcissistic leadership:* the constructive and the destructive, the high level and the low level, the healthy and the pathological. Unlike destructive narcissistic leaders like Hitler, Stalin, or Mao, who derived their sense of self-worth, power, and superiority from putting others down, humiliating them, or murdering them, creative, constructive, reparative, and high-level narcissistic leaders like Napoleon Bonaparte (Falk, 2007), Mustafa Kemal Atatürk (Volkan & Itzkowitz, 1984), and Obama receive their narcissistic gratification from raising others to their own level rather than from putting others down, hurting them, or killing them. Abramsky observes that Obama "radiates confidence... in the ability of the country to adapt to his presence and to his ideas" (2009, p. 87).

This book uses Obama's memoir *Dreams from My Father* as its chief primary source. Obama himself admitted in his introduction to that book that "for the sake of compression" he had created "composites" of some of the people he had known and that "some events appear out of precise chronology" (1995, p. xvii). He added that "the names of most characters have been changed for the sake of their privacy." Was he also acting on legal advice to avoid being sued by any of his characters? In fact, Obama's memoir is a *roman à clef*. Journalists and scholars have uncovered the real names of many of his characters (Boylan, 2008; Calmes, 2009; Essoyan, 2008; The Irish Times, 2009; Goldman & Tanner, 2008; Helman, 2008; Hoover, 2007; Jorgensen, 2006; Lakshmanan, 2008; Littwin, 2007; Ramos, 2008; Scharnberg & Barker, 2007; Smith, 2008; Springen, 2008; Sweet, 2007; Tapper, 2008; Thanawala, 2008; Wills, 2008). I have used those real names in this book whenever appropriate.

This study is not designed to explore each of the strengths and virtues of Obama's personality separately: rather, it explores the personal life history that gave him his capacity for leadership and the psychological strengths and virtues that make up his character. If you find any weaknesses or conflicts in his personality, why, that is merely human, and his ability to achieve what he has attests to his emotional power to overcome such weaknesses.

Much like the *Diagnostic and Statistical Manual*, which outlines psychiatric symptoms and syndromes without explaining their etiology, the *Character Strengths and Virtues* handbook lists character traits and virtues but does not explain how they come about, what the developmental psychological processes are that create strong, happy, and virtuous individuals. It would take considerable probing into a person's life history and application of psychoanalytic knowledge to understand and explain how these come about. This is what this book aims to do. I realize that this no modest undertaking, even though my ambitions may not be as "fierce" as those of my subject (Obama, 2006a, p. 243).

Indeed, like any top political leader, Obama has great ambition, yet he also has humility, calmness under pressure, extraordinary self-control, and moderation. He knows that he is superior to most people yet often describes himself as "one of you," and he often makes people feel that way, too. That Obama could attain such an extraordinary achievement despite what we shall see was a difficult early psychological background attests to his emotional strength and intelligence. Despite his unusual and in some ways unhealthy family-of-origin background, as we shall see, Obama created for himself a psychologically healthy family with a bright, successful, able, and caring wife and two happy daughters. He is doing well politically despite fierce opposition from "Tea Party" types. It is therefore vital to ask the psychological question, how did this young man from a broken family reach this extraordinary achievement and status at such a young age, rather than become a marginal, wayward youth? What emotional stuff is he made of? How did he overcome his early abandonment by his father? And did it have to do with his quest for power and his achievement of it?

Abramsky thinks that, to Barack Obama, the 16th president of the United States, Abraham Lincoln (1809–1865), Obama's chief historical identification figure, is "a man of many ghosts": the great debater, the reluctant pragmatist, the oratorical master, and the idealist (2009, p. 59). Similarly, during the presidential election campaign of 2008 the editors of *Time* magazine called Obama "a man of five faces": the face of the black man, the face of the healer, the face of the novice, the face of the radical, and "the face of the future" (Von Drehle, 2008). The U.S. historian David Brinkley thinks that Obama sees his "polyglot" life story as a modern-day equivalent to the vision of the 26th president of the United States, Theodore Roosevelt (1858–1919), who saw the American West as a physical space within which to heal the North–South divide after the American Civil War (1861–1865). Brinkley believes that Obama sees his own task as healing the black-white divide and generating a new multiracial space in America (Abramsky, 2009, p. 50).

One might add some more faces to those outlined by *Time:* the face of the unifier, the face of the pacifier, the face of the hope giver, the face of the mediator, the face of the conciliator, the face of the realist, the face of the idealist, the face of the community builder (see Abramsky, 2009, p. 53). Human nature does not play by the rules of logic. Some of Obama's faces may seem contradictory, but together they make up the man. In fact, much more than these faces makes Obama what he is. A man this complex and successful is not easy to decipher. He is unique, and his biography cries out for a psychoanalytic interpretation. We need to look below the surface and try to decipher not only his conscious mind but also his unconscious in order to understand how Obama came to be what he is. Given the extraordinarily high hopes pinned on him not only by his own people but by the entire world, he is bound to disappoint some of us. Let us therefore try to decipher this extraordinary and fascinating man through the lens of psychoanalysis.

Chapter 1

"GRAMPS" AND "TOOT"

Synopsis: Barack Obama's maternal grandfather, Stanley Dunham, whom Barack called "Gramps," found his mother dead when he was eight years old. She had committed suicide. Unable to mourn his terrible loss, he unconsciously denied his grief and through this psychological defense developed a restless hypomanic personality. At one point during his adolescence he punched his high school principal in his rage, was expelled from the school, and began riding trains back and forth across the United States. Gramps later became a fast-talking and restless furniture salesman, moving his family to various states numerous times. When his only child was born a daughter, he was sorely disappointed, for he had wanted a boy, and he named her Stanley Ann after himself. The pattern of emotional abandonment went on through the generations. Gramps was jovial and loved his grandson, and he was a father figure to him, but he later declined, disappointing the adolescent Barry. His wife, Madelyn, whom Barack affectionately called "Toot" and "Tutu," was more stable but also more rigid, and she had touch of racism as well, which became apparent in her attitude to black people. Along with his busy mother, these two people raised Barack during his adolescent years in Hawai'i, and his ultimately negative identification with them was part of his prolonged struggle to establish his own racial, ethnic, religious, and other identities.

Barack's maternal grandparents were crucial in his life in at least two ways: First, they gave birth to his mother, whose character and relationship with him in his early life shaped his entire development, and, second, they raised him at different times in his infancy, childhood, and adolescence as if he were their own son. Barack fondly called his white maternal grandfather Gramps and liked him very much as a boy. However, Gramps suffered from a self-destructive hypomanic personality disorder. In clinical psychology, psychiatry, and psychoanalysis, *hypomania* designates a mood state characterized by a persistent and pervasive "high" and irritable mood, and the thoughts and behavior patterns consistent with such a mood state. Hypomanic people have a "flight of ideas" (a rapid flow of thoughts) and a decreased need for sleep and rest, are extremely outgoing and daring, and have a great deal of energy.

Unlike patients suffering from psychotic mania, hypomanic personalities are fully functioning: Gramps was a successful furniture salesman for many years. The hypomanic personality disorder differs from psychotic mania by the absence of delusions and hallucinations and by its lower degree of impact on the patient's functioning. In psychiatry, hypomania is a feature of bipolar disorder (manic-depressive illness), cyclothymia, and schizoaffective disorder. Hypomania can also have a benefit in creativity and productive energy. Many people with hypomanic personalities consider it the gateway to their success, and a vast number of creative people have experienced hypomania or other symptoms of bipolar disorder. The classical symptoms of hypomania include mild euphoria, the flight of ideas, endless energy, and a desire and drive for success.

The downside of hypomania, however, is that it conceals a denial of depression, an unconscious psychological defense. This was the defense that the eight-year-old Gramps fell back on when he discovered his mother's body after her suicide. When this defense broke down due to reverses in his life, Gramps became enraged and depressed, and even had suicidal thoughts. Barry was aware of Gramps's unrealistic ambitions and, after Barry returned from Indonesia, he noticed Gramps's personal and professional decline, depression, and instability (Obama, 1995, p. 15). Barry was disappointed in his grandfather, and, during his adolescent years, he constantly fought with Gramps. He later believed that this struggle had taught him empathy (Obama, 2006a, p. 80). His white maternal grandmother, Madelyn, whom he affectionately called Tutu or Toot, had a rigid but strong and stable personality and had a quiet but powerful influence on the young Barry, who called her "a rock of stability" (Obama, 2006a, dedication).

It would therefore be useful and important to study the personalities and life histories of Barack's maternal grandparents, and even those of their parents. Barack's maternal great-grandfather, Ralph Waldo Emerson Dunham (1894–1970), a Kansas coffeehouse owner and auto mechanic who during World War II worked for Boeing Aircraft, was named after the great

American philosopher Ralph Waldo Emerson (1803–1882). This may have expressed the impossibly high expectations Ralph's parents had for him, which he could never fulfill. On October 3, 1915, the 21-year-old Ralph married the 15-year-old Ruth Lucille Armour, a teenager from Illinois (born September 1, 1900) whose family had moved to Kansas. A teenage bride, mother, and housewife, Lucille later killed herself as a result of the conflict and strife in her marriage to Ralph.

Was it a shotgun marriage? Was she pregnant? Lucille gave birth to their first son in August 1916, when she was not yet 16. He was named Ralph Waldo Emerson Dunham, Jr., after his father, a narcissistic gesture on the father's part. Their second son, Stanley Armour Dunham (1918–1992), Barack's maternal grandfather, was born on March 23, 1918, and received his mother's maiden name as his middle name. Psychologically, the first son, Ralph, was the father's son, whereas the second, Stanley, was the mother's.

In the 1920 U.S. federal census of Sedgwick County, Kansas, of which Wichita is the seat, Ralph and Lucille Dunham and their two sons were found living with Lucille's parents, the Armours. In 1930, the children Ralph Jr. and Stanley were living with their maternal grandparents in Butler County, Kansas, of which El Dorado is the seat, while their father, Ralph Sr., was living with his own parents in Sedgwick County. In between these two dates, Stanley had suffered a terrible loss and trauma: His mother killed herself on November 25, 1926, when she was 26 and he was only eight years old. She had committed suicide after several years of strife and rage at her womanizing husband, and in the throes of a severe depression.

Ralph could never fulfill his parents' impossible expectations of him, while his unhappy wife Lucille paid the price for his feelings of inferiority and abandonment by his parents, which he tried to assuage by womanizing. Whether Lucille had been a "good enough mother" to her two sons, in the terms of the British psychoanalyst Donald Woods Winnicott (1896–1971), is uncertain, as she may herself have been a needy child who felt abandoned by her parents when they gave her away at the age of 15. Winnicott's good-enough mother empathizes with her baby and tries to provide what the infant needs, but she also leaves a time lag between the demands and their satisfaction, and progressively increases it. "The good-enough mother...starts off with an almost complete adaptation to her infant's needs, and as time proceeds she adapts less and less completely, gradually, according to the infant's growing ability to deal with her failure" (Winnicott, 1971, p. 12).

Barack knew about the suicide of his maternal grandfather's mother and its effect on his grandfather, who had become hypomanic after his mother killed herself (Obama, 1995, p. 14). Even before his mother's suicide, the boy Stanley must have felt the pain of the strife between his parents. His mother may also have confided in him his father's unfaithfulness to her. In his memoir, the adult Barack empathized with his grandfather's pain at this terrible loss and trauma. He understood that his grandfather lived in his fantasies, that he unconsciously or subconsciously identified his own personal suffering with that of black Americans, that, like Barack himself, he had been abandoned by his own father, that people talked about his mother who had "gone away," and that as a child he had been abused by other children, who called him a "wop," the derogatory American slang term for an Italian American (Obama, 1995, p. 21).

In fact, of course, Barack's great-grandmother had not "gone away": she had killed herself, and this act of abandonment marked her son for life. For the rest of his life, he was restless and hypomanic, he moved his family numerous times, and his career suffered many reverses. After his daughter Ann and her son Barry left Hawai'i for Indonesia in 1967, Gramps declined, losing his job and becoming depressed.

Barack's memoir dwelled on his beloved Gramps and Toot with little mention of their own parents. Yet at the age of eight, Gramps had had the terrible misfortune of discovering his mother's dead body. He must have been deeply shocked and traumatized, enraged at his mother for abandoning him, profoundly hurt, and depressed. The traumatized, abandoned, enraged, and grieving boy Stanley suffered a further trauma soon thereafter, when his father regressed emotionally, abandoned his family, and went back to live with his own parents (Meacham, 2008). Stanley and his elder brother Ralph were sent to live with their maternal grandparents—the very same thing that would happen to his grandson Barack.

The eight-year-old Stanley had thus lost both his parents in rapid succession. This was too painful for him. Unable to mourn his losses, Stanley's grief and bereavement, through the unconscious defensive psychological process of denial, were replaced by hypomanic aggression, restlessness, rebellion, and violence. He became loud, boisterous, aggressive, quick to anger, and violent. Meacham, 2008; Obama, 1995, p. 14). He became a rebel and a drifter, a charmer and a dreamer. He was described as "gregarious, friendly, impetuous, challenging and loud" and as a manipulative furniture salesman "who could charm the legs off a couch" (Jones, 2007).

Stanley rebelled against his parent's strict Baptist faith and against many other accepted social traditions. In 1940, when he was 22, the gregarious Stanley, who came from a blue-collar Baptist family, met the 18-year-old Madelyn Lee Payne (1922–2008), a strictly brought-up, stable, but rigid and reserved Wichita girl from a white-collar Methodist family, whom he married and who became Barack's white grandmother (Niven, 2009, p. 9). Madelyn had been born in Peru, Kansas, the daughter of Rolla Charles

Payne and Leona McCurry Payne. In Barack's memoir, he described his maternal great-grandparents as stern Methodists who brought up their children in a strict fashion, forbidding life's pleasures to them (Obama, 1995). There was a strange blend of masculinity and femininity in the family. Both Madelyn Lee and her father Rolla Charles bore names that could be either masculine or feminine. Barack's mother would also get a masculine name.

Brought up strictly and puritanically, at the age of three, Madelyn moved with her parents to Augusta, Kansas. She was one of the best students in her high school graduating class in 1940. Despite her strict Methodist upbringing, she liked to go to Wichita, Kansas, to see big-band concerts. While in Wichita, she met the Kansas-born Stanley from the oil town of El Dorado, Kansas, who was from the other side of the railroad tracks. Stanley attended El Dorado High School. The lower-class orphan Stanley courted his girlfriend Madelyn even though her parents, who were Methodists and middle class, disapproved.

The boy Barry seems to have had mixed feelings about his Tutu. On March 18, 2008, during his presidential campaign, following the surfacing of the controversial videos of Barack Obama's racist antiwhite pastor Jeremiah Wright, Jr., he delivered a speech on race relations in Philadelphia's Constitution Center, entitled "A More Perfect Union." In that speech Obama described his maternal grandmother as something of a racist but claimed that he could no more disown her or the Reverend Wright than he could the black American community (Obama, 2008, p. 58).

Two days later, in an interview on Philadelphia's WIP radio station, Senator Obama explained this remark about his grandmother's racism by saying that she did not really "harbor racial animosity" but that she was "a typical white person" who feared people she did not know. He added that white fear of blacks was an inbred reaction and that it was part and parcel of American society. Obama's use of the phrase "typical white person" made headlines, as he seemed to say that white people were inbred racists. It was first highlighted by the *Philadelphia Daily News* (Gross, 2008) and then picked up by political commentators for *The Huffington Post*, ABC News, and other mass-communication media. In a CNN interview with Larry King, a famous American television interviewer, the latter asked Senator Obama to clarify his "typical white person" remark. Obama replied that white people in America typically fear street crime by black people and have negative inbred stereotypes of black people. Obama paid tribute to his grandmother, saying that she had helped raise him and that he loved her (Mucha, 2008).

Was Madelyn racist and enlightened at the same time? The marriage of Stanley to Madelyn took place on May 5, 1940, just as Madelyn was graduating from high school, against her parents' wishes. In fact, the marriage occurred on the night of Madelyn's high school prom (Jones, 2007). In the United States a *prom*, which is short for *promenade*, is a formal black-tie dance or a gathering of high school students, held at the end of senior year to celebrate their high school graduation.

During the first two years of their marriage, Stanley and his wife Madelyn had no children. They kept their marriage secret, to avoid provoking the wrath of their parents. Madelyn only told her parents that she was married after she got her high school diploma in June 1940 (Jones, 2007). Why did they wait two years to have a child? Was it because Stanley, who had lost his mother as a child, feared to lose his wife or child as well? In any event, he wanted a boy, but he had a girl. With his emotional, hypomanic character, he was deeply disappointed. Barack's mother had to start her life in 1942 with the heavy burden of her father wanting her to be a boy.

Defying the disapproval of Madelyn's parents, then, the young couple married in 1940 and, according to their grandson, they eloped just before the Japanese attack on Pearl Harbor in late 1941 (Obama, 1995, p. 15). In January 1942 Stanley enlisted in the U.S. Army as a private at Fort Leavenworth, Kansas, while his wife Madelyn worked on a Boeing Aircraft bomber-assembly line in Wichita, Kansas. Stanley, however, remained at Fort Leavenworth that year and was not deployed to Europe until 1943, and Madelyn became pregnant in February 1942. Their daughter, Stanley Ann Dunham Obama Soetoro (1942–1995), was born on November 29. Stanley served with the U.S. Army's 1830th Ordnance Supply and Maintenance Company, Aviation, rising to the rank of sergeant. During the Allied invasion of German-occupied Normandy in June 1944, his unit helped support the Ninth Air Force, an air force unit in the U.S. Air Combat Command. The Allied invasion began on June 6, 1944, better known as D-Day. *D-Day* is a term used in military parlance to denote the day on which a combat attack or operation is to be initiated. After two years of military service in Europe (1943–1945), where he saw no real combat, Stanley was discharged from the U.S. Army at Fort Leavenworth on August 30, 1945.

In 1944, before the Allied invasion of Normandy, Stanley and his older brother, Ralph Jr., met by chance in London's Russell Hotel when Ralph was staying there and Stanley came for rations. Ralph took part in the Allied invasion of Normandy, while Stanley went on serving in his ordnance unit. Ralph landed at Normandy's Omaha Beach on June 10. The Ninth Air Force was deployed to France on June 16. Along with the Eighth Air Force, the Ninth Air Force had to destroy the German *Luftwaffe* in the air and on the ground so as to bring about complete Allied air supremacy in Normandy and elsewhere prior to D-Day and after it. Operational missions involved attacks on rail marshaling yards, railroads, airfields, industrial plants, military installations, and other German targets in France, Belgium, and the Netherlands. Other targets were German Atlantic Wall defenses along the English Channel coast of France.

After the war, the restless, nomadic, and hypomanic Stanley kept moving around the United States. At first he found work as a furniture salesman in El Dorado, Texas, but soon moved his family to California, where he enrolled at the University of California at Berkeley under the G.I. (Government Issue) Bill, which provided free education for U.S. war veterans. Soon, however, Stanley dropped out of school, which may have exacerbated his feelings of failure. He then moved his family to Oklahoma, then to Texas, then back to Kansas, where Stanley managed a furniture store, then, according to Barack, to several Texan towns, and then to Seattle, Washington, where Ann finished high school. She was called Ann by those who liked her but teased as "Stan" by those who didn't. They finally settled in Hawai'i in 1960 (Obama, 1995, p. 15).

In fact, Ann had wanted to go to Chicago rather than to Hawai'i. In 1959, when Ann was still 16, she had been accepted by the University of Chicago, but her father would not let her go there on her own (Obama, 1995, p. 123). She, however, nonetheless went to Chicago as an *au pair* girl, living with a Chicago family and taking care of their children in exchange for room and board and a small allowance. It was the first time she ever lived outside of her parents' house. In 1960 she graduated from high school, and her family moved to Hawai'i, where she attended the University of Hawai'i at Manoa. Manoa is the name of a valley and also of a residential neighborhood of the city and county of Honolulu, and it was home to the flagship campus of the University of Hawai'i.

At the University of Hawai'i in Manoa, Ann met the Kenyan student Barak Hussein Obama (1936–1982) and presumably married him in 1961, in Hawai'i's Maui County, when she was already pregnant with his child. There is some evidence, however, that they were not married at the time of Barack's birth in August 1961 and that Ann left Hawai'i for Seattle with her baby boy shortly after giving birth to him (Corsi 2009a, 2009b; A. Klein, 2009; LeFevre, 2009). Ann's father, the hypomanic, restless, boisterous, and tempestuous Stanley, who often lived in fantasy as much as in reality, styled himself a freethinker. He apparently raised no objections to his daughter's marriage to Obama and cherished his grandson Barack.

Chapter 2

A GIRL NAMED STANLEY

Synopsis: *When Stanley Ann Dunham was born in November 1942, her father Stanley had so much wanted a boy, and was so immersed in himself, that he named her Stanley Ann. As she grew up, Ann had to get used to the pain of being called "Stanley" or "Stan" by those who disliked her or wished to tease her. She grew up a special, intelligent, unconventional, eccentric, feminist girl, with no boyfriend in high school, while idealizing black people and foreigners. After she attended the special Mercer Island High School on Lake Washington, her father moved the family to Hawai'i, where Ann attended the local university. She quickly fell in love with a black Kenyan student named Barak Obama, who already had a wife and children back in Kenya. She became pregnant by him, married him, and had their only son, Barack, in August 1961, when she was not yet 19. She had many strengths and virtues, including honesty, courage, and empathy, but she was also immature in her idealization of her narcissistic and abusive Kenyan husband. He abandoned his wife and son when he left for Harvard University in 1963, and the following year he and Ann divorced. Barack thus lost his father when he was two years old, a fact that marked him for life. Among other things, he had to be his mother's comfort in her emotional pain.*

Let us go back to February 1942, when Madelyn Dunham conceived her first and only child, the future Stanley Ann Dunham Obama Soetoro. Madelyn's husband Stanley Dunham had enlisted as a private in the U.S. Army on January 18 at Fort Leavenworth, Kansas. With his military unit, he and his wife lived in Fort Leavenworth, where their daughter was born on November 29. Stanley Dunham named her Stanley Ann, after himself. The name expressed his wishes and expectations for her, and Ann's psychological destiny, therefore, was in some ways to try to be both a girl and the boy that her father had wanted her to be. Ann was a strong-willed girl, and her parents were rebellious, progressive, and non-conventional. Her father had joined the army, and her mother worked at a Boeing Aircraft plant in Wichita, Kansas.

On April 5, 1945, Charles Payne (born 1925), a younger brother of Ann's mother Madelyn and thus a maternal great-uncle of Barack, was among the U.S. soldiers of the U.S. 89th Infantry Division who liberated the German death camp at Ohrdurf, a satellite of the notorious Buchenwald forced-labor and concentration camp, outside Weimar. On June 5, 2009, U.S. President Barack Obama, during his visit to Buchenwald, a day before he helped commemorate the 65th anniversary of D-Day, in France, said that his great-uncle had been so traumatized by the horrors he saw at Ohrdurf that he could not speak for months thereafter. Payne himself had just told this to a German news magazine (Payne, 2009).

At the end of World War II, in the summer of 1945, when Ann was barely three, Stanley returned to Kansas, where he was discharged from the U.S. Army. He moved his family to California, where he studied at the University of California at Berkeley, but he soon dropped out. They then moved to Texas, then to Oklahoma, then back to Kansas, and then to Seattle, Washington, where he was a furniture salesman and his wife worked at a bank, and finally to Hawai'i. We shall examine the grandparents' lives in greater detail later when discussing their daughter, Barack's mother, and the life of Barack himself.

While Barack's Kenyan father and his absence were crucial to his emotional development, psychoanalysts regard the mother and her early relationship with her baby as crucial to the development of the personality and emotions. This is the first and most important physical and emotional relationship in our life, and its effect on the individual's development is incalculable. Let us take a close look, then, at Barack's extraordinary mother, her personality, and her emotional relationship with her son.

Stanley Ann Dunham Obama Soetoro (1942–1995) was a special and formidable woman, but her life was complex, fraught with difficulties and pain, and at times tragic. She was twice married and twice divorced, and she died of cancer at the age of 53. Ann was the only child of Stanley Armour Dunham and Madelyn Lee Payne Dunham. She was born in Kansas during World War II, while her father was serving in the U.S. Army, and her mother was working at the Boeing Aircraft plant. Stanley had wanted a son to bear his name. Perhaps he did not want women because the woman he had most loved and trusted, his mother, had abandoned him by killing herself.

So, when Ann was born, she was given her father's first name, Stanley. The matter of masculine and feminine given names in Ann's family of origin is complex and fascinating. Just as Ann's mother Madelyn had an ambiguous middle name, Lee, Ann's first name was Stanley, after her hypomanic father, who had wanted a son and was deeply disappointed when his daughter was born. He named her Stanley, which expressed his wish for a boy. To be a girl, the little Stanley Ann had to struggle against a father who wanted her to be a boy. At the same time, her father was a crucial influence and an ambivalent identification figure for her. She is referred to as Ann in some documents and as Stanley Ann in others. When she went to college in Hawai'i in 1960, she called herself Ann, dropping her first name. In 1992 she signed her Ph.D. dissertation S. Ann Dunham, even though she had been married and divorced twice and had two more last names (Dunham, 1992). In other words, Ann kept going back to her father's name, however ambivalently.

What kind of parenting did Ann receive? Ann's mother, Madelyn, was a "rock of stability," as her grandson put it, but also a rigid, strict, and pedantic woman. She was a career woman who was often promoted at her job but a relatively reserved mother, as opposed to her hypomanic and boisterous husband, who was warm, loving and effusive, and at times explosive. Barack has described his grandmother as "quiet yet firm," in contrast to his "boisterous" and oft-drinking grandfather, whom he described as "jolly" and emotional. Barack affectionately called him Gramps and his grandmother Toot. Both Madelyn and her daughter Ann were to die of cancer—the daughter first, in 1995, and the mother much later, in 2008. Curiously, in his memoir, Barack passed over his mother's birth in 1942 in total silence (Obama, 1995, p. 15). Sasha Abramsky believes that despite Barack's "protestations of filial love for his mother," he loved her less than it seems (Abramsky, 2009, pp. 42–43). This view is confirmed by Barack's discussion of his mother's immaturity in his memoir (Obama, 1995, pp. 123–125).

In fact, Barack seems to have loved his maternal grandmother more than he did his mother. To Barack, Ann's mother was Toot or Tutu (Hawai'ian for "grandmother"), the grand matron of her family. She died of cancer in Hawai'i just before Barack's election as president. On the night of November 2, 2008, in Hawai'i (November 3, 2008, in the continental United States), the Obama campaign announced that Barack's maternal grandmother, Madelyn Dunham, had "died peacefully after a battle with cancer" in Hawai'i. Barack and his half sister, Maya Kassandra Soetoro-Ng, released a statement saying that "she was the cornerstone of our family, and a woman of extraordinary accomplishment, strength, and humility." (Zeleny, 2008a). At his final election rally in Charlotte, North Carolina, on November 3, Barack Obama said, "She was one of those quiet heroes that we have all across America. They're not famous. Their names are not in the newspapers, but each and every day they work hard. They aren't seeking the limelight. All they try to do is just do the right thing." (Zeleny, 2008a).

Yet Ann seems to have identified more with her hypomanic and boisterous father, whose first and last names she bore, than with her quiet yet firm, pedantic, and strict mother, the "rock of stability." Barack called his mother "reckless" (Ripley, 2008). Had Madelyn done the right thing when she defied her own parents on her prom night to marry the lower-class Stanley from the other side of the tracks? The Paynes were Methodists, while the Dunhams were Baptists. Unlike the white-collar Paynes, the Dunhams were a blue-collar family. In 1953–1954, when she was 11 years old, Ann suffered from severe asthma, a disease with psychosomatic components. This may have been her reaction to emotional events in her family, including the frequent moves, over which her parents may well have argued heatedly.

The illness made Ann an eccentric loner, who was "teased mercilessly for her name" and was called "Stanley Steamer" or "Stan the Man" (Obama, 1995, p. 19). Ann withdrew into herself, perhaps burying her anger and humiliation in her loneliness. Racism was rampant at that time. When Ann befriended a black girl at school and invited her to her home, she was taunted by the other schoolchildren as a "nigger lover" and a "dirty Yankee." One of the kids threw a stone at the black girl and at Ann, who were lying side by side on the grass in Ann's courtyard. Ann was rescued by her mother, but the black girl was shaking, and Toot's eyes shone with tears. She invited the two girls inside her home. Enraged at what the white children had done, Gramps went to speak to the school principal and called the parents of the offending children to "give them a piece of his mind." They told him to tell his daughter that "white girls don't play with coloreds in this town" (Obama, 1995, pp. 19–20).

Indeed, white racism was so widespread and black anger so deep that by 1954 race relations were coming to a boiling point in the United States. The U.S. Supreme Court made a landmark decision in the case of *Brown vs. Board of Education* to desegregate U.S. schools and to force segregationist schools, colleges, and universities to accept "Negroes" as well as "white" people. Yet in reality blacks feared to apply, and schools persisted in their segregation. Less than 1% of black schoolchildren in the southern United States attended integrated schools, and the University of North Carolina admitted three black students in 1955 and four in 1960. In 1961 two black students were admitted to the University of Georgia. Even at Columbia University in New York, no more than five blacks were enrolled in 1960. During the 1950s, Harvard Law School had no more than two or three blacks in its graduating class each year. U.S. politics, including the executive, the legislature, and the judiciary, were equally race-segregated (Niven, 2009, p. 5).

Meanwhile, in Ann's family, there were endless dramas and disloca-tions. Gramps was a warm-hearted but hypomanic man with a hot tem-per, and Ann's relationship with her father was strained. Stanley was unstable, crude, and ham-fisted, an abusive father at times, and Ann was often angry at him or ashamed of him (Obama, 1995, p. 21). Ann grew into an eccentric, different, special girl. In 1955, when Ann was not yet 13 and going into the seventh grade, her parents moved with her to Seattle, Washington, where Gramps worked as a furniture salesman for the Standard-Grunbaum Furniture Company.

In Seattle, the Dunhams rented an apartment in the Wedgwood Estates in Seattle's Wedgwood neighborhood so that Ann could attend the Nathan Eckstein Middle School, on the border of Seattle's Wedg-wood and Bryant neighborhoods. It was named after Nathan Eckstein, a German-born Jewish Seattle businessman, school board member, and former director of the Seattle public schools. The school was originally opened as a junior high school in 1950 but later became a middle school, where a group of two to eight teachers from different disciplines worked as a team with the same group of students of the same grade level, each teacher teaching a different subject. This format facilitated interdisci-plinary studies, where the teaching team teaches the same topic from the perspective of different disciplines. The middle-school philosophy also advocated assigning students in each team to a homeroom. By hav-ing their homeroom daily for various discussions and activities, middle schools try to foster a sense of belonging in students to ease social and emotional tensions during the students' early adolescence. The Nathan Eckstein Middle School is still known for its strong academic program, vast elective offerings, and award-winning music programs.

Ann's studies at the Nathan Eckstein Middle School did not last very long, however. In 1956 her parents moved to the Shorewood Apartments on Mercer Island, a Seattle suburb, so that their daughter could attend the new Mercer Island High School on Lake Washington, which had just opened. There, progressive teachers taught open-minded students the importance of challenging social norms and questioning authority. Ann's liberalism was encouraged by her parents and by the Unitarian Church that she attended (Niven, 2009, p. 9). Ann, with her idealistic and defiant char-acter, was a natural liberal. She became a lifelong feminist, liberal, rebel, and maverick. During her son's presidential campaign in 2008, a Seattle journalist interviewed her former classmates:

> As a suburb, Mercer Island was still in its infancy. The 1950 census counted about 5,000 people, almost all white. Sanctioned deer hunts had stopped just a few years before the Dunhams arrived. Stanley Ann Dunham's classmates, many of whom had lived on the island their whole lives, viewed Dunham as a novelty. "She had a really ironic sense of humor, sort of downbeat and she was a great observer," said Iona Stenhouse, of Seattle, a former classmate. "There was an arched eyebrow, or a smile on her face about the immaturity of us all. I felt at times that Stanley thought we were a bit of a provincial group." (J. Martin, 2008)

Did Ann feel superior to the other students? Was this an unconscious defense on her part, or was she really superior? In fact, Ann was immature herself (Obama, 1995, pp. 123–125), yet her former classmates at Mercer Island High School believed that Barack had "inherited" his mother's "uncommon" character. Certain it is that as a child he partially identified with her, as she was the most important adult in his early life. In psychoanalytic terms, the infant and child Barry (as Barack Obama was known during his childhood and adolescence) internalized or introjected his image of his mother. Ann Dunham, as her name was then, for her part ambivalently identified with her father. At times she used the name Stanley Ann, and at other times she signed her name S. Ann Dunham. She took the Mercer Island High School lessons personally and seriously. She deeply felt that she didn't have to be like every other girl—in fact, she could even be like the boy her father had wanted her to be. She didn't have to date or marry or have children. Unlike the other girls, she apparently had no boyfriend in high school (J. Martin, 2008). A former classmate remembered her as "intellectually way more mature than we were and a little bit ahead of her time, in an off-center way" (Jones, 2007).

Chip Wall, another former classmate of Ann's, said, "She was not a standard-issue girl of her times ... She wasn't part of the matched-sweater-set crowd ... If you were concerned about something going wrong in the world, Stanley would know about it first ... We were liberals before we knew what liberals were." (Jones, 2007). Yet another former classmate of Ann's has called her "the original feminist" (Ripley, 2008). She was unconventional and eccentric. She was also described as quiet, cerebral, and fearless. Indeed, Ann was courageous. But, as her son later discovered, she was also emotionally immature, difficult, stubborn, and reckless. Ann was an only child, which exacerbated her psychological predicament, as her father had no other child to fill the role of the son he craved, so that she had to be that boy.

In the summer of 1960, after Ann graduated from Mercer Island High School, the peripatetic Dunhams left Seattle and moved to Honolulu, Hawai'i, where her father obtained a new salesman's job. Not yet 18, Ann enrolled in college at the University of Hawai'i at Manoa, majoring in anthropology, being greatly interested in people of other cultures than hers. In college, she "quickly moved into the orbit of an older group of opinionated, left-leaning graduate and international students, including the charismatic and politically sophisticated [Barak] Obama" (Niven, 2009, p. 9). As we shall see, the emotionally immature Ann had wild-eyed, idealized images of free, happy, singing and dancing black people, such as were seen in the Brazilian carnival in the film *Black Orpheus* (*Orfeu Negro*), by the French director Marcel Camus, which was released in 1959 and which she saw soon after its release (Obama, 1995, pp. 123–125).

In the leftist, international orbit at the University of Hawai'i at Manoa, the 18-year-old Ann quickly met and fell in love with the 24-year-old Kenyan student Barak Hussein Obama (1936–1982), whom she soon married in 1961, after he got her pregnant. His first name meant "blessing" in Swahili. We know that his first name was Barak rather than Barack from an article that he published in the *East Africa Journal* after his return to Kenya (Obama, 1965). He was the school's first African student under the Airlift Africa program initiated in 1959 by the prominent Kenyan politician Thomas Joseph Odhiambo Mboya (1930–1969) of the Luo tribe.

Mboya had developed a close relationship with Kwame Nkrumah of Ghana, who, like Mboya, was a Pan-Africanist. In 1958, during the All-African Peoples' Conference in Ghana, convened by Nkrumah, the 28-year-old Mboya was elected as the conference chairman. Barak Obama came to Hawai'i in 1959, the year in which Hawai'i was admitted to the American union as a state, while Kenya became independent in 1963—the year Barack Obama was abandoned by his Kenyan father. Kenya's first president was the Kikuyu Kamau wa Ngengi (1894–1978), better known as Jomo Kenyatta. He was an autocrat, and he did not like any challenge to his authority from his ministers or from anyone else. The Luo had to settle for the second-fiddle role.

The Luo Mboya became Kenya's minister of justice and constitutional affairs, and later its minister for economic planning and development, but he was tragically assassinated in 1969, possibly at the orders of Kenyatta himself, who saw the ambitious Mboya as a rival and a threat to his own rule. Barak Obama's fate was also tragic. After he returned to Kenya in 1965, he criticized Kenyatta's government publicly, getting himself in serious trouble with Kenyatta. This would lead to his blacklisting, unemployment, alcoholism, ruin, road accidents, the loss of his legs, and finally his untimely death (Obama, 1995, pp. 214–215).

Chapter 3

A PATERNAL GRANDFATHER
NAMED "THE TERROR"

Synopsis: *The Obama family saga and tragedy can be traced back to Barack Obama's paternal grandfather, Hussein Onyango Obama (1895–1979), of the Luo tribe, who was among the major causes of his son Barak's emotional troubles and tragic life. Onyango, who converted to Islam and took an Arabic name, was hard, punitive, and violent, and a very difficult and emotionally castrating father. He was mean, suspicious, tyrannical, and very proud, and he got himself in trouble with the British colonial rulers in Kenya, whom he served. He was a cook and servant for the British army. His wife Akumu, the mother of his son Barak, ran away from him, abandoning her two children, Sarah and Barak. Barak was raised by Onyango's third wife, Sarah Onyango Obama (born 1922), whom Barack called "Granny" in his memoir. Barak's abandonment by his mother affected him deeply.*

In his memoir, Barack wrote that his father was born "in a place called Alego" on the shores of Lake Victoria in Kenya (Obama, 1995, p. 9). In fact, Barak Hussein Obama was born in 1936 in the village of Kanyadhiang, outside Kendu Bay, some 27 miles south of Kisumu, on the shores of Lake Victoria. He was raised in the village of Nyang'oma Kogelo, which is part of the larger Alego. The area of Alego, and particularly Kogelo, was notorious for its medicine men or witch doctors and was nicknamed *Alego tat yien* (Swahili for "Alego roof of medicine"). This name was given to Alego because of its people's wide knowledge in traditional medicine, witchcraft, and charms. Normally, their medicine and charms were not used to harm others but to protect the innocent from evildoers. The languages spoken in Alego at that time were Luo, Swahili, and English.

Barack's paternal grandfather, Onyango, was in fact an emotionally disturbed man, whom his family called "the Terror" (Obama, 1995, p. 369). The dates of Onyango's birth and death are recorded in his grandson's memoir (Obama, p. 376). Some sources give different birth and death dates (1870–1975), but they may be erroneous. Onyango was so abusive toward his wives and children that his granddaughter Auma, Barack's favorite half sister, blamed him for her family's problems (Obama, p. 371). When his grandson Barack visited Onyango' ancestral village in 1988, he found an old British registry book from about 1930 saying that his grandfather had been living in the port city of Kisumu, in Nyanza Province, on Lake Victoria, and was already missing six of his teeth at the age of 35 (Obama, pp. 425–426).

After converting to Islam, at an unknown date, and taking the Arabic first name of Hussein, Onyango had several wives. His first wife was named Helima, but he had no children by her. Next, he married a young Luo woman named Akumu, who did not love him and who had been promised to another man. She took the Arabic name of Habiba ("beloved" in Swahili) when she converted to her husband's religion of Islam. Onyango had two children by Akumu: Sarah and Barak. Akumu loved another man, and she did not love the hot-tempered Onyango. She was rebellious, and there was much strife between her and her domineering husband. She eventually ran away from Onyango, abandoning her two children. In 1938 Onyango married a 16-year-old woman named Sarah—his first daughter's namesake—and he later claimed to have married a white woman in Burma while there with the British army during World War II (Obama, 1995, pp. 375, 403–408).

Barack's father, Barak Hussein Obama, born in 1936, was thus the second child and eldest son of Onyango and his second wife, Akumu. The Obamas were members of the Luo tribe, a major Kenyan ethnic group and the chief rival of the Kikuyu (other tribes in Kenya include the Kalenjin, Maasai, Kamba, and Meru). Onyango raised his son Barak as a Muslim, but at an early point in his life Barak became an atheist. He was a goatherd and a student (Obama, 1995, p. 9; 2004). His relationship with his father, who was a harsh and violent disciplinarian, was strained, and he was also abandoned by his mother, who divorced his father when he was a child.

Onyango traveled widely, enlisting in the British military in Kenya and visiting Europe, Arabia, India, Burma (now Myanmar), Ceylon (now Sri Lanka), and Zanzibar (now Tanzania). In 1939, when World War II broke out and his son Barak was three years old, Onyango went to Burma as a cook to a British officer. His third wife, "Granny" Sarah, went to live with his wives Akumu and Helima, and life was easier. In 1942 Onyango returned home to Kenya with the picture of the white woman whom he claimed to have married in Burma. Some time later he decided to move his family from Kendu Bay back to Alego (Obama, 1995, pp. 408–409). While still living near Kendu Bay, Barak attended the Gendia Primary School and moved to Ng'iya Intermediate School once his family relocated to Siaya District.

Onyango was born into an animist Luo family, which, like other African animists, revered the spirits of its ancestors. He was "a prominent farmer, an elder of the [Luo] tribe, [and] a medicine man with healing powers" (Obama, 1995, pp. 408–409). He briefly converted to Christianity and took the last name of Johnson, but soon thereafter converted to Islam, which suited his male-supremacy beliefs much better. He was circumcised and took the first name of Hussein. He worked as a cook and butler for important white men like Lord Delamere and for *Wazungu* missionaries in Nairobi (Obama, pp. 370, 401, 407). Lord Delamere was Hugh Cholmondeley, the Third Baron Delamere (1870–1931), the successor to the Delamere baronetcy in the English county of Cheshire after 1887. He was one of the first and most influential British settlers in Kenya. *Wazungu* is the Swahili word for "people on the move" and is used in East Africa as a derogatory term for people who keep moving around the country. After this service, Onyango became a farmer and did well in his affairs. He named his son by his second wife Barak, meaning "blessing" in Swahili. We know that his name was spelled Barak—not Barack—in Kenya from the article he published in 1965 in the *East Africa Journal*.

One of the reasons Barack's paternal grandfather Onyango converted to Islam may have been to have more than one wife: Islam allows four. Onyango had at least four (Helima, Akumu, Sarah, and the white woman from Burma). Akumu tried to escape her husband several times, once after her daughter Sarah was born and again after her son Barak was born, but Onyango went after her and brought her back home each time, "for he believed that the children needed their mother" (Obama, 1995, p. 408). This means that Barak experienced an abandonment by his mother already in his infancy.

Though his son Barak was Akumu's son, Akumu ran away from her abusive and unloved husband in 1945, when Barak was nine years old, going back to Kendu Bay, where she came from. Akumu had given birth to another child, a girl, whom she named Auma, the same name that her son Barak would give to his own daughter (Obama, 1995, p. 412). Akumu woke up her elder daughter Sarah in the middle of the night and told her that she and Barak should follow her to Kendu Bay "as soon as they were older" (Obama, 1995, p. 412). In fact, Akumu abandoned her children. Barak was raised by Onyango's third wife, Sarah. This abandonment by his mother affected him deeply. He felt empty and worthless, for otherwise his mother would not have left him. He was also enraged and depressed. In response, he developed a narcissistic, arrogant, and self-destructive personality. Unconsciously, he may have blamed himself for his abandonment by his mother: "If I were worthy of her love, she would not have abandoned me." This unhappy, abandoned child was to become Barack's father. He was very bright and did well in his studies, but inside him was a great void that he tried to fill with women, success, wealth, and fame.

Chapter 4

A NARCISSISTIC AND SELF-DESTRUCTIVE FATHER

Synopsis: *Barack Obama's father, Barak Obama, was born in 1936 to his father, Hussein Onyango Obama, "the Terror," and to his young mother, Akumu, who did not love his father. He grew up a very intelligent young boy, but he was also a goatherd. His father often upbraided and punished him, both physically and psychologically. Barak had, on the one hand, a grandiose image of himself as the best and the brightest in everything and, on the other hand, a poor self-image due to his father's punitive upbringing and his abandonment by his mother, which he may have blamed himself for. As a young man Barak married a beautiful teenage Luo woman named Kezia, who bore him a son and was pregnant with their second child when he abandoned her and left for the United States to study at the University of Hawai'i on the Airlift Africa program. He did well but remained arrogant, with what the psychoanalyst Donald Woods Winnicott (1965) has called a "false self, always presenting himself as greater than he was." He changed the spelling of his first name to Barack to make it more American—and to avoid charges of bigamy. He married Stanley Ann Dunham in 1961, after he got her pregnant, but when he was admitted to Harvard University in 1963 for graduate study in economics, Barak abandoned her and his son Barack. After returning to Kenya and to his wife Kezia in 1965, he got into trouble with the authorities, lost his job, drifted into alcoholism, and suffered road accidents, which ended in his early death at the age of 46. His son Barack was to discover all this only after his father's death.*

Barak was highly intelligent, and as a teenager he won a scholarship to a school in the Kenyan capital of Nairobi. But he was also arrogant, always thinking himself better than everybody else. Barack Obama's "Granny," Sarah Onyango Obama, who raised his father after Akumu's escape, gave him a good description of his father's narcissistic personality, which was already clear in his boyhood. Among its hallmarks were his arrogance and his lack of empathy. He was such a good student that he often skipped school because he was bored with his teachers. He could learn in a few hours what other students took days and weeks to learn. Granny told Barack that whenever his father was not first in his class, which was rare, he was terribly upset (Obama, 1995, p. 415). She added that Barak often laughed and boasted about his cleverness.

Granny Sarah obviously liked Barak, her adopted stepson, and she tried to paint as flattering a picture of him to his son Barack as she was able. She thought that Barak did not mean his boasting cruelly, that he was kind and good-natured, that he had no idea that other people envied him or resented his high intelligence. When he was a grown-up man, he often insulted in public former classmates who had become important or wealthy people. Barak made many enemies without intending to offend them. He had no empathy for other people's feelings (Obama, 1995, pp. 415–416). Indeed, Barak's narcissism was self-destructive. It was his unconscious defense against the unbearable feelings of abandonment and worthlessness that he may have felt even before his physical abandonment by his mother, and certainly after it.

After escaping her husband Onyango, Barak's mother Akumu married another man and moved to Tanganyika (now Tanzania). According to Granny, Akumu's elder child Sarah remembered her mother's instructions. One night in 1945 she woke up her brother Barak, and the two began to walk toward Kendu Bay, where she thought her mother lived. But they lost their way, became dirty, hungry, tattered, and miserable, were reduced to begging, and were finally taken in by a woman who took pity on them. The woman called Onyango, and when he came and saw his poor children he wept for the first and last time in his life (Obama, 1995, p. 413). Sarah and Barak never tried to run away again, but Sarah remained loyal to her mother, Akumu, and she resented Granny Sarah's taking her mother's place (Obama, pp. 412–413, 428).

Barak, however, never forgave his mother her abandonment of him. He took his father's side, acted as if Akumu no longer existed, and called Granny his mother. Granny Sarah, who did not like her namesake stepdaughter, told Barack that her stepdaughter Sarah had become much like her father Onyango. In a gender-role reversal, Sarah seems to have identified with her father, whereas Barak seems to have become more like his mother. Onyango was a harsh and stern father, if not an abusive one. He made his children work hard and would not let them play with the "filthy and ill-mannered" children of his neighbors (Obama 1995, pp. 413–414). His wife, Granny Sarah, broke his rules behind his back when he was away, trying to give the children some freedom and joy (ibid., p. 414).

Along with his harsh treatment by his father, Barak's abandonment by his mother, Akumu, was the crucial event in his life. Rather than grieve and mourn, he became mischievous, rebellious, and violent, causing his father many problems with their neighbors. Granny Sarah tried to patch things up, not always successfully. There was also tension between Barak and his sister Sarah, who envied him his education and what she saw as his preferential treatment by their father. Sarah married and moved away from Alego but after her husband died she returned there (Obama, 1995, p. 420). Barak was very intelligent but also very haughty, and he often corrected the mistakes of his teachers before the whole class. The teachers were enraged, and he was caned many times by the headmaster, but his character became increasingly narcissistic. He would come home from school and boast of his cleverness and of always being the first in his class (Obama, p. 415). Did Barak's academic prowess give him a feeling of superiority that protected him from the feelings of helplessness and worthlessness after he was abandoned by his mother?

In 1949, during the Kenyan revolt against the British colonial rulers, Onyango was arrested by the British on charges of belonging to an illegal rebel group. Onyango was arrested by the British *askaris* (African soldier-policemen working for the British colonialists) on the false allegations of an informer that he was a rebel and a subversive. Granny Sarah told Barack that his grandfather's arrest and imprisonment were due to a denunciation by an African whom Onyango had offended. He was detained for six months without trial. He was tried in a British court, but the records of his trial cannot be found, as the British destroyed all their colonial courts records that were over six years old. Onyango was tortured by the British and their Kenyan police. He returned home from prison skinny, dirty, and lousy and felt deeply humiliated. Onyango's helpless rage was boundless (Obama, 1995, pp. 417–418).

Maseno is a town in the Kisumu District of Kenya's Nyanza province, located along the Kisumu-Busia highway, northwest of Kisumu, the provincial capital. In 1950 the 14-year-old Barak was admitted to Maseno's Mission School (now the Maseno School), an exclusive Christian boarding school run by Anglican missionaries. The head teacher, B. L. Bowers, who ran the school from 1951 to 1969, described Barak in his records as "very keen, steady, trustworthy and friendly. Concentrates, reliable and out-going" (Oywa, 2008). Barak did well at school but was so arrogant, mischievous, and rebellious that in 1953 he was expelled from the Maseno Mission School.

According to Barack's Granny Sarah, his 17-year-old father Barak was badly beaten by his furious father Onyango and then sent to "the coast," where he would work as a clerk. In fact, Barak took a job in Mombasa, Kenya's port city on the Indian Ocean, in the office of an Arab merchant, only to leave shortly thereafter following an argument with his employer, without even collecting his pay. He then got a lower-paying job, and when he visited his father and told him what had happened, Onyango shouted at his son that he was no good and would never amount to anything. Barak tried to lie to his father about his wages, but his father exposed his lie and told him to go away because he had brought shame on his father (Obama, 1995, pp. 418–419). The humiliation and helpless patricidal rage that the young Barak felt must have been overwhelming.

At the age of 18, in 1954, Barak met a beautiful teenage Luo woman from Kendu Bay named Kezia Aoko, and some time later he married her in a Luo tribal village ceremony. There are no records of this marriage, and its date is uncertain. Onyango and Barak's sister Sarah opposed the marriage, but Granny Sarah told Barack that she had talked Onyango into consenting. According to Granny Sarah, Barak's son Roy (who later became a proud Black Muslim and changed his name to Abongo Malik) was born "one year after Barack and Kezia were married" and his daughter Auma "two years later" (Obama 1995, p. 420). It is hard to say when exactly the two children were born. Granny Sarah told Barack that by 1956 Barak already had Roy, yet she also said that Kezia was pregnant with Auma when Barak left for the United States in 1959 (Obama, 1995, p. 420). Some sources say that Roy was born in 1958 and Auma in 1960.

From 1952 to 1959 Kenya was under a British-imposed state of emergency arising from the native *Mau Mau* revolt against British colonial rule. During this period native African participation in the British Kenyan political process increased rapidly. But the meetings of the Kenyan rebel organizations were outlawed. In 1956 Barak was arrested at one of those meetings, and his furious father Onyango refused to bail him out of jail. The first direct elections for Africans to Kenya's Legislative Council took place in 1957. According to Barack's Granny, after working in Mombasa, his father Barak worked for the Kenyan railway in Nairobi, but he was fired from this job, too. Granny also said that Barak attended the political meetings of the Kenya African National Union (KANU; Obama, 1995, pp. 419–420). In fact, as in many other cases, her information is inexact: for during the 1950s there was as yet no KANU. There was the Kenya African Union (KAU), which merged with other Kenyan tribal parties to form the KANU in 1960.

In 1958–1959, although he was deeply depressed for a while, his self-esteem in tatters, Barak nevertheless made it. He was released from jail and later met two American ladies who helped him take a correspondence course and a high school exam at the U.S. embassy in Nairobi. One of these women was Elizabeth Mooney Kirk (1914–2004), known by many as Betty, who spent her entire life advancing adult literacy. She worked with Dr. Frank Charles Laubach (1884–1970), a Christian evangelical missionary known as "the apostle to the illiterates," using his "each one teach one" method. Kirk traveled and taught worldwide, including India, Africa, and the United States. While working in Kenya, she provided the financial support for Barak to come to the United States to study. The paragraph in his son's memoir about this event is very poignant. The son tells us about his father's feverish work and burning ambition to succeed on his tests at the U.S. embassy in Nairobi and to get admitted to a U.S. university. During the months between taking the examinations and receiving their results, Barak became anorexic, and Granny feared that he might die. Finally, when he received the letter telling him that he had passed the exams, he shouted with happiness, and Granny laughed along with him, because Barak had become his old self again, laughing and boasting about his unrivaled abilities (Obama, 1995, p. 421).

However emotionally troubled, narcissistic and self-destructive, the young Barak was also resourceful and determined, and perhaps as fiercely ambitious as was his son after him (Obama, 2006a, p. 243). His grandiose self demanded that he attain ever-greater achievement. He was tireless in his efforts to get admitted to a U.S. university, which he saw as the key to a successful career. For many months he wrote to scores of U.S. universities until at last he was accepted by the University of Hawai'i at Manoa. In 1959 Barak abandoned his pregnant wife Kezia and his son Roy (now Abongo Malik Obama) and left for the United States (Obama, 1995, p. 422). In so doing, he was doing to them what his mother had done to him.

THE FATHER'S NAME CHANGE

Once in the United States, Barak Hussein Obama changed the spelling of his first name to Barack. Upon his return to Kenya, however, he again used his original name (Barak Obama, 1965). In his son's birth certificate of 1961 the father's name is given as Barack. Why did the father change the spelling of his name from Barak to Barack? And why did he change it back to Barak in Kenya? Did the father have two different identities, a Kenyan one and an American one? The online copy of Barack Obama's birth certificate as released by his campaign has its number blacked out. The date of birth is August 4, 1961. Most sources have Barack born at the Kapi'olani Maternity and Gynecological Hospital in Honolulu, Oahu Island, Hawai'i, although some scholars believe that he was born in Honolulu's Queen's Medical Center.

Some enemies of President Obama, as well as some conspiracy theorists, have questioned the authenticity of this online birth certificate and challenged it in court, but their lawsuits were dismissed by the U.S. Supreme Court. Moreover, on August 13, 1961, the *Honolulu Advertiser* reported the birth of a son to Mr. and Mrs. Barack H. Obama on August 4, as did the *Honolulu Star-Bulletin*. But facts do not deter right-wing conspiracy theorists, and Barack has more than his fair share of these. One of them, Webster Griffin Tarpley (born 1944), an extreme leftist, has written an "unauthorized biography" of the 44th president to prove that Obama is a right-wing "foundation operative" and an agent of "Wall Street finance capital," controlled by corporate power and by Zbigniew Brzezinski, George Soros, and Goldman Sachs … (Tarpley, 2008a).

All human extremes are dangerous and indicate inner turmoil. Though most of Obama's enemies are in the extreme right wing of American politics, Webster Tarpley is an example of extreme left-wing paranoid conspiracy theories. He is an author, lecturer, and critic of U.S. foreign and domestic policy. Tarpley seriously believes that the September 11, 2001, attacks on the United States were the work of a rogue network of the U.S. military-industrial complex and U.S. intelligence agencies. He claims to have uncovered "false-flag" terror operations by a rogue network in U.S. military intelligence working with "moles" in the private sector and in corporate mass-communication media, and believes that such false-flag operations date back to the gunpowder plot in England in 1605.

To me, the most important thing about Barack's birth certificate is his father's name change from Barak in Kenya to Barack in the United States. The conscious reason for this may have been to escape the charge of bigamy, but he may also have wanted to escape his Kenyan identity and to assume an American one. Barak, who left Kenya for the United States in 1959 under the Airlift Africa program organized by the Kenyan leader Tom Mboya (1930–1969), seems to have been the first African student at the University of Hawai'i at Manoa. Philip Ochieng, a Kenyan Luo friend of Barak's who later became a prominent Kenyan journalist, went to another U.S. university on the same airlift. Barak was a brilliant but tragic man (Ochieng, 2004, 2009). One of the first Kenyan nonreligious Muslims, after his return to Kenya, Barak would get himself in trouble with the Kikuyu-dominated Kenyan government of Jomo Kenyatta, which would cause his downfall, alcoholism, road accidents, and early death.

Muslim custom allows a man four wives. As we have seen, Barak's father, Onyango, had at least three, and Barak was his eldest son, the son of Habiba Akumu, his father's second wife. However, after a certain age, and definitely after his parents separated when he was nine, Barak was raised by Onyango's third wife, Sarah. His mother's relations with her husband were not good, and she left her family and divorced her husband in 1945. Granny Sarah thus became Barack's step-grandmother. Since she speaks only Luo and Swahili and Barack does not speak those languages, their communication is limited. When the 27-year-old Barack visited Kenya in 1988, Barack's favorite half sister, Auma, interpreted between him and Granny (Obama, 1995, pp. 331–334).

Given the chronic tensions between his parents, it is possible that Barak's mother Akumu was not always psychologically available to him, that she may not always have been a good-enough mother for him (Winnicott, 1953). She tried to run away from her husband at least twice, after each of her children was born, and she finally abandoned him when Barak was nine. This was a crucial psychological issue for Barack's father: he was abandoned by his mother, first psychologically, then physically. He, in turn, would abandon his own son and wife when his son was two years old. This was a crucial event in his son Barack's life, the source of his quest for a father and a family, for his identity and his life's work and destiny.

It was no accident that Barak was married four times (his wives were Kezia Aoko, Stanley Ann Dunham, Ruth Nidesand, and Jael Otieno). His son Barack has called him a womanizer, but, like the legendary Don Juan, he may have been trying to fill an inner void. Having been abandoned by his mother, his marriage to Ann, at least, may have been an unconscious attempt, however unsuccessful, to repair his feelings of abandonment, ending up, however, with his own abandonment of his wife. As we know, in his youth he married a young Luo woman named Kezia in a tribal village ceremony. He later said that he had divorced her, but his second wife, Ann, told her son Barack that there was no legal document either to prove that marriage or to show a divorce (Obama, 1995, p. 126). In 1959, Barak left Kezia and Kenya to study at the University of Hawai'i in Manoa, having received a scholarship there. He and Kezia had four children, one before he left her (when she was pregnant with their second child), one soon after he left, and the other two after he returned to Kenya from the United States.

Some Obama biographers think that Kezia, rather that Barack's mother Ann, was Barak's true love. Indeed, Barak seems never to have divorced Kezia, who now lives in England. When he married Ann, Barack's mother, he was still married to Kezia, and he returned to her when he returned to Kenya. As bigamy was illegal in the United States, Barak did not report his previous marriage, stating that he was unmarried. This may have been a reason for giving his first name as Barack in the United States, to conceal his Kenyan marriage. In Kenya, as an official Muslim, Barak was legally entitled to four wives. In the United States he would have been considered a bigamist.

Barak had eight children by his four wives: four children with Kezia (Roy, Auma, Abo, and Bernard), one with Ann (Barack), two with Ruth (Mark and David), and one with Jael (George). Barak was an abusive husband and father. His stepmother, Granny Sarah, told his son Barack that Barak had abused his children just as his own father had abused him, in a critical, aggressive, rejecting, and disparaging manner (Obama, 1995, p. 424). Disparaging others was the only way the self-destructive narcissistic Barak could feel good about himself. In stark contrast, his son Barack feels good by bringing others up to his own level.

In his memoir, Barack describes his father Barak as domineering, imperious, grandiose, and uncompromising. In psychoanalytic terms, his father suffered from a severe narcissistic personality disorder. The young Barak had a grandiose self. He was fiercely ambitious, and he wanted to study in the United States and to become famous, rich, and great. In Kenya, in 1959, an airlift program offering Western educational opportunities in the United States to outstanding Kenyan students was organized by Mboya, the most prominent Luo politician in the Kenyan government of the Kikuyu leader Kenyatta.

At that time, the Kikuyu-Luo rivalry in Kenya had not yet led to the kind of murderous tribal riots that occurred almost fifty years later, in 2007–2008, after a Kenyan election was stolen by the third president, Mwai Kibaki (born 1931), a Kikuyu. In those riots, Luo tribesmen brutally murdered many Kikuyus, saying, "It's not that we don't like Kikuyus—it's because they think they have a right to rule this country forever, even if it means stealing votes." Yet political assassination was common even then. The first two presidents, Kenyatta and Daniel arap Moi, had some of their political rivals assassinated. The 38-year-old Mboya was murdered in 1969, and many Kenyans suspected his murder was ordered by Kenyatta.

The bright but arrogant young Barak was awarded a scholarship in economics, and in 1959, at the age of 23, he enrolled at the University of Hawai'i at Manoa, where the next year Ann Dunham was to arrive. In what was to become a pattern of abandonments, he left behind his pregnant wife Kezia and their infant son. Kezia was to become Barack's stepmother. If we think of Barak's rejection by his father Onyango and his abandonment by his mother Akumu, the suicide of Barack's maternal great-grandmother, Lucille Armour Dunham, and Ann's rejection by her father Stanley because she was not a boy, we can see that Barack's parents both came from families with histories of emotional abandonments and rejections. This may be one unconscious reason why Barak and Ann were attracted to one another: each saw himself or herself in the other. Barack would have to deal with this issue himself after his own abandonment by his father.

Barack has attributed his father's admission to the University of Hawai'i at Manoa to John and Robert Kennedy's African Student Airlift initiative. In fact, that initiative began after his father came to the United States. Barak came from Kenya to the United States in 1959 on the initial Airlift Africa program initiated by the young Kenyan leader Tom Mboya, with which the Kennedys became associated only in 1960 after a visit they received from Mboya. The Kennedys contributed $100,000 to Mboya's program (Dobbs, 2008; Niven, 2009, pp. 8–9).

The first Airlift Africa project began in 1959, four years before Kenya gained its independence from Great Britain. In the first airlift, through the efforts of Mboya and the U.S. African-American Students Foundation, 81 native Kenyan students were granted scholarships to top-level colleges in the United States, and a special plane was chartered to bring them there. Repeatedly, however, the U.S. State Department was asked to help finance this project, and repeatedly it turned down those requests. The money was raised by a direct appeal to the public.

The second Airlift Africa initiative was organized in 1960. In response to letters from Ralph Bunche (1903–1971), the African American Nobel Peace Prize winner, a prominent United Nations official, and a former director of the African-American Students Foundation, accredited colleges offered scholarships for African students in the United States. The college-accrediting agencies in the United States are private educational associations of regional or national scope that develop evaluation criteria and conduct peer evaluations to assess whether or not those criteria are met. The U.S. Department of Education does not itself accredit colleges and universities, although it does publish its own criteria for such accreditation.

The new African Student Airlift program of 1960 included students not only from Kenya but also from Uganda, Tanganyika and Zanzibar (now Tanzania), Northern Rhodesia (now Zambia), Southern Rhodesia (now Zimbabwe), and Nyasaland (now Malawi). About 230 students were selected, and money was raised in Africa from Africans to provide for the students' living expenses in the United States. The original supporters of Mboya's 1959 program for Kenyans to study in the United States included prominent civil rights activists like Harry Belafonte,

Sidney Poitier, Jackie Robinson, Martin Luther King, Jr., and Elizabeth Mooney Kirk, the literacy advocate who provided most of the support for Barak's early years in the United States and recommended him to several U.S. colleges. This information is in Mboya's papers, which are part of the Hoover Institution Archives at Stanford University.

If Barak Obama was raised as a Muslim, he did not remain one for long. According to his son Barack, Barak had been raised as a Muslim but had rejected his father's religion, and when he arrived in the United States at the age of 23 he was "a confirmed atheist, thinking religion to be so much superstition" (Obama 2006a, p. 242). Auma, Barak's daughter by his wife Kezia and Barack's favorite half sister, has said that her father "was never a Muslim although he was born into a Muslim family with a Muslim name" (Rice, 2008). In fact, Hussein is an Arabic rather than a Muslim name. Whether or not his father was ever a Muslim preoccupied the young Barack long before he himself embraced Christianity in 1988. His mother's family had moved to Hawai'i in 1960, a year after Barack's father arrived from Kenya. It is likely that during his first year in the United States Barak dated other women before he met Ann.

What made the teenage Ann fall in love with the black African student from Kenya? Her son by that Kenyan, Barack, had psychological insight into this: it was her immature idealization of blacks. It dawned on Barack that his mother had entertained an immature fantasy of "childlike blacks" as an unconscious revolt against her strict white middle-class parents, a fantasy that carried with it "the promise of another life: warm, sensual, exotic, different" (Obama, 1995, p. 124). In other words, Ann fell in love with the Kenyan Barak for immature emotional reasons derived from her early upbringing and childlike fantasies. It was also a narcissistic love, as each of them saw his or her image in the other. It was also exogamy, which, Sigmund Freud believed, is an unconscious defense against incestuous wishes (Freud, 1953).

Sasha Abramsky has rightly called our attention to Barack's ambivalence about his mother, which becomes obvious when one observes the striking difference between his laudatory public statements about her and the paucity of the space he has given her in his writings: "After all, while Obama is eloquent in his protestations of filial love for his mother, he actually writes about her far more sparingly than he does [about] many other important people in his life" (Abramsky, 2009, pp. 42–43). In Barack's statements his mother remains "something of an enigma" (p. 43), and even though her son portrays her as the source of his faith and his values, as an early feminist, and as a fighter for good causes, she always remains in the background, whereas Barack devoted a 442-page book to his father, in which his maternal grandparents play a larger role than his mother. Even in his second book, her name is second to that of her mother (Obama, 2006a, dedication).

WERE BARACK'S PARENTS MARRIED?

The divorce decree of Barack's parents, issued in 1964, states that they had married on February 2, 1961, in Wailuku, Maui County, Hawai'i. Had Barack not seen that decree, or did he prefer to ignore it, when he wrote that his parents married in 1960 (Obama, 1995, p. 12)? Since he was born on August 4, 1961, did he prefer to think that his parents were married before his mother became pregnant in November 1960? Very significantly, Barack later added an important caveat: "How and when the marriage occurred remains a bit murky, a bill of particulars that I've never had the courage to explore" (Obama, p. 22). Did Barack fear that the marriage had never taken place? There is some evidence that his parents were not married at the time of his birth (Corsi 2009a, 2009b; A. Klein, 2009; LeFevre, 2009). This evidence was collected by Obama's right-wing enemies. No marriage document, however, has been made public.

Hawai'i's Maui County is composed of four islands: Maui, Lanaii, Kahoolawe, and Molokaii. Maui is the second largest of all of Hawai'i's islands, smaller than Hawai'i Island but bigger than Oahu. If the information in the divorce decree is true, why did Barack's parents not marry on Oahu Island, where Honolulu, its Manoa Valley, and the University of Hawai'i at Manoa are located? Did they elope, as Ann's parents had done? On February 2, 1961, Ann was eighteen and three months pregnant with Barak's child. Their son, Barack, was born six months later, on August 4, 1961. As her son later realized, Ann had fallen in love not with his real father but with her image of the wild, free, sensuous black man, and her immature idealization of her husband was bound to lead to severe disappointment and divorce (Obama, 1995, pp. 123–124).

The adult Barack was puzzled by the fact that his middle-class white maternal grandparents had let their daughter marry a black African man. How could such conventional, conservative, white people from Kansas consent to their daughter committing "miscegenation" (Obama, 1995, pp. 12–13)? At that time *miscegenation*, the American term for a marriage or sexual union of a white person with a black one, not only was condemned by most Americans but was also illegal in many states of the United States. Both Ann's parents and Barak's father Onyango opposed the marriage, the latter vehemently. Onyango wrote Ann's father threatening to have his son's passport and U.S. visa revoked: he did not want his family blood sullied by his son's marriage to a white woman. Did Onyango forget his own marriage to a white woman in Burma?

At the time of the wedding of Barack's parents in February 1961—if in fact it occurred—miscegenation or interracial marriage was legal in Hawai'i and in 27 other states of the United States, but it was still illegal in 22 states, and 96% of Americans opposed it (Niven, 2009, p. 9). Looking back on it, the adult Barack thought that his parents' marriage had been very "fragile and haphazard" (Niven, p. 22). Trying to understand why his father left him when he was a baby was a lifelong psychological occupation for Barack. In fact, his entire memoir, *Dreams from My Father*, and perhaps his entire life, can be read as a story of his quest for his absent father and at the same time a quest for his own identity as separate from that of his father. Barack has had a lifelong ambivalent identification with his father, whom he has idealized and admired and yet at the same time has also felt ashamed of. Sasha Abramsky (2009, p. 48) thinks that the reader of *Dreams from My Father* senses the young Barack's rage at his father but that this anger "rapidly dissipates as he channels his talents into working for social change." This channeling is known in psychoanalysis as displacement and sublimation, and indeed Barack's success is in part due to his capacity to sublimate his anger into social and political activity, along with his great emotional resiliency, which we shall discuss in greater detail in the following.

By the time of Barack's birth in 1961, political and legal challenges to racial segregation and discrimination in the United States were increasing. Black groups like the Student Nonviolent Coordinating Committee and the Congress on Racial Equality were confronting racial segregation and the Kennedy administration, which treated it with great caution. The civil rights movement was gaining many white adherents, many of them Jews. In 1961 civil rights activists who called themselves freedom riders rode interstate buses into the segregated southern United States to test the enforcement of the U.S. Supreme Court decision in *Boynton vs. Virginia*.

Boynton vs. Virginia was a landmark U.S. Supreme Court ruling in 1960 that marked a peak in the U.S. civil rights struggle and in the freedom rides that were its chief tactic. In 1946 the U.S. Supreme Court had banned racial segregation in interstate bus travel. In 1947 the American civil rights activists had tested the enforcement of the Court ruling in the South with a Journey of Reconciliation in which whites and blacks rode a bus together into the South. They encountered violent opposition, but their legal struggle went on, and in 1960 the U.S. Supreme Court's *Boynton vs. Virginia* ruling extended the 1946 Court decision to include bus terminals, restrooms, and other facilities associated with interstate travel. The majority opinion was written by the 74-year-old white liberal Justice Hugo Lafayette Black (1886–1971).

The freedom riders were buoyed by the *Boynton vs. Virginia* ruling, and their freedom rides went on in greater force. After John F. Kennedy was elected president of the United States in 1960, his younger brother, Robert F. Kennedy, the new U.S. attorney general, intervened on the side of the civil rights activists. Nonetheless, they were often severely beaten by furious Southerners, who felt their entire way of life, which rested on prejudice, racism, defensive projection, and feelings of superiority, threatened by the freedom rides. Racist Southern police, rather than arresting the violent attackers, often arrested the freedom riders. Due to the emotional power of racism, it took many U.S. Supreme Court rulings over several decades to desegregate the United States and bring about racial equality, at least on paper. The U.S. federal government failed to enforce its own rules and the Supreme Court's decisions, and the freedom riders were determined to change what to them was an unbearable situation. The freedom riders were blacks and whites riding various forms of public transportation together in the South to challenge local laws or customs that enforced segregation.

Notwithstanding this political and racial background, the marriage of Barack's parents, if it ever took place, leaves many psychological questions unanswered. Did Barak really want to marry Ann? Was he forced to marry her by her pregnancy? Where is their marriage license? Did Barak plan to stay with Ann and his child? In any event, he would soon leave her. It was no accident that Barak, who gave his first name as Barack on his son's birth certificate, named his son after himself. With his narcissistic grandiose self, he wanted a copy of himself, a narcissistic mirror image of himself. The middle name, Hussein, was his own as well as his father's name. For the father, Barak, however bright and capable, had a self-destructive narcissistic personality, which, eventually, led to his ruin after he went back to Kenya. There he got himself in trouble, had serious accidents, drank alcohol, and finally died in another accident.

In U.S. politics, meanwhile, people like Robert Moses, Ella Baker, Bayard Rustin, Stokely Carmichael, Diane Nash, John Lewis, Bob Zellner, and other prominent American civil rights figures led thousands of black and white activists in the struggle for black civil rights. They took their struggle to the heart of Southern racial segregation in Mississippi, Alabama, and Georgia, former African-slave-owning states whose white residents could not abide black equality. Many civil rights activists were arrested, placed in prison farms, fire-hosed, beat up with truncheons, and even killed. These violent dramas were publicized by the sensation-hungry (if not bloodthirsty) mass-communication media, and, after a prolonged struggle, racial segregation gave way to racial integration and the enfranchisement of black Americans (Niven, 2009, p. 7).

At the time of these civil-rights activities in the late 1950s, Barack's father was applying to graduate school in the United States. He was admitted in 1959. In 1962, when Barack was a year old, his 26-year-old father, Barak (now renamed Barack), who was getting his bachelor's degree from the University of Hawai'i, was accepted both by the New School for Social Research in New York and by Harvard University in Cambridge, Massachusetts, for graduate study. The young father preferred the prestige of Harvard to the financial advantages at the New School. When Barack was two, in 1963, his father moved to Massachusetts, abandoning his wife and son. The ostensible reason was that he could not afford to take them with him. The deeper reason may have been his wish to escape his difficult and strong-willed wife, and his lifelong pattern of abandonments by both his parents.

In late 1963 President Kennedy was assassinated, being succeeded by his vice president, Lyndon B. Johnson. In 1964 the first Civil Rights Act was enacted by the U.S. Congress and signed into law by President Johnson. In 1965 the Voting Rights Act desegregated the United States and integrated blacks into its society. In 1968 the second Civil Rights Act was signed into law by Johnson. Yet the actual situation of black people in the United States took decades more to improve, and even during the 1980s and 1990s being black in the United States was a serious disadvantage.

In 1981, a year before his father's death, Barack's mother Ann told him that it was not his father's fault but *her* fault that his father had left him, and also the fault of his paternal grandfather, who was threatening to have Barak's passport and U.S. student visa revoked, as he did not approve of his son's marriage to a white woman. Onyango was obviously overlooking his own marriage to a white woman in Burma. Barack's mother added that his father had gone to Harvard because he always had to show that he was better than everybody else (Obama, 1995, pp. 125–126, 422). Indeed, many times Barak presented himself as greater than he was (Obama, pp. 216, 394–424). Like the brilliant Indian-born British Muslim psychoanalyst Mohammed Masud Raza Khan (1924–1989), he had what Khan's therapist, the British psychoanalyst Winnicott, had called a false self (Hopkins, 2006).

After his father left him in 1963, Barry's mother Ann was the dominant person in his emotional life during the early, formative years of his infancy and childhood. As he later put it in an interview with an American journalist, "the values she taught me continue to be my touchstone when it comes to how I go about the world of politics" (Jones, 2007). Barack understood, however, that his mother was emotionally immature (Obama, 1995, pp. 123–127). Her love for his father, too, was immature and idealized. The infant Barry must have *felt* his mother's immaturity and neediness. With his father absent, the toddler Barry was raised by his immature mother and her parents and was free to idealize his father as he wished to imagine him, or according to the idealized stories that his mother and her parents told him about his father. But he also had to deal with an abandoned and grieving mother, who may have sought solace in her baby son for her abandonment by her husband. In a sense, Barry had to be the father to his own mother.

Separation, rejection, and abandonment were key psychological motifs in Barak's life. After only a few months of separation, Barak returned to Hawai'i in early 1964 to divorce Ann. Back in Massachusetts, he received his master's degree in economics from Harvard University in 1965 and then returned home to Kenya, where he quickly published his antigovernment article (Obama, 1965). Despite having only a master's degree from Harvard, he constantly called himself Dr. Obama (Obama, 1995, p. 216). This was part of his narcissistic false self. Barak repeatedly presented himself as greater, richer, and more important than he really was (Obama, pp. 394–424). Barak saw his son only once more, in late 1971 and early 1972, when Barack was 10 years old.

At Harvard University, Barak had met an American-born woman named Ruth Nidesand, a teacher and a person of some means, whose age remains a mystery. According to Barack's Granny, Ruth later followed Barak to Kenya without his knowledge, despite the fact that he already had another wife there, Kezia, whom he had not officially divorced. Barak was reluctant to marry Ruth, but she was stubborn and domineering. She became Barak's third wife, after Kezia and Ann, and had two children by him, Mark and David. There was much strife in the marriage of Barak and Ruth, as both were stubborn, narcissistic personalities.

According to Barack's Granny Sarah, his stepmother Ruth demanded that his father Barak divorce and renounce his first wife, Kezia, who went back to her home village in Kendu Bay. Kezia's children, Roy and Auma, who wished to continue their studies in Nairobi, had to leave their mother and move in with their father Barak in Nairobi. Ruth refused to accompany Barak when he brought Roy and Auma to visit their mother, Kezia, in Kendu Bay, nor would she let her husband bring her children David and Mark to see Kezia. Barak's father Onyango repeatedly insulted his son in public, telling everyone that Barak's wife would not cook for him, which was a shameful thing for a married man in his society. When Barak returned from Nairobi to visit his father's family, he tried to impress everyone by driving a big car, wearing fine clothes, and bringing them expensive gifts, but he would stay only a short time, because his old father Onyango, who by now could hardly walk, see, or bathe, always tried to put him down and humiliate him. Even in his old age, Onyango was still the terror that he had been all his life (Obama, 1995, pp. 423–424).

After a few years of marital strife, Barak and his third wife Ruth divorced—bitterly—after which Ruth reportedly married a Tanzanian man surnamed Ndesandjo (his first name has remained a mystery, and his last name is suspiciously similar to her own), who, she said, made her a gift of Nairobi's Madari Kindergarten, which she still runs. Is this Tanzanian man a figment of Ruth's imagination? If not, was she in love with him, or was she pregnant by him? What was he doing in Kenya? Ruth was a narcissistic woman, and if Mr. Ndesandjo does exist, it may have been the similarity between her last name and his that helped make her fall for him. In any event, by his father's various wives Barack has many half brothers, half sisters, half aunts, half cousins, and half uncles. In his *Dreams from My Father* Barack describes his real father as exceptionally gifted but also as wild, boastful, and stubborn.

Back in 1963 Kenya had gained its independence from Great Britain and was ruled by Jomo Kenyatta. Upon his return to Kenya in 1965, Barak was hired by an oil company, but he did not last long at this job, due to his infuriating character. He then worked as an economist in the Kenyan ministry of transportation, and later as a senior economist in the Kenyan ministry of finance. Barak's life, however, ended in self-inflicted tragedy. Upon his return to Kenya he published a paper entitled "Problems Facing Our Socialism" (Obama, 1965), attacking the Kenyan government's blueprint for national planning. This blueprint was entitled "African Socialism and Its Applicability to Planning in Kenya" and had been produced by Mboya's ministry of economic planning and development. According to some U.S. journalists, Mboya was offended and angry. The man whom he had helped get a U.S. education had turned against him (Dobbs, 2008; Fornek, 2007b).

In U.S. politics, meanwhile, during the 1960s, race relations were undergoing a dramatic transition. Barack's Harvard biographer thinks that by the time Barack was four or five years old, in 1965–1966, the idea of a black U.S. president was no longer an impossible dream "even for a boy born in Honolulu to a black Kenyan father and a white mother from Kansas" (Niven, 2009, pp. 7–8). During the U.S. presidential primary election campaign of 2008, Hillary Clinton's aides dredged up an essay written by Barack as "a kindergarten student in Indonesia" saying that he wanted to be president (Niven, p. 8). In fact, Barack attended kindergarten in Hawai'i and two primary schools in Indonesia, a Catholic school and a public Muslim school. According to his own memoir, Barack spent two years at the Muslim school and two years at the Catholic school, yet at least one American journalist claimed that he spent three years at the Catholic school and then only one year at the Muslim school (Barker, 2007; Obama, 1995, p. 154).

The "Indonesian" schoolboy known as Barry Soetoro apparently wrote *two* different essays about wanting to be president. At the Catholic school in Jakarta, Fransiskus Strada Asisia (Francis of Assisi School), Barry wrote an essay entitled "I Want to Become President," as his first-grade teacher, Israella Pareira Darmawan (born 1944), told the Associated Press (January 25, 2007). Darmawan remembers him as an exceptionally tall and curly-haired child who quickly picked up the local language and had sharp math skills. In third grade, also at the Catholic school, Barry wrote an essay titled "I Want to Be a President." His third-grade teacher at this school, Fermina Katarina Sinaga, had asked her class to write an essay titled "My Dream: What I Want to Be in the Future." Barry wrote "I want to be a President," she told the *Los Angeles Times* (March 15, 2007).

Meanwhile, as in many other third-world countries, there were many political assassinations in Kenya, some of them ordered by Jomo Kenyatta, who died in 1978, others by his successor Daniel arap Moi, who would later stage a *coup d'état* in 1982. Mboya, who like Barak was a Luo, was assassinated in 1969 by the Kikuyu thug Nahashon Isaac Njenga Njoroge, who was convicted for the murder and hanged. After his arrest, Njoroge reportedly asked, "Why don't you go after the big man?" meaning Kenyatta, a Kikuyu, since the Luo Mboya was seen as a possible contender for the presidency.

The mostly Kikuyu tribal elite around Kenyatta has been blamed for Mboya's death, which has never been the subject of any judicial inquiry. During Mboya's funeral, a mass demonstration of Luo tribesmen against the attendance of President Kenyatta led to a big skirmish, with two people shot dead. The demonstrators believed that Kenyatta was involved in the death of Mboya, eliminating him as a threat to his political career, though this is still disputed.

While the boy Barry was in Indonesia, Kenyatta continued to rule Kenya. In late 1971 Barak Obama returned from Kenya to Hawai'i, where he spent a month with his ex-wife, her parents, and his son, until early 1972. As Barack described it in his memoir, *Dreams from My Father*, his father Barak was a Luo, and his conflict with Kenyatta, a Kikuyu, had destroyed his career. But had Barak not sought the conflict early on, he might have survived and thrived. Barak's life deteriorated into drinking and poverty, from which he never fully recovered. His friend, the prominent Kenyan journalist Philip Ochieng, who had come to study in the United States on the same airlift as Barak, has described Barak's difficult personality and drinking problems (Ochieng, 2004).

After returning to Kenya in early 1972, Barak lost both his legs in an automobile accident and subsequently also lost his job. His father Onyango died in 1975 or 1979, depending on one's sources. After years of alcohol abuse, joblessness, poverty, and road accidents, Barak died in 1982, at the age of 46, in another car crash in Nairobi. Was it an unconscious suicide? Certainly Barack's father Barak, however bright and capable, was also a tragic, abusive, self-abusive, and self-destructive person.

Barak is buried next to his father Onyango in the village of Nyang'oma Kogelo, in Kenya's Siaya District, in Nyanza Province, where he grew up. While Onyango's grave has a plaque engraved with his name and with the years of his birth and death, there is no plaque or inscription on Barak's tombstone (Dobbs, 2008; Fornek, 2007b; Obama, 1995, p. 376). Philip Ochieng (2004) remembered his friend Barak as "charming, generous and extraordinarily clever" but also as "imperious, cruel and given to boasting about his brain and his wealth." Barak's narcissistic arrogance, his false self, brought about his personal ruin and his untimely death.

As we have seen, at some point in time, perhaps when he left Kenya for the United States in 1959, Barak Obama had begun to spell his first name Barack, the English rather than the Swahili spelling. Just as her mother Madelyn's parents had opposed her marriage to her father, so, when Ann became engaged to Barack Sr. (this has been his official name in the United States after his son's birth), both her parents and his father opposed the marriage. Even though he claimed to have married a white woman in Burma himself, Barak's father Onyango objected to his son marrying a white woman, when he already had a black wife back in Kenya. Nevertheless, the two young people defied their parents. Barak was as stubborn as his wife. As we have seen, according to their divorce decree of 1964, Barack Hussein Obama and Stanley Ann Dunham were married on February 2, 1961, in Wailuku, Maui County, Hawai'i. Ann was pregnant. Their son Barack was born in Hawai'i on August 4, 1961. Ann was not yet 19 when she had her first child.

Chapter 5

THE FATHERLESS CHILD
AND HIS UNHAPPY MOTHER

Synopsis: *Barack Obama was born in 1961 in Honolulu. During his child-hood and adolescence, he was called Barry. As a toddler he grew up in a family with considerable strife between the parents, which ended with his abandonment by his father, Barak, when he was two years old. This meant that he had no father figure to identify with other than his maternal grandfather, "Gramps," who was "boisterous," jovial, and loving but also hypomanic and unstable and who often moved his family to other cities and states. His maternal grandmother, "Toot," also loved him, and Barack loved her too, as he did his mother, but he also had to comfort his mother in her distress. His mother, Stanley Ann Dunham, brought him up in such a way that he acquired many character strengths and virtues, including integrity, persistence, empathy, and caring, but she was also immature in some ways, such as her wide-eyed idealization of black people and foreigners, perhaps a reaction to her mother's covert racism. Barack at times felt that he had to protect his sensitive, vulnerable mother. Later, in his adult life, his community, his city, and his country would play the unconscious role of his mother in his feelings, and he would set out to organize, protect, rule ,and repair them. Due to his quest for a father, older men would play the role of substitute father figures with whom he alternately identified.*

The black American spiritual singer Paul Robeson (1898–1976) sang, "Sometimes I Feel Like a Motherless Child" in his wonderful basso profundo voice. Barry Obama might have sung, "I Always Feel Like a Fa-therless Child." The adult Barack called his mother "the dominant figure in my formative years ... The values she taught me continue to be my touch-stone when it comes to how I go about the world of politics" (Jones, 2007; Ripley, 2008). He also recalled that his mother had made great efforts to raise him on "Sunday School values" such as honesty, empathy, discipline, delayed gratification, and hard work, adding that as a child he had not fully grasped the extent of his mother's emotional influence on him (Obama, 2006a, p. 243).

In his memoir Barack called his mother "the kindest, most generous spirit I have ever known" and said that "what is best in me I owe to her" (Obama, 1995, p. xii). He also dedicated his second book to his maternal grandmother and to "my mother, whose loving spirit sustains me still" (Obama, 2006a, dedication). There was some unconscious idealization in this memory, as Ann had been a complex and immature person with many different aspects, not all of them so positive (Abramsky, 2009, pp. 42–43). She could also be childish, immature, and reckless. She must have provoked her son's anger more than once. Yet she did have the kind-ness, generosity, empathy, and compassion that are part of her son. And among her values were honesty, fairness, straight talk, and independent judgment. In psychoanalytic language, Barack's primary object in his early life, his mother, was an object of ambivalent identification for him.

What was Ann like as a mother? What kind of relationship did she have with her infant son? Did she leave his father shortly after Barry was born and take him with her to Seattle? What were those Sunday School val-ues that she taught her son Barry? One of them was empathy (Obama, 2006a, p. 80), and Barack seems to have plenty of it, as his feelings for poor people and his indefatigable fight for health-care reform indicate. Was Ann mature enough to be a good-enough mother in Winnicott's terms? As we have seen, Chip Wall, a former classmate of Ann's who is now a retired philosophy teacher, has said, "She was not a standard-issue girl of her times ... She wasn't part of the matched-sweater-set crowd.... If you were concerned about something going wrong in the world," Stanley would know about it first ... [She was] "a fellow traveler ... We were liberals before we knew what liberals were" (Jones, 2007). Wall used to make after-school runs to Seattle with Ann to sit and talk—for hours—in the city's coffee shops.

Ann was an idealistic dreamer and a Unitarian or an atheist. Steven Niven, Barack's Harvard biographer, thinks that Ann's values were not necessarily religious. Like her first husband, Ann was an agnostic or an atheist, and her values were "largely secular," even though the U.S. civil rights movement had been influenced by Christian idealism. Barack later thought that this idealism was romanticized and that his mother had an immature tendency to idealize black people as childlike, happy, singing, dancing, free, and spontaneous people (Obama, 1995, p. 124). His biographer, however, thinks that "there was nothing romantic in [Ann] Dunham's determination, while still only in her twenties, to raise her son, and to pursue her studies" (Niven, 2009, pp. 9–10).

Ann's best friend in high school, Maxine Box, told an American journalist, "She touted herself as an atheist, and it was something she'd read about and could argue … She was always challenging and arguing and comparing. She was already thinking about things that the rest of us hadn't" (Jones, 2007). Tim Jones thinks that the parental traits that would mold Barry Obama—a different world view from the majority, "an initial rejection of organized religion, a questioning and defiant nature"—had been formed during his early life "in the nomadic and tempestuous Dunham family, where the only child was a curious and precocious daughter of a restless father who wanted a boy so badly that he named her Stanley—after himself" (Jones, 2007).

Why did Ann marry a black man from an African culture she knew little about? The American word *miscegenation* is related to the scholarly term *exogamy*. Sigmund Freud (1953) thought that exogamy—marrying outside your tribe, clan, race, nation, or religion—was an unconscious defense against incestuous wishes. If indeed Ann was deeply—though ambivalently—attached to her father, whose first and last names she bore, then marrying someone who was as unlike her father as possible was exogamy, and she may have married the Kenyan as a way of telling herself, "It is not my father I want, it is someone totally different." We may have further proof of that in the fact that she later married an Indonesian. Both exogamous marriages failed, however, perhaps due to her neurotic choice of mates and her difficult character. The two families' tradition of physical or emotional abandonments, beginning with the suicide of Barry's maternal great-grandmother, Ruth Lucille Armour Dunham, was continued by Barry's father and mother. Her first husband abandoned her and her son, and she abandoned her second husband.

PARENTAL STRIFE AND SEPARATION

Barak Obama, a narcissistic person who always needed to feel superior to everybody else, was also a womanizer, as we know from his life in Kenya before and after his stay in the United States. It is quite likely that he had affairs with other women and that he did not like his American wife's independent-mindedness. The relations between Barak and Ann may have been strained even before Barak left his wife and son to study at Harvard University. It is also likely that Ann sought comfort in her only child, Barack. In this sense, Barack had to be his mother's psychological parent from the outset, right after his birth. Nonetheless, Ann was a good-enough mother to Barack: the incredible strength of his personality indicates that he did receive good-enough mothering from his mother during his infancy, however troubled her relationship with her husband may have been.

There is some evidence that Barak abused his wife physically during their fights and that Ann left her husband in Hawai'i a few months after Barack's birth and went back to Seattle. Some of her former friends in Washington State recall her visiting Seattle with her baby in late 1961 or early 1962 (Botkin, 2007; Brodeur, 2008; Maraniss, 2008; J. Martin, 2008; Montgomery, 2008). By January 1962, she had enrolled at the University of Washington in Seattle and was living as a single mother in the Capitol Hill neighborhood of Seattle with her baby son Barry, while her husband Barak continued his studies in Hawai'i (P. Dougherty, 2009; LeFevre, 2009; LeFevre & Lipson, 2009; J. Martin, 2008; Neyman, 2009). If that was the case, then the baby Barry fortunately lost sight of his father much earlier than the age of two and did not witness the fights between his parents, or his enraged father's violence toward his mother, at least for one year.

This information sounds reliable. According to the directors of the Seattle Museum of the Mysteries, Ann's friend Mary Toutonghi, a speech pathologist in Alaska who lived in Seattle during the early 1960s,

> recalls as best she can the dates she baby sat Barack as her daughter was 18 months old and was born in July of 1959 and that would have placed the months of babysitting Barack in January and February of 1962 … Anna [Ann] was taking night classes at the University of Washington, and according to the University of Washington's registrar's office her major was listed as history. She was enrolled at the University of Washington in the fall of 1961, took a full course load in the spring of 1962 and had her transcript transferred to the University of Hawai'i in the fall of 1962. Along with the Seattle Polk Directory, Marc Leavipp of the University of Washington Registrar's office confirms [that] 516 13th Ave. E. [516 Thirteenth Avenue East] was the address "Ann Dunham had given upon registering at the University" (LeFevre & Lipson, 2009; cf. Neyman, 2009)

Some time in 1962 or 1963 Ann returned to Hawai'i and to her husband with her infant son Barry. The marital strife and wife abuse resumed. As we have seen, Barry's Kenyan father, Barak, who had left his African wife in 1959, left his American wife and their son in 1963, when Barry was two years old, to attend graduate school at Harvard University in Massachusetts. Obviously, his ambitions and his studies were not the only reasons Barak left his wife and son. Why did he not take them along with him to Cambridge, Massachusetts? Was he fleeing a difficult and independent-minded wife as well as pursuing his career? Did he tire of his marital and paternal responsibilities? Was he an inadequate husband and father? With his self-destructive and narcissistic personality, Barak was hardly the good father that his son needed. The toddler Barry was exposed to his black father's physical presence but also to the violent quarrels between his parents. As an adult, one of the primary themes of his emotional life has been his quest for mediation, conciliation, and conflict resolution.

It is not clear how Ann reacted to her abandonment by her husband, nor how it affected the two-year-old Barry. One might imagine that his father's sudden disappearance left a void in the two-year-old boy's emotional life. At the same time, he now had his mother all to himself. Yet this same mother now clung to him for emotional sustenance. Certain it is that his fantasy father's image played a very important role in his emotional life. In the summer of 1963, upon his graduation from the University of Hawai'i at Manoa, Barak was interviewed by the *Honolulu Star-Bulletin*. He criticized various aspects of his education there yet praised the interracial harmony in Hawai'i (Obama, 1995, p. 26).

The adolescent Barry discovered this interview while he was attending Honolulu's prestigious Punahou School in the 1970s. He was pained and puzzled by the fact that his father had totally omitted any mention of his mother and of himself. Was the reporter too intimidated by his father's "imperious manner" (Obama 1995, p. 27) to ask the obvious question, or had the editor cut out such mention, or did Barry's father omit any mention of his family because he was already planning his "long departure," not caring very much about his wife and son? Or were Ann and Barry still in Seattle? In any event, it may be no accident that throughout his adult life, and in politics, Barack would try to bring about reconciliation and harmony among people in conflict.

The child Barry struggled hard to understand his abandonment by his father and who was to blame for it. Was it his father? Was it his mother? Was it his grandparents? Did he ever think that he himself was the cause of his father's leaving the family? In his memoir he wrote that he did not blame his mother or her parents for this (Obama, 1995, p. 26). Does this mean that deep in his heart he blamed his father for abandoning him? Or could he have felt guilty himself? As an adolescent boy, he was disappointed, enraged, and confused, and he longed for the father that he never had. He wrote in his memoir *Dreams from My Father* that he was too young to know that he was supposed to have a live-in father, just as he was too young to know that he needed a race (Obama, p. 27). In fact, he must have *felt* that he needed a live-in father. He may have *displaced* his need for a father to his need for belonging to a race, community, or nation.

Barry's parents were divorced in 1964 in the Circuit Court of the First Judicial Circuit in Hawai'i. The senior Obama obtained a master's degree in economics from Harvard University and returned to Kenya in 1965, where he obtained a position in the Kenyan government. As he had done with his father, and as he would do many times afterward, he presented himself as greater than he was, calling himself "Dr. Obama" (Obama, 1995, p. 216, 394–424). His was a "false self," in Winnicott's phrase. Tragically, he got himself in trouble with the Kikuyu-dominated government of Jomo Kenyatta, and, later in life, he drank too much and became a bitter alcoholic. He briefly saw his son again in Hawai'i in late 1971 and early 1972, returned to Kenya, lost his job, became an alcoholic, drove recklessly, lost his legs in road accidents, and was killed in an automobile accident in 1982. The father's life ended in tragedy, and his son was alternately proud and ashamed of him. Yet, Barack wrote, "even in his absence his strong image had given me some bulwark on which to grow up, an image to live up to, or disappoint" (Obama, p. 129).

In 1987 Barack lost another key figure in his early life—his Indonesian stepfather, Lolo Soetoro, who died in Indonesia. Whether or not Soetoro formally adopted Barry, he had given him his name, and they had lived together in Indonesia from 1967 to 1971. They had met again in 1980, when Barry was a student at Occidental College in Los Angeles and Lolo went there for medical treatment for his liver ailment (Obama, 1995, p. 47), and in 1981, before Barry went to Columbia, when he traveled to Pakistan with some of his Pakistani college friends and also to Indonesia to see his mother, half sister, and stepfather (Goldman & Tanner 2008). Lolo had taught Barry how to defend himself in a tough world, and Barack liked him very much (Obama, pp. 30–31).

According to his friends and neighbors, Lolo had been more of a free spirit than a devout Muslim. Lolo died of a liver ailment at the age of 51 and was buried in the Tanah Kusir Cemetery in Jakarta. The loss may not have been as painful to Barack as that of his biological father, yet Lolo had been an actual father to Barry for at least four years, whereas his real father had abandoned him in his infancy. This was another loss that Barack needed to mourn in his emotions. It may be no accident that the following year he decided to go to Kenya for the first time in his quest for his father's image.

A perceptive American journalist has observed that the absence of Barack's father made him stronger and spared him the emotional damage his father would have caused him. As this journalist put it in the title of his article: "Cerebral and Cool, Obama Is Also Steely, and His Strength Comes from the Absence of a Father" (Meacham, 2008). The young Barry had idealized his absent father in his fantasies before he learned the truth about him in 1988. In his memoir *Dreams from My Father* he described the painful shattering of his idealizations. In an obvious exaggeration and idealization, his maternal grandfather Gramps had told Barry that his father Barak could do anything, that he "could handle just about any situation" (Obama, 1995, p. 8). Unconsciously projecting his own grandiose self on his son-in-law, Gramps told Barry many wondrous things about his father. Barack's mother Ann, the daughter of Gramps, who knew better, dared not contradict him openly: the most she would say was that he was exaggerating.

Barry himself, however, by the time he was a teenager in Hawai'i, began to doubt the truth of the stories that his mother and grandparents told him about his father (Obama, 1995, p. 11). Barry's mother Ann told him that his father was "domineering" and "uncompromising"—without ever calling him selfish or narcissistic—but she also added that he was "a very honest person" (Obama, p. 8). Barack himself, after he had learned the bitter truth about his father, told the journalist Jon Meacham (2008) that "My father was a deeply troubled person. My father was an alcoholic. He was a womanizer. He did not treat his children well." The teenage Barry may have unconsciously displaced his rage at his father to his grandfather. By the time he was 16, he was arguing with his grandfather all the time (Obama, 2006a, p. 81).

The absent father, or rather Barack's fantasy of him, was a very important influence in Barack's life. Meacham (2008) was aware that the absence of Barack's father was a very crucial element in his life. Barack himself was also aware of this. When Meacham asked him why great leaders either had a strong father or none at all, Barack replied that to run for the presidency of the United States, he had to have "pretty high expectations" of himself and that, with his father absent, he always felt that he had to prove his own worth to himself and that he had tried to live up to his larger-than-life image of his father. Barack thought that he was not too well adjusted or else he would not be running for the presidency. This made Meacham laugh, as it was a well-known joke among his colleagues that normal people never become presidents. He was surprised to hear this "joke" as a matter-of-fact statement from a presidential candidate.

Indeed, incredible as it may seem, Barry's abandonment by his father at the age of two, or possibly even in his early infancy (if his mother had indeed left his father and gone back to Seattle then), may have been a blessing in disguise for him. It was a crucial element in his development. While filling him with painful feelings of abandonment, loneliness, emptiness, sadness, and anger, it also enabled him to forge his own identity, to try to outdo his father, to avoid the unhealthy aspects of his father's character, and to steel himself for his career, which led to a happy family and to the presidency of the United States of America.

Chapter 6

A STEPFATHER
FROM INDONESIA

Synopsis: *Still idealizing foreigners, in 1965 the young mother Stanley Ann Dunham Obama met an Indonesian student at her university, Lolo Soetoro (1936–1987), who proposed to her. He had been traumatized as a boy during the Indonesian fight for independence against the Dutch colonial rulers. Lolo's father and eldest brother were killed, and the Dutch army burned down the family's home. The traumatized Lolo fled with his mother into the countryside to survive. Barack described Lolo quite affectionately in his memoir, as handsome, pleasant, a good tennis player, with an even smile and imperturbable temperament. As we have seen, Barack Obama was known as "Barry" in his childhood. From the time Barry was four to when he was six Lolo endured endless chess games with "Gramps" and long wrestling sessions with Barry (Obama, 1995, pp. 30–31). Lolo married Ann in 1966 and in 1967 returned to Indonesia with her, after his government recalled its citizens who were abroad. Barry had a likable stepfather, who adopted him as his own son, and gave him the name of Barry Soetoro. Some of Barack's even and imperturbable temperament is due to his identification with his adoptive stepfather.*

Barry's mother Ann was an immature but tough woman. She survived many emotional hurts. After an initial period of traumatization following her abandonment by her first husband, her separation from him, and their divorce, Ann went on with her life. Her divorce decree was issued in March 1964, due to "grievous mental suffering." Ann had inner strength, and within less than a year she met Lolo Soetoro, who had also been traumatized as a child, at the East-West Center in Honolulu, an educational and research organization established by the U.S. Congress in 1960 to strengthen relations and understanding among the peoples and nations of Asia, the Pacific, and the United States. This organization had originated in 1959 as a University of Hawai'i at Manoa faculty initiative. Lolo was the same age as Ann's first husband, Barak Obama. An orphan, he had also been abandoned by a father (who died).

The Indonesian nationalists had declared their independence from their Dutch colonial rulers in 1945. This had led the Dutch to arrest many Indonesian nationalist leaders and to raid Indonesian homes. Lolo was the 9th of 10 children of a man from Yogyakarta, a center of classical Javanese art and culture and the republican capital of Indonesia during the Indonesian national revolution and war against the Dutch colonial rulers, who were defeated and driven out of the country in 1949. The four years of war against the Dutch left Indonesia war-torn, poor, hungry, and traumatized. Its first president was Soekarno (Sukarno), who had led the nationalist struggle. *Bahasa Indonesia*, a Classical Malay dialect, was formally adopted as the national language. Benedict Richard O'Gorman Anderson, a well-known American scholar of international studies, government, and Asian studies, has called Indonesia a "synthetic nation" and an "imagined community" (B. Anderson, 1983).

After's Lolo's father and eldest brother were killed, and the Dutch burned down the family's home, the traumatized 10-year-old orphan Lolo fled with his mother into the countryside to survive. He was quite intelligent, and when he grew up, he attended Gajah Mada University in Yogyakarta and got his bachelor's degree in geography. He later obtained a scholarship from his workplace to study for a master's degree at the University of Hawai'i at Manoa, where in 1965 he met Barry's mother, Ann. Here the two traumatized and abandoned young people were drawn to one another due to their common emotional problems.

The adult Barack wrote that his mother's announcement that she was going to marry Lolo and move with him "to a faraway place" had not surprised him and that he had not objected to her new marriage. In a telling and poignant passage in his memoir, he recalled asking his mother whether she loved Lolo, at which she almost cried. She hugged him for a long time, clinging to him for affection and comfort, which made Barry feel "very brave, although I wasn't sure why" (Obama, 1995, p. 31). Did he feel brave because he sensed that his mother was fearful and he was not? Was it because he felt he was his mother's protector? Did his mother almost cry because she did not love Lolo? Did she hug Barry so long because she needed his protection and his love?

Lolo and Ann married in 1966, when she was about 24 and he was about 30. (Their marriage document is not available publicly. As in the case of Ann's first marriage, attempts to locate it have not been successful.) In the meantime, there was political upheaval in Indonesia. President Sukarno, Indonesia's first president, who had ruled the country since it became independent in 1949, was getting old and his government weak. In 1965 Major General Suharto foiled a *coup d'état* against Sukarno, which Suharto then blamed on the Communists. The Indonesian Communist Party was outlawed, and Suharto led a violent anti-Communist purge, in which over half a million people were killed. Suharto then wrested power from the weakened Sukarno, who relied on the Communists for support, and was inaugurated president in March 1968.

In 1966, during the unrest after the ascent of President Suharto, the Indonesian government recalled its citizens from abroad. Lolo returned to Indonesia, where he was interrogated and conscripted into the army. He worked as a geologist for the Indonesian army in the jungles of New Guinea, where leeches sucked the blood from his legs. Ann followed him to Jakarta with Barry a year later, in 1967. After a three-day stopover in Japan, they flew on to Indonesia. "Walking off the plane in Djakarta, the tarmac rippling with heat, the sun bright as a furnace, I clutched her hand, determined to protect her from whatever might come" (Obama, 1995, p. 32).

This is an extraordinary statement: the six-year-old son felt that he had to protect his 25-year-old mother. The parent-child roles were reversed. In the same way, the adult Barack Obama seeks to protect mother America and to heal her from her financial and social ailments. America would take the place of his idealized mother. He would reform her health care system, her banking and financial system, her criminal justice system, her military service system, her immigration system: he would create a new and better Mother America.

Chapter 7

PROTECTING HIS MOTHER

Synopsis: *One of the most poignant moments in Barack Obama's memoir* Dreams from My Father *is when he landed in Indonesia with his mother and felt that she needed his protection rather than the other way around. Barry was only six years old when this happened in 1967, while his mother was 25: "Walking off the plane in Djakarta, the tarmac rippling with heat, the sun bright as a furnace, I clutched her hand, determined to protect her from whatever might come" (Obama, 1995, p. 32). Later, as president of the United States, he would reform and protect Mother America. This was the pattern of his relationship with his mother. While his mother raised him, brought him up, educated him, made him get up at 4 A.M. each morning to study, sent him to two good schools (a Catholic one and a Muslim one), and made him take correspondence courses, she was also a vulnerable woman who needed his protection. She had a child by Lolo, a daughter named Maya, and this half sister of Barry's played an important role: He was no longer the only child and had to share his parents with her. But the relations between Ann and Lolo became strained, and she planned to leave him and return to the United States with her two children.*

As we have seen, while Barry's mother Ann was liberal, progressive, an atheist, and a feminist, she was also immature in some ways. She idealized blacks and foreigners and acted impulsively and at times recklessly on her emotions. What was it like for the infant Barry to have an 18-year-old white, rebellious, feminist, unconventional, stubborn, restless, immature, and self-willed mother? When Amanda Ripley interviewed the son about the mother, he called her "reckless." "When I think about my mother," Obama told Ripley recently, "I think that there was a certain combination of being very grounded in who she was, what she believed in. But also a certain recklessness. I think she was always searching for something. She wasn't comfortable seeing her life confined to a certain box" (Ripley, 2008). Psychologically, Barry had to adjust to his mother's recklessness. In many ways, his father, too, was reckless and also self-destructive. So Barack would have to learn to be as careful in this world as he could—which he has been, and very much so.

One might say that Barack had to fight hard to find the right place in his mother's heart. She was a complex and difficult individual. She did not get along well with her first husband, Barack's Kenyan father Barak Obama, who left her when Barack was two years old, nor with her second husband, Lolo Soetoro. After her abandonment by Barack's father, she may have clung to her little boy for comfort, which placed him in the unhealthy situation of being a father to his mother and of having to take care of her, protect her, and comfort her, until she married the Indonesian Lolo in 1966 and even during the years they lived in Indonesia (1966–1970). Many years later, in an unsigned note placed in Jerusalem's Wailing Wall, written on King David Hotel stationery and later retrieved by an Israeli tabloid, he asked God for "protection, humility and wisdom" (Camp, 2008; Smith, 2008).

TRAUMA AND RACIAL AWAKENING

At the age of nine, probably after the birth of his half sister Maya on August 15, 1970, Barry was attending the public Muslim school, where the other schoolkids derisively called him a "Negro." At about that time Barry one day found himself in the library of the U.S. embassy in Indonesia, where his mother taught English to wealthy Indonesian businessmen. There, he later recalled, he ran into a copy of a *Life* magazine issue that awoke his racial consciousness and was a turning point in his life (Obama, 1995, pp. 29–30, 51–52). In it, he later recalled, was a story about a black man who had been physically and mentally scarred by his efforts to bleach, lighten, or "peel off" his skin, with two accompanying photographs. Reading this article was a violent trauma for Barry, provoking much anxiety. This trauma started off his racial consciousness.

In fact, two U.S. journalists have found that the *Life* magazine story and the shocking photographs mentioned by Barack do not exist, nor are they to be found in the black magazine *Ebony* or in any other known U.S. magazine (Scharnberg and Barker, 2007). In other words, Barack's recollection of the *Life* magazine story was a later distortion of an actual childhood memory. In psychoanalysis, such a memory is known as a *screen memory* because it conceals deeper and more painful memories. The interpretation of this screen memory may be that Barry wanted to be white like his mother or that he *ambivalently* accepted his father's black identity, or a combination of the two. At the Muslim school that he attended at that time, the other kids called him a Negro, which was an offensive appellation at that time, like "nigger" in America.

The mulatto boy Barry felt that trying to be white was no use: it would only scar him physically and emotionally. It was not just the color or race issue; it was also an identity issue: Am I like my father? Am I like my mother? Whom do I identify with? Who am I? Reading this article traumatized Barry and made him insecure. He later recalled that he still trusted his mother's love but that he had begun to understand that her view of the world and of his black father's place in it was idealized (Obama, 1995, p. 52). It was not only a racial awakening for Barry but also a realization that his mother's perception of the world was unreliable, that her reality testing was flawed, and that he had to rely on himself alone to understand this cruel world and to face it with confidence and strength.

The adult Barack recalled that reading that *Life* magazine article gave him a serious anxiety attack. He felt hot, his stomach tightened, and his vision blurred. He wondered whether his white mother and her black boss knew about this horror story. He wanted to jump out of his seat, run over to them, show them his terrible discovery, and ask them to explain it and to reassure him about it. Yet he was afraid to do this. He could not name his fear, but he felt attacked, ambushed, shocked. The nine-year-old Barry was traumatized by this article, although his mother had told him about ignorant racists, and he knew about the dangers of illness, accidents, and bad fortune. He even knew about greed and cruelty. Yet he had not known about those unseen foes who could attack and damage him without his knowledge. He was overwhelmed by his anxiety. Back home he could not figure out whether he was abnormal or whether the world of the grown-up people among whom he lived was insane (Obama, 1995, pp. 30, 51–52).

If in fact that *Life* magazine article does not exist, as Scharnberg and Barker (2007) have shown, could Barack have forgotten the name of the magazine when he wrote his memoir? Could he have confused *Life* magazine with another magazine? Were there any other U.S. magazines that dealt with black people trying to become white and that the nine-year-old Barry Soetoro could have found in the library of the U.S. embassy in Jakarta in 1970?

Could the *Life* magazine article that so traumatized the nine-year-old Barry have been the article published in *Look* magazine in 1949 by Walter Francis White (1893–1955), a Negro whose skin, like his name, was so light that he could easily have passed for a white man? Rather than use his fair skin to pass himself off as a white man, however, White courageously stuck with his black race. In 1931 he became the head of the National Association for the Advancement of Colored People, which he led until his death. He even became known as "Mr. NAACP" (Janken, 2003; White, 1948). In the last decade of his life, however, White became so deeply disillusioned with the chances of improving the lot of the Negroes (as African Americans were then called) that he published an article in *Look* magazine advocating that Negroes bleach their skin and undergo plastic surgery to look like white people (White, 1949).

Or could the *Life* magazine article that so deeply shocked and scared the boy Barry have been the essay published in *Time* magazine about the changing situation of the Negroes in America (Time Magazine, 1966)? Neither of these articles, however, contains the traumatizing and anxiety-provoking story that the adult Barack remembered as having awakened his racial consciousness. Could his screen memory of the *Life* magazine article have masked deeper, more personal fears that had to do with his relationship with his mother, or his shock at the birth of his half sister, which had occurred a short time before his reading of the *Life* magazine story?

EMOTIONAL RESILIENCE

Trying to understand Barack's distorted memory of the *Life* magazine article, the *Chicago Tribune* journalists thought that "some of these discrepancies [between the memoir and the reality] are typical of childhood memories—fuzzy in specifics, warped by age, shaped by writerly license. Others almost certainly illustrate how carefully the young man guarded the secret of his loneliness from even those who knew him best. And the accounts bear out much of Obama's self-portrait as someone deeply affected by his father's abandonment yet able to thrive in greatly disparate worlds" (Scharnberg & Barker, 2007).

Indeed, one of the chief psychological riddles about Barack is his emotional resilience. What about him made it possible for him to thrive so well personally, politically, and in the family he created for himself, despite the emotional difficulties of his early life, his abandonment and his loneliness, his troubled adolescence, his inner struggle with his father's image and ghost, and the adversities he encountered as a community organizer in Chicago? How was he able to transform himself from a troubled young black American in an acute identity crisis into the first African American president of the United States of America?

It is indeed amazing that by the age of nine Barack had forged the ambivalent identification with his idealized father and the successful separation and individuation from his clinging mother that would sustain him and help him thrive. Barack likes to think of himself as a rare combination of black and white, rich and poor, high-brow and low-brow, sophisticated and simple, liberal and conservative, mainstream and marginal, a man who embodies all the contradictions and diversities in American society and in the human species. As Scharnberg and Barker (2007) have pointed out, his mother, his grandparents, and his stepfather were just as diverse: "Not as well known is the fact that the many people who raised him were nearly as diverse as the places where he grew up. There was his mother, Ann, a brilliant but impulsive woman; his grandmother Madelyn, a deeply private and stoically pragmatic Midwesterner; his grandfather Stanley, a loving soul inclined toward tall tales and unrealistic dreams."

The Danish-German-American psychoanalyst Erik Homburger Erikson (1902–1994) defined *ego identity* as the awareness of the fact that there is a self-sameness and continuity to the ego's synthesizing methods and a continuity of one's meaning for others. (Erikson, 1959, 1968). Erikson himself had his own identity problems: he was the son of a Danish Jewess who was an unwed mother before she married a German Jewish physician, who adopted Erik; he never met his real father. Erikson later converted from Judaism to Christianity. For Barack, the quest for his ego identity, including his personal, ethnic, religious, racial, communal, and national identity, went on throughout his young life. After his mother took him with her to Indonesia in 1967, Barry, who had a Swahili first name (Barack) and an Arabic middle name (Hussein), lived in this Muslim country for four years. In addition, his paternal grandfather had been a Muslim. Yet his father had not been a Muslim, and he did not wish to be a Muslim either. In Indonesia he was called Barry Soetoro: Barry had been his nickname, and his stepfather Lolo may have adopted him. The name Barry may also have indicated an identity separate from that of his father Barak (Erikson, 1959; Falk, 1975–1976). Indeed, it was at about the time of his father's death that he went back to his legal name of Barack.

In his memoir, Barack recalled how as a young black college student, after some heated discussions with fellow black students, he learned to conceal his violent emotions about his race and about racism and racial tensions (Obama, 1995, p. 87). As a little boy in Indonesia, the adopted Barry had already developed his incredible control of his feelings through the unconscious process of isolation, which separates thoughts from their associated feelings. For example, when he arrived in Indonesia at the age of six, he ran into frightening creatures and scenes: a huge figure of Hanuman, the Hindu monkey god; a huge ape or monkey named Tata who looked so threatening that Barry kept his distance from him; and a hen being beheaded, with all the gory sights and details (Obama 1995, pp. 33–34).

Rather than recall his fear, shock, disgust, or other painful feelings in his memoir, Barack recalled his dinner of chicken stew afterward and his feeling that he could hardly believe his good fortune (Obama, p. 35). It takes a good deal of unconscious emotional isolation not to experience violent emotions: the perceptions and thoughts are isolated from the painful feelings they evoke.

Barry's adoptive stepfather, Lolo, who had fun-wrestled with him in Hawai'i, now taught him to seriously protect himself against other boys' violence. Barry had strong emotions: When another boy ran off with his friend's soccer ball and then hit Barry on the head with a rock, he bitterly complained to his stepfather that the other had cheated unfairly (Obama, 1995, p. 35). Lolo parted Barry's hair calmly and said that his head was not bleeding, and that was the end of that. But the next day Lolo began to teach Barry boxing, and Barry took to Lolo as a replacement for the father who had abandoned him. Barack later fondly recalled his life in Indonesia from age 6 to age 10 as pleasant and adventurous (ibid., p. 37).

Despite his wife's objections, Lolo, a moderate Indonesian Muslim who also practiced some parts of the Hindu and animist religions that were common in Indonesia (Obama, 1995, p. 37), worked on the offshore oil rigs of Mobil Oil, the U.S.-based international oil company, as a government-relations consultant. It is not clear whether Lolo legally and officially adopted Barry Obama, who used the name Barry Soetoro in Indonesia, or whether he only acknowledged him as his son. This later gave rise to many lawsuits by Barack's foes alleging that he was not a natural-born citizen of the United States and that he had lost his U.S. citizenship by becoming an Indonesian citizen. All these suits failed in the U.S. courts, but the matter is still being pursued by some anti-Obama fanatics. In Lolo and Ann's divorce decree of 1980, one child above the age of 18 is listed, who must be Barack. Barry obviously liked his stepfather. In *Dreams from My Father*, he described Lolo affectionately as well mannered, even-tempered, imperturbable, graceful, and easygoing, and he described the personal and economic struggles that Lolo had to deal with after he returned to Indonesia from Hawai'i. Yet he did not forget to add that, in the Hawai'ian language, the word *Lolo* meant "crazy," a fact that amused Gramps a lot—and probably made Barry laugh too (Obama, pp. 30–31).

Many of the things that Barack omitted from his memoir are no less important that those he dwelled upon. For example, he did not mention a wedding ceremony when his mother married Lolo (Obama, 1995, p. 31). Did they marry legally? Also, in his letters from Indonesia to his grandparents in Hawai'i, Barry omitted any mention of several horrific events that might well have traumatized a lesser boy. Barry matured quickly in Indonesia and was intellectually and emotionally precocious. He quickly learned that the real world was violent, harsh, and full of painful surprises, but he also knew that his grandparents lived in an idealized world, and he sought to spare them the pain of hearing about the harsh reality he was experiencing and of bothering them with questions they could not answer (Obama, pp. 35–38).

For a boy so young to think so maturely is truly extraordinary. Did the nine-year-old Barry really think like this, or was it the adult Barack who later reconstructed his past in this fashion? His mother gave him all the attention and comfort he craved, but she could not defend him against the violent world they lived in. It was his stepfather who taught Barry how to face this violent world and how to protect himself. Barry liked Lolo. He learned to be tough with beggars, servants, and almost everybody else. Lolo told him that he could not afford to be soft or compassionate, because he would have to pay dearly for it. Lolo told Barry that his mother was soft and that men had to be tough and sensible (Obama, 1995, p. 39). Yet, for all the toughness that Lolo tried to teach Barry in order to help him protect himself, Barry Soetoro eventually became the compassionate and empathic Barack Obama, the man who would organize poor black people in Chicago into self-helping communities and finally rule the United States in a way meant to help the poor and the needy.

Lolo also taught Barry how to control his feelings. The imperturbable Lolo never showed his own emotions, and Barry never saw him angry or sad. When his legs hurt badly from the leeches sucking his blood in New Guinea, he said that he could not afford to worry about his hurt, because he had to fight his way through this cruel life. Lolo taught Barry that he must always be strong, or else other men would take advantage of him, exploit him, take what he owned from him, hurt him, and otherwise cause him pain and grief. So Barry had to be strong, or else ally himself with strong men (Obama, 1995, pp. 40–41). This was a lesson that Barry never forgot.

In many ways, Barry's stepfather Lolo filled the role of his absent father and gave Barry basic skills that helped him survive and thrive. Barry's mother, Ann, however, for all her toughness, felt lonely in Indonesia. Her initially good relations with her second husband Lolo turned sour, especially when he wanted to leave Jakarta and work on Mobil Oil's offshore rigs. In Hawai'i, Lolo had told Ann that he would teach at a university, that the newly independent Indonesia held endless promise. But now, in Indonesia, he barely spoke to her. In fact, Lolo had become depressed (Obama, 1995, p. 42). Like Barry's biological father, Barak, his stepfather Lolo, who had been traumatized and orphaned as a child, tried to drown his sorrow in alcohol. Suspicious and closed up in himself, he tried to avoid words and feelings. His job as a geologist paid little.

In his memoir, Barry tried to understand why his mother's second marriage had also fallen apart. He thought that Ann felt she was a burden on Lolo. She taught English to Indonesian businessmen at the U.S. embassy, and her income helped, but she still felt lonely. Some of her Indonesian students made passes at her, and she was not very happy with the Americans at the embassy either. She learned that the military *coup d'état* in which Suharto had replaced Sukarno had killed hundreds of thousands of Indonesians. She learned about the graft, shakedowns, bribes, nepotism, and corruption of Indonesia's top officials, all the way up to the president (Obama, 1995, p. 44).

Barry recalled that Lolo never told Ann about his emotional pain. One of Lolo's cousins, however, told Ann that his return to Indonesia in 1966 had been traumatic for him. He had been held and questioned by the military, conscripted into the army, and sent to New Guinea, where the Indonesian army was bloodily suppressing a native Papuan revolt against its occupation of West Papua, which it had annexed and renamed West Irian (later Irian Jaya). As a young soldier wading through the tropical marshes of Papua, Lolo had been prey to leeches. This was his second major trauma after he was victimized and orphaned by the Dutch as a child. His cousin told Ann not to be too hard on her husband. Ann, and through her Barry, saw the blatant abuse of power by Indonesia's politicians, diplomats, and generals. Barack recalled that his mother saw power as a curse. She identified with its victims, while her son would seek power in order to cure its evils and not feel powerless himself.

Lolo Soetoro had been the victim of the ruthless power of the Indonesian authorities. Barry himself, however, saw how crucial power was to survival. It was no accident that he later became a politician and finally attained the most powerful position in the world. Power is an antidote to early feelings of powerlessness, and such feelings were plentiful both in Barry's unconscious mind and in Indonesia (Obama, 1995, pp. 46–47). Lolo and Ann began to argue when Lolo wanted to leave her and work for the U.S. oilmen who had offshore drilling enterprises. Barry overheard their arguments, but he does not say how he felt. It is painful and traumatic for a child to hear his parents fighting. He fears that they will separate and that he will lose one of them.

In July 1970 Ann sent the almost-nine-year-old Barry back to Hawai'i to spend his summer vacation with her parents. They were delighted to have him back and gave him everything they could to make him happy—ice cream, cartoons, days at the beach. Barry had a great time that summer. Ann was about to give birth to her second child. Barry knew that when he returned to Indonesia at the end of August, he would have a half sibling. For Ann, sending Barry home to her parents was a step on the way to a final return home the following year, as she was planning to leave her husband and return to Hawai'i with her two children. Her second marriage was on the rocks. The following year, when she told Barry her plans, she would remind him of the great summer he had the year before (Obama, 1995, p. 54).

On August 4, 1970, Barry celebrated his ninth birthday with his grandparents in Hawai'i. Shortly thereafter, on August 15, a major event occurred in his life: His mother Ann gave birth to his half sister, Maya Kassandra Soetoro. The nine-year-old Barry had to contend with a new rival for his mother's and stepfather's affection. In his memoir he said nothing of his feelings on that very important occasion (Obama, 1995, p. 47). It was at that time, however, that he later recalled having read the *Life* magazine story that so badly traumatized him and awakened his racial consciousness. Could the birth of his half sister have been so traumatic and painful for the only child Barry? Or could it have been the fact that at that time he had begun to attend the Muslim public school, where the other kids called him a Negro?

The following year the 10-year-old Barry was sent by his mother back to Hawai'i, and soon thereafter Maya too was taken there by her mother. When Maya grew up she got a Ph.D. in international comparative education from the University of Hawai'i and married the Chinese Canadian Konrad Ng, who was teaching at one of Hawai'i's universities. They had a daughter whom they named Suhaila. With her diverse cultural and spiritual background, Maya Kassandra Soetoro-Ng became a Buddhist. She is now a 40-year-old history teacher at the Roman Catholic La Pietra Hawai'i School for Girls in Honolulu, and she also teaches night classes in her field at the University of Hawai'i at Manoa, her parents' and her own alma mater. Maya is fond of her half brother Barack and is often interviewed about him in the mass-communication media.

The adult Barack recalled that his mother had pushed him to integrate himself into the local Indonesian culture, making him an independent, unspoiled, well-behaved American schoolboy, unlike the other, spoiled American children in Jakarta (Obama, 1995, p. 47). She also taught him to disdain ignorance and arrogance, which helped him build his character. Ann educated her precocious son, among other things, with correspondence courses in English, records of the African American singer Mahalia Jackson, and speeches by Dr. Martin Luther King. Did she wish to inculcate "black consciousness" in him? Did she miss her first husband, the black African Barak Obama? For three years (1967–1970), from age six to age nine, Barry attended a Catholic boys' school, the Fransiskus Strada Asisia (Francis of Assisi School), in Jakarta, where he was registered by his stepfather Lolo as "Barry Soetoro, an Indonesian Muslim"

(Barker, 2007). The registration document was later used against him by his rivals during the U.S. presidential campaign, who sought to show that he was not a U.S. citizen and not a Christian.

After three years at the Catholic school, for one year, from age 9 to age 10, Barry attended a public Indonesian Muslim school, the Besuki School, also known as the Sekolah Dasar Negeri Menteng 01 (Menteng 01 State Elementary School), Menteng being Jakarta's "Beverly Hills" (Barker, 2007). In his memoir, Barack curiously reversed the order of the two schools and recalled that he had spent two years at each school (Obama, 1995, p. 154). One is left to wonder about the causes of this curious memory distortion. After Barry had enrolled in the Muslim school, however, Ann supplemented his education with a U.S. correspondence course. During his year at the Muslim school, his last year in Indonesia, his mother woke him up at 4 A.M. each morning to do English-language correspondence lessons until 7 A.M., so he could catch up with his peers in America, where she planned to send him back. Ann was very ambitious for her son, whom she may have unconsciously seen as an extension of herself. When he complained to her about his early starts, she told him that it was no fun for her either (Obama, p. 48).

In Indonesia, Ann worried about Barry's health, fearful of losing him, and was upset by the rampant corruption and abuse of power. Ann was a tough woman. Barack described her as a soldier for peace, liberty, and equality. The adult Barack wrote about her with great affection and admiration, saying that he owed his mother the best parts of his character (Obama, 1995, pp. 49–50), yet he mentioned her sparingly relative to his father and grandparents (Abramsky, 2009, pp. 42–43). Did he deny the negative feelings he had for her? No child can avoid having mixed or ambivalent feelings for his parents. In the face of Indonesian vices, Ann taught him what she held to be life's cardinal virtues and values: honesty, fairness, straight talk, independent judgment. But in Indonesia, those values were impractical: They did not work against the rampant poverty, corruption, and insecurity.

Until 1981, when he moved from Occidental College in Los Angeles to Columbia University in New York, and perhaps even until his father's death in 1982, Barack did not use his first name (Obama, 1995, p. 118) but instead was called Barry, his nickname, which he used as his formal name as well. His name Barry Soetoro in Indonesia may indicate his adoption by his stepfather, Lolo Soetoro. When he was nine years old, in 1970, his mother placed him in Jakarta's public Muslim Besuki School, in the upper-class Jakarta neighborhood of Menteng.

Contrary to claims by his rivals during the presidential campaign, the Besuki School that Barry Soetoro attended from 1970 to 1971 was not a

Muslim *madrassah* but a public school. It taught children of all faiths as well as Muslims. The language of instruction was Indonesian, or *Bahasa Indonesia*, a Classical Malay dialect that had been declared the official language of Indonesia when Indonesian independence was declared in 1945 (which led to the war of 1945–1949 against the Dutch), following the 1928 unifying-language declaration in the Indonesian Youth Pledge. The Besuki School had been founded in 1934 by the Dutch colonial rulers of Indonesia as the Carpentier Alting Stichting Nassau School, teaching the children of the Dutch and Indonesian nobility. After Indonesia's independence in 1949, it became a public school. The Indonesian government took over the school in 1962. It was run by the Raden Saleh Foundation, named after Raden Saleh Syarif Bustaman (1807–1880), a well-known Indonesian painter from the noble Indonesian family of the legendary Kijai Ngabehi Kertoboso Bustaman (1681–1759), ruler of the old Mataram Kingdom and Sultanate. The school's name was abbreviated as *SDN Menteng 1*, and it was a public school attended by both Indonesians and foreigners. At the Besuki School, Barry was aloof from the other children. By the age of nine, he had already developed the self-control, isolation of feeling, and extraordinary control of feelings that would become a hallmark of his character. This may have been his defense against feelings of abandonment, rage, and fear, and it worked very well.

When he was 10 years old, in 1971, Barry's mother Ann decided to send him home to Hawai'i to attend the Punahou School, an elite, private, coeducational, nonsectarian college-preparatory school in Honolulu, to which he had won a scholarship (Niven, 2009, p. 10; Obama, 1995, p. 54). Unhappy in her marriage, Ann was actually planning to leave her husband and return to America herself. She had also been worried about Barry's poor education at the Indonesian Muslim Besuki School, and she had a hard time taking care of her two children as a working mother. Ann was planning to follow her son back to Hawai'i along with her daughter within the year.

The adult Barack later recalled that returning to Hawai'i and living with his grandparents had seemed like a good idea to him, but that when he arrived in Hawai'i he found his grandparents badly changed. His grandfather had lost his furniture-salesman job and was working unhappily as an insurance salesman, and they had moved from their big house into a small apartment in a high-rise building on a major Honolulu thoroughfare. He felt as if he were living with strangers (Obama, 1995, pp. 54–55). His unhappy description implies that had he known about the decline and fall of his grandparents, he would not have wanted to go back to them, and that he may well have experienced his mother's sending him away as another abandonment, this time by his mother. He may have had deeply ambivalent feelings about it.

Did Barry feel that he could or should have done anything to save his mother's second marriage? Did he feel responsible or guilty for the problems between his mother and his stepfather? It is certain that he liked his stepfather Lolo very much and that the impending separations between him and his stepfather, him and his mother, and his mother and his stepfather did not make him happy. Yet there was nothing he could do about it. When his mother told him about sending him home to Hawai'i, it did not sound bad to him. She assured him that she and his half sister Maya would join him within the year. Yet his feelings changed later, especially after he returned to Honolulu and saw his grandfather's personal decline (Obama, 1995, pp. 54–55).

Ann sent her son Barry to Hawai'i, although the decision was painful for her, as she planned to follow him there with her daughter Maya within the year. In 1971, at the age of 10, Barry went back to Honolulu to live with his white maternal grandparents and to attend the prestigious Punahou School, which was 90 percent white. Back home in Hawai'i, Barry Soetoro became Barry Obama again, resuming his father's identity. But his maternal grandfather, Gramps, had undergone a significant change for the worse. He had left the furniture-sales business to become an unsuccessful insurance salesman and had become alternately irritable, morose, depressed, and desperate (Obama, 1995, p. 55). Barry missed his mother. His Harvard biographer thinks that even though she shuttled between Indonesia and Hawai'i throughout his adolescence, Ann's "absence from her son's daily life (and his from hers) left a significant void at a time when the teenage Obama was beginning to examine his own racial identity" (Niven, 2009, p. 11). Niven thinks that Barack ultimately identified with his black African father, but this identification was deeply ambivalent, and it is more accurate to say that the young Barry identified with his *idealized fantasy image* of his absent father.

Barry felt that his maternal grandparents had become strangers to him. Gramps and Toot were not getting along very well, either. While Gramps was not making much money any longer and was living in fantasy, Toot had a senior job at the Bank of Hawai'i, which helped pay Barry's tuition, with some assistance from his scholarship. Toot disapproved of her husband's grandiose plans for writing poetry, painting, and building a dream house, as well as other projects that were unrealistic and well-nigh impossible (Obama, 1995, p. 55). Barry was a bright student, but, as we shall see, he did not totally identify with the black student community. At the end of 1971 he saw his father for the first and only time since age two, and it was not a happy meeting.

As in her first marriage, there were serious conflicts between the strong-willed Ann and her husband Lolo in Indonesia. For one thing, after the birth of her daughter, Ann wished to return to work, to pursue her career, while Lolo wanted more children. "He became more American, she once said, as she became more Javanese" (Scott, 2008a). Missing her son and her parents and unhappy in her marriage, after Barry left, in late 1971, Ann left Lolo and Indonesia, taking their daughter Maya with her, returning to Hawai'i, and reuniting with her son Barry and with her parents.

In his memoir, Barack does not tell us how he *felt* about the breakup of his mother's second marriage. Lolo and Ann still saw each other occasionally during the 1970s, when Ann returned to Indonesia for her anthropological fieldwork, but they did not live together again. They were legally divorced in 1980 in Hawai'i, and at that time Ann helped Lolo travel to Los Angeles for the treatment of his liver disease, which would kill him seven years later. In Los Angeles, Lolo met his stepson Barry for the last time. Lolo died in 1987, at the age of 51. Barack did not even mention this loss in his memoir. A year later, Barack would travel to Kenya to search for the ghost of his own father.

During most of the 1970s, Barry's mother was divorced from her first husband and separated from her second one. Ann kept shuttling between Hawai'i and Indonesia, between her family and her career. She kept in touch with both her ex-husbands, however. She was not estranged from either, and she encouraged her two children to keep in touch with them. In 1974 she returned to graduate school at the University of Hawai'i at Manoa, while raising Barry and Maya with her parents' help.

In 1975 Ann returned to Indonesia to do the fieldwork for her Ph.D. in anthropology at the University of Hawai'i, taking her five-year-old daughter Maya with her. Did she miss her second husband Lolo? Her son Barry chose to stay in Hawai'i. Did he have negative feelings for his mother? Barry remained at the Punahou School and lived with his maternal grandparents. He later thought that he was forging his identity. Ann acquiesced to his decision, despite it being personally painful for her. We shall see later what this meant for Barry.

Adolescent boys often rebel against their fathers in an effort to create their ego identity through that struggle. Barry had no father, and he was deeply disappointed in his formerly strong and "boisterous" grandfather, who had declined and become old, depressed, small, and weak before his very eyes (Obama, 1995, p. 89). Barry now had very mixed feelings about his grandfather. Around 1977, when he was 16 years old, Barry fought with his grandfather all the time. Barry unconsciously displaced his rage at his father onto his grandfather. He later realized that "without a father present in the house, my grandfather bore the brunt of much of my adolescent rebellion" (Obama, 2006a, p. 81).

A couple of years later, when he was a 17-year-old high school senior, Barry slowly realized that it was better for him to empathize with Gramps than to fight with him. Barry's gift for rhetoric gave him an advantage over Gramps, and he usually won his arguments with his grandfather, making him very upset. As he grew older, however, he began to have empathy for his mother's father. Barry began to think about his grandfather's past emotional suffering and to understand "his need to feel respected in his own home" (Obama, 2006a, p. 81). The teenage boy began to see that obeying Gramps would not hurt him much, whereas it would give his grandfather the sense of self-worth and mastery that he badly needed. Fighting Gramps tooth and nail became self-debasing for Barry.

This was an incredibly mature insight for a 17-year-old high school student. Was it Barry's mother Ann who had helped him transform himself from her father's antagonist to his psychotherapist? Ann, who worked for many years in Indonesia on her Ph.D. dissertation in anthropology (Dunham, 1992), was shuttling between Indonesia and Hawai'i, and she still had a considerable influence on her son Barry. The adult Barack recalled that it was his mother who had taught him empathy. Whenever she saw cruelty, thoughtlessness, abuse, exploitation, and other ways in which people hurt one another, she would look Barry square in the eyes and ask him, "How do you think that would make you feel?" (Obama, 2006a, p. 80).

Despite his adolescent upheaval, Barry could apply his mother's question of empathy to his grandfather, empathize with him, and adapt himself to his needs. Few teenagers can do this, and few people have the empathy that Barack has. He thus has an extraordinary combination of realism and idealism, fierce ambitions and great empathy and compassion. Barack still considers empathy the most important personal quality.

Yet Barry's mother also repeatedly left him during his adolescence, to travel to Indonesia for her fieldwork in anthropology. How did *that* make *him* feel? Barry's mother was a complex individual. Being a former weaver, among her various other occupations, she decided to study Indonesian village industries, in particular, blacksmithing. Why did Ann study blacksmithing and not weaving, for example, with which she had firsthand experience? Did this have to do with her love for her black first husband or for black people in general? Ann went to live in Yogyakarta, her second husband's birthplace, which was also the center of Javanese handicrafts and the former republican capital of Indonesia during the war of independence against the Dutch in 1945–1949.

In 1992, after her father's death and before her son's marriage, the 49-year-old Ann earned her PhD in anthropology from the University of Hawai'i at Manoa with a doctoral dissertation entitled *Peasant Blacksmithing in Indonesia: Surviving and Thriving against All Odds* (Dunham, 1992).

She signed it S. Ann Dunham—no first name, no Obama, no Soetoro. Survival against all odds was a major theme in Ann's life. By the time she turned 50 on November 29, 1992, the formidable Stanley Ann Dunham Obama Soetoro, too, had survived and thrived against all odds, despite her dislocations, abandonments, and divorces. Two years later, however, she was diagnosed with terminal cancer, and she died in 1995.

In Indonesia, Ann also became active in microcredit, the extension of small loans to poor people designed to spur their entrepreneurship. As these individuals lack collateral, steady employment, and a verifiable credit history, they cannot meet the minimal qualifications to gain access to traditional credit. Microcredit originated with the Grameen Bank in Bangladesh, created by Muhammad Yunus (born 1940), a Fulbright scholar at Vanderbilt University in Tennessee and a professor of economics at the University of Chittagong in Bangladesh. This bank has helped poor people create their own small businesses, begin to make money, and become relatively well-to-do.

When Yunus started microcredit, even the international economic-development organizations, including the World Bank and the International Monetary Fund, rejected his ideas as unfeasible. The enormous success of microcredit in getting people out of poverty spurred bankers worldwide to realize that poor people can safely be given loans without incurring undue risk. Large banks are offering microcredit to poor borrowers, and microcredit has become a respectable and legitimate form of financial activity. The United Nations has formally embraced microcredit and declared the year 2005 the international year of microcredit.

In Asia, Ann also pursued a career in rural development, championing women's work and microcredit for the poor, first with Indonesia's oldest bank, then with the U.S. Agency for International Development, the Ford Foundation, and Women's World Banking, and finally as a rural-development consultant in Pakistan. She had ties to leaders of organizations working for human rights, women's rights, and grassroots development in Indonesia and elsewhere. Ann never ceased to work and to fight for the underdog. Perhaps she felt like one herself. But she paid heavily for her hard-driving life: In 1992—the year of her father's death, of receiving her PhD degree, and of her son's wedding—she fell ill with uterine cancer, which was diagnosed too late, two years later, and she died within three years, in 1995. Barack would suffer yet another loss and abandonment, perhaps the most painful of them all.

MOURNING HIS LOSSES

Barack had suffered a series of painful abandonments and losses, from his desertion by his father when he was two years old, to his separation from his mother at age 10, to the death of the old neighbor that he liked in New York in 1981, the death of his father in 1982, the loss of his stepfather in 1987, and the shattering of his idealized father image in 1988. In early 1992 the 30-year-old Barack suffered another serious personal loss when his maternal grandfather, the formerly warm, jolly, and boisterous Stanley Armour Dunham, whom Barack affectionately called Gramps, who had given his daughter Ann his own first name, and whose mother had killed herself when he was eight, died at the age of 73, after many years of personal decline and bouts of depression.

The death of her father was also a great loss for Barack's mother, Ann, as her father had been the dominant emotional influence in her life, for better or for worse. But it was also a loss for her son Barack, who had loved his grandfather and had been loved by him, even though Gramps had declined emotionally for the previous 20 years. Was Ann able to mourn her losses? In the same year, 1992, she received her PhD in anthropology. In 1994, when Barack was 33, Ann was diagnosed with ovarian and uterine cancer; she moved back to Hawai'i to be near her widowed mother, Madelyn. Stanley Ann Dunham Obama Soetoro died of cancer in Honolulu in 1995 at the age of 52, after a bitter struggle with her health insurers, who refused to pay her medical expenses. Barack was unable to save her. Later, during his first year as president, in 2009, he would devote his greatest efforts to health-care reform in America, which he successfully achieved when the U.S. Congress passed his health-care reform bill in late 2009, which Obama would sign into law in early 2010.

In late 1992, the year in which so many important events occurred in his life, Barack married Michelle LaVaughn Robinson, whom he had met three years earlier and became engaged to in 1991. Having lost his loving grandfather, he gained a loving wife. Barack had met Michelle in 1989 during his first summer break from Harvard Law School, while working as a summer associate at the Chicago law firm of Sidley Austin. This firm was owned by Newton Norman Minow (born 1926), a former chairman of the U.S. Federal Communications Commission, whose "Television and the Public Interest" speech of 1961, referring to U.S. television as a "vast wasteland," is often cited by writers and speakers. At Sidley Austin, one of the oldest law firms in the world, Barack and Michelle were among the few black employees. He was 28 years old, she was 25, and both were graduates of Harvard Law School (Niven, 2009, pp. 17–18). After they began to date, Michelle took him to her home to meet her family, and Barack hit it off with her brother Craig, a professional basketball player and coach.

In 1995, Barack, who had suffered many losses and abandonments, suffered yet another loss when his mother died. Barack's emotions may have ranged from grief to rage to guilt for not saving his mother. But

Barack was highly resilient emotionally: he had overcome his earlier traumas, and he had learned how to mourn his losses. Psychological resiliency has been studied by the French Jewish psychoanalyst Boris Cyrulnik, whose books may help explain Barack's resiliency. Cyrulnik, who was born in 1937, lost his own parents when he was seven years old. They, like six million other Jews, were murdered by the German Nazis. Nonetheless, he overcame his loss and his trauma and became an eminent psychiatrist.

In his 20 books in French and 2 in English (Cyrulnik, 1993, 2003), he studied how people find the inner strength to rise above childhood trauma. Cyrulnik found that 1 in 2 people experience emotional trauma and that 1 in 10 remains a lifelong prisoner of that suffering. The others, however, overcome their trauma. Cyrulnik studied why some children are permanently damaged by their difficult childhoods, while others, like Barack Obama, grow up into secure, creative, loving adults. Like Barack's own book *The Audacity of Hope* (2006a), Cyrulnik's books, based on his broad clinical experience with the victims of childhood trauma, offer a message of hope for the victims of deprivation, separation, abandonment, emotional and sexual abuse, and parental violence.

In Barack's memoir *Dreams from My Father* he constantly struggles with the ghost of his father (Obama, 1995). Cyrulnik, too, described how the ghosts of the past keep whispering to the child within the adult (Cyrulnik, 2003). Through dozens of vivid clinical examples, Cyrulnik described the psychological ingredients of resiliency, the ability to heal the wounded self and to move on, to mourn one's losses, to make sense of what happened in the past, and to form new emotional and social ties. Affection is a vital need, Cyrulnik believed, and those who are deprived of it in their early life will attach themselves intensely to anybody and anything that rekindles the spark of life, whatever the emotional cost. From the earliest parent-child bonding to the sexual turbulence of the teenage years, Cyrulnik, himself a successful survivor, studied what makes for success or failure in the emotional struggle to gain freedom from early pain. Certainly Barack's case is a very good example of emotional resiliency.

We have seen Barack's lifelong ambivalence about his mother (Abramsky, 2009, pp. 42–45; Obama, 1995, pp. 123–125). In late 1995 Barack was waging his first campaign for political office in Illinois and was not present with his mother at the time of her death in November. After he was informed of it, he at once flew to Hawai'i to join his half sister Maya in taking leave of their dead mother. His emotions at that time can only be guessed at: was he enraged at her for abandoning him by dying? Did he feel grief, guilt, or relief? In her will, the unconventional Ann had wanted her corpse cremated. There was therefore no funeral and no burial. Following a memorial service at his mother's alma mater, the University of Hawai'i at Manoa, Barack and Maya spread their mother's ashes in the Pacific Ocean on the south side of Oahu Island. Barack hurried back to Chicago, where he was waging a fierce political battle against another mother figure, the older black politician Alice Palmer, who had sponsored him for her vacant state senate seat, only to try to take it from him after she lost her primary race for the U.S. Congress.

Barack's memoir *Dreams from My Father* was published in 1995, just before his mother's death. By dying, Barack's mother had abandoned him, just as his father had done. Barack's emotional task was to mourn the loss of his mother and to reconcile his ambivalent feelings for her within himself. Mourning is a long and painful process, and it is often incomplete or partial. It may be too painful to grieve, to go through bereavement, to accept one's loss and abandonment. Barack made his motherland, America, his new mother. By running for president and by protecting America, taking care of her, and saving her from her many woes, he could once again protect his mother, as he felt he had to do when he was six years old and they reached Indonesia (Obama, 1995, p. 32; Ripley, 2008). This time he has all the power he needs to protect America and care for her properly.

As we have seen, Barack's lifelong inner struggle with the ghost of his abandoning father is crucial to understanding his extraordinary, unique, and complex personality. A perceptive American journalist has pointed out the great discrepancy between Barack's idealized youthful image of his father and his later disappointment with him in his memoir:

> "All my life, I had carried a single image of my father, one that I had sometimes rebelled against but had never questioned, one that I had later tried to take as my own," Obama writes in *Dreams From My Father*. "The brilliant scholar, the generous friend, the upstanding leader—my father had been all those things." But, as an adult, he learned there was a darker side to his Harvard-educated father. "A bitter drunk? An abusive husband? A defeated, lonely bureaucrat?" Obama wrote. "To think that all my life I had been wrestling with nothing more than a ghost!"... "He and my mother divorced when I was only two years old, and for most of my life I knew him only through the letters he sent and the stories my mother and grandparents told," Obama said in speech he delivered this year just before Father's Day. (Fornek, 2007b, based on Obama, 1995, p. 220, and on Obama's speeches)

If in fact Barack's parents were married in 1961, Barack's mother may have left his father when he was still a baby, and they divorced in 1964, when he was not yet three. As another perceptive journalist understood, it is easier to grow up without a father than with a seriously disturbed one (Meacham, 2008). Barack was lucky to have been spared his father's disturbed personality and his tragic life as a result of his father's abandonment of him. Though initially traumatized by this abandonment, through his grandparents' stories he invented for himself a highly idealized father, identified with him ambivalently, and sought to outdo his father. With his real father absent, he was free to imagine one that was great, wise, and wonderful, until he discovered otherwise after his father's death in 1982—in fact, only when he first came to Kenya in 1988.

Such were the emotions that characterized Barry's young life: abandonment, loneliness, grief, solitude, the search for a father figure, the idealization of the real father, the escape into solitude, the ambiguous ego identity, the quest for a new and clearer identity, the longing for friendship and love. His father was narcissistic, arrogant, and self-destructive. For example, as Barack's maternal grandparents told him, his father drove on the left-hand side of the road in America, as they do in Kenya (a former British colony), and instead of admitting his dangerous mistake complained about the stupid traffic regulations in America.

Barry's father had frequent outbursts of violent narcissistic rage, which he tried to rationalize. He abused his wives and children. Barry's maternal grandparents told him many fantastic stories about his father, making him out to be a very powerful and important man. Gramps told Barry that his father's self-confidence was the key to his success (Obama, 1995, pp. 6–7). It was not until he was 27 that Barack discovered the extent of his father's flaws and self-destruction. Yet, as we shall see, self-confidence is a major aspect of Barack's character. In this, as in many other things, he identified with his *idealized* image of his father.

EMOTIONAL INTELLIGENCE AND FREUDIAN SLIPS

The feelings that were aroused in the 27-year-old Barack by his discovery of his flawed father were very powerful and painful. In my view, his unconscious defense against them was emotional isolation, discipline, and detachment, in an attempt to achieve total control of his feelings. He had developed this emotional defense in his early life. As a perceptive American journalist put it,

> If there is one quality that those closest to Obama marvel at, it is his emotional discipline. This is partly a matter of temperament, partly *an effort by Obama to step away from his own feelings* so he can make dispassionate judgments. "He doesn't allow himself the luxury of any distraction," said Valerie [Bowman] Jarrett, a close adviser. "He is able to use his disciplined mind to not get caught up in the emotional swirl." ... It is not that Obama does

not experience emotion, friends say. But he detaches from it, observing it instead. "He has the qualities of a writer," said [David] Axelrod, his strategist. "I get the sense that he's participating in these things but also watching them." Obama watches and assesses no one more avidly than himself. (Kantor, 2008; italics added)

Valerie Bowman Jarrett (born 1956), who is now a senior advisor to the president for public engagement and intergovernmental affairs, knows a thing or two about painful emotions. In 1983 she married her childhood boyfriend, the physician William Robert Jarrett (born 1953). She separated from him in 1987 and went through a painful divorce in 1988. William died five years later, in 1993, at the age of 40, of a sudden heart attack. Valerie's boss, Barack, also knows about painful emotions, but he has an extraordinary degree of emotional intelligence in dealing with people, and this is one of the secrets of his success. Emotional intelligence involves correctly perceiving people's emotions and one's own, using them skillfully, understanding emotions, and managing emotions, as well as empathy, self-awareness, self-management, social awareness, and relationship management (Goleman, 2006; Matthews, Zeidner, & Roberts, 2002). Barack has the extraordinary ability to observe his own feelings and to control them rather than to express them outwardly.

Barack is aware of his extraordinary ability to stay calm, his incredible emotional control, even under great provocation. In *The Audacity of Hope*, he humorously advised his reader to ask his wife Michelle about this. He does not take the right-wing pundits who always hound him, such as Ann Coulter, Sean Hannity, Glenn Beck, or Rush Limbaugh, very seriously, preferring to think of them as bloodhounds and sourpusses. He does not feel that being called names is so terrible (Obama, 2006a, p. 27). In a courageous move, on March 17, 2010—four days before the crucial vote in the U.S. Congress on his heath-care-reform bill, which he won—President Obama agreed to be interviewed by Fox News, his great right-wing nemesis. His interviewer, Brett Baier, constantly and rudely interrupted Barack, and the president repeatedly had to ask Baier to let him finish, calling him by his first name. Barack did not seem to get angry, however, whereas Baier was visibly upset.

Nor is Barack given to exaggeration or overstatement. He sees reality, however painful, in proportion. When his Democratic colleagues in the U.S. Senate complained to him about the evils of American politics, Senator Obama told them that there had been much worse abuses in American political history, such as the infamous Alien and Sedition Act under President John Adams, the illegal and unhindered lynching of countless innocent people for a hundred years under several dozen U.S.

administrations, and the detention of Japanese Americans in internment camps during World War II under Franklin Delano Roosevelt. He suggested that they all "take a deep breath." (Obama 2006, p. 27). When his supporters asked him how he could function amid all the smear campaigns against him, Barack told them that there were much worse situations to be in, such as Nelson Mandela's in apartheid South Africa, Aleksandr Solzhenitsyn's in Soviet Russia, or any political prisoner's in China or Egypt.

Barack developed this extraordinary ability early in his life, in his emotional relationship with his mother, and then learned emotional self-control from his stepfather. But when he discovered his father's tragic past and his idealization of his father was shattered, his unconscious processes of emotional control, discipline, detachment, and isolation were reinforced. This is why Barack seems cool, almost detached, non-spontaneous, and never very angry, euphoric, sad, upset, or desperate. He always seems in total control of himself, active, and happy, and he never displays undue emotion. His self-confidence and self-control are supreme. His total control of his feelings is the most remarkable quality of his personality, the one most vaunted by his aides and friends.

Barack's self-confidence was evident in Chicago in 1985–1988, where he organized the black community, and at Harvard Law School in 1988–1991, where he was the first black president of the *Harvard Law Review*. The American legal scholar Geoffrey R. Stone (born 1946) met Barack when both of them were teaching U.S. constitutional law at the University of Chicago Law School. Stone has published several books on this subject (Stone, Seidman, Sunstein, & Tushnet, 1986, with several later editions and supplements), all of which have won prestigious awards. In an interview with Sasha Abramsky (2009, p. 86), Stone, who himself does not lack for self-confidence, spoke of Barack as someone who felt quite good in his own skin. Stone thought that Barack's body language, voice, gestures, and movements conveyed a sense of equality, if not command.

People who are as self-controlled and self-confident as Barack Obama rarely display or express their innermost feelings, especially not the painful ones that every human being has: anger, fear, longing, loss, grief, sadness, abandonment, bereavement, jealousy, anxiety, depression, envy. However, these feelings may come through inadvertently through slips of the tongue and other "parapraxes," as Freud called them. For example, on August 23, 2008, when introducing his running mate, Barack said, "So let me introduce to you *the next president*—the next vice president of the United States of America, Joe Biden" (italics added). Barack's slip of the tongue can be understood if we think of Biden as a father figure to Barack and of Barack's lifelong quest for the good father that he never had. It was only through this Freudian slip that his painful feelings about his father came through.

Born in 1942, old enough to be Barack's father, Biden had lost his first wife and child in a car accident, while Barack's father was likewise killed in an accident. Biden was a much better father than Barack's father was. He had recovered from his loss and trauma and rebuilt his life, while Barack's father had destroyed his. Biden created a new family, as did Barack. In Barack's unconscious mind, Biden may be the good father that he wanted, who therefore has priority over him. It was like saying, "Here is my new father." Interestingly enough, when it was Biden's turn to accept his nomination, the Delaware senator called the presumptive Democratic nominee "Barack America." One can only wonder what in Biden's unconscious feelings caused this curious slip.

Barack's odyssey had begun with his childhood in Hawai'i and had taken him to Indonesia, "the markets and slums of Jakarta," then back to Hawai'i, Los Angeles, New York, Chicago, Harvard University, Springfield, Illinois, and Washington, D.C. The occasions on which Barack displays his painful feelings in public or loses control of them are rare. One such occasion was the launch of his new book *The Audacity of Hope* in 2006. When he spoke of his work as a U.S. senator in Washington and of the emotional price that his wife and daughters were paying for it, due to his absence from home, tears began to stream down his cheeks. Barack felt that he was abandoning his family. This may have reminded him of his own abandonment by his father, of the price that he and his mother paid for it. It brought out the pain that he had been denying, repressing, or isolating all his life. His wife Michelle calmed him down with a kiss. Michelle, who was born in 1964, the year Barack's parents divorced, seems like a perfect match for Barack. "He loved Michelle.... This is a person who could help him manage the pressures of the life he thought he wanted," said Jerry Kellman, Obama's community-organizing mentor in Chicago. Barack was also looking for the kind of partner who could join him on his climb (Kantor, 2008a).

Kellman, the head of Chicago's Calumet Community Religious Conference, who hired Barack as a community organizer in 1985 and whom Barack called "Marty Kaufman" in his memoir (Obama 1995, p. 140), was Barack's first community-organizing mentor and his most influential one (Abramsky, 2009, p. 8). Kellman "liked the young man's intelligence, motivation and acutely personal understanding of how it felt to be an outsider. He also remembers that Mr. Obama drove a hard bargain" (Kovaleski, 2008). Barack concealed Kellman's name in his memoir, as he did many others. An American journalist thought that Barack had made a great impression on Kellman's board of directors: "Obama, only 24, struck board members as 'awesome' and 'extremely impressive,' and they quickly hired him, at $13,000 a year, plus $2,000 for a car—a beat-up blue Honda Civic, which Obama drove for the next three years organizing more than twenty congregations to change their neighborhoods" (Moberg, 2007).

Barack himself considers his often-difficult three-year period as a community organizer in Chicago's South Side a very important education. An American journalist wrote that "Mr. Obama's three-year stretch as a grass-roots organizer has figured prominently, if not profoundly, in his own narrative of his life. Campaigning in Iowa, Mr. Obama called it 'the best education I ever had, better than anything I got at Harvard Law School,' an education that he said was 'seared into my brain.' He devoted about one-third of the 442 pages in his memoir, *Dreams From My Father,* to chronicling that Chicago organizing period" (Kovaleski, 2008). Barack later wrote that he had learned empathy and compassion, like most of his other values, from his mother and also from her father (Obama, 2006a, pp. 80–81, 243). But it was here, in Chicago's South Side, working with the poorest and most underprivileged black people, that he also acquired his empathy and compassion and developed his emotional intelligence. And he also may have had a good father figure in Kellman, even though—or because—he was a white man.

It may sound surprising or strange, but I believe that Barack's absentee father may have been one of the most powerful emotional forces of his entire life. He forged for himself an identity in which his imaginary father played a major role, as he tried to emulate the idealized image of his father in his mind. Not until six years after his father's death, in 1988, did he confront the truth about his father by going to Kenya and visiting his family. Throughout his life his fantasies about his father, and his quest for a good father figure, played a major role in his emotional development.

We can now see how the son of two complicated, immature, problematic, and difficult parents forged his own identity, how he became a self-made man, how he overcame his trauma, sublimated his rage, and created a family. Abramsky thinks that Barack's story is almost mythological because it is so improbable. Barack's life and career are a living contradiction of social codes and accepted notions. Abramsky calls Barack "a walking one-man diaspora, a man who can't be defined, or rather confined, by his many heritages, but who instead has to weave those heritages...into a coherent narrative of identity ... He is ... his own creation" (2009, p. 49). In plain English, Barack is a self-made man.

We know relatively little about Barack's early childhood. Much of it comes from his memoir, *Dreams from My Father* (Obama, 1995) and from *The Audacity of Hope* (Obama, 2006a). What we do know is complex and ambiguous, and there are some factual errors and confabulations in the memoir. One thing is clear throughout, though: his father has continued to preoccupy Barack throughout his life. He first visited Kenya and found out the bitter truth about his father in 1988, the year before he met his future wife, Michelle. In 2006, on his third trip to Kenya, Barack flew his wife and two daughters from Chicago to join him in a visit to his father's birthplace, the village of Nyang'oma Kogelo, in Kenya's Siaya District, in rural western Kenya.

Dreams from My Father relates how Barack tried to understand himself and his origins following his father's death, which was no doubt a traumatic event for him. By traveling to all the places of his childhood and youth, and then to Kenya, his father's birthplace, he sorted out his life in an admirable way, emotionally, by reconstructing it through travel and imagination. Fantasy is a way of dealing with painful reality. And Barack emerged emotionally triumphant. He married and has a healthy family that is very different from his father's. And then he has also made it to the pinnacle of power in the United States and has used his power to improve his motherland.

Barack was 21 when he received a phone call from his aunt Jane in Kenya in late 1982 telling him that his 46-year-old father had died in a car crash. "I felt no pain," Barack wrote after the call, "only the vague sense of an opportunity lost" (Obama, 1995, p. 128). He did not go to Kenya to visit his father's grave and meet his paternal family for another six years. He must have repressed or denied the pain, because, as the perceptive mixed-race British politician Oona Tamsyn King pointed out, after several more years and several hundred pages of *Dreams from My Father*, the pain finally came out (King, 2007). Throughout his journey, Barack tried to deal with "the puzzle of being a black man" (Obama 1995, p. 442), but the deeper issues were "Who am I?" and "Why did my father abandon me?" and "Why did I grow up in a white family?" and "Am I like my father?"

Of his childhood, Barack recalled that he had wondered why his father never returned to him; "that my father looked nothing like the people around me—that he was black as pitch, my mother white as milk—barely registered in my mind" (Obama, 1995, p. 10). In his memoir, he described his struggles as a young adult to reconcile the conflicting social perceptions of his multiracial heritage. But his struggle with his own identity was hard, for he also wrote that he had used alcohol, marijuana, and cocaine during his teenage years in high school to "push questions of who I was out of my mind" (Obama 1995, p. 93). At the Civil Forum on the Presidency in 2008, Barack called his adolescent drug use his "greatest moral failure." Being a mixed-race child, raised mostly by his white grandparents, Barack desperately sought to believe that white and black people could get along, even though his own parents could not. King (2007) thought that Barack felt that "otherwise his existence must be at best a mistake, at worst a lie." But the puzzle of being the black son of a white mother always concealed his deeper, personal puzzles, such as the causes of his abandonment by his father.

It is hard to say what kind of mothering the infant Barack received, but, despite his mother's difficult character, or because of it, judging by his own strong character, his emotional intelligence, and his ability to overcome adversity, the basic relationship with his mother must have been a good one, and he writes about her with much affection in his memoir. At other times, however, he also notes her immaturity (Obama, 1995, pp. 123–127). Later on, however, the relationship of care and protection was reversed, as we have seen, and when they came to Indonesia the six-year-old Barack felt that he wanted to protect his mother (Obama, p. 32; Ripley, 2008).

Oona King has a unique personal background that helps her understand Barack. King was born in 1967 to the African American civil rights activist Preston King (born 1936) and his British Jewish activist wife, Murriel Hazel Stern, who was also committed to social justice issues. King is thus not only half white and half black but also half British and half American. Like Barack's, her parents separated and later divorced when she was a child, although her father has kept in touch with her. She has pointed out that as Barack's memoir's title, *Dreams from My Father*, suggests, it is mostly concerned with his black Kenyan father, who abandoned Barack as a baby and whose life ended tragically. King thought that the "wound of parental abandonment, added to the search for identity within white mainstream society, means that his journey of self-discovery must uncover the black part of him, not the white part" (King, 2007). The question "Why did my father abandon me?" seems to cry out for an answer on every page of *Dreams from My Father*.

In college, Barry Obama was an outsider to both whites and blacks. He felt unable to fit in with the white students yet constantly had to prove himself "black enough" to the black ones. In his memoir, when a black "brother" whom he named "Marcus" (his real name was Earl Chew) claimed (falsely) that his choice of reading—*Heart of Darkness* by Joseph Conrad—is a racist tract, Barack told a sympathetic "sister" named Regina, "I read the book to help me understand just what it is that makes white people so afraid [of black people]. Their demons. The way ideas get twisted around. It helps me understand how people learn to hate." "And that's important to you?" asked Regina. "My life depends on it," Barack thought to himself (Obama, 1995, p. 103). Deeper inside him may be the questions, "Did my father hate my mother? Was she afraid of him or he of her? Is that why he left us?"

As part of his psychological strengths and virtues and his emotional intelligence, Barack has integrity and authenticity. King feels that

> there is an authenticity to [*Dreams from My Father*] that makes you think he might really be driven by the quest for common ground; the desire to diagnose the phenomenon of hate, and to come up with a prescription; the desire to prove that what unites us is greater than what divides us. *This desire to bring harmony is not purely a Ghandi-esque [sic] display of altruism, but also an act of survival.* He finds some of the answer to what feeds hate in his grass-roots work. He tries to bring hope to desperate communities in sink estates around the decaying hulk of Chicago's industrial past, and has a surprising level of success. You have to admire him for it, especially "if you've ever tried to mobilize local communities mired in poverty and depression." (King, 2007; italics added)

By working to repair the broken lives in his chosen community, was Barack unconsciously trying to repair his own broken family?

FROM THE PERSONAL TO THE POLITICAL

As a young man, the American political scientist Harold D. Lasswell (1902–1978) pioneered the psychoanalytic study of political action. Lasswell (1930) believed that political leaders deal with their personal conflicts by unconsciously displacing them to the public arena and rationalizing their actions in terms of the public good. This may well have been true of Barack, who, like Lasswell, later taught at the University of Chicago. Rather than explore the personal question of his black father's relationship to him, or to his white mother, he has explored the public political issue of black-white relations and acted to improve them.

Barack, however, is often aware of his rationalizations. His father, too, had rationalized his self-destructive behavior, which had led him into joblessness, poverty, alcoholism, accidents, and untimely death. At Occidental College in Los Angeles, in 1979–1980, the freshman Barry shared a dormitory with a beautiful green-eyed girl with "honey skin and pouty lips" whom he named "Joyce," the green-eyed, honey-skinned daughter of an Italian father and a "multiracial" mother, who considered herself "not black but multiracial" and resented black people forcing her to choose her race or telling her that she could not be who she was (Obama, 1995, pp. 99–100).

Barack noticed that for all of Joyce's talk about being multiracial, she avoided black people. In 1987, when he was a black-community organizer in Chicago, he feared that he, too, like Joyce, was trying to escape what he was and to be what he was not, white or multiracial. He feared that he was rationalizing his behavior, that he was trying to escape poverty, boredom, or crime, or his black skin color. Barack feared that if he went to a "white" law school, he would be caving in to the centuries-old pattern that began when white men came to black Africa, a pattern of trying to escape his black identity and his racial destiny, of fleeing into the white man's culture and surrendering to his power (Obama, 1995, p. 277). One of the most important things for Barack was to maintain his sense of independence and control, not to feel powerless or driven by the will of others.

Barack visited Kenya three times: in 1988 to visit his family and his father's grave, in 1992 to introduce his future wife Michelle to his African family, and in 2006 to make a political visit. As a U.S. senator, in 2006, Barack gave a speech at the University of Nairobi, condemning corruption in the Kenyan government, which triggered personal attacks on him by Kenyan leaders (Nairobi Star, 2008; Moracha & Mosota, 2006; Wamalwa, 2006). Barack told his audience that Kenya would have to struggle mightily to eradicate poverty and to find its economic potential unless it abandoned its entrenched corruption and tribalism: "If the people cannot trust their government to do the job for which it exists—to protect them and to promote their common welfare—all else is lost," Barack said, adding "and this is why the struggle against corruption is one of the great struggles of our time" (Klatell, 2006).

Was Barack unwittingly speaking for his dead father, who had attacked the Kenyan government, as well as for his dead mother, who had fought corruption? Was he blaming the Kenyan government rather than his own father for his father's tragic fate? Was he trying to preserve his idealized image of his father despite everything he knew about him? Certain it is that his political speech had deep personal roots, just as Lasswell believed.

Just as the first Kenyan president, Jomo Kenyatta, had punished Barack's father for his public attacks on his government, so its third president, Mwai Kibaki, tried to punish Barack himself. Referring to the bloody tribal conflict between the Kikuyu and the Luo—and specifically between the Kikuyu president Kibaki and his Luo rival prime minister Raila Odinga—the Kenyan government's Kikuyu spokesman, Alfred Mutua, at first dismissed U.S. Senator Barack Obama as an inexperienced young man who could not teach Kenya how to manage its affairs and who had been caught up in Odinga's "ethnic politics." Two years later, when Barack was about to become the president of the United States, Mutua "forgot" his attack on Obama, changed his tune, and praised the young candidate (Nairobi Star, 2008).

In 2009, however, U.S. President Obama chose to visit "democratic" Ghana over "corrupt" Kenya on his first visit to sub-Saharan Africa as president. The mixed-race politician Oona King thinks that Barack's personal *exploration* of African American rage in the face of white discrimination was coupled with his *incomprehension* of why black people are always so angry. But, though *Dreams from My Father* deals with race and class, its real strength is in revealing the flawed human psychology, both black and white, that can lead any person toward misunderstanding, prejudice, despair, poverty, and tragedy (King, 2007).

THE CHARISMA OF THE "FOREIGNER" AND OUTSIDER

Barack Obama has always been something of an outsider in his own community, yet he has belonged to the "ultimate insider clubs" such as Columbia, Harvard, and the U.S. Senate (Kantor, 2008a). Matthew McGuire, a Chicago financier who contributed to Obama's presidential campaign, seems to have understood this. The American journalist Jodi Kantor, who interviewed McGuire, observed that "Obama is often called a permanent outsider—racially, geographically, politically. But his story is more complicated than that. 'He's been an outsider at Columbia and Harvard,' said Matthew McGuire, a friend. 'He was an outsider but within the ultimate insider clubs.' Within those and other powerful institutions, Obama has always appointed himself critic. After becoming the first black American president of the *Harvard Law Review*, Obama gave a speech to black students and alumni so rousing that a few recall it nearly two decades later. 'Don't let Harvard change you,' went the refrain" (ibid.). Indeed, among the qualities that attracted voters to Barack during the presidential campaign were precisely those of the outsider and the critic, or, as the Canadian psychoanalyst Irvine Schiffer (1973) has put it, the charisma of the foreigner and of the fighting stance.

During the 2008 U.S. presidential campaign, the Republican nominee John McCain and his running mate Sarah Palin attempted to portray Obama as a foreigner, as not quite American, a celebrity, an elitist, a friend of terrorists, or a radical leftist (Niven, 2009, p. 42), which may have enhanced his charisma in the eyes of most Americans. While Niven thinks that none of these efforts to depict Obama as "other" quite stuck, the charisma of the foreigner is rooted in our own developmental history, and it is in the eye of the beholder. As the psychoanalyst Schiffer points out, the psychological corollary of "familiarity breeds contempt" is that "foreignness breeds charisma" (1973, p. 24). More precisely, the partly foreign, or a combination of the familiar and the foreign, is a key ingredient of charisma. This striking psychological phenomenon has to do with our early symbiosis and individuation, with many people being fixated in an incomplete individuation-differentiation process from their mothers, where the mother's body seems both familiar and foreign at the same time. The more immature the person, the more charismatic his leader may appear to him or her (Schiffer, 1973, pp. 25–26, 58–60).

But the charismatic Barack was lonely in his youth. Much of Barack's *Dreams from My Father* is a meditation on this loneliness (King, 2007). On his first day at the Punahou School, Barry met a new boy, whom he called "Frederick" in his memoir (Obama, 1995, p. 59), but whose real name was Ronald Loui (Ramos, 2008). Gramps accompanied Barry to the school and tried to ease his entry into the new environment by engaging "Frederick" in conversation and by trying to get him to be Barry's friend. In a reversal of the usual "don't do anything I wouldn't do," the grandfather humorously told his grandson not to do anything he *would* do; "Frederick" found Gramps funny (Obama, 1995, p. 59). Yet Barry felt lonely and abandoned by both his parents.

Barry's literary talent helped him relieve the pain of his loneliness. At the Punahou School, Barry joined a literary club, writing poems and short stories. These adolescent literary works have not survived, but Abramsky's interviewees thought that the poems were "of mediocre caliber" (2009, p. 67). In 2008, during his presidential campaign, Barack told a popular magazine that his favorite writers were Toni Morrison, William Shakespeare, and Ernest Hemingway (Wenner, 2008). He also liked the books of Aleksandr Solzhenitsyn, Herman Melville, Ralph Waldo Emerson (the name of his mother's uncle), W.E.B. DuBois, Graham Greene, Doris Lessing, John Steinbeck, E. L. Doctorow, Philip Roth, and Studs Terkel (Abramsky, 2009, ibid., based on articles in the *New York Times*, *Los Angeles Times*, and salon. com). Abramsky thinks that Barack likes realist writers who write about his favorite themes of overcoming hardship and obstacles, corruption, intrigue, inequality, war, and duty.

King (2007) thinks that, even at the Punahou School, Barack was an outsider in search of a real community, a community that he finally found in Chicago. This is an important psychological observation, for a community is like a large family, and political entities can represent personal objects in our unconscious mind. If you replace the word *community* with the word *family*, then the young Barack was always looking for an alternative family, one that would accept and never abandon him. And he finally found his community-family, first on Chicago's South Side, then in the Illinois senate, then in the U.S. Senate, and finally in America herself. He was the only African American U.S. senator among his colleagues and then became the first African American president. That was his new white-black family.

Chapter 8

ADOLESCENCE AND THE QUEST FOR IDENTITY

Synopsis: *Perhaps due to her immaturity, Stanley Ann Dunham Obama Soetoro tended to idealize her mates and then to become disillusioned with them. By 1971 she was getting ready to separate from her second husband, Lolo Soetoro, in Indonesia and to return to her parents in Hawai'i. She sent her son Barry (as Barack was called during his youth) home ahead of her. Thus he lost his primary masculine identification figure. Later that year, she too came to Honolulu with her daughter Maya. Back in the United States, Barry Soetoro once more became Barry Obama, and this was how he registered at the Punahou School, an elite high school in Honolulu. Barry's father visited him in late 1971 and early 1972, and that summer Barry and his mother, half sister, and maternal grandmother traveled around the continental United States. His grandfather, "Gramps," had declined, lost his taste for traveling, and was no longer a good identification figure. During Barry's adolescent years at Punahou, he was still torn between his various identities, white and black, American and African, and he had to go through the second separation-individuation phase of adolescence, in which he needed to forge an identity separate from that of his mother, who had been the dominant figure in his formative years. Barry was influenced by several older black father figures who gave him a sense of his identity and belonging. Ann was worried that her son Barack might turn out like her father. He proved her wrong by being accepted to Occidental College in Los Angeles, where he applied after falling in love with a girl from Brentwood, a Los Angeles suburb, who was vacationing in Hawai'i.*

There are many poignant passages in *Dreams from My Father*. Barack constantly recognizes his own privileged position, but his empathy for less-privileged others is considerable. In one passage, when he comes back to Hawai'i from Indonesia in 1971, at the age of 10, he stands in the American immigration control line, behind a Chinese family who had been lively and animated during the flight from Jakarta to Honolulu. Fearful of U.S. officials, the Chinese family members try to remain inconspicuous, looking apprehensively at the customs officer's hands as he calmly examines their papers and their bags (Obama, 1995, p. 53). The U.S. customs official then turns to the 10-year-old Barry, asks him if he is an American, checks his passport, and waves him through ahead of the Chinese (King, 2007; Obama, 1995, pp. 53–54).

In his memoir, Barack feels for the poor Chinese immigrants and does not like the immigration official's discrimination in his favor. Oona King (2007) thinks that Barack's background gives him a heightened ability to understand different and opposing worldviews. He believes in the power of words: "If I could just find the right words, things would change," he has said (King, 2007). In 2004 he proved this point at the Democratic National Convention in Boston when he was chosen as its keynote speaker. His keynote address made him an overnight celebrity and a political sensation. Barack sees himself as a self-made man of destiny, and Sasha Abramsky thinks that "the extraordinary response to his keynote address...only shored up his already strong sense of destiny calling" (2009, p. 75).

Barack's keynote address, entitled "The Audacity of Hope," a title based on the Reverend Jeremiah Wright's sermon "The Audacity to Hope," propelled him to national prominence. In the 17 minutes it took him to deliver the speech, Barack was catapulted to sudden fame, with many political analysts rightly predicting that he would enter the next presidential race. Abramsky (2009, p. 66) believes that Barack wrote this speech himself, even though he had good speechwriters. Barack was immediately commissioned to write a book, and, in 2006, he published *The Audacity of Hope*, a book-length account that expanded on many of the themes he had addressed in the keynote speech. Like his 1995 memoir, it became an instant best seller.

Oona King thinks that *Dreams from My Father* proved that Barack is a "listening" politician; he could not otherwise have depicted the myriad lives that are described in the pages of this book. It also demonstrates his capacity to provide a compelling narrative for the human condition. The book's epilogue ends with him at his wedding in 1992, toasting a happy ending (King, 2007). Becoming America's first African American president is a good new beginning. But on a deeper level, Barack's entire career may be seen as an attempt to fix broken families and shattered lives, to knit together broken communities. By fixing America's troubles, he may unconsciously be trying to overcome his own early feelings of helplessness at being unable to fix his mother's broken marriages, his father's self-destruction, and the deaths of both.

Barack's memoir, *Dreams from My Father*, is a somewhat idealized account of his life, as Barack also had to come to terms with his father's failed life in Kenya after his return there from the United States, his entanglement with the Kenyan authorities, and his tragic death. It was in Kenya, in 1988, during his first visit there, that Barack discovered a nation with several dozen different tribes, each of them with negative stereotypes of the others. It was also in Kenya that he recognized the dichotomy that had been his lifelong existence between the graves of his father and his grandfather. He tried to make sense of everything, but he cannot make sense of his father's tragic life.

Despite Barack's caveat in his introduction to his memoir that his characters were "composites of people I've known" and that "some events appear out of precise chronology," several *Chicago Tribune* journalists searched assiduously for discrepancies between *Dreams from My Father* and Barack's real-life events:

> More than 40 interviews with former classmates, teachers, friends and neighbors in his childhood homes of Hawaii and Indonesia, as well as a review of public records, show the arc of Obama's personal journey took him to places and situations far removed from the experience of most Americans. At the same time, *several of his oft-recited stories may not have happened in the way he has recounted them.* Some seem to make Obama look better in the retelling, others appear to exaggerate his outward struggles over issues of race, or simply skim over some of the most painful, private moments of his life. The handful of black students who attended [the prestigious] Punahou School in Hawaii, for instance, say they struggled mightily with issues of race and racism there. But absent from those discussions, they say, was another student then known as Barry Obama. (Scharnberg & Barker, 2007; italics added)

Barack Obama called himself Barry through high school and his first two years in college. This was his name among his classmates. Was he trying to fit in with the American scene, to be accepted, to avoid further rejection or abandonment, not to feel an outsider anymore? Was it his way of distinguishing himself from his father? Around 1981 or 1982, around the time of his father's death, he began to use his official name of Barack H. Obama. It was as if he was taking over his father's identity. Barack's emotional turmoil as a youth was not about race. It was about the much more personal issues of abandonment and loneliness. Another mixed-race classmate in Hawai'i, the Japanese American Keith Kakugawa, had this to say about Barack:

> [Kakugawa]...said he does recall long, soulful talks with the young Obama and that his friend confided his longing and loneliness. But those talks, Kakugawa said, were not about race. "Not even close," he said, adding that [Barack] Obama was dealing with "some inner turmoil" in those days. "But it wasn't a race thing," he said. "Barry's biggest struggles then were missing his parents. His biggest struggles were his feelings of abandonment. The idea that his biggest struggle was race is [bull]." (Scharnberg & Barker, 2007)

Abandonment was the primary issue of Barry's life. His father had abandoned him at age 2, and his mother had sent him away to Hawai'i from Indonesia when he was 10. He may well have felt this, too, as an abandonment by her.

Successively identifying with those who raised him, Barry internalized their emotional qualities, especially those internalized objects of his whom he liked and those that helped him thrive. This internalization capacity was a unique ability. It is hard to understand how he could avoid internalizing his mother's impulsiveness and recklessness while making her hard work and her drive part of himself. Perhaps his jolly grandfather's deep love for him made up for his father's abandonment of him and for his mother's toughness:

> One of those friends [of Barack Obama], Neil Abercrombie, then a graduate student in the sociology department, frequently would see young Obama around [Honolulu] with his grandfather Stanley, whom Obama called "Gramps." "Stanley loved that little boy," said Abercrombie, now a Democratic congressman from Hawaii. "In the absence of his father, there was not a kinder, more understanding man than Stanley Dunham. He was loving and generous." A close friend of Obama's from their teenage years, Greg Orme [whom Barack named "Scott" in his memoir], spent so much time with Dunham that he, too, called him "Gramps." Orme recalled that years later, at Obama's wedding reception in Chicago [in 1992], Obama brought the crowd to tears when he spoke of his recently deceased maternal grandfather and how he made a little boy with an absent father feel as though he was never alone. (Scharnberg & Barker, 2007)

Barack had loved his hypomanic, jolly, and boisterous grandfather as much as Gramps loved him. The personality of his maternal grandfather may be another key to his emotional well-being and to his achievements. However, during Barry's adolescence, after Gramps had lost his job and his house, declined, became weak and depressed, and was a shadow of his former self, Barry became disappointed with him and often fought with him. Only in his senior year in high school could he empathize with his grandfather, feel for him, and try to give him a sense of command and self-respect.

Gramps died on February 8, 1992. This was a great loss to Barack. He had been with his future wife, Michelle, since 1989. He married her later that year, on October 3, not long after his mother finally got her doctorate in anthropology from the University of Hawai'i. In some ways, the new family that he created for himself made up for his losses and abandonments. He was going to be the good father that his father never was and that Gramps had been to him when he was a child. He is also many things his mother was *not* and that her mother was: a stable, protective, good parent who keeps his kids in one place, does not drag them to faraway places, does not uproot them unnecessarily, and does not keep changing their environment, their schools, or their friends—until his move to the White House in January 2009 inevitably did this to them.

Barack's daughters, Malia Ann and Sasha (Natasha), who live in the White House with their parents, attend Sidwell Friends School, a prestigious Quaker school in Washington that is known as the Harvard of Washington's private schools. Vice President Joseph Biden's grandchildren also attend that school. Presidents Theodore Roosevelt, Richard Nixon, and Bill Clinton had sent their children to Sidwell Friends School. Albert Gore III, a son of former U.S. Vice President Al Gore, graduated from there. Founded in 1883 by Thomas Sidwell, the school's motto is *Eluceat omnibus lux* (Let the light shine out from all), alluding to the Quaker concept of the inner light within people. All the students attend the weekly Quaker meeting for Christian worship.

Barack developed his mature ego identity through his ambivalent identifications with his problematic parents and grandparents, though he seems to have had a positive identification with his maternal grandfather: he wanted to be like Gramps, not like his mother Ann or his father Barak. Nonetheless, some of his mother's character did become his through unconscious identification, and he acknowledged her to have been a great influence on his life.

> But Obama is his mother's son. In his wide-open rhetoric about what can be instead of what was, you see a hint of his mother's credulity. When Obama gets donations from people who have never believed in politics before, they're responding to his ability—passed down from his mother—to make a powerful argument (that happens to be very liberal) without using a trace of ideology. On a good day, when he figures out how to move a crowd of thousands of people very different from himself, it has something to do with having had a parent who gazed at different cultures the way other people study gems. (Ripley, 2008)

What was the mother-son relationship like? Ann was a hypersensitive woman. "She cried a lot," says her daughter Maya Soetoro-Ng, "if she saw animals being treated cruelly or children in the news or a sad movie—or if she felt like she wasn't being understood in a conversation" (Ripley, 2008). When they arrived in Indonesia when he was six, Barack later recalled, he felt that he had to protect his mother (Obama, 1995, p. 32). So, in a reversal of roles, the child felt that *he* had to protect *his mother*. This is an extraordinary role reversal: normally it is up to mothers to protect their children. From an early age, Barack had to learn to protect a needy person, to be his mother's parent. Today, he is out to protect and help America, which has replaced his dead mother in his emotions.

In Indonesia, he was known as Barry Soetoro. At the Roman Catholic *Fransiskus Strada Asisia* (Francis of Assisi School) in Jakarta, which Barry attended from age six to age nine, the other kids called him a "Negro," which was a racial slur in Indonesia. It was the time of his racial awakening, which he later thought was due to reading a *Life* magazine story at the U.S. embassy about an American Negro who had tried to bleach his skin. Yet, incredibly, he later said that he was not offended by being called a Negro and was already displaying his leadership qualities, not only protecting his mother but also leading other boys:

> Still, all of his teachers at the Catholic school recognized leadership qualities in him. "He would be very helpful with friends. He'd pick them up if they fell down" [Obama's former teacher Israella Pareira] Darmawan recalled. "He would protect the smaller ones." Third-grade teacher Fermina Katarina Sinaga, now 67, has perhaps the most telling story. In an essay about what he wanted to be when he grew up, Obama "wrote he wanted to be president," Sinaga recalled. "He didn't say what country he wanted to be president of. But *he wanted to make everybody happy*" (Scharnberg & Barker, 2007; italics added; see also Barker, 2007)

To Barry, being president meant taking care of people, protecting them, making them happy—perhaps also making his mother cry less and be happier.

In August 1970, Barry's half sister Maya Kassandra Soetoro was born. Barry was then nine years old and spending the summer with his maternal grandparents in Hawai'i. The birth of his sister meant that he had a new rival for his mother's affections. At that time his parents moved, and when he returned to Indonesia in the fall he was sent to the Besuki School, which was a public secular school.

With his middle name of Hussein, Barry Soetoro could have passed for a Muslim, but he did not even try. Rather, he acted like the American boy that he was. He sat in the back of the class, drawing the popular American cartoons of Batman and Spiderman. But the other kids were calling him a Negro, a derogatory term at that time. Did he want to be omnipotent like those cartoon characters? His capacity for emotional detachment was showing. He thought that he was not offended by being called a Negro. Yet he later had that screen memory of reading the nonexistent horror story in *Life* magazine about the American Negro who had tried to bleach his skin—at exactly that time. When he was 10, he was gone—back to Hawai'i, when his mother sent him back to her parents in 1971 to attend the Punahou School, the elite private college-preparatory academy. He would no longer be called a Negro. His mother Ann was already preparing to end her unhappy second marriage.

His eight years at the Punahou School in Honolulu (1971–1979), from 5th grade to 12th grade, marked Barry's transition to adolescence and his quest for his identity. In fifth grade in grammar school, the 10-year-old Barry rejected the friendship of the only other black child in his grade, a girl whom he called "Coretta" in his memoir—a namesake of Dr. Martin Luther King's widow; her real name was Joella Edwards (Calmes, 2009). When the other boys said that "Coretta" was Barry's girlfriend, he angrily said that she was not, yelled at "Coretta" to leave him alone, and shoved her away from him, at which she gave him a hurt, disappointed, and accusing look and ran away. The adult Barack felt guilty about this cowardly and hurtful act and rued it as born of fear (Obama, 1995, pp. 60–62, 111).

In late 1971, two weeks after his mother returned from Indonesia to Honolulu with his half sister Maya, the 10-year-old Barry saw his biological father for the first and only time since he was abandoned by that father as a baby. The father had returned to Hawai'i from Kenya after learning that his son had returned there from Indonesia. Barry was living with his maternal grandparents. Ann rented an apartment for Barak and herself downstairs from her parents. The tense meeting between the son and his father, which took place at the home of Barry's maternal grandparents, lasted one month. At first admiring his father's mysterious power (Obama, 1995, p. 67), Barry later could not wait for his father to leave. Here is the poignant memory as described by a perceptive journalist, based on Barack's own memoir:

> He last saw his father in 1971, when he was 10 years old. Remarried and living in his native Kenya, Barack Obama Sr. sent word that he wanted to visit his son in Hawaii over Christmas. To the son, he had become a ghost, an opaque figure hailed as brilliant, charismatic, dignified, with a deep baritone voice that reminded everyone of James Earl Jones. All the boy knew was that his father had gone off to study at Harvard and [had] never come back. Now, the old man would put flesh on the ghost. On the day his father arrived, young Barack, known as Barry then, left school early and headed toward his grandparents' apartment, his legs leaden, his chest pounding.

He nervously rang the doorbell. His grandmother opened the door, and there in the hallway was a dark, slender man wearing horn-rimmed glasses and sporting a blue blazer and scarlet ascot. (Merida, 2007)

The "old man" Barak Obama was 35 years old when he saw Barry. The meeting between the 10-year-old boy and the father who had abandoned him was tense, poignant, and heartrending. The father had been seriously injured in a road accident in Kenya and had a bad leg, due to his alcoholism and his narcissistic and self-destructive personality. Like his father, he believed that children should be brought up strictly and firmly. In fact, the father was doing to his son what his own father had done to him. At one point during his visit, the father would not let his son watch *How the Grinch Stole Christmas* on television, precipitating a crisis between father and son, as well as between the father, his ex-wife, and her parents.

When we read how Barack later recalled his first and only meeting with his long-absent father, we can sense the anger, love, hate, ambivalence and even sadness in the boy's reaction to his father. The 10-year-old Barry rejected his abandoning father's attempts at creating an emotional closeness between them. He was stiff, unresponsive, indifferent, and cold. Barry's father was hurt. His maternal grandmother, "Toot," tried to soothe her son-in-law's feelings by saying that Barry was a little timid. That did not help matters very much. The angry and abandoned boy kept his distance from his abandoning and unloved father (Obama, 1995, p. 65).

The father and son may have been groping their way toward one another, but the son could neither forget nor forgive his father's abandonment of him. He observed his father's every move and found his father to be much weaker and more fragile than he had thought he was. Barry had idealized his father as a great man, a king or a prince, an omnipotent and omniscient figure, but he now saw a damaged and fragile man with a bad leg, walking with the aid of a cane, with the yellow eyes of a malaria patient. The father smoked and drank beer but after about an hour seemed so weak that Barry's mother told him that he looked tired and should take a nap (Obama, 1995, p. 65). Barry was obviously disappointed with his father.

The television show *How the Grinch Stole Christmas*, which Barak would not let his son watch, is based on a book by the American children's author Dr. Seuss (Theodor Seuss Geisel, 1904–1991). It is a story about the Grinch, a bitter, green, cave-dwelling, catlike creature with a heart "two sizes too small." He lives on top of snowy Mount Crumpit, a steep, 3,000-foot-high mountain north of Whoville, home of the merry and warmhearted creatures called the Whos. The Grinch's only companion is his faithful dog, Max. He has no friends. From his perch high atop Mount Crumpit, the Grinch can hear the noisy and merry Christmas festivities that take place in Whoville. Envious of the Whos' happiness, he makes plans to descend on the town and, by means of burglary, deprive them of all their Christmas presents and decorations and thus "prevent Christmas from coming." However, the Grinch finally learns that despite his success in stealing all the Christmas presents and decorations from the Whos, Christmas comes just the same. He realizes that Christmas is more than just gifts and presents but a giving state of mind. His heart grows three sizes larger, and he returns all the presents and trimmings and is warmly welcomed into the community of the Whos.

For a while then 10-year-old Barry was fascinated by his father's charming effect on people, by his charisma, his deep, sure voice, and his apparent self-confidence. Barry was fascinated by his father's strange power and even wished that his father would stay (Obama, 1995, p. 67). But then things turned sour. As time went by, tension built up between Barry's narcissistic black father and his white grandparents. Gramps bitched about Barak sitting in his chair, and Toot complained about being made to wait on him. Barak's ex-wife Ann and her son felt caught in the middle between Barak and Ann's parents. When Barry wanted to watch his favorite television show, *How the Grinch Stole Christmas*, his father exploded at him furiously, telling him that he had watched enough television and should go to his room, do his homework, and not disturb his parents and his grandparents (Obama, p. 67).

The father may have been furious at Barry for paying more attention to the television set than to him, or he may have unconsciously displaced his anger at Ann's parents onto Barry. This was a moment of crisis between father and son. Barry's grandmother Toot thought that she had a solution to the crisis, but that was wishful thinking. Barry's grandmother turned off the television set in the living room and told Barry to turn on the show on the set in his own room, but Barry's father refused to let him do that, saying that Barry had been constantly watching television and that he had to study now. Barry's mother Ann tried to intervene, saying that the show would not last very long and that *How the Grinch Stole Christmas* was Barry's favorite show, but Barak was adamant and threatened Barry with his anger (Obama, 1995, pp. 67–68).

By this time Barry was very angry at his father and deeply disappointed in him. The father in his turn was angry at Barry, who had left the room in a rage. In the living room, his father continue to argue heatedly with his mother and her parents. Toot told Barak that he had no right to come in after eight years of absence and bully everyone. Barry sulked angrily, went to his room, slammed the door in his fury, and listened to his father and mother arguing with his grandparents. Barak told Gramps and Toot that they were spoiling Barry, and Ann took Barak's side against her parents.

Even after Barak had left and Toot came into Barry's room to tell him that he could watch the end of the show, Barry felt shocked, traumatized, deceived, angry, bewildered, and fearful. He later recalled that when he saw the Grinch in the show being transformed from an evil creature into a kind one, he thought that it was a lie. His father was mean and could not be changed. He wished his father would leave as soon as possible (Obama, 1995, p. 68).

Barry had defeated his father: he had watched the end of the show, despite his father's prohibition. Yet it was a hollow victory: the 10-year-old Barry was shattered by the disintegration of the fantasies he had entertained about his father and his grandparents. The Grinch could no more be transformed into a kindhearted creature than his parents and grandparents could transform themselves into easygoing people who got along smoothly with one another. Here is how an American journalist summarized the father's visit with Barry and the heartrending scene in the Dunham family home when Barak would not let his son watch his favorite show:

> For a month, the father hung around [his in-laws' home], speaking to his son's fifth-grade class, taking the boy to a Dave Brubeck [jazz piano] concert, but never quite re-establishing himself [as Barry's father]. The trip's pivotal moment came one night as Barry prepared to watch *How the Grinch Stole Christmas*, the annual Dr. Seuss special. The father said the boy had watched enough television and insisted that he go to his room to study. Barry's mother and grandparents intervened in what became a heated family argument. But they proved no match for the strong-willed father, who in an instant had reclaimed the paternal role he had long ago abdicated. (Merida, 2007, based on Obama, 1995, pp. 67–68)

What a disappointment with his father Barry had suffered! How angry he must have been! The father who had abandoned him as an infant was now denying him the simple pleasure of watching his favorite television show. At the Punahou School, he had proudly told his classmates that his father was a prince, the son of the Luo king: that was what he *wished* his father to be (Obama, 1995, p. 63). But Barry's father Barak had been brought up by a father, Onyango, with a very firm hand: in fact, it had been a violent hand. Barak now wanted to bring up his son the same way. The father was doing to his son what his own father had done to him, and what he himself had done to his other children. The abused child had become an abusive father.

The 10-year-old Barry was so disappointed and angry with his father that he could not wait for his father to leave. His mother, however, tried to mollify Barry. His grandmother sent Barry to his father's apartment to get his dirty laundry. When Barry entered, his father was half-naked, and his mother was ironing his clothes. She looked as if she had been crying. Barak tried to get Barry to sit beside him on the bed, but Barry only wanted to give his father his grandmother's message and then leave his parents. His mother then came to his room and tried to mollify Barry, telling him that his father really loved him but that he was pig-headed at times (Obama, 1995, p. 68). Barry was not convinced. He still treated his father with mistrust and even hostility.

When his father was invited to Barry's school to speak to his classmates, Barry was in agony: he had told his classmates that his father was a great African prince. Now his father would reveal himself as the ordinary man that he was. How would he explain his lies about his father to his classmates? Mabel Hefty, Barack's homeroom teacher, was excited about the Kenyan's visit. She and her class were joined by the Hawai'ian mathematics and science teacher, Pal Eldredge, and 30 kids from Mr. Eldredge's homeroom. To Barry's great surprise, his father's talk to his class was very successful. His father impressed the two teachers and their pupils, as well as Barry himself, who could now well be proud of his father. Yet did not say so in his memoir. His feelings about his father were deeply ambivalent, as was his identification with his father. His father remained a mysterious figure to him, unclear, nontransparent, almost incomprehensible. Barack could not understand why he imitated his father's speech or gestures (Obama, 1995, pp. 69–71).

On the day before Barak left for Kenya, he gave his son Barry a basketball and two small 45 rpm eight-minute single-track vinyl records of African music and taught him how to dance to its sounds (Obama, 1995, pp. 71, 129). Since that time the basketball has always been associated with his father in Barack's unconscious mind, and he excelled at the game in high school and college. Playing basketball became an important activity in Barack's life. It is still his favorite sport and his most frequent leisure activity. By playing basketball he can regain his lost father.

Before leaving, Barak placed one of the two small records on his son's phonograph turntable and began to dance to the African music, despite his bad leg. Barry was impressed and moved. This was his last memory of his father. After his father left him, Barry idealized him again and continued to identify with him, however ambivalently. It was not until many years later, in 1983, a year after his father died, that he had a sad dream about meeting his father in jail (which we will analyze later in this book) and not until 1988 that he discovered the bitter truth about his father, which he may have known intuitively. In fact, as a perceptive American journalist has observed, Barry may not really have wanted his father to leave when he did (Meacham, 2008).

Barack's handling of his father's absence is an example of Barack's emotional resilience. The French Jewish psychoanalyst Boris Cyrulnik, himself a Holocaust survivor who successfully overcame his massive trauma, has devoted decades to the study of psychological resilience (Cyrulnik, 2003). Meacham (2008) thinks that Barack's resilience came from his unyielding struggle "to fill the hole left by an absent father." The father had put his career above his wife and child, abandoning them to study at Harvard. The journalist discussed the famous photograph of Barry with his father at the Honolulu airport during their one and only meeting, when Barry was 10 years old. Both father and son are smiling, but whereas the father seems to be looking away, Barry seems to be holding his father's hand tightly, "as though he would like to hold on forever. He never saw his father again" (Meacham, 2008).

When Barry's mother and her baby daughter, Maya, left Indonesia for Hawai'i in 1971, Maya's father, Lolo, stayed behind in Indonesia. In this way, from her point of view, Maya, too, was abandoned by her father when she was a baby. It was a separation that would be followed by a divorce. For four years (1971–1975) Ann, Barry, and Maya lived in a small apartment near the Punahou School, near Ann's parents. After two failed marriages, Ann had come back home to her parents. She depended both on her children and on her parents. In 1975, when Ann returned to Indonesia for her fieldwork in anthropology, Barry refused to go with her. His independence, his separateness from her, was becoming a major psychological issue for him (Obama, 1995, p. 75).

The adult Barack thought that his adolescent inner struggle had to do with his racial identity. With his parents away, his thoughts and feelings turned to his racial-identity struggle. He consciously sought to become a black American, without quite knowing what it meant (Obama, 1995, p. 76). In fact, his struggle was for what the psychoanalyst Erik H. Erikson (1902–1994) called ego identity, for separation and individuation, and for what the psychoanalyst Peter Blos (1904–1997) called the second individuation process in adolescence (Blos, 1979, 1998). It was a struggle for his existence as a separate being. He was moving away from Gramps, who had become a negative identification figure for Barry as he declined and slipped into card-playing and bar-hopping. Barry had to create his own identity out of his ambivalent identifications with his parents and substitute parents.

The teenage Barry felt isolated at Honolulu's Punahou School, where black students were few and most students were white, Polynesian, or Asian. The adult Barack recalled attending parties at the local military base named Schofield Barracks, 30 miles from Honolulu, where there were many black soldiers. His black classmates of that time, however, who complained about racism from whites and Asians alike, recalled that he was isolated from them. Barry was forever the outsider. A black classmate named Rik Smith recalled that "we'd all do things together, but Obama was never there," adding that they often brought along the few other black underclassmen. "I went to those parties up at Schofield [Barracks] but never saw him at any of them" (Scharnberg & Barker, 2007).

BASKETBALL AS A LINK TO THE FATHER

Longing for social acceptance, Barry found his way into the Punahou School community by playing basketball, his unconscious emotional link to his father, at which he excelled (Obama, 1995, pp. 78–79). He later remembered attending at least one party at Schofield Barracks with his black friends (Obama, pp. 83–84). Did Barry feel that he was a black man at the Punahou School? He knew that he was different. He was the son of a black man but also of a white woman, being raised by a white family. He was forging his own highly complex racial identity. And perhaps he did not wish to be the son of the man who had abandoned him, out of deep feelings of anger at his absent father.

Barry's way of being accepted at the Punahou School included his skill-ful basketball playing. In retrospect, the adult Barack saw his adolescent basketball playing as a travesty of a black boy's adolescence, which itself imitated and exaggerated the peacock-like strutting of young American whites (Obama, 1995, p. 79). Yet his basketball playing was his uncon-scious link to his father, and during his adolescence the camaraderie of his fellow players was very important to him. Through the commu-nity of his peers, he was creating his identity, that of a black man who nevertheless wished to put race aside.

In fact, basketball has a psychological world all its own. In America, basketball is dominated by tall black players like Earvin Johnson, Jr. (born 1959), better known as "Magic" Johnson. As the famous American basket-ball coach Phil Jackson has pointed out, a good basketball player respects both the game and his team's opponents. He is aggressive without anger or violence, he lives in the reality of the game but is calmly focused in the midst of chaos, and he thinks of his team members as well as of himself. Unconsciously, the coach is the father figure who has a sensitive interaction with his team players, his "sons." Jackson was a good psychological coach. Along with being called the "Zen Master," he was known as the master of mind games and as a good leader. He was thought to wage psychological warfare on his team's opponents (Jackson & Delenhanty, 1995).

We have seen that basketball playing is one of Barack's unconscious links to his dead father. To Barack, basketball and politics are "full-contact sports" (Obama, 2006a, p. 22). Abramsky believes that "Obama thinks of power as a ball intercepted by different countries at different moments in time" (2009, p. 77). Good team play in basketball can lead to good teamwork in politics, and good leadership in basketball can help achieve good political leadership. Jackson's team, the Chicago Bulls, won six U.S. National Basketball Association championships. In 2001, when he coached the Los Angeles Lakers during the NBA finals against the Philadelphia 76ers, Jackson had Tyronn Lue, a player on the Lakers team who was comparable in size and height to the 76ers star Allen Iverson, wear a sock on his arm during the Lakers' practice sessions, to simulate Iverson's use of a compression arm sleeve as part of his game-time attire. Philadelphia's mass-communication media considered this to be yet another psychological-warfare tactic of Jackson's, but Jackson's main idea was to simulate what a game against Iverson would be like, right down to Iverson's tattoos and cornrows, which Lue also had (Jackson & Delenhanty, 1995).

In 1975 Barry's mother was away in Indonesia. After majoring in anthropology at the University of Hawai'i at Manoa, studying at Honolulu's East-West Center, and attaining her bachelor's and master's degrees, she had decided to go back to Indonesia for her doctoral fieldwork, and perhaps also to see her ex-husband, Lolo. She took her daughter Maya with her. Barry was 14. He decided to stay in Hawai'i. Apparently, his ties to his grandparents were more important to him now than his ties to his mother. While his memoir is full of praise for his mother, his actual feelings for her were more complex. Indeed, when she left with his half sister Maya, he moved back in with Gramps and Toot, who loved him very much. There was no more sibling to compete with for his mother's love. And his restless and reckless mother was away.

Barry played on his high-school basketball team. He was good at the game and a good team player. Through basketball, he got love and comradeship from his teammates. He learned how hard and painful it was be black in America, how rampant and pervasive white racism was, highly dosed with arrogance and obtuseness (Obama, 1995, p. 80). Yet he could not hate white people as some of his fellow black students did, for his mother and her parents were "white folks" and he was half white himself. It was hard for him to sort out his enemies from his friends, to know whom to identify with. It was very important for him not to lose his control over his emotions. He learned to shuttle between his two racial groups, trying to fit into each one. Nonetheless, white people's derogatory comments about black people always set him on edge (Obama, p. 82).

During his adolescence, Barry went through a prolonged and painful quest for his identity, or an identity crisis as the psychoanalyst Erikson

(1959) has called it. Who was he? Which community did he belong to? He felt that being black meant feeling powerless (Obama, 1995, p. 85). To avoid feeling helpless in the face of white discrimination against blacks, he read the writings of African American leaders and thinkers like James Baldwin, Ralph Ellison, Langston Hughes, Richard Nathaniel Wright, and W.E.B. DuBois but failed to find in them the answer he was seeking. In the end, he found no comfort in all those books. Underneath their intellect, irony, humor, and love they were full of pain, uncertainty, and self-loathing. The power of those painful feelings was such that these authors felt defeated, gave up, and withdrew to Africa, to Europe, or into the heart of their black community (Obama, p. 86).

For the adolescent Barry, searching for an identification figure, that left only the extremist black leader Malcolm X (Malcolm Little, 1925–1965), whose autobiography Barry was reading (Little, 1965). Malcolm X, who after his pilgrimage to Mecca was also known by his Muslim Arabic name of El-Hajj Malik El-Shabazz, was a black American Muslim minister, public speaker, and human rights activist who had been assassinated when he was not quite 40 years old. The self-made late-adolescent Barry identified with Malcolm's attempts to recreate himself, as well as with his forthright speeches, his pride, his ideals of respect, order, and discipline, and above all his will power (Obama, 1995, p. 86).

Like Barry, Malcolm X was a mulatto: his black mother had been raped by a white man and had become pregnant by him. Malcolm had a traumatic childhood. He was raised by an adoptive black father, who was murdered when Malcolm was a young boy. This stepfather had taught Malcolm about black pride and independence. The young Malcolm personally encountered many incidents of white racism against blacks. He was placed in foster homes and, feeling rejected and abandoned, and full of rage, became a juvenile delinquent. At the age of 20 Malcolm was arrested, tried, and sentenced to an 8-to-10-year prison term.

During his seven years in prison (1945–1952), Malcolm Little became a Muslim and joined the black nationalist Nation of Islam. As a rejection of his parental names and an assertion of his self-made-man status, he called himself Malcolm X. He was paroled for good behavior at the age of 27 and became one of the leaders of the Nation of Islam, along with Elijah Muhammad. His eloquence made him its chief spokesman. For 12 years (1952–1964) Malcolm spoke for the Nation of Islam. Muhammad, however, was jealous of Malcolm's prominence, and the rivalry between the two leaders caused Malcolm to quit at the age of 39. He converted to Sunni Islam and went to Mecca on the sacred pilgrimage.

In the last year of his life (1964–1965) the formerly antiwhite black-racist leader Malcolm X publicly renounced racism and traveled through Africa and the Muslim world seeking racial and religious harmony. As his answer to the Nation of Islam, he founded two new organizations, the religious Muslim Mosque and the secular Organization of Afro-American Unity. However, his prominence and his black-pride stance made him many enemies among white racists. In 1965 Malcolm X was murdered, just like his adoptive stepfather. He was not yet 40 years old. The murderers were three white men.

Barry had several reasons to identify with Malcolm X, his mulatto identity being only one of them. Malcolm Little had dropped his last name and called himself Malcolm X, which may have meant that he had a diffuse sense of identity. Barry, too, had changed his last name from Obama to Soetoro and back to Obama. But Barry could not identify with Malcolm's violence nor with his antiwhite racism. The adult Barack recalled that as an adolescent he had had fantasies of becoming Malcolm's follower, but he was dissuaded by recalling that Malcolm had wished to rid himself of the white blood that he had in him as a result of the rape of one of his female forebears by a white man. Barack could never identify with that wish: to preserve his self-esteem, he had to keep his white mother's blood or, psychologically, her internal image in him (Obama, 1995, p. 86).

Barack's Harvard biographer thinks that "for all that his parents' marriage was short-lived, Obama had little doubt that, unlike Malcolm's, his own dual heritage was conceived in love, not violence" (Niven, 2009, p. 11). However, the psychological processes of separation and individuation, and of ego-identity formation, whose first phase occurs during infancy and whose second phase takes place during adolescence, were not easy for the young Barry. He could not cut himself off from his white mother and from her parents any more than he could from his black father. In the same way, as an adult, in his "More Perfect Union" presidential-campaign speech in 2008, he said that he could no more disown his racist black pastor Jeremiah Wright, Jr., than he could his black father, his white family, or America's black people. It took another racist speech by Wright for Barack to be able to make a clean break with him. And so Barry continued to struggle for his racial and ego identity.

Barack's Chicago mentor, Jerry Kellman, told him about other black community organizers and political leaders that he could identify with, such as Myles Horton, the founder of the Highlander School in Tennessee, a training center for young community organizers during the Great Depression of the 1930s, which followed the U.S. stock-market crash of 1929; Ella Baker, the black American civil rights pioneer who had created citizenship schools in the southern United States; Bob Moses, a leader of the Student Nonviolent Coordinating Committee. Moses had told the historian Charles Payne (a namesake of Barack's maternal great-uncle) that a good community organizer had to make personal contact with the person he was dealing with, and that change had to come from the bottom up (Payne, 1995, p. 98). Abramsky thinks that the young leaders who attended those schools learned "not only the importance of voting" but also "the transformative power" that they could exert on others through their personal activity (2009, p. 62).

Barack believes in the transformation of people, in their ability to change radically, just as he transformed himself from a troubled adolescent into the successful president of the United States. When he was 10 years old, he received his only visit ever from his father, who would not let him watch his favorite television show. There followed a noisy and unpleasant argument between his parents and his grandparents, and the unhappy 10-year-old Barry concluded that it was all a lie, that his father and grandparents would never become happy and pleasant people that it was fun to be with. He could not wait for his father to leave (Obama, 1995, p. 68). Later, however, Barack made transforming himself and other people his major preoccupation (Abramsky, 2009, pp. 63–64).

Barry also sought a father figure and an identification figure in a man he called "Frank" in his memoir, an old black poet from Kansas who had settled in Hawai'i many years earlier (Obama, 1995, p. 76). The African American historian Gerald Horne thinks that this was none other than Frank Marshall Davis (1905–1987), a black journalist, poet, radical political activist, and Communist who had moved to Hawai'i many years earlier on the advice of the famous "Negro" singer Paul Robeson (Horne, 2007a; Niven, 2009, p. 11). As Communism is anathema to most Americans, Barack denied during his presidential campaign of 2008 that "Frank" was Frank Davis, but it is nonetheless possible that Horne was right.

During U.S. Senator Joseph McCarthy's witch hunt of Communists in the late 1940s and 1950s, the leftist Davis was investigated by the House Un-American Activities Committee for comments he had made in the *Honolulu Record*, as well as for political activities that McCarthy alleged were connected to the Communist Party. The traumatized "Frank" told Barry that "white" universities were no good, that they only taught blacks to compromise and surrender to whites. Barry rejected the extremist "Frank," too, as his emotional or spiritual father figure (Niven, 2009, p. 12; Obama, 1995, p. 97).

For Barry's maternal grandfather Stanley Armour Dunham, whom Barry called "Gramps," Barry was the son he had so much wanted. When Barry graduated from Honolulu's Punahou School in 1979 at age 18, his preference for his fond grandparents over his absentee mother was clear. "On page 271 of the 1979 *Oahuan* [the Punahou School yearbook], Barack's entry reflects the crossroads he found himself at as he prepared for life beyond Hawai'i. He thanked 'Tut and Gramps,' his nicknames for Madelyn and Stanley Dunham, but did not mention his faraway mother" (Scharnberg & Barker, 2007). Ann often returned to Hawai'i for visits but got her Ph.D. degree only in 1992, the year Gramps died and Barack married. By that time she had cancer. She was not an ideal mother for Barack, even though he idealized her in his memory.

In the absence of both his parents, the adolescent Barry built himself from within as a self-made man. It was his way of dealing with his abandonment. The journalist Jon Meacham understood this psychological secret. Without paternal love, Barry had to "build his own universe," to create a psychological space within which "the failings and flightiness of others could do him the least harm" (Meacham, 2008). In his interview with this journalist, Barack admitted that he had always measured himself against his image of his father: "A man's either trying to live up to his father's expectations or make up for his father's mistakes....In my case, both things might be true" (ibid.). Meacham thinks that Barack had also had to forge his own identity, to feel good in his own skin, to reconcile his black identity with being raised by his white grandparents.

Barry had struggled with the racial issue throughout his adolescence and early adulthood. At one point his grandmother Toot was scared by a black panhandler at a bus stop and later refused to take the bus to work, while her husband Gramps refused to drive her there. The aging Gramps declined, became depressed, lost his job, and lost his stature in Barry's eyes (Obama, 1995, p. 89). His grandmother was right to be scared, "Frank" told Barry, because black people *did* hate white people: they had a reason to do so, for the humiliating way the whites treated them. Barack was shocked. He lost his self-confidence and felt "utterly alone." (Obama 1995, p. 91). Barry felt that he was the only one who could deal with his anxiety and with his identity crisis. Nobody else, not "Frank," not Gramps, not Toot, not his mother, could help him feel otherwise.

Chapter 9

IN HIS FATHER'S
FOOTSTEPS

Synopsis: *At Occidental College in Los Angeles, from 1979 to 1981, Barry Obama (as Barack was still known at that time) became involved in black politics, fighting against South African apartheid and for other causes. He also had two wealthy Pakistani friends. But throughout his stay at Occidental College, Barry was struggling with the race issue and with his own identity. He could not identify with the black-power extremists nor with blacks who hated whites. He also kept questioning himself, his own credentials as a black man, and he felt that he was not genuine. He felt alienated and alone. One of the girls, a big, dark junior from Chicago, whom he called "Regina" (the name means "queen"), made him feel at ease, so he did not have to lie to her. Barry told her that he read the "racist" novel* Heart of Darkness *by Joseph Conrad because it helped him understand how white people learned to hate black people, and he told himself that his life depended on this understanding (Obama, 1995, p. 103). He identified with an idealized image of his absent father as a strong, wise, great man. He finally came away from Los Angeles with a stronger and clearer sense of his identity as a black man. But his black identity would be built on positive foundations: He never identified with black extremists like Louis Farrakhan or Malcolm X. He would become a political activist and a community organizer, but he would try to achieve harmony and conciliation between the races, not confrontation and war.*

In 1978, when Barry was 17, his mother Ann, who had been shuttling between Hawai'i and Indonesia, returned to Hawai'i from her doctoral fieldwork in Indonesia. She was shocked by her father's physical and emotional decline and by her son's drinking and smoking marijuana. Her worst fear was that her son Barry would become a failure like her father—that he would drink, take drugs, and become a good-for-nothing loafer (Obama, 1995, pp. 94–95). Barry, however, proved her fears unfounded by getting admitted to "several respectable schools" (Obama, p. 96). He chose Occidental College in Los Angeles, not for its academic merit but because he had met a pretty girl from the Los Angeles district of Brentwood and had fallen in love with her.

After graduating from Honolulu's Punahou School in 1979, the 18-year-old Barry moved to Los Angeles to attend Occidental College and see his Brentwood girlfriend. He did not say in his memoir what happened to their affair. Since her family lived in Brentwood, she probably did not live in the college dormitory and was therefore not the beautiful green-eyed honey-skinned multiracial girl whom he called "Joyce" in his memoir, who shared his dormitory during his freshman year and whom all the black "brothers" at Occidental College were chasing (Obama, 1995, pp. 99, 277).

In Indonesia, Barry Obama had been known as Barry Soetoro, and he had used the nickname Barry throughout high school in Hawai'i. He would also use it in college, until he moved to New York. For some time in his late adolescence, Barry was restless like his maternal grandfather, "Gramps." In 1979, the year Barry graduated from high school, his paternal grandfather, Hussein Onyango Obama, known as "the Terror," died in Kenya at the age of 84. Barry's father, Barak, then 43, had had a very strained relationship with his hot-tempered, tyrannical, critical, and rejecting father. When Barak came to his father's home to make the arrangements for his funeral and burial and sorted through his father's belongings, that was the only time his stepmother, "Granny" Sarah, had ever seen him cry. After his father's death, however, rather than mourn and accept his loss, the abusive and self-abusive Barak continued to destroy himself through his alcoholism and his road accidents, and drove his children away from him by behaving meanly toward them, just as his father had done to him (Obama, 1995, p. 424). Being abandoned by his father at a very early age, Barack had the great fortune of not suffering directly from his father's serious emotional disturbance.

Throughout his stay at Occidental College in Los Angeles, Barry was struggling with the race issue and with his own identity. He could not identify with the black-power extremists nor with blacks who hated whites. He also kept questioning himself, and his own credentials as a black man. He felt alienated and alone (Obama, 1995, pp. 91, 100–101). He also felt like a liar, as if he were telling two lies, one about other black people, the other about himself (Obama, p. 102). Luckily for him, one of the girls, a big, dark junior from Chicago named Regina (her name means "queen" in Latin), made him feel at ease, so at least he did not have to lie to her. When a fellow black student or "brother" named Earl Chew, whom he called "Marcus" in his memoir, accused him of reading a "racist" book—*Heart of Darkness* by Joseph Conrad—Barry told Regina that he read the "racist" novel because it taught him how white people learned to hate black people, and he told himself that his life depended on this kind of understanding (Obama 1995, p. 103).

Barry told Regina that his real name was Barack, which meant "blessed" in Arabic, and that his grandfather was a Muslim. In fact, "Barak" or "Baraka" is a noun that means "blessing" in Swahili. He did not say whether his father was a Muslim, nor whether he was one, or wished to be. She told him about her childhood. Regina, too, like Barry, had had an absent father. Barry envied Regina her happy family memories with her uncles, cousins, and grandparents. Regina laughed and said she wished she had grown up in nonracist Hawai'i. His conversation with Regina changed Barry for the better and gave him renewed self-confidence (Obama, 1995, p. 105). His voice began to come back and to become strong and sturdy, as it is today. The adult Barack saw his voice as "that constant, honest portion of myself, a bridge between my future and my past" (Obama, 1995, p. 105). But why did a single talk with Regina change Barry so much? Was it because the big, dark "queen" from Chicago was like a good mother to him, who let him become his true self and gave him the compassionate understanding that his anxious mother could not?

In 1980, after he met his stepfather Lolo Soetoro in Los Angeles (Lolo had come for treatment of his liver ailment), the 19-year-old Barry became politically active at Occidental College. He first became involved in the South Africa divestment campaign, in which American student groups like the Student Nonviolent Coordinating Committee (SNCC), the Students for a Democratic Society (SDS), and the African-American Student Foundation (AASF) lobbied 55 U.S. universities to divest themselves financially from investment companies affiliated with the white South African apartheid regime. Barry contacted the banned African National Congress in South Africa and invited its envoys to speak on the Occidental College campus.

The young Barry discovered that his words carried weight, that people listened to him, that his words gave him influence and power. He became "hungry for words...that could carry a message, support an idea" (Obama, 1995, p. 105). Public speaking became very important to him, as it still is. It was his words—and his character—that won him the presidency of the United States, the words in his "Audacity of Hope" keynote address at the Democratic National Convention in 2004, his "More Perfect Union" presidential-campaign speech in 2008, his campaign slogans "Yes We Can" and "Change We Need." Was it the power of his father's words to his high school class in early 1972 that Barack wanted to possess? He now believed in the power of words to transform people, and his mouth and the words it produced became paramount in his emotional life. His words gave him power; his words made up for his helplessness in the face of his father's absence.

Barry's first public speech was given to an Occidental College audience, and it was about the atrocities of South Africa's apartheid. It was cut short, however, when two white students dressed as South African paramilitaries dragged him off the stage according to a preplanned script that he had helped write himself. Despite this fact, Barry did not like the interruption, and when Regina congratulated him on his speech at a party that night, he told her he would never speak again because he had no right to speak for black people, as if he were not black enough (Obama, 1995, p. 108). Here was his ambivalence about his black father again. He confessed that the main reason for his speech was that it made him feel important, powerful, and wanted and that it gave him a cheap thrill. Regina did not believe him and told him that he was trying to run away from himself and that the struggle was not about him but about people who needed his help (ibid.).

Thanks to Regina and to other black people he liked and respected, Barry began to resolve his identity crisis in college. He realized that he was acting out of fear, just as he had when he rejected the friendship of the 10-year-old black girl "Coretta" in grammar school. Barry suffered from a chronic fear that he did not belong, that no community truly accepted him, that he had to conceal his true identity to be accepted, that the world was always judging him (Obama, 1995, p. 111). In fact, it was an unconscious projection of his own self-judgment, his difficulty in accepting himself as he was. He still needed a false self. Later, he would find his true identity and no longer need to conceal or disguise who he was.

Saying that he was always an outsider, a marginal man, was a striking and powerful statement for a man who would become the first African American president of the United States. Barry felt that above all else he needed determination, the kind of emotional strength and will that made it possible for his friend Regina to resist all the forces that tried to bend her to their will (Obama, 1995, p. 111). Barry felt that his "many grandmothers," both real and imaginary, including his father's mother, his fantasy image of Regina's grandmother, Lolo's mother, "the copper-skinned Mexican maid" and "the tight-lipped, chalk-colored face of Toot," demanded it of him. He felt that did not have to choose between them: He should have the courage to accept them all. Indeed, his determination to achieve his goals and live out his values has been remarkable.

We do not know much about Barry's two years at Occidental College except that he became active in campus black politics and met his ailing Indonesian stepfather Lolo. The affair with the Brentwood girl that brought him to Los Angeles must have ended in heartbreak after some time. These two years from age 18 to age 20 were mainly a preparation for his young adulthood in New York. In any event, he came away from Los Angeles with a stronger, clearer, and more balanced sense of his black racial identity (Niven, 2009, p. 12). In other words, he knew he was a black man or an African American, but he also knew that he could never identify with black extremists like Louis Farrakhan or Malcolm X. He would become a political activist and a community organizer, but he would try to achieve harmony and conciliation between the races, not confrontation or war.

Chapter 10

NAME CHANGE AND IDENTITY STRUGGLE

Synopsis: *In 1981 Barry Obama left Occidental College; traveled to Indonesia, Pakistan, and India; and then moved from Los Angeles to New York to attend Columbia University. Some time before or after his father's death in 1982 he reverted to his given name of Barack (Obama, 1995, p. 118). The name change was significant, as it was his father's name, and as it also meant he was no longer the adolescent Barry. He was still leading a marginal life, living on the border of Spanish Harlem, moving between the various communities, and leading a kind of monastic existence in Sin City. He devoted himself very seriously to his studies and to political activism, despite the injunctions of friends to make money and take care of himself. In late 1982 his paternal aunt Jane called him from Kenya to tell him that his father had died in a road accident at the age of 46. Barack did not feel grief, "only the vague sense of an opportunity lost" (Obama, 1995, p. 128). But he continued to struggle inside himself with his father's ghost, and during a trip to Kenya in 1988 he would learn the bitter truth about his tragic father. Nonetheless, he was able to construct his own identity out of the positive elements in his father's personality—his generosity, his intelligence, his ambition. In 1983 he had a fascinating dream about his dead father, which revealed that he still harbored very powerful and deeply ambivalent feelings about his father. His identification with his African father had been equally ambivalent. For two years after graduating from Columbia in 1983 he held some unsatisfactory jobs in New York and wavered about what to do with his life, who and what he wanted to be. There was a period when he was broke and unemployed.*

Like the young Barack, Philippe Wamba (1971–2002) was an African American editor and writer. He was born in California to an African American mother from Detroit and her African husband Ernest Wamba dia Wamba (born 1942), a Congolese scholar who became a rebel leader and later a senator in the Democratic Republic of the Congo. The Wambas moved to Boston, then to the Tanzanian capital of Dar es Salaam ("abode of peace"). Wamba then returned to the United States and went to high school in New Mexico, where he attended the United World College U.S.A. before going on to college at Harvard University in Massachusetts and to graduate school at Columbia University in New York. Wamba claimed to fuse in his own person the African culture, as represented by his father, and the African American culture, as represented by his mother.

Wamba, 10 years Barack's junior, walked the fine line between his two cultures in much the same way as Barack did. As he put it himself, "although balancing two cultures within the same family sometimes involved shifting identities in shifting contexts, in some way my family managed to situate itself on the boundary between cultural and continental communities" (Wamba, 1999, p. 53, cited in Abramsky, 2009, pp. 49–50). After getting his graduate degree from Columbia, Wamba worked on a variety of writing and publishing projects.

At the age of 28 Wamba published a memoir that was promoted by his mentor, the African American Harvard scholar Henry Louis Gates, Jr., who has also played a significant role in Barack's life. The memoir received some good reviews (Wamba, 1999). Wamba was profiled in the *New York Times Magazine* in connection with the publication of this book. He later became the editor-in-chief of the now-defunct online magazine *Africana*, founded by Gates. Like Barack's father, however, Wamba died in a car crash in Kenya, where he was conducting research on African youth movements, at the age of 31. After his death, the Harvard African Students Alumni Network announced plans to raise funds in his memory to promote traffic safety in Africa. Gates spoke at his funeral, saying "Philippe lived on no man's hyphen" (Tuttle, 2003).

In 1981 the 20-year-old Barry Obama took advantage of a special transfer program that existed between Occidental College in Los Angeles and Columbia University in New York to apply for that program and was admitted to Columbia, an Ivy League school near Harlem in Manhattan. Before moving to New York, however, he traveled to Indonesia to visit his mother Ann, his half sister Maya, and his stepfather Lolo, then spent three weeks in Pakistan with his Pakistani college buddy Wahid Hamid, and then visited India before returning to Los Angeles. After that, he drove across the United States from Los Angeles to New York to attend Columbia University.

The Columbia campus is in uptown Manhattan, near Harlem, which has a black part and a Puerto Rican or Spanish part. As Barack later recalled, he seized an opportunity to grab an apartment in Spanish Harlem that was being vacated by a female friend of a friend of his from Los Angeles (Obama, 1995, p. 113). Who was Barack's friend in Los Angeles whose lady friend in New York was vacating her apartment? Was it one of Barack's Pakistani friends at Occidental College—Imad Husain, now a Boston banker; Mohammed Hasan Chandoo, now a financial consultant in Armonk, New York; or Hamid, now a vice president at Pepsico in New York City, who had traveled with Barack to Pakistan, where they stayed with the Chandoo family in Karachi?

Be that as it may, Spanish Harlem, also known as El Barrio and East Harlem, is a predominantly Spanish-speaking Latino neighborhood in Harlem, in the northeastern part of New York City's borough of Manhattan. Why did the African American Barack not rent a place in black Harlem? Surely at least one was available? Was it because of his diffuse racial identity, his feeling of being an outsider in his own community? Throughout his four-year stay in New York (1981–1985), Barack lived on the border between two neighborhoods. During his three years of black-community organizing in Chicago's predominantly black South Side (1985–1988) he did not live in the South Side, which he helped organize, either.

When the 20-year-old Barry reached the New York apartment he had rented, after a long and arduous journey across the United States, he found the door locked, and no one answered the door buzzer. Not quite knowing what to do, he sat on the stoop downstairs and read a letter he had just received from his unhappy father, urging him to visit Kenya and meet his family. His ties to his father had greatly weakened, and their correspondence had all but stopped (Obama, 1995, p. 114). Struggling for his racial and personal identity, Barry did not know where he belonged, what he would do with his life, where he would live, or what he would do. He finally fell asleep outdoors. When he woke up in the morning, he washed himself at an open fire hydrant alongside a homeless man. He then went to the home of "Sadik," a Pakistani friend whom he had met in Los Angeles (Obama, p. 113), whose real name was Sohale Siddiqi (Goldman & Tanner, 2008). Like his countrymen and friends in Los Angeles, "Sadik" became Barack's best friend in New York.

In New York City, Barry Obama changed his first name back to Barack, his given name (Obama, 1995, p. 118). He does not say when exactly he changed his name, and he may have used both "Barry" and "Barack" for some time until his father died in late 1982. The name change was an acceptance of both himself and his like-named father Barak, and a rejection of his adolescent identity. Barry had been the spoiled adolescent at the Punahou School and at Occidental College; Barack was the budding young adult at Columbia. His Harvard biographer thinks that Barack led an ascetic life in "small, uncluttered apartments" (Niven, 2009, p. 12), feverishly reading numerous books on politics, philosophy, and literature. Barack felt that he badly needed a community in which he would put down stakes and test his social commitments. This community would be his new family, the kind of family he had never had.

While dozing off on the Spanish Harlem staircase, Barack remembered Earl Chew, whom he called "Marcus," his black "brother" at Occidental College who had been involved in black politics but who became very extreme and had joined the Malcolm X crowd. In a public debate, an older Iranian student had accused the black slaves in America of not fighting to the death against their white owners. Barack in turn had attacked the Iranian for how his people stood by idly while the Shah's brutal Savak thugs murdered and tortured his Iranian opponents. But his friend "Marcus" had become increasingly less communicative and more extreme, and he later dropped out of school. Barack thought that "Marcus" needed his help as much as Barack needed help from "Marcus"—that neither of them quite knew where they belonged or who they were (Obama, 1995, pp. 116–118).

After all those years, Barack still carried within him the bitter pain of his abandonment by his father. When he looked down at the street, it looked abandoned to him. He wondered whether he or any of his "brothers" knew where they belonged. They longed for a member of an elder generation to help them find their identity or heal their divided souls. Barack's own father sent him a letter once a year, "full of dime-store advice" (Obama, 1995, p. 118). Barack was bitter. One can feel in those words Barack's rage at his absent father as well as his longing for him. His father might have given him a clearer sense of his own identity, racial and otherwise. But the father was away in Africa, and Barack had to painfully search for and find his own identity.

As we have seen, either before or after his father's death, Barry Obama switched from using his nickname of Barry to using his first name of Barack (Obama, 1995, p. 118). Name changes involve identity issues (Falk, 1975–1976). Barack later recalled that his name change occurred in 1981, when he arrived in New York, and his Harvard biographer bought the story (Niven, 2009, p. 12). Memory, however, can be tricky, and the change may have occurred in 1982, after he had learned of his father's death. If it did, it would indicate an identification with his long-idealized dead father.

Was Barry's move from Occidental College in Los Angeles to Columbia University in New York an unconscious echo of his father's move from the University of Hawai'i to Harvard University when Barry was a toddler? Both Columbia and Harvard were Ivy League schools, and both were across the United States. Barry now adopted his father's first name as well. Some perceptive American journalists have thought that Barry's choice of name was "part of his almost lifelong quest for identity and belonging—to figure out who he is, and how he fits into the larger American tapestry" (Wolffe, Ramirez, & Bartholet, 2008). Barack himself told these journalists that at Occidental College he had been feeling as if he was at a "dead end" and "that somehow I needed to connect with something bigger than myself" (ibid.). That "something bigger" was America, unconsciously a maternal figure. The former Barry Soetoro was now Barack Obama, like his father. In his endless quest for identity, he had come to identify with his idealized image of his black African father.

The young Barack had come to New York full of noble sentiments about finding himself, making amends for his "misspent youth," and making himself useful to his black community. His Pakistani friend, "Sadik," tried to disabuse him of his naïveté, telling him that New York was a jungle where only the fittest and most aggressive people survived and that he had to look after himself first. "Sadik" took Barack around New York and showed him the selfishness and greed of its people and its sky-high prices. Barack gave up his apartment on 109th Street in Spanish Harlem for lack of heat, and "Sadik" took him in and helped him sort out his legal and financial affairs.

The two friends shared an apartment in Harlem. The Pakistani "Sadik" told the American Barack to fight tooth and nail for his own survival. But Barack's personal change in New York was not what "Sadik" had expected. Rather than becoming more self-centered, aggressive, predatory, and fighting for his own survival, Barack stopped using alcohol and drugs, which he had done as a teenager, ran three miles daily, fasted on Sundays, began studying seriously, kept a daily journal, and wrote poetry. He stopped going to bars and nightclubs, refusing "Sadik's" invitations with various excuses. When "Sadik" accused him of becoming a bore, Barack thought that he was right: Barack feared New York City's allure and its power to corrupt. He defended himself by resisting New York's temptations, leading a somewhat ascetic or monastic life, and applying himself to his studies at Columbia and to his quest for identity (Niven 2009, pp. 12–13; Obama, 1995, p. 120). His love affair with the Brentwood girl in Los Angeles, which must have ended unhappily, had broken his heart and may have made him desist from new ones for some time.

Although he did not mention it at all in his memoir, in 1981 Barack had flown back to Indonesia, which he had left 10 years earlier, to visit his mother Ann, his stepfather Lolo, and his half sister Maya. On his way back to the United States he stopped for three weeks in "Sadik's" native country of Pakistan. During his two years at Occidental College in Los Angeles, Barry had befriended another Pakistani student, Wahid Hamid, who traveled with Barack to Pakistan. Barack had flown to Indonesia from Los Angeles rather than from New York. His Pakistani friend Hamid is now vice president at a major U.S. company, and according to public records, he donated the maximum amount permitted by law to the Obama presidential campaign and raised funds for it (Rohter, 2008).

The 20-year-old Barack did not know in 1981 that his father had become a hopeless alcoholic in Kenya, that he was destroying his own life through drinking and road accidents, and that he would soon die of his self-destruction. He wrote little about his father in this part of his memoir, *Dreams from My Father*. Yet Barack had crossed the United States to the East Coast to attend an Ivy League school—just as his father had done 18 years earlier. He majored in political science, with a specialization in international relations. He lived on the East Harlem or Spanish Harlem border with black Harlem, between the Puerto Ricans and the blacks. In New York he realized as never before the violence, ferocity, and depth of the tribal and class wars between whites and blacks, between Jews and blacks and Hispanics, between every class and every race in America. Even in the stalls of Columbia University's bathrooms there were graffiti written by Jews and blacks, each calling the other racist names. Barack felt as if there was no more room for understanding and compromise (Obama, 1995, p. 121). Racial and ethnic strife was everywhere.

But it was precisely that elusive middle ground, that multiracial, multicultural, and multiethnic identity, that Barack so desperately sought. The young Barack struggled with his identity, not knowing where exactly he belonged, whom to identify with, where to live, what to be, who he was. He had to choose which race or class to identify with, which community to belong to, but he feared that once he made that choice, there would be no going back, and he might rue his decision. He spent a whole year walking all over Manhattan trying to decide which ethnic or racial group he belonged to (Obama, 1995, p. 122). He was not only trying to figure out New York's secrets and its social fabric but also, and especially, trying to find who he was and where he belonged.

On August 4, 1982, Barack celebrated his 21st birthday in New York. He had finished his junior year at Columbia. That summer, in a somewhat depressed mood, he received a visit from his mother Ann and his younger half sister Maya, who had flown from Hawai'i to see him. Maya found Barack very "skinny" (Obama, 1995, p. 122). She and Ann stayed with Barack for several weeks, first in his rented apartment, then in a friend's apartment. Barack took on the role of his father, scolding his half sister for watching television instead of reading the novels he had bought for her and instructing his mother on political and economic matters (Obama, p. 123). His half sister Maya, whom he called "my sister," worried about his emotional health, lest he become a freak. Barack, however, was far from freaking out: in fact, he was quickly maturing.

During that visit in the summer of 1982, Barack realized for the first time the depth of his mother's immaturity when she dragged him and his half sister Maya to a revival theater—an American movie theater re-screening old films—to see *Black Orpheus* (*Orfeu Negro*). The film is a modern Brazilian version of the ancient Greek myth of Orpheus, who goes into the underworld to take his dead beloved Eurydice back from the underworld god, only to lose her again when he looks back at her on their way out. The film had been made in Brazil in 1959 by the French film director Marcel Camus (1912–1982) and was based on the play *Orfeu da Conceição* (Orpheus of Conception) by the Brazilian poet Vinicius de Moraes (1913–1980). It was set in the context of Rio de Janeiro during the Carnival, and the main characters were named Orfeu (Orpheus) and Eurydice, as in the Greek myth.

During the screening of *Black Orpheus*, Barack later recalled, his mother Ann gazed wistfully at the screen, entranced by the black Brazilian dancers and by their happy, rhythmic dancing. Ann had seen the film once before, in 1959 when she was 16, when she was an *au pair* girl in Chicago, and she had been enthralled by it. Barack recalled realizing that his mother had always imagined black people as childlike, warm, sensual, and exotic, the very opposite of Joseph Conrad's savages in *The Heart of Darkness* (Obama, 1995, p. 124).

Barack felt embarrassed for his immature mother and irritated with her. His obvious irritation, which may have concealed a deeper anger, was unconsciously displaced from his mother to the other people in the theater. His half sister Maya told Barack afterward that the film was "corny," as was their mother's taste in films (Obama, 1995, p. 125). Actually, *Black Orpheus* is a poetic art film with considerable psychological insight. But to Barack, his mother's reaction to the film demonstrated her immaturity in the choice of her first husband, which had led to his own abandonment by this father.

The adult Barack later idealized his mother, saying that he owed to her all that was good in him. Yet he also realized that she had been immature and that she had repeatedly abandoned him emotionally. As Sasha Abramsky rightly notes (2009, pp. 42–43), despite his protestations of filial love for his mother, Barack wrote relatively little about her. Barack has an intuitive psychological understanding and a high emotional intelligence.

He understands that mixed-race white-black love affairs conceal a longing for something that one feels wanting in oneself. This was the unconscious reason his white mother had fallen in love with his black father. But the tensions between the races were there to stay. "Whether we sought our demons or salvation, the other race would always remain just that: menacing, alien and apart" (Obama, 1995, p. 124). In his political life, Obama would wage an endless battle against this racial apartheid.

During her visit with him in the summer of 1982, Barack's mother Ann once more tried to take the blame for his father's abandonment of him upon herself (Obama, 1995, p. 125). She told him that her parents had not approved of her marriage to his father and that his paternal grandfather, Hussein Onyango Obama, had written her father, Stanley Armour Dunham, a nasty letter saying that he did not approve of the marriage and threatening to have his son's passport and visa revoked. But the main thing Barack understood about his mother at that time was how immature and childlike her love for his father had been and that the mother who had raised him was herself needy and childlike (Obama, p. 127). This is what he must have felt in his early childhood, and this may also have been why he felt he had to protect his mother when they arrived in Indonesia.

Barack lived in New York for four years (1981–1985). He graduated with a bachelor's degree from Columbia University in 1983 and held a few unsatisfactory jobs from 1983 to 1985. During the year before his father died (1981–1982), Barack had enclosed himself in his solitude for his own emotional protection. He felt safer in his solitude than in his interpersonal relationships, which often ended in frustration, disappointment, anger, and hurt (Obama, 1995, p. 4). His solitude protected him from contact with people who would hurt him or abandon him. Yet he still needed a father figure. He took a liking to an old, lonely man who lived in his Spanish Harlem building, who might well have been his father, and helped him carry his groceries up the stairs. But the old man never thanked him and then abandoned him by dying on the staircase. Barack once more felt grief, loneliness, and abandonment. It was if he had lost another father. His real father had remained a myth and a mystery to him, "both more and less than a man" (Obama, p. 5).

FATHER'S DEATH

Barack turned 21 on August 4, 1982. Three months later, in November 1982, just before his mother's 40th birthday, he received the news of his father's death in Kenya through a telephone call from his paternal aunt Jane, a sister of his father's first wife, Kezia. Barack was living in New York, on the shifting boundary of Spanish Harlem (Obama, 1995, pp. 3–5).

Borders have their own unconscious emotional symbolism in our mind (Falk, 1989a, 1989b). Living on the boundary, never quite belonging to any community, being a stranger to every community, was part of the outsider identity that Barack had forged for himself. He had solved his problem of abandonment and as-yet-unclear identity by developing his solitude and escaping into it. After he received the news of his father's death, he called his mother, Ann, who cried out in anguish at the news, then his paternal uncle in Boston, with whom he had "a brief, awkward conversation" (Obama, 1995, p. 127). Barack did not mention his uncle's name, but it was probably his poor Uncle Omar (Bone, Crilly, & Macintyre, 2008; Obama, 1995, p. 307). He wrote his father's family in Kenya to express his condolences.

Apparently Barack did not feel that *he* needed any condolences. He recalled that he "sat down on the couch, smelling eggs burn in the kitchen, staring at cracks in the plaster, trying to measure my loss." He did not say that he felt any grief or pain. His father had been a myth to him, "both more and less than a man" (Obama 1995, p. 5). He later recalled that he felt neither pain nor grief at his father's death, "only the vague sense of an opportunity lost" (Obama, p. 128), and saw no reason to pretend otherwise. He did not feel the need to mourn the loss of his father, as he had already lost him many years before, when he was 2 years old, and again when he was 10, after his father had visited him in Hawai'i. Barack did not fly to Kenya for his father's funeral, nor did he go there for another six years, until after he had not only graduated from Columbia but also done three years of community-organizing work in Chicago. Did he fear to know the unhappy truth about his father?

DREAMING ABOUT HIS FATHER

Only about a year after his father's death and after he had graduated from Columbia University was the 22-year-old Barack finally able to let himself feel his grief at the loss of his father, which he had denied. His grief did not break out in a wakeful state, however: That would have been too painful for him. It broke out in the unconsciousness of a dream.

Let us examine Barack's fascinating dream about his father, as he openly related it in his memoir (Obama, 1995, pp. 128–129). As we shall see, this dream reveals that Barack badly missed his dead father and still had powerful and ambivalent feelings for him. A psychoanalytic interpretation of a dream requires that the dreamer supply his associations to each part of the dream, what each scene and figure reminds him of. Sigmund Freud called dreams "the royal road to the unconscious." Freud's psychoanalysis relied heavily on the dreamer's associations to the dream in order to interpret it appropriately. However, as Barack did not tell us his associations to the dream, it is hard to interpret it properly. I shall try nevertheless, because the dream is important and revealing about his mind. Moreover, as I cannot quote the dream verbatim, due to fair-use word-count limit and Obama's publisher's denial of permission to exceed that limit, I encourage you to look up the dream in Obama's *Dreams from My Father*.

The chief psychological function of the dream is to keep the dreamer asleep despite the emotional pain and anxiety aroused by the content of the dream. In his dream, Barack was traveling with some friends and was sitting beside a heavyset old white union man who was traveling to meet his daughter and was reading a book about the mistreatment of old people (Obama, 1995, p. 128). Could this man have stood for Barack's maternal grandfather, "Gramps," who, like the man in the dream, had a daughter—Stanley Ann, Barack's mother? As we know, Barack felt that he had been mean to his grandfather during his adolescence. Or could the old man in the dream have been a cross between three old men—Gramps, Barack's old man (his dead father), and Barack's old neighbor, who had died on the staircase of his New York apartment house the year before, shortly before Barack received the news of his father's death? Barack had mentioned that by the time he returned to Hawai'i from Indonesia at the age of 10, his grandfather was old and broken, a shadow of his former self. In this dream, the old white man was senile, retarded, and, in fact, no longer even a man, for he turned into a little black girl. Then a young Hispanic waitress entered the scene. She laughed under her frown and signaled to them to keep quiet or to keep a secret (Obama, p. 128).

It is hard to say who or what the black girl in the dream symbolized in Barack's unconscious mind. One little black girl who stood out in *Dreams from My Father* was Joella Edwards, whom he called "Coretta" in his memoir, the grade-school classmate whom the other boys called his girl-friend and whom he had rejected. Barack had not only rejected "Coretta" in fifth grade, when he was 10 years old, but also, and at the same time, his white old grandfather, Gramps, who had become depressed or retarded by the time the 10-year-old Barack returned to Hawai'i from Indonesia and whom Barack had also rejected during his adolescence. This asso-ciative similarity may explain why the old white man in the dream was transformed into a small black girl.

It is less clear who or what the young Hispanic waitress in the dream represented, nor what secret she was sharing with Barack and his friends. Could the secret have been that of the tragic life of his father, of his father's character defects, which Barack had always suspected but never quite knew for sure? The waitress's frown may have expressed Barack's anger at his father, while the laughter under it might be his way of denying his father's faults or his love of his father.

Next came a "dream within a dream" or rather a "sleep within a dream" episode. It was a prelude to Barack putting his father on trial for his misdeeds. In his dream, Barack fell asleep, only to wake up utterly alone. His friends, the old man, the black girl, and the Hispanic waitress were gone. Barack's father was in jail. Barack sat on a curb outside a rough-stone building. Inside, a judge and a lawyer argued about the fate of Barack's father. While the judge wanted to set his father free, the lawyer argued vociferously for keeping Barack's father in prison (Obama, 1995, p. 128). Was the rough-stone building a courthouse or a jailhouse, or did it have another function? Why was Barack's father in jail? Could the lawyer who objected so vigorously to his being released from jail have stood for Barack himself? Was he accusing his father of his crimes of abandoning his son, his wife abuse, his alcoholism, his self-destructive narcissism, and his false self?

Now, in his dream, Barack finally came face to face with his dead father, who was not unlike the dead father's ghost in Shakespeare's *Hamlet*. Barack entered his father's jail cell, where he saw his father in deathly shape: he was emaciated, wore nothing but a loincloth, and had a large head and no hair on his body; his face was pale and ashen, his black eyes shone, and he looked like a ghost. There was also a "tall, mute guard" in the room. Yet, at the same time, his father smiled and motioned to the guard to step aside (Obama, 1995, pp. 128–129).

Who was that tall, mute guard in the dream? Freud believed that the dream work is neither logical nor rational nor realistic: it is built on unconscious associations and symbolism. For example, the large head of Barack's father may have symbolized his intellect, whereas his loincloth may have symbolized his sexuality. Barack himself may have played several roles in this part of his dream, including the judge, the lawyer, the jailer, and the guard all at once. After all, the entire dream was about him and his father.

Then came the most moving scene in the dream. His father was amazed that Barack was so tall and so thin and had gray hair. Barack realized that his father was right. He went up to his father and hugged him. Then he began to weep. It was the first time he cried since his father died. The strong Barack felt ashamed of his crying but could not help it (Obama, 1995, p. 129). Barack had felt too ashamed to weep for the loss of his father in his waking life, and even in his dream he felt ashamed of his weeping, as if real men never wept or expressed their sadness. While the father in his dream told Barack that he loved him, he was more like Barack's son than his father. "He seemed small in my arms now, the size of a boy" (Obama, p. 129).

In the dream, then, Barack was both his father's son and his father's father. The poor, sad father was in jail—perhaps symbolizing a psychological jail of his own making, the jail of his self-destruction—and Barack wished to console him and save him. The jail may also have symbolized his father's self-destruction. After Barack embraced him, the father withdrew to his cot and became incredibly sad. Barack tried to cheer him up, to no avail. Barack tried to free his father from jail, but the father would not hear of it and asked Barack to leave (Obama, 1995, p. 129).

The father's sadness in the dream was overwhelming, and so was Barack's. In this fascinating dream, Barack played many different roles with his father: he was his father's son, his father's father, his judge, his jailer, his prosecutor, his guard, and his would-be savior. So far, the dream had succeeded in keeping Barack asleep despite the painful emotions in it. But by now the sadness in the dream had become too painful, the anxiety too great, and Barack woke up crying for his poor father. He quickly realized the many roles that he had played in his dream. He took out his dead father's letters to him and recalled his one and only meeting with his father, when he was 10 years old. Barack fondly remembered the basketball that his father had given him, the African dancing that his father had taught him, and his idealized lifelong image of his father as a strong man, against which he had always measured himself (Obama, 1995, p. 129). Playing basketball and dancing have remained his unconscious link to his father to this day.

But why did Barack see himself in his dream as his father's jailor and his savior, as his father's son and his father's father at the same time? Was it because deep in his heart he had wanted to jail his father and punish him for having abandoned him, and yet he also loved his father and wished that he had saved him from his tragic fate? The dream—and Barack's *Dreams from My Father*—clearly tells us how important the absent father had been to the young Barack. His entire life had been spent measuring up to his fantasy image of his father. Having woken up from his dream, Barack felt that this dream meant that he had to do something about his dead father. He had to search for his father's ghost and talk to him again (Obama, 1995, p. 129).

Can a man search for his dead father, find him, and talk to him? What was the meaning of Barack's wishful fantasy? It was with this dream and on this note that Barack ended the chapter in his memoir about his studies at Columbia University. His dead father was more important to him than both New York and Columbia. Around the time of this dream in 1983, he decided to become a community organizer. It would take him another two years to find such a community and another three years to organize it. Barack would also organize his new family this way. But it was not until 1988 that he would go to Kenya in search of his dead father.

Chapter 11

THE COMMUNITY AS FAMILY

Synopsis: *In 1985, after two years of unhappy aimlessness in New York, Barack's emotional and personal salvation came from Jerry Kellman, whom he called "Marty Kaufman" in his memoir. Kellman was an American Jewish black-community organizer in Chicago, the "black metropolis" that had absorbed masses of black people from the southern United States. He offered Barack a job helping him organize Chicago's poor black South Side community to better their lot. This fit into Barack's identity struggle, and he accepted. Barack remembered his "cold and gray" visit to Chicago in 1972, when he was almost 11 years old, and thought the city much prettier now (Obama, 1995, pp. 144–145), but now he was 24, and he got to know the misery of Chicago's poor black people. Barack spent three years (1985– 1988) as a community organizer, achieving only a modest success in fighting City Hall and the entrenched interests and powers, despite Chicago having a black mayor in Harold Washington. Barack at first loved and admired Washington as a new father figure, but he grew weary and frustrated with the endless impediments put in the way of organizing the powerless residents of Chicago's poor housing projects into a group with some political say. Yet he was accepted and loved by the people he organized, and his roots in the black community grew deeper. The black community of Chicago became his new family. In the fall of 1987 the 26-year-old Barack met the 46-year-old Reverend Jeremiah Alvesta Wright, Jr., the pastor of Trinity United Church of Christ, who became yet another father figure to Barack. It was Wright who baptized the atheist Barack into Christianity, who later married him, and who also baptized his daughters. But in 2008 Wright's antiwhite and anti-American sermons came to light, became a major embarrassment to Barack during his U.S. presidential campaign, and Barack was forced to break with him.*

Through his academic achievement, through his basketball playing, and through his public speaking, Barack proved to himself that he could do as well as his idealized father, or even better. As we have seen, ever since he was 10 years old, playing basketball and dancing had been his unconscious way of maintaining his ties to his father. The brilliant and hardworking Barack graduated from Columbia with a Bachelor's degree in political science in 1983, at the age of 22, having written an undergraduate thesis on nuclear disarmament (Abramsky, 2009, p. 79). This would later become a central theme of his work as a legislator.

After graduating from Columbia, Barack spent two aimless and unhappy years (1983–1985) in New York, working on several unsatisfactory jobs while searching for the right opportunity to organize a black American community. Barack later saw a clear thread running from his early life to his community organizing, starting with his parents and their families of origin, through his life in Indonesia, Los Angeles, and New York, and ending with his father's death (Obama, 1995, pp. 133–134). Was that narrative his triple quest for a father, a family, and an identity?

From 1983 to 1985 Barack burned with the desire to organize a black community, which was a thinly veiled type of political action. Just as his father had written from Kenya to all those American universities until he was accepted by the University of Hawai'i, Barack wrote to every American civil rights group he could think of and to every African American elected official in the United States to offer his community-organizing services. He had no takers (Obama, 1995, p. 135). His application for community and civil rights work was rejected by the office of Harold Washington (1922–1987), the new black mayor of Chicago. Barack was discouraged. His Harvard biographer thinks that Barack had idealized the civil rights struggle (Niven, 2009, p. 13). He had no idea what it was really like to live in a poor black ghetto.

In 1983 Barack was hired as a research assistant by Business International Corporation, a publishing and consulting firm helping American companies operate abroad and advising them on how to do business (and bribe officials) in other countries (Obama, 1995, p. 135). Barack was not happy with his first job. He was the only black person with a college education at this company. The only other black employees at Business International Corporation were the secretaries and the security guard, who advised the idealist Barack to look after his own career and to make money rather than seek to organize communities.

Although he was well paid by Business International Corporation and was promoted to financial writer, Barack later portrayed his first employer in his memoir as a symbol of the greedy capitalism of the 1980s and himself as an idealist who hated his job (Obama, 1995, p. 136). Some of his fellow employees think that Obama exaggerated the company's greed, "perhaps to portray his community organizing career as a more self-sacrificing choice than it actually was" (Niven, 2009, p. 13). Barack himself, however, truly believed that community organizing was more important than making money. When he moved to Chicago two years later, he felt that he was right in sacrificing his career for his ideals.

In his memoir, Barack recalled that by 1983 he had decided to become a black-community organizer (Obama, 1995, p. 133). Nonetheless, he spent another two years in New York, working at different jobs and trying to decide who and what he wanted to be. During that time, Barack's half sister Auma Obama, a daughter of his father Barak Obama by his first wife, Kezia, called him from Germany, where she was studying, announcing that she would visit him in New York during a forthcoming trip to the United States with some friends. Auma had gone to Heidelberg for her studies and had a white German boyfriend there, which Barack did not know. They had corresponded intermittently, and Barack had considered traveling to Germany to see Auma (Obama, pp. 136–137).

Barack, whose other family members were far away in Kenya and Hawai'i, was very excited about Auma's imminent visit, and made preparations. Sadly, a few weeks later Auma called him again from Germany, two days before her scheduled arrival, saying that she was not coming after all, as their half brother David Ndesandjo, a son of their father Barak and his third wife, Ruth Nidesand, had just been killed in a motorcycle accident. Barack was sorely disappointed.

David had been a troubled teenager in constant conflict with his father and mother, who sounds like a difficult person from press reports. Ruth had divorced Barak and married a Tanzanian man surnamed Ndesandjo, a mysterious figure whose first name does not seem to be mentioned in any public document. David's tragic death had traumatized Auma. In her anguish, she cried and asked Barack why those terrible things always happened in their family (Obama, 1995, p. 137). Like a good father or elder brother, Barack tried to help her calm down. It was like an ancient Greek tragedy, and, like all tragedies, it was psychological. Full of murderous rage at his parents, the troubled David might have committed an unconscious suicide. In 1988, when Barack visited Kenya, Auma told him that David's death had broken everybody's heart in their family, especially that of his half brother Roy (now Abongo Malik Obama), with whom David had been living (Obama, p. 339).

The Greek tragedy had played itself out in the Obama family in Kenya: Barack's father had also been killed in a road accident. Barack left his office and wandered the streets of Manhattan, deeply shaken by his half sister's call. He thought of Auma's crying, of the accident that killed his half brother David, of his African family that carried his blood, of how he could save Auma from her sorrow, of the wild, unspoken dreams that David had possessed, and, finally, he blamed himself for his lack of feeling: why did he not cry at David's death? (Obama, 1995, pp. 137–138). Barack could not understand his own emotional detachment, how he could feel no grief at his loss. Yet he realized later that Auma's telephone call had changed his life. A few months later he resigned from Business International Corporation.

In 1984 Barack was offered a new job by a New York civil rights group, organizing its conferences, but he declined it, as he wanted direct contact with his community. For three months he worked for the New York Public Interest Research Group, trying to convince minority students at the City College of New York of the importance of recycling. The New York Public Interest Research Group was the New York State affiliate of Ralph Nader's Public Interest Research Group, a political nonprofit organization in the United States and Canada. Founded by the consumer advocate Ralph Nader, it was composed of self-governing affiliates at the state and provincial level (Obama, 1995, p. 139). It was a national and grassroots advocacy and lobbying organization working for consumers and ordinary citizens against special-interest lobbyists. Barack was already showing his preference for civil rights and public-interest work over corporate-interest activity.

After three months at the New York Public Interest Research Group, however, Barack left this job, too, feeling this was not what he really wished to do. For a week he worked for a black politician's race, which failed, and he never got paid for this. Six months later he was broke and unemployed, living like a pauper. He attended a fiery political talk at his alma mater, Columbia University, by Stokely Carmichael (1941–1998), the Trinidad-born former leader of the Student Nonviolent Coordinating Council and black-power firebrand, who now called himself by the African name of Kwame Touré. Barack came away from Carmichael's speech discouraged and dispirited. Carmichael struck him as either crazy or a holy man with no practical ideas about how to better the lot of black people in America.

The 23-year-old Barack became despondent. He felt that the American civil rights movement had died, that there was no more hope for blacks, and that even the best-intentioned black leaders could be driven out of their mind by intransigent white racism. At one point Barack found himself talking to himself, with some former classmates carefully avoiding his glance. He was in bad emotional shape and had all but despaired of community organizing (Obama, 1995, pp. 139–140).

In 1984 Barack was still groping his way, trying to cement his identity, trying to know who he was, partly by helping others in need, but also looking for a new family. His salvation came in 1985 when he finally received a call from "Marty Kaufman," a Jewish community organizer in Chicago who had started a community-organizing drive there and wanted a trainee to help him out. The man's real name was Jerry Kellman, but Obama concealed his name in his memoir, just as he did those of most of the people in it. After a long interview, "Marty" offered Barack a job organizing poor blacks in churches in Chicago's South Side. His appearance did not inspire confidence, and something about him made Barack wary. "Marty" seemed too sure of himself, and he was a white organizer in a black community. Yet Barack took the job (Obama, 1995, pp. 140–143). He had been eager to find such a job for two years, and he was not going to miss this opportunity. Kellman himself recalled his relationship with Barack as follows:

> In 1985, I needed to hire a community organizer. I found myself in New York City, across from a 25-year-old recent college graduate. I wanted to convince him to give up a comfortable life and a bright future to come to Chicago to take up the toughest of challenges for a salary of just $10,000 a year. It was not difficult to convince Barack to take the job. All I had to do was describe what had happened to people on the south side of Chicago. The region had once been the largest producer of steel in the entire world, but the mills had shut down one by one. Other industries began to close, then stores and offices. Without jobs, neighborhoods unraveled and kids became easy prey for gangs and drugs. Two weeks later, using $2,000 we gave him to buy a car, Barack arrived in Chicago. Many before had quit in frustration at the challenges of organizing. Not Barack. If something didn't work, he'd stay up all night long until he figured out what went wrong and how to fix it. With his help, "people who had been shut out of decisions and robbed of dignity all their lives found their voice and found one another." (Kellman, 2008)

Actually, Barack was 24 years old when he met Kellman and came to Chicago. After two years in Los Angeles and four years in New York, much of them spent in his painful quest for his identity, Barack had left for Chicago to work as a black community organizer with Kellman. The car he bought was a small, beat-up blue subcompact Honda Civic. His Harvard biographer thinks that in the six years that had passed since he left Hawai'i, Barack had acquired "a stronger, less conflicted sense of his racial identity" (Niven, 2009, p. 14).

Barry had been to Chicago once before for three days, in the summer of 1972, just before his 11th birthday, and he remembered it as a cold and gray city (Obama, 1995, p. 144). He remembered two shrunken European heads in Chicago's Field Museum. They had been shrunk by Native Americans, and he saw their shrinking as their magical effort at taking control of the feared enemy, much as when he had eaten tiger meat with his Indonesian stepfather (Obama, 1995, p. 145). By the time he was 24, in 1985, the issues of power and control were becoming central to Barack's emotional life. He could not stand the feelings of helplessness and powerlessness. Years later, he related how people who did not know him tried to figure him out, to classify him into a racial category or otherwise pigeonhole him. He thought that such people could guess at the violent conflict within him, at his ambiguous identity, at what it must feel like to be half black, half white without belonging to either race (Obama, p. xv).

In an interview with the *Washington Post* on July 27, 2004, the day of his keynote address at the Democratic National Convention, when he was running for the U.S. Senate, Barack put it differently: "I've always been clear that I'm rooted in the African-American community but not limited to it" (Obama, 2009a, p. 68). Well, not quite always: in his youth he had been unclear about his racial identity and about belonging to the black community. By leaving New York in 1985 to organize the black community in Chicago, however, he was opting for his father's race—but not against his mother's. His quest for identity was fused with his quest for political power, an unconscious antidote to the feelings of helplessness he had suffered due to his abandonments.

It was no accident that Barack had chosen Chicago as the city where he wished to organize a black community. The "black metropolis" of Chicago (Drake & Cayton, 1945) had attracted masses of black migrants from the southern United States, mostly descendants of slaves or mixed-race offspring of black and white people. In America, mulattoes like Barack are usually considered black. Chicago was the most important center of black culture in America at that time (Niven, 2009, p. 14).

The year was 1985, 13 years after his first visit to Chicago in 1972, yet Barack erroneously recalled that 14 years had passed (Obama, 1995, p. 145). Did he have bad memories of his first visit to Chicago? Did the time that had elapsed seem longer to him? Chicago now seemed much prettier to him than it had been in 1972. In his imagination he now saw many faces from his life, connected his own life with those faces, and in his mind he tried to possess Chicago, making it his own (Obama, p. 146). The city of Chicago, where his mother had stayed in 1959, may have had an unconscious maternal role in Barack's mind.

One of the people who influenced black American politics in the 1980s was the thinker Saul David Alinsky (1909–1972), an American Jewish political activist who had founded modern community organizing in America. Alinsky had conceived and developed the political practice of organizing communities to act in their common self-interest (Alinsky, 1971;

Horwitt, 1989; Knoepfle, 1990). Organizations like the Student Nonviolent Coordinating Committee, the Congress on Racial Equality, and the Students for a Democratic Society, and labor leaders like César Chávez (1927–1993), embraced Alinsky's ideas. In 1969 Hillary Rodham Clinton (born 1947) wrote her college senior thesis at Wellesley College on Alinsky.

Barack Obama read Alinsky's writings when he began to organize Chicago's black community (Niven, 2009, p. 15). He also read Peter Drucker (1909–2005), the American management expert, whose writings Barack's mentor, Jerry Kellman, considered relevant to community organizing, to politics, and to business (Abramsky, 2009, p. 8; Drucker, 1999). Kellman's Calumet Community Religious Conference and Barack's Developing Communities Project used Alinsky's model of community agitation, in which paid organizers learned how to "rub raw the sores of discontent" in order to challenge those in authority (Alinsky, 1971).

In the early 1960s, Dr. Arthur Brazier (born 1921), a black Pentecostal minister of the Apostolic Church of God in Chicago's South Side neighborhood of Woodlawn, had created the Woodlawn Organization, a successful 20,000-strong community that applied Alinsky's ideas to better its living conditions (Niven, 2009, p. 15). Woodlawn had escaped the Chicago race riots that erupted after Dr. Martin Luther King's assassination in 1968. Brazier's example was a guiding light to the young Barack. He would follow Alinsky's theories and their application by Brazier. Leaders must listen to their followers, and change must come from the bottom up.

Unlike the unhappy state of helplessness and despair that Barack had felt in New York, in Chicago he now had a happy sense of control, power, and hope. Since 1983 Chicago had been run by Mayor Harold Washington, the first black mayor of that city. From New York, Barack had written the mayor about his search for community organizing, but his letter had gone unanswered. Chicago's black people spoke of "Harold" with much familiarity and affection (Obama, 1995, pp. 146–147). In Barack's unconscious mind, Washington became the Great Father with whom or against whom his life was to be played out. His feelings about the mayor were just as ambivalent as his emotions about his father. And just as Barack's father had died suddenly less than three years before Barack left New York for Chicago, two years after Barack's arrival in Chicago, Mayor Washington would die of a sudden heart attack.

POWER THROUGH ORGANIZING PEOPLE

His move to Chicago in 1985 changed Barack's life and cemented his black identity. He was going to fix the broken pieces of a poor community, which unconsciously stood for his broken family. Kellman had created the

Calumet Community Religious Conference, an organization of 20 suburban Chicago churches. Eight Chicago inner-city churches in the South Side had joined the "city arm" of the Calumet Community Religious Conference (Obama, 1995, p. 150), the Developing Communities Project, which now became Barack's organization. But there were many obstacles: The labor unions had not signed on to these organizations, and political battles were being waged against the Calumet Community Religious Conference and Developing Communities Project in Chicago's city council. Barack was getting his first taste of local politics.

Roseland was a rough South Side Chicago neighborhood, so crime-ridden that even black people tried to avoid it when driving in Chicago. From 1985 to 1988 Barack directed the Developing Communities Project, a Catholic-church-based community organization involving eight Roman Catholic parishes in Greater Roseland on Chicago's far South Side. Barack learned his political-leadership skills during those three years. During all this time, Barack idealized his dead father, tried to emulate him, and never went to Kenya to discover the bitter truth about him. It was better to keep his father's ideal image intact in his mind. He also hoped to be mayor of Chicago one day.

Barack's Harvard biographer thinks that he achieved "a modest success" in his Chicago community-organizing work from 1985 to 1988 (Niven, 2009, p. 15). Despite his initial happy feeling of power, Barack often felt frustration, anger, and a sense of failure (Obama, 1995, pp. 144–163). After his first community rally, held by Kellman's Calumet Community Religious Conference in a suburban school, Barack felt disappointed. The rally reminded him of a boring political meeting or a sports event (Obama, p. 152). Yet the fact that all those churches white and black had come together in one group made him feel good. His warring white and black identities, those of his internalized mother and father, found reconciliation and peace in this meeting.

Despite Barack's reservations about Kellman, his white mentor inspired Barack. "Marty" could bring black and white people together, cheer them up, give them a feeling of self-confidence, mobilize their feelings of community belonging and solidarity. He made them believe in their own power over that of their politicians and the television, newspapers, and bureaucrats and got them to find what bound them together rather than what split them apart (Obama, 1995, p. 152). Barack was beginning to like Kellman; in fact, he even wanted to emulate him.

Ironically, despite his dislike of politicians, Barack was to become one of the greatest of them all. Kellman had Barack interview numerous people who were involved in community organizing out of what Kellman considered self-interest. Barack felt that he could have power if he found an issue that people cared about and took them into it. To his mother, power had been a curse, a cause of corruption, injustice, and violence (Obama, 1995, p. 45). To Barack, power was an antidote to his unconscious feelings of abandonment and helplessness. He later wrote that he liked the ideas of issues, action, power, and self-interest: they signified toughness, self-control, lack of emotion, politics rather than religion (Obama, p. 155). In the world of power politics, he felt in his element. Here the painful feelings about his abandonment by his father and about his racial identity vanished, and the good feeling of power and control filled his being.

In the mid-1980s, Chicago was a place of racial strife and upheaval, one of the most segregated cities in the northern United States. It resembled present-day Detroit, where the city is almost all black, the suburbs almost all white. Barack spent three full weeks working day and night on his interviews with the black community organizers. Time and again, Barack heard the painful life stories of the black people he interviewed, stories of poverty, hardship, and migration, stories of violent encounters with the white world. These stories reminded him of those that his maternal grandparents had told him, but whereas their stories had been about racial harmony, these unhappy stories were all about racial strife, rage, and grief (Obama, 1995, p. 156).

Was not that, however, what had happened when his parents met? His black father had abandoned his white mother and himself, his father's life ended in tragedy, and his mother came to grief in her relationship with his father. Barack noted that along with the stories of success and accomplishment that he heard from the black people he interviewed, there were also worrisome and ominous ones, stories of boarded-up homes, decaying storefronts, aging church rolls, street gangs, broken families, kids feeding potato chips to crying toddlers, painful stories of suffering and loss, stories of ephemeral progress that might easily be reversed (Obama, 1995, p. 157).

While some black individuals may have advanced and improved their lives, the collective black experience in Chicago's South Side was one of constant decline, and many upwardly mobile blacks got caught up in middle-class white attitudes, not really caring about the lot of their poor brethren. Some black people avoided driving through violent, street-gang-ridden areas like Roseland. As a home builder had done in Detroit in the 1940s, building a six-foot-high concrete wall nearly half a mile long between his all-white development and the adjacent black neighborhood (Okrent, 2009), the upwardly mobile black people of Chicago tried to cordon off their new, middle-class neighborhoods from the rough decaying ones. Barack, however, sought the ideal of collective redemption, of saving the entire community, which unconsciously may have stood for his new family (Obama, 1995, p. 158).

When Barack proudly presented his report to Kellman after three weeks of interviews, however, this "white father" told Barack that he needed to avoid the side issues and map out the core problems that bothered black people. Barack was deeply hurt. He was incensed with what he saw as Kellman's unjust criticism and left his office in a foul mood. Later, however, he courageously admitted to himself that Kellman was right. This occurred toward the end of his interviews, when he spoke with a heavyset black lady whom he called "Ruby Styles" (Obama, 1995, p. 159). To the best of my knowledge, her identity has not been uncovered.

"Ruby Styles" was a black office manager in Chicago's North Side who lived in the South Side. "Ruby's" son, whom Barack called "Kyle" in his memoir, was getting into trouble at school and was involved with a street gang, one of whose members had already been shot. She feared for her son's life. With the keen sense of a good politician, Barack decided to try to organize a community meeting with the police district commander and the Baptist church pastor, Reverend Reynolds, whose church was on the block on which Kyle's friend had been shot (Obama, 1995, p. 159).

Barack's well-meaning plans for conciliation, however, ran into a serious snag in the shape of a racist black Baptist pastor named Reverend Smalls, a tall, brown-skinned clergyman who showed up at the young Barack's meeting with the Reverend Reynolds and his church leaders. Reverend Smalls hated Jews and Catholics, and he told Barack "Obamba," as he mistakenly called him to Barack's great irritation, that he had already told his Jewish boss, Kellman, that the black people of Chicago did not need any meeting with the police. Smalls said that Jews, Catholics, and whites were racists, that since the election of the black Washington as mayor of Chicago, the aldermen and the police were on their side, and that there was no need to protest their actions. Smalls told Barack he was on the wrong side of the fence, and after that none of the participants took the flyers that he had prepared. Barack's first political initiative had fallen flat. The meeting with the police was a small disaster (Obama, 1995, pp. 160–162).

Kellman, however, taught his young trainee his budding political skills by pointing out his mistakes. He told Barack that the Kyle Styles gang problem was not an issue that impressed people greatly, that he should have prepared "Ruby Styles" more carefully for the meeting and set out fewer chairs. Above all, Barack needed to get to know the leaders of the Chicago black community, for only they could get the members of his community to come out and attend a meeting on cold Chicago evening. When Barack asked Kellman angrily why he had not warned him about Reverend Smalls, Kellman replied that he had warned Barack that Chicago was a highly polarized city and that politicians always try to divide people and control them. Smalls was a politician in a clerical collar. After much unhappy reflection, Barack thought that he was worse than a heretic, because he no longer believed in anything anymore (Obama, 1995, p. 163).

Indeed, Barack did not know what or whom to believe anymore. He felt frustrated and helpless. The black metropolis of Chicago had been a magnet for poor black people from the South, and many of them lived in run-down tenements on the South Side. When Barack discovered the Altgeld Gardens public-housing project in Chicago's South Side, he was horrified. Altgeld Gardens had a 97% black population. It had been built in 1945 with 1,498 housing units, consisting primarily of two-story row houses spread over 190 acres. It had been built for "Negro" war veterans returning from World War II and was originally owned by the U.S. federal government, but it had been given to the Chicago Housing Authority in 1956. Located in an industrial area on Chicago's far South Side, Altgeld Gardens was named after John Peter Altgeld, an Illinois governor in the 1890s. As one of the first public-housing developments ever built in the United States, it is considered an historic landmark. But it was a hellhole for its residents.

Barack found Altgeld Gardens with its "two thousand apartments" a terrible dump and a place to house poor black people, suffering from the heavy, putrid stench of the Chicago Metropolitan Sanitary District's sewage-treatment plant to its north and from very bad maintenance (Obama, 1995, p. 164). Barack later wrote that Altgeld Gardens was not the worst of Chicago's black slums. Chicago's high-rise projects like the Robert Taylor Homes and the Cabrini Green were even worse—dirty, smelly dens of violent crime (Obama, 1995, p. 165).

The Robert Taylor Homes had been completed in 1962 and named after Robert Taylor, a black Chicago activist and Chicago Housing Authority board member who had resigned from the housing authority in 1950 after the city council had refused to endorse building locations throughout Chicago that would induce racially integrated housing. The Taylor Homes had been the largest housing project in the United States and was intended to offer decent affordable housing, with over 4,000 apartments. Cabrini Green was another housing project on Chicago's North Side. Both were the epitome of poor housing, and only those who could not afford decent housing lived there.

Among their other ailments, the buildings of Altgeld Gardens contained high quantities of toxic asbestos in their construction materials, which remained there until a grassroots campaign in the 1980s fought for its removal. Barack, then a local community organizer, took part in this campaign, even if he did not initiate it. Altgeld Gardens still has one of the worst concentrations of hazardous pollutants in North America. Barack found Altgeld Gardens hopeless and neglected. It had never been maintained properly, and the Chicago Housing Authority no longer even pretended to try to maintain it (Obama, 1995, pp. 165–166).

For Barack himself, as a black-community organizer, things had gone rather badly. There were no public meetings, marches, sit-ins, or freedom songs, nothing to show for his efforts. The community he organized had eight Catholic churches with all-black congregations but white priests, which comprised the Developing Communities Project. The white priests remained because nobody else would replace them, and the black women who helped Barack organize the Developing Communities Project complained about Kellman's indifference and arrogance (Obama, 1995, pp. 166–167). Kellman himself, however, thought that these black women were upset because he would not hire them to run his program.

Due to fierce competition from low-wage steelmakers elsewhere, many of Chicago's steel mills had closed, and many poor black people had lost their jobs. One company, Ling-Temco-Vought, now known as LTV Steel, still survived. In 1986 Kellman held a meeting with steelworkers-union officials, urging them to work with the churches, the city, and the banks to preserve the jobs that LTV Steel was preparing to eliminate. But the white Irish union president and his two black aides were more interested in discussing LTV's offer to cut some jobs so as to preserve others. One of Barack's black aides, whom he called "Angela" (her real name was Loretta Herron), said she had not understood Kellman's ideas, and Kellman himself was stunned by the union leaders' blindness to their being manipulated by LTV's management. Barack himself thought that Kellman had badly miscalculated, that keeping LTV Steel open had no relevance to the plight of the black people on Chicago's South Side, and that it would not make a dent in the rolls of the poor black unemployed.

Sigmund Freud believed that in the "primeval horde" of human evolution the son killed his father, ate his flesh, and thereby identified with him. Shakespeare's Macbeth, who murders King Duncan of Scotland and takes his place (an unconscious form of patricide), speaks of his "vaulting ambition" (*Macbeth*, act 1, scene 7, lines 25–28). The young U.S. Senator Barack Obama thought that he had got his "fierce ambitions" from his father (Obama, 2006a, p. 243), and indeed he ultimately made it to the pinnacle of power. He believed that his fierce ambitions came from his ambivalent feelings for his father, from his wish to earn his father's love and to avoid his father's failures (Obama). But Barack's Chicago mentor, Kellman, was not the father Barack wanted. Barack needed a better identification figure, such as Mayor Washington.

Barack recalled five activists who worked for his Developing Communities Project in Chicago. He called them "Angela," "Mona," "Shirley," "Will," and "Mary." The real names of the first three were Loretta Augustine-Herron, Margaret Bagby, and Yvonne Lloyd (Abramsky, 2009, pp. 23–25, 30–31, 35, 174, 213–215; Smith, 2008; Springen, 2008; Sweet, 2007). There was also another aide named Linda Randle. The older black women tried to fatten Barack up with cookies but failed (Springen, 2008). To the best of my knowledge "Will" and "Mary" have not been identified. "Mary" was the only white person among Barack's aides.

While Barack had some modest successes in the black community of Chicago, his mentor Kellman had almost none. The black women in Barack's Developing Communities Project loved him but were so unhappy with Kellman and with the failure of his public initiatives for them that they threatened to resign from Barack's organization. This threat may have revived Barack's painful feelings of abandonment. In an unusual outburst of emotion, Barack asked them pointedly what would happen to the poor black street-gang boys if they quit. He was able to get these ladies to stay on for a few more months, but some of the suburban Chicago churches were already dropping out of Kellman's Calumet Community Religious Conference.

Barack had a hard time deciding which of his fellow organizers should stay and which should be replaced. He liked the dark-haired white lady whom he called "Mary," a grade-school teacher at a local Catholic school (Obama, 1995, p. 170). "Mary's" father, like his own, was absent, and so was her husband. Like Barack's mother, she had married a black man who had abandoned her and left her in the Chicago slum with their two daughters. "Mary," like Barack himself, was alone and lonely. She was one of only five white people left in West Pullman, a poor neighborhood in the far South Side of Chicago (Obama, p. 175).

Barack had a hard time in Chicago. Many of his plans either fell through or failed to win the cooperation of the people he wanted to organize. The way Barack saw it, the black mayor, Harold Washington, was "maintaining and working the levers of power" but had no larger vision for the black community of his city (De Zutter, 1995). Barack later said that the "potentially powerful collective spirit that went into supporting [Harold Washington]"— the coalition of blacks, Hispanics, and progressive whites—was "never translated into clear principles, or into an articulable agenda for community change" (ibid.). Much as he tried, there was no way Barack could get any of the big Chicago manufacturers to move their offices or plants from the well-scrubbed white Chicago suburbs to black hellholes like Altgeld Gardens.

During his community-organizing activity in Chicago, Barack met a Black Muslim activist whom he called "Rafiq al Shabazz" in his memoir and whose real name was Salim al-Nuriddin. "Rafiq" was the Black Muslim president of the Roseland Unity Coalition, which militated for the black cause and had helped elect Harold Washington mayor of Chicago (Obama, 1995, p. 180). "Rafiq" is now active in the Healthcare Consortium of Illinois. "Rafiq's" given name had been Walter Thompson, but he had changed his "slave name" to an Arabic one, and Barack gave him the Arabic name of Malcolm X, al-Shabbaz. "Rafiq" told Barack that he had found his Muslim religion under the stewardship of a Chicago Muslim leader *unaffiliated* with Louis Farrakhan's Nation of Islam and then changed his name to an Arabic one (Obama, p. 196).

As Barack knew, the Nation of Islam, an extremist and racist U.S. black-power hate group, had a colorful history. It was founded in Detroit in 1930 by a Negro named Wallace Dodd Ford, who changed his name to Wallace Fard Muhammad, with the self-proclaimed goal of resurrecting the spiritual, mental, social, and economic condition of the Negroes of America. From 1934 to 1975 the Nation of Islam was led by Elijah Muhammad (Elijah Poole, 1897–1975), who from 1952 shared the leadership with Malcolm X. Malcolm X left the Nation of Islam in 1964 and was assassinated in 1965. From 1975 the Nation of Islam had been led by Muhammad's son, Warith Deen Muhammad (1933–2008), who dissolved the organization in 1978. The extremist Black Muslim leader Louis Farrakhan (born Louis Eugene Walcott in 1933) had resurrected it and become its leader.

Even though "Rafiq al Shabbaz" (Salim al-Nuriddin) was not a member of the Nation of Islam, he was a black-power activist like most other U.S. Black Muslims. The antiracist, postracial Barack was bound to come into conflict with the racist "Rafiq." And even though Farrakhan's Nation of Islam promoted the belief that Allah would bring about a universal government of peace, it was racist, thuggish, militant, and violent. From 1978 the racist and anti-Semitic Farrakhan had been the leader of the Nation of Islam, whose national center and headquarters were located in Chicago, which was also home to its flagship Mosque No. 2 (Mosque Maryam). Even the black Southern Poverty Law Center in Montgomery, Alabama (the former capital of black slavery and antiblack segregation), which monitors hate groups and militias in the United States, included the Nation of Islam in its list of active hate groups in the United States.

Even with "Rafiq," who was not a member of Farrakhan's hate group, Barack realized who he was dealing with: an antiwhite racist. With his black lady assistants, Barack met a plump black man named Foster, who had just resigned his post as president of the local Chamber of Commerce. "Rafiq" and Foster were bitter about the lot of black people in Chicago and all over America. Barack later thought that it was the incoherence and disorder of their lives that made them so bitter (Obama, 1995, p. 183).

After a series of frustrating, exasperating, and futile meetings with Chicago politicians, functionaries, bureaucrats, and community leaders, none of whom seemed to really care about the plight of the South Side's black people, the budding politician Barack finally found himself an issue: All of the Mayor's Employment and Training programs were north of 95th Street; none of them were on Chicago's South Side. He would request a public meeting with the city official in charge of the Mayor's Employment and Training programs and would publicly ask him or her to open a job intake and training center on the South Side (Obama, 1995, p. 184).

This was an example of how the young Barack could turn adversity into an advantage, how he could "thrive against all odds," the phrase used by his mother in the title of the doctoral dissertation that she completed a few years later (Dunham, 1992). Indeed, in 2005 Barack gave a commencement speech to the graduating class at Knox College in Galesburg, Illinois, saying that America was "a journey to be shared and shaped and remade by people who had the gall, the temerity to believe that, against all odds, they could form 'a more perfect union' on this new frontier" (Obama, 2006c; cited in Abramsky, 2009, p. 73).

THE MAKING OF A PSYCHOLOGICAL POLITICIAN

Remembering his previous failures, Barack Obama prepared himself well for his requested meeting with the director of the mayor's employment and training program, a Hispanic lady whom Barack called "Cynthia Alvarez." He organized and prepared all the churches of his Developing Communities Project and of Kellman's Calumet Community Religious Conference, prepared a script for the meeting, and tried to get many black people to attend.

On the day of the meeting with "Alvarez," Barack's stomach was tied up in knots of anxiety. Unconsciously, he was a child preparing to face a bad mother or a witch. Some 100 mostly black people turned up for the meeting. When "Alvarez" arrived, she turned out to be a big fat Latino accompanied by two white lackeys (Obama, 1995, p. 185). When pressed for an answer on Barack's demand, "Alvarez" tried to avoid giving one. Finally, under pressure from one of Barack's lady colleagues, who demanded "a yes or no answer," she did promise to have a mayor's employment and training job intake and training center on the South Side within six months.

Barack felt happy and victorious after winning this promise from a top Chicago city official. It was his first public victory. He finally had some real power. He felt elated and almost omnipotent. Barack later recalled having thought euphorically that he could organize all of Chicago, that he was as good as Mayor Washington, that he could share Chicago's leadership with the mayor (Obama, 1995, p. 186). But soon thereafter a meeting out on the street with a black drunkard who had disturbed the meeting brought him to his senses. When Barack tried to help the drunken man, the latter hurled abusive epithets and curses at him. The drunken man's voice slowly died down as he walked away (Obama, p. 186). A shaken Barack realized that his work would be much tougher than he had thought.

But would "Cynthia Alvarez" keep her promise and open the mayor's employment and training center in the South Side? What power did Barack have to make her do so? The fiercely ambitious Barack worked tirelessly, day and night, and during the cold Chicago winter he often froze while trying to get from one meeting to another. He ran himself down, and his boss, Kellman, suggested he take more time off and build a life for himself. Yet, while Barack may have felt lonely on weekends, he had created emotional bonds with the older leaders of the community. He heard many wrenching personal stories from his community members, stories of illness, personal crises, tragedy. Barack realized that his true self-interest was to find himself, to know himself, that it was up to him to understand and decipher the life stories of the people he was organizing, both terrible and wonderful (Obama, 1995, p. 190).

Even more important, the wrenching stories of his fellow community leaders gave Barack a sense of identity, purpose, and belonging. Their stories helped him make sense of his life and of his world, and they gave him the sense of purpose and belonging that he had been seeking. It was no accident that this quintessential outsider lived outside Chicago's South Side. Yet, even though he did not live there, the South Side community became his, and he belonged to it, perhaps even more than he had ever belonged to his own family or to any other group. Not only was there a real black community in the South Side, which he could find if he cared to look for it, but he felt that his work was like a poem, and that under the dark surface of black life there was a whole bright world that people would gladly give him if he only cared to ask (Obama, 1995, pp. 190–191). It took a great deal of courage, optimism, and even idealism to see such a bright side to the dark, violent, and unhappy life of Chicago's South Side.

Barack told us little in his memoir about his love life or sexual life. While he had a fair number of love affairs before he married, the only two he mentioned were the Brentwood girl in 1979, a relationship that made him go to college in Los Angeles, and the white girl in New York whom he dated for about a year. His fat black lady assistants in Chicago jokingly complained that his subcompact Honda Civic had room only for the thin young women he was dating—jealous, perhaps, that it had no room for them (Obama, 1995, p. 179). Barack had several black girlfriends, he told his half sister Auma, and they had broken his heart no less than the white one

(Obama, p. 211). All his other meetings with women in his memoir seem nonsexual. When recalling his Harvard Law School years he mentioned no girlfriend. It is only when he returned to Chicago in 1989 and met Michelle that his love life was reawakened.

One of Barack's close aides, the stocky black lady whom he called "Ruby Styles" in his memoir, who was fearful of her teenage son, Kyle Jr., getting in trouble, proved a wonderful organizer. Barack recalled her as highly talented, intelligent, hardworking, stable, motivated, and capable (Obama, 1995, p. 191). "Ruby" was like an adoptive black mother to Barack. Barack took a liking to her erratic adolescent son Kyle as if Barack were his older brother. Indeed, inarticulate though he was, the fatherless "Kyle Jr.," who, like Barack, was named after his own father, reminded Barack of his own turbulent adolescence. However, when he saw Kyle's mother "Ruby" wearing contact lenses that made her brown eyes look blue, Barack disapproved, and it got him thinking about all the emotional complexes that black people had about themselves and their self-esteem problem. It may have reminded him of that imaginary *Life* magazine story of the black man who bleached his skin.

The issues of self-esteem, self-confidence, self-love and self-hatred were paramount in Barack's emotional life. White people, by first enslaving African Americans and then segregating and humiliating them, had done great damage to their self-esteem. Black people would never discuss the painful feelings they had about themselves in front of white people. Most white people looked on black people as bearers of psychopathology. Barack was an astute psychological observer. He saw the big difference between black people's private conversations and their public utterances, and he distrusted black leaders who promoted black pride as a panacea for all black people's woes, as in the "black is beautiful" bumper stickers of the 1960s and 1970s. The emotional afflictions of black Americans went far deeper than that (Obama, 1995, p. 193).

Self-esteem was both a private and a public issue for Barack. If he had his own problems with his own self-esteem, so did all black people. His fellow black leaders could not specify what they meant by self-esteem. They denied the ills of black American society, such as children's abandonment by their fathers, single motherhood, alcohol and drug abuse, illiteracy, crime and lack of religious faith (Obama, 1995, pp. 193–194). Barack's observations of black people's emotional ills are impressive for someone who had never studied psychology. He was describing his own feelings about himself as well as those of his community members. He realized that the self-esteem talk would not by itself solve black people's problems. He needed to give black people jobs, to teach black children survival skills, before they could all feel proud of themselves. He had erected an artificial wall between psychology and politics, between economics and feelings, which "Ruby" had shaken up.

The tendency to separate politics from psychology is part of splitting, black-and-white thinking. As the American psychiatrist and psychoanalyst John Edward Mack (1929–2004) put it, "The proper place to begin our effort to understand (not to excuse), it seems to me, is with the question of causation. For no matter how loathsome we may find the acts of 'fanatics,' without understanding what breeds them and drives them to do what they do in a particular time and place, we have little chance of preventing further such actions, let alone of 'eradicating terrorism'" (Mack, 2002, p. 174).

STRUGGLING WITH BLACK RACISM

The young Barack had to deal with black self-hatred and with black hate of blacks themselves. Some blacks even used the derogatory word *nigger* for their children, friends, or enemies. He noticed that black people often struck out at themselves before they struck out at whites. Barack felt that he could not separate the emotional strengths of his "brothers," their language, humor, and stories, from their emotional afflictions (Obama, 1995, p. 195). The stories he heard from his fellow black leaders had been born out of their painful experience with white racism. Barack wondered whether a healthy black community could be forged without first curing it of black people's nightmarish fear of white people's hate of them (Obama). It would take him years to answer that question, and he would still be trying to do so as president of the United States.

Barack briefly allied himself with "Rafiq al Shabbaz," the Black Muslim leader in the Chicago neighborhood of Roseland, who helped him in his "sticky negotiations" with "Cynthia Alvarez," the mayor's employment and training director, about the new job intake and training center that the mayor's employment and training project was to open in Chicago's South Side. "Rafiq" wanted the new office located in a storefront near his Michigan Avenue office. Barack's Developing Communities Project colleagues were not happy about Barack's alliance with the leader of a black hate group, who was obviously paranoid about whites. Barack had to yell and to shout "Rafiq" down just to get him to slow down his hate-filled diatribes and his paranoid white-conspiracy theories. Nonetheless, Barack had a grudging admiration for "Rafiq's" tenacity, bravado, and sincerity (Obama, 1995, p. 196).

Barack had read *Leviathan* by the English political philosopher Thomas Hobbes (1588–1679), which spelled out his doctrine of the foundation of states and legitimate governments, based on social-contract theories. Hobbes had written *Leviathan* during the English Civil War of 1641–1651, a series of armed conflicts and political struggles between the English parliamentarians and royalists, and much of the book is devoted to demonstrating the necessity of a strong central authority to avoid the evil of civil war. Hobbes had described human life as nasty, brutish, and short, with "all against all," and Barack thought that "Rafiq" lived in a Hobbesian world, where distrust of whites and everyone else was the basis of his life. "Rafiq" believed that every racial, ethnic, and religious group must look after its own (Obama, 1995, pp. 196–197).

Barack did not want any part of the blind hatred of whites that "Rafiq" promoted. He believed that solidarity, self-reliance, discipline, and communal responsibility could promote the black cause and advance black nationalism, and that the black community could tell white America where it was wrong and cause it to change, just as the civil rights movement had done in the 1960s. But "Rafiq's" political and psychological message was "the blanket indictment of everything white" (Obama, 1995, p. 198). It was an extremist stance, splitting the world into "black and white," where black was good and white was bad. Reality was not like that at all. It was much more complex.

Barack could not accept "Rafiq's" message, which implied, as whites did, that blacks suffered from cultural or genetic inferiority. The black nationalist message was too simplistic and unrealistic: whites had planted self-loathing in the minds of blacks, and so all that black people had to do was rid themselves of it. Just as Sasha Abramsky intuitively understood Barack, the young Barack intuitively understood that with its unceasing attacks on the white "race" the hate group called the Nation of Islam was unconsciously using psychological tricks and subterfuges on its own people and even on itself (Obama, 1995, pp. 198–199).

One of those unconscious processes was displacement, by which Barack meant criticizing black people while excluding oneself from those very people. This was why the Nation of Islam could reform criminals and drug addicts. Another subterfuge was using black-power and black-is-beautiful slogans to artificially boost the self-esteem of black people who feel rejected by white American society—not only the self-esteem of addicts and criminals but also that of young black college students who barely make it out of the violence of Chicago's streets and of young black lawyers who join a lawyers' club only to encounter a stony silence from their white colleagues when they walk into the clubhouse (Obama, 1995, p. 199).

Barack was torn between his genuine quest for harmony and conciliation between the races and the appeal of "Rafiq's" racist insistence on black nationalism and the hatred of whites. He realized that black people's anger against white people was deep but that it was all repressed or turned against themselves. He recalled the incidents he had witnessed or read about in which blacks tried to make themselves look white, he remembered the black teenagers who called each other "nigger," and he thought that "Rafiq" had been right in trying to displace that bottled-up anger. He thought that a black politics that did not address the problem of black rage toward whites was not good enough (Obama, 1995, p. 199).

Barack was sorely tempted to embrace an angry black politics that would not suppress black rage against whites or, if you like, the Nation of Islam politics. But, in his own personal case, such a stance would mean being enraged with his own white mother and with her white parents. As Barack himself wrote, a racist, antiwhite, black-power politics went against his mother's values, faith, and morals: it was a black-and-white view of the world that would ignore and distort a reality with many shades of gray, in which it was not skin color or race that mattered but the individual's worth, goodwill, malice, ignorance, or indifference. Barack was not sure, however, whether he personally or other American blacks could afford this morality, as it might weaken black resolve and sow confusion in the black ranks. For some time Barack was strongly drawn to Malcolm X and to black nationalism, but he soon realized that "Rafiq" had a very small following and that whatever power he had came from his ability to shout down his opponents (Obama, 1995, pp. 199–200).

Barack realized that the idea of black nationalism had dissipated into grievances that did not lead to any concrete action that bettered the lives of black people. Even the largest and most important black nationalist group in America, Farrakhan's Nation of Islam, had a limited active membership in its political base of Chicago, and even its physical presence in the poor black South Side neighborhoods was meager. Barack was ambivalent about Farrakhan and his racist newspaper, *The Final Call*, which was sold at major Chicago intersections. Farrakhan's paper used attention-grabbing racist headlines like "Caucasian Woman Admits: Whites Are the Devil" and printed Farrakhan's antiwhite speeches and anti-Semitic propaganda. It also advertised videotapes of Farrakhan's speeches and a line of toiletries under the brand name of Power, which Black Muslims were supposed to buy and use: this was Farrakhan's way of getting his black "brothers" to buy from other blacks rather than from whites (Obama, 1995, p. 201).

Barack, to whom powerlessness was unbearable and power was crucial, thought that the failure of Farrakhan's Power brand-name campaign was due to the barriers that faced any black business in America but also to the ridiculousness of the lofty Minister Farrakhan being reduced to selling toothpaste. Even black store owners would not display his brand in their stores for fear of alienating their white customers. The Nation of Islam had a strident antiwhite message that enabled them to let off steam by cursing the white race, but it did not do much to find jobs for black people or to advance their lives (Obama, 1995, p. 202).

Barack gradually realized that all the black-racist conspiracy theories about whites were yet another self-deceptive trick, another subterfuge, another unconscious defense. Black people's rage against white people always had a ready market, just like sex or violence on television. People were eager to blame others for their own failures or misfortunes. Anti-Semitism, Asian baiting, and white hating were easy for black people to embrace and fall into. Barack's fellow black leaders told him that black people needed a chance to let off steam occasionally. Barack was concerned not just about the damage and pain that such black-racist talk caused but also about the gap between black-racist black-power talk and black-power action, which he felt corrupted both language and thought, encouraged the dangerous denial of reality, and destroyed vital accountability (Obama, 1995, p. 203).

Barack thought that of all the racial and ethnic groups in America, the blacks could least afford to deny their own reality. Unwavering honesty and an absence of delusions had kept the black people going, but now, he later wrote, black people were losing their hold on reality, falling prey to their rage, hatred, despair, and other unhealthy emotions. He would not let himself fall into that trap. The only healthy way to gain self-esteem, Barack felt, was "to align word and action" (Obama, 1995, p. 204), an intentional or unintentional takeoff on the famous line in William Shakespeare's *Hamlet*, "to suit the action to the word, the word to the action" (act 3, scene 2).

The young Barack was mature enough to realize that black-power notions of purity, whether of blood, race, or culture—simplistic divisions of reality into black and white—could no longer help black Americans gain self-esteem any more than they did him. He needed a course of political action that would do this properly (Obama, 1995, p. 204). In 1986 he left Chicago for a two-week home visit to Hawai'i, to see his mother, half sister, and grandparents. Upon his return he took "Ruby Styles," his "adoptive" black mother, to Chicago's North Side, to watch a black play by Ntozake Shange (born 1948), a feminist black American playwright.

Shange has written mainly about race and feminism. She won the Obie Award, or Off Broadway Theater Award from *The Village Voice* newspaper, for her play, *For Colored Girls Who Have Considered Suicide When the Rainbow Is Enuf*. She also wrote *Betsey Brown*, a novel about a black American girl who runs away from home. The play was a very emotional dance-drama about the cruel fate of black women. "Ruby" was deeply moved, and she kissed Barack on the cheek. He, in turn, squeezed her hand quickly. He drove his "adoptive mother" in his subcompact Honda Civic to her home on Chicago's South Side.

In 1987 Barack finally met his half sister Auma, who is about a year older than him and who had planned to visit him a few years earlier, before their half brother David was killed in a Kenyan motorcycle accident. Auma had been born in 1960, while their father was away in Hawai'i. She had studied for a master's degree in linguistics at the German university of Heidelberg from 1981 to 1987. Then she finally made it to the United States and came to Chicago to see her half brother. As soon as he met Auma at the airport, Barack felt that he loved her intensely and that he did not know the causes of his love for her; he began to mistrust his love after she was gone (Obama, 1995, pp. 207–208).

Barack had longed for a true family for many years. His immature mother and her problematic parents were not emotionally satisfying, let alone his disturbed, absent father. Perhaps rightly so, Auma found Barack as bossy as the "old man," their father, who was all of 46 years old when he died (Obama, 1995, pp. 208–209). Barack took his sister Auma to his office to meet his women staffers. They all liked Auma and him very much. Barack learned that Auma had a German boyfriend and became jealous of him (Obama, p. 210). He told Auma about his white girlfriend in New York—of whom he had said nothing in his memoir when describing his New York years. When he visited that girl's parents' home with her, he told Auma, he realized that his world and hers were separated by a gulf bigger than the distance between Kenya and Germany (Obama, p. 211). Why did Barack choose Kenya and Germany to illustrate the gap that separated him from his white girlfriend? Was not the United States farther away from Kenya than Germany? Was he unconsciously telling Auma to break up with her German boyfriend, just as he had done with his white girlfriend?

Auma asked Barack what had happened to him with his white girlfriend after their visit to her parents' home. Barack told her that he and his white girlfriend began to grow apart. They began to quarrel, and when they thought about their future, their life together no longer felt so warm. When he took her to a new black comedy by a black playwright, the mostly black audience clapped and yelled and jumped and chanted, and his girlfriend later asked him why black people were so angry. Barack told her that black people could not forget all the harm that white people had done to them, just as the Jews could not forget the Holocaust. His girlfriend disagreed, and they argued vociferously in public. Back in their car, she began to cry and told Barack that she would have liked to be black but that she could not: was she not enough for him as she was? (Obama, 1995, p. 211).

Barack had broken up with his white girlfriend, and he wanted Auma to break up with her white boyfriend as well. Auma thought that his was a sad story, but Barack did not seem very upset. He told her that some black women had also broken his heart "just as good." He had become very good at controlling his feelings. Auma, for her part, was afraid of getting married. She may have been deterred by the example of her mother Kezia, whose marriage to the old man—Barak was all of 46 years old when he died—was tragic and ended in divorce, and in the old man dying in a road accident. Auma did not marry her German boyfriend. She did, however, finally marry someone else. After graduating from the German university of Heidelberg in 1987, she went back home to Kenya and later returned to Germany for her graduate studies at the University of Bayreuth, in the German state of Bavaria, where she was awarded a Ph.D. degree in 1996. Her doctoral dissertation was about the conception of labor in Germany and its literary reflections. Auma then moved to London, and in 1996 she married an English businessman named Ian Manners but they later divorced, and Auma returned to Kenya. They have a daughter named Akinyi (born 1997).

When Auma visited Barack in Chicago, at first they did not talk much about their dead father, who, after all, was the most important link between them. The subject was too painful. When they finally broached it, Auma told Barack that the "old man" had had a very "scattered" life and that she did not really know him all that well. In fact, she was very angry with him. Auma had been born when Barak was in America, and she told Barack that she did not see their father until she was four and her brother Roy was six (Obama, 1995, p. 212).

Auma was born in 1960. In 1965, when their father Barak returned to Kenya from the United States, he brought along his third wife, Ruth Nidesand, and then took Auma and her brother Roy away from their mother, Kezia, to live with him in Nairobi. Ruth became Auma's unloved and unloving stepmother. Barack asked Auma why she had not stayed with Kezia. Auma said that she had in fact asked her mother why she had let Barak take her away from her; Kezia told her that Ruth refused to share Barak with another wife and that Kenyan fathers got to keep their children in case of a divorce (Obama, 1995, p. 213).

Barack was angry at the old man not only for abandoning him as an infant but now also for forcing Auma to leave her mother. He was struggling with his powerful ambivalent feelings about his father. Auma answered Barack's persistent questions about their father by telling him that during the first years back in Kenya the old man had done well, was well connected, and knew the top government people. But after the assassination of the Luo leader Tom Mboya in 1969 and the subsequent Kikuyu takeover of Kenya, Barak spoke up in public against tribalism and against "unqualified" men taking the best government jobs. Barak's narcissistic grandiosity was such that he always thought he knew best, and he publicly criticized Kenyan cabinet members. Finally, President Jomo Kenyatta himself summoned Barak and fired him from his job, telling him that he would not work again until he was barefoot (Obama, 1995, p. 215).

In fact, Barack learned from Auma that his father had been his own worst enemy. After he got himself fired, no one, public or private, would hire him again. He was blacklisted. When he found a job in Ethiopia, Kenyatta's government revoked his passport, and he could not leave Kenya. When he had to accept a lowly job with the Water Department, Barak felt so degraded that his entire self-esteem fell to pieces, and he became anxious and depressed. His lifelong narcissistic defenses had broken down: his feelings of omnipotence and omniscience, his narcissistic grandiosity. He began to drink alcohol heavily in order to escape his unbearable feelings of worthlessness and helplessness and to calm his anxiety. He then lost most of his friends. The proud Barak refused to apologize to Kenyatta, and his situation became worse and worse. He abused his wife Ruth, who in turn began to mistreat her stepchildren, Auma and Roy. Ruth finally left Barak after his first serious road accident (Obama, 1995, pp. 215–216).

It must have been very painful for Barack, who had idealized his father, despite his ambivalence, to hear those heartrending stories about him. He also learned that his drunken father had had a serious car accident in which the other driver, a white farmer, was killed and that he spent almost a year in a hospital, which he left with a bad leg. After that, Auma said, the old man (who was only 35) went to Hawai'i in late 1971 to get his wife and son, Ann and Barack, but he returned to Kenya without them, he lost his job with the Water Department, and things became even worse. Barak, Auma, and Roy did not have a place to live. They finally found a run-down house in a poor neighborhood of Nairobi, and their life was terrible. Barak's self-esteem was shattered, and he became angrier and more violent. Yet he denied his terrible reality and acted as if he were the great Dr. Obama (Obama, 1995, p. 216), which, although Barack did not say so in his memoir, his father, who had only a master's degree, had never really been.

It was a family tragedy. The adolescent Roy Obama constantly fought with his father and finally left the Obama home in a fit of fury. Later, Roy, who had also become an alcoholic, straightened out his life by embracing Islam and his African heritage. He took his Luo tribal name of Abongo and the Swahili name of Malik, became a Muslim, and had sworn off pork, smoking, and drinking by the time of his younger brother's wedding in 1992. Roy became a militant Luo activist. Auma, for her part, was saved from her father by Nairobi's Kenya High School, where one of the headmistresses gave her a scholarship so that she could move out of her father's house into the boarding school (Obama, 1995, p. 217).

Auma told Barack that after Kenyatta's death in 1978, and the accession to the Kenyan presidency of Daniel arap Moi, their father's situation had improved. He got a new job with the Kenyan Ministry of Finance and once more had some money and some influence. Yet he remained very bitter and did not regain his self-esteem and self-confidence. Even though he could afford to buy a house, he lived alone in a Nairobi hotel room and had different women for short spells of time. He did not know how to be a good father to Auma either. When Auma got her scholarship to Heidelberg in Germany in 1981, she left Kenya without saying goodbye to her father, with whom she was still very angry. Auma later met him again in Germany, and they flew together to London, but in 1982 the old man—who was only 46—died after another road accident.

While telling Barack about their father, Auma had very painful memories. At one point, she suddenly clutched the photograph of their father and began to sob and shake violently. Barack once more took the fatherly role toward her, even though he was the younger of the two. He comforted her by putting his arms around her as she wept, feeling how Auma's sorrow swept through her in waves (Obama, 1995, p. 219). Auma told Barack how cheated she had felt when Barak died: she had just begun to know him, and, had he lived, he might have explained himself. She finally pulled herself together and stopped crying. In his memoir, however, before telling how she calmed down and fell asleep, Barack did not say what *he* felt about his family's tragedy.

Auma told Barack that their father had cherished Barack's mother Ann's letters to him, that he used to show her those letters and tell her sadly but proudly that there were still some people who cared for him (Obama, 1995, p. 219). The narcissistic Barak, who had thought that the whole world owed him its love, must have felt that the whole world had abandoned him. It was only after his half sister Auma had fallen sleep that Barack could face his own emotional reaction to her story. He felt shaken and discombobulated. His idealized image of his father had been shattered. His father may have been a brilliant scholar, a generous friend, and an upstanding leader, but he had also been a wife abuser, an alcoholic, and an irresponsible father who abused or abandoned his own children. Barack had seen his father only once, for one month, when he was 10 years old, during Christmas and New Year's of 1971–1972. He had not witnessed his father's physical, emotional, social, professional, and financial decline, nor his tragic death (Obama, p. 220).

Barack was struggling with a major emotional upheaval. His lifelong idealized image of his father had been shattered. He had seen signs of weakness in his grandfather, "Gramps," in his stepfather, Lolo, and in others, but he had not suspected it in his own "great" father. He realized for the first time that he had been unconsciously projecting onto his image of his father the greatness that he wished to have in himself, that he had wanted to be as great as the black leaders Dr. Martin Luther King, Malcolm X, W.E.B. Dubois, and Nelson Mandela.

The minor black leaders whom Barack had met in Hawai'i, Los Angeles, New York, and Chicago could not even approach such high standards. Barack respected their struggles, but his expectations of himself were those that he had imagined his father had of him, those of an idealized father whose imaginary voice was calm, clear, and strong, who could tell him what was right and what was wrong, and what was expected of him. He remembered his traumatic meeting with his father when he was 10 years old, when his father told him that he did not work hard enough, that he should stop watching television and start working hard on his homework. It was as if his father was telling him to get up and help in the struggle of the black people (Obama, 1995, p. 220). Needless to say, Barack heard in his father's imaginary voice what he was actually telling himself.

While Auma's story had dealt a grievous blow to Barack's idealized image of their father, the one he had tried to live up to all his life, it had also given him an oedipal triumph over his father. Having learned of his father's shortcomings and failures, Barack was no longer bound by the imagined expectations of a dead father whom he no longer looked up to. Auma's story had liberated Barack from his father's imagined authority over him. After Auma had fallen asleep, he thought about his father having been an alcoholic wife abuser, a failed lonely bureaucrat, while he, Barack, had no such failings. He felt euphoric and thought that if Auma had not been in the room with him, he would have burst out laughing. He was now free to do whatever he pleased, as he could never do worse than his no-good father (Obama, 1995, pp. 220–221).

Not only has Barack not done worse than his father, he has done immeasurably better. At about the same age as his father died an alcoholic wreck in a road accident, Barack would become the first black president of the United States of America. Yet, while he felt liberated from his father, he feared that he would unwittingly follow in his father's footsteps and destroy himself, just as his father had done. How could he be sure that he was not as self-destructive deep down in his soul as his old man had been? Yet he thought that he had been saved from despair by the knowledge that his dead father could no longer dominate him (Obama, 1995, p. 221).

Barak was 46 years old when he died, yet to his son Barack he was still the old man. The oedipal triumph of the young son over his old father is evident in the memoir, but so is the son's sadness and his fear that his fate would be that of his father. He still was not even sure what had really happened to his father, how he had lost his vigor and his promise, how his great ambitions had developed. He still longed for the father whom he had met when he was 10 years old, and he realized that his father must have been just as anxious about their meeting as he himself had been. His father had returned from Kenya to Hawai'i after more than six years of absence to face his American past, his wife and his son, and try to salvage what was best in him. Barack regretted not having told his father his true feelings, just as his father had not been able to tell him his. Barack felt that he and Auma had paid a very heavy emotional price for that silence with their father (Obama, 1995, p. 221).

As we have seen, Auma and Barack's father Barak had been raised by his stepmother, Sarah, whom Barack called "Granny." Before leaving Chicago, Auma told Barack about their grandfather's estate in Kenya, which she called "Home Square." Granny still lived there, it was a beautiful place, and Auma often felt homesick for Home Square when she felt lonely and cold in Germany. She remembered with nostalgia Granny telling her funny stories about their family, and the cow and the hens and the cooking fire and the tree under which the old man lay buried (Obama, 1995, pp. 221–222). In fact, Auma was idealizing her home in Kenya, and the estate's real name was *Home Squared*, a name given by Nairobi kids to their home away from home, which was in no way a name particular to their grandfather's estate (Obama, p. 369).

Auma's visit with Barack in 1987 was a turning point in his life. Before she left Chicago, she urged him to come to Kenya and visit their father's grave. The following year Barack would do just that. He really could not complete his dealing with his father's ghost until he actually came to see the places where his father grew up, where he lived, and where he died. In 1988, six years after his father's death, Barack would finally travel to Kenya for the first time. There he would hear the entire family saga from Granny Sarah, through Auma's translation from the Luo.

In the spring of 1986 Barack had his first political achievement: the mayor's employment and training center in Roseland, on Chicago's South Side, which had been promised many months earlier by "Cynthia Alvarez," the director of the mayor's employment and training department, finally opened. Mayor Washington himself came to cut the ribbon. Barack had asked his staff to get the mayor's commitment to attend the Developing Communities Project rally that he had planned for the fall of that year. But his staff was so awestruck by the mayor's presence and by having their pictures taken with him that they completely forgot to ask the mayor about attending the planned rally. Barack was terribly frustrated, a budding politician whose first moves were being foiled. His old friend "Will" told Barack that he was too impatient, that he was never satisfied, that he always wanted things to happen fast, as if he had something to prove. "Will" told

Barack that he did not have to prove anything to them, that they loved him, and that Jesus loved him (Obama, 1995, p. 226). Later, Barack learned patience from his wife, Michelle.

Actually, Barack needed to prove to himself how capable he was. He doubted the value of his work. He wanted to show the people of Altgeld Gardens, Kellman, his father, and, above all, himself that what he did was real, significant, and important (Obama, 1995, p. 230). Barack's Developing Communities Project was the surrogate family he had been looking for. One of the black women who worked with him, Yvonne Lloyd, whom he called "Shirley" in his memoir, spoke of him like a mother who was proud of her son (Obama, 1995, p. 227). Yet he was still not satisfied. He felt that he had to make up for his father's mistakes, to do better than his father, but he still was not sure what those mistakes had been, and he still did not think he knew how to avoid making them himself (Obama). Barack was still tormented by his conflicted internal image of his father, "as if I was following him into error, a captive to his tragedy" (Obama).

Barack has confessed to having "fierce ambitions" (Obama, 2006a, p. 243). One of his biographers, the American Jewish journalist David Mendell, thinks that Barack, like his father, can be arrogant and pretentious. Mendell called Barack "imperious, mercurial, self-righteous and sometimes prickly ... He is an extraordinarily ambitious, competitive man with persuasive charm and a career reach that seems to have no bounds ... He is, in fact, a man of raw ambition so powerful that even he is still coming to terms with its full force" (Mendell, 2007, p. 7). Mendell described Barack as suffering from "a mild case of megalomania" (Mendell, 2007, p. 7, cited in Abramsky, 2009, p. 89).

According to Sasha Abramsky, the American journalist Evan Thomas attended a meeting in South Carolina in which Barack acted cocky and arrogant, boasting of having been on Oprah Winfrey's television show (Abramsky, 2009, p. 89). Some men who met Barack in 1997, when he was a freshman state senator, found him arrogant, immature, brash, and self-righteous. His African American colleagues Donne Trotter (born 1950) and Rickey Hendon (born 1953) found Barack "too big for his boots, too cocksure, too eager for the spotlight" (Abramsky, p. 90).

The American political activist John Cameron, who met Barack at about the same time, found the young Barack "pretentious" and "insufferably ambitious." Cameron is the political director of the Illinois branch of the American Federation of State, County and Municipal Employees and has been the secretary-treasurer of the Illinois affiliate of Citizen Action, a liberal American group. Cameron told Abramsky that Barack's office was full of copies of his book *Dreams from My Father*. Recalling Barack angrily, Cameron asked Abramsky rhetorically, "Publishing your own autobiography at age thirty-four, you think that's not in-your-face arrogance? Who is this guy? He's just a kid and he's already written his autobiography." Cameron had been sure that Barack was "heading for a fall" (Abramsky, 2009, pp. 89–91).

However, as Abramsky correctly points out (2009, p. 89), Barack was acutely aware of his unfortunate tendency to narcissistic arrogance, and he had worked very hard to overcome it, ever since he was elected to the Illinois senate in 1996 and began to serve in early 1997. Fortunately for Barack, while his father's arrogance and narcissistic grandiosity had destroyed his life, Barack himself succeeded in conquering his arrogance: his character strengths and virtues, his empathy, his compassion, and his humility won him the love of most of the people he worked with. He was not self-destructive like his father but rather a self-made man. Already as a community organizer in Chicago, he was surrounded by an adoring "family" of close aides and coworkers who loved him and appreciated what he was doing for them.

Barack made himself independent of his "white father," Jerry Kellman. He separated his inner-city Developing Communities Project from Kellman's suburban Calumet Community Religious Conference. Kellman had hired another organizer for his Calumet Community Religious Conference and was starting a new organization in Gary, Indiana, a Chicago suburb with many of the social, economic, and racial problems that plagued Chicago. But, as Barack later observed, Kellman had made no real attachments to Chicago or to the people he worked with. While Kellman got his love and warmth from his wife and son, the single Barack had to get his from his surrogate family, the Developing Communities Project family (Obama, 1995, p. 228).

Despite the formal separation of their two organizations, Barack still had weekly meetings with Kellman, who kept telling him that he was not making any serious headway in Roseland or the entire South Side. Barack realized that the people running Altgeld Gardens were a small group of older blacks driven by their anxieties and by their greed (Obama, 1995, p. 229). Just as he had always compared himself to his idealized image of his father, the ambitious Barack now measured himself up against Mayor Washington, whom he liked and wanted to succeed (Obama, p. 230). The mayor had become the surrogate father now, the idealized father.

In reality, Mayor Washington was far from ideal. As a lawyer serving in the Illinois state house, he had filed problematic if not fraudulent U.S. tax returns and was accused of not performing services he owed his clients. His first term in office as mayor was marred by ugly, racially polarized battles in Chicago's city council, dubbed "Council Wars," an allusion to the popular *Star Wars* films. A 29–21 city-council majority, led by the white Democrat-turned-Republican alderman Edward Robert Vrdolyak (born 1937), refused to enact Mayor Washington's reform legislation and prevented him from appointing reform nominees to city boards and commissions. Washington's other first-term mayoral woes included an overall-city-population loss, an increase in crime in Chicago, and a massive decrease in the number of riders on the Chicago Transit Authority. Chicago's chronic South Side violence helped earn the city the unflattering nickname of "Beirut on the Lake," and many people wondered whether Chicago would ever recover or would face the more permanent declines of other major inner cities in the U.S. Midwest, such as Detroit and St. Louis. Yet Barack was in love with Mayor Washington, his newly found idealized father figure. Where his real father had failed, his idealized father figure Harold Washington had to succeed. Barack had enormous expectations of Mayor Washington, no less great than he had had of his own dead father. Washington had appointed many black people to key city posts, and Barack was very excited about this great achievement for black empowerment (Obama, 1995, pp. 230–231). Unconsciously, Barack was projecting his own grandiose self on Washington.

Yet Barack was also realistic enough to realize that Mayor Washington's political triumphs and his great achievements for black people were partial, temporary, and precarious. The black housing projects of Chicago were still dens of crime, drugs, and neglect, their denizens as poor and desperate as before. Barack thought that his black mayor felt as trapped as any of the black officials who ran those slums, because he had "inherited" the tragic history of the black people in America and was powerless to change the system from within. Like Barack himself, Mayor Washington seemed to him a prisoner of his own fate (Obama, 1995, p. 231).

The young Barack was haunted by what he called "fate," the fate of the black people in America, his father's tragic fate, and his fear of falling into the same fate as his father. Barack was depressed for some time (Obama, 1995, p. 231). He overcame his depression by finding a new mother figure, Dr. Martha Collier, a black Chicago school principal who ran the Carver Elementary School on the southern edge of Altgeld Gardens. She quickly became his new surrogate mother. Collier told Barack that the schoolchildren's joy and happiness always vanished after a few years. She invited the young Barack to speak to her parents' group. Most of them were young single mothers in their late teens or early twenties, who had been raised by single mothers themselves. It was a self-perpetuating generational tragedy. The fathers were mostly absent.

While Barack felt paternally toward the black mothers, they felt maternally toward him and asked him why he was not married. Some of his matronly black associates and aides in Chicago may have been attracted to him or even have fallen in love with him. He was an attractive young man, and many black women liked him, but he was interested only in "skinny girls," they complained. Barack's plan was to improve basic services in Altgeld Gardens despite the foot dragging by the Chicago Housing Authority. He wanted the young parents to form the nucleus of a genuinely activist tenants' organization. Barack passed out complaint forms at the parents' meeting. One of the women, Sadie Evans, drew his attention to a newspaper clipping that said that Altgeld Gardens was full of poisonous asbestos and that the Chicago Housing Authority was soliciting bids from contractors to remove it. With his sharp political instincts, Barack sensed a good new issue, more powerful still than the mayor's employment and training center in Roseland. He asked for a volunteer to call Mr. Anderson, the director of the Altgeld Gardens project. Only the seemingly shy Sadie volunteered, but Barack was surprised to learn the same day that she had already set up a meeting with Anderson. Barack accompanied her to the meeting with the project director.

The toxic-asbestos issue at Altgeld Gardens became a springboard to Barack's political career. It was perhaps his most confrontational effort so far, to pressure the Chicago Housing Authority to remove the asbestos from the Altgeld Gardens apartments. The on-site manager, Anderson, did not take any action, saying falsely that there was no asbestos in the residential units. Sadie wanted to see a copy of the tests that had been conducted, and a defiant Barack pushed the Altgeld Gardens residents into confronting Chicago Housing Authority officials in angry public meetings. The Chicago Housing Authority director avoided them, but his assistant finally met them and promised to start testing the asbestos and set up a meeting with the director (Obama, 1995, pp. 236–241). These meetings caused the Chicago Housing Authority to send its workers to seal the asbestos in the buildings. But the anti-asbestos project gradually ran out of steam and money. In fact, some Altgeld Gardens tenants still have asbestos in their homes, according to Linda Randle, an Altgeld Gardens resident who worked with Barack in the 1986 anti-asbestos campaign (Walsh, 2007).

Barack, however, felt that his dramatic confrontation with the Chicago Housing Authority and his bus ride home changed him dramatically. It gave him a sense of power that he had not had before and that has not left him since (Obama, 1995, p. 242). It hinted at greater things, spurred him on, helped him transcend his violent and conflicting emotions of elation and disillusionment, and made him wish to repeat the experience, to feel once again the sense of victory over the powers that be (Obama). Barack got a good deal of publicity out of his fight with the Chicago Housing Authority. To him, he later wrote, the most wonderful thing about it was to see the poor Altgeld Gardens people regain the say in their own lives that they had forgotten they had (ibid.). Barack, too, was reclaiming a power he had had all along, and it made him ecstatic. It was the power to affect other people, to move them, to get them to act in their own interest. It was the power of the leader.

Barack's public meeting with the Chicago Housing Authority director, a black man in his early forties, turned into a farce, and then into pandemonium as the director struggled with the activist Linda Randle for control of the microphone. The director left in a huff, and a black alderman's aide told Barack that the whole thing had been staged by Ed Vrdolyak, the mayor's white opponent, and that the white men were just trying to make Mayor Washington look bad. Mrs. Reece, the plump, pincushion-faced president of the Altgeld Gardens tenants' council, who saw Barack as a rival, publicly accused him of embarrassing the Altgeld Gardens community. But, for all the embarrassment, the asbestos issue picked up momentum in the mass-communication media, and Barack felt that he and his black community had the right to feel victorious, as the following day the employees of the Chicago Housing Authority were all over Altgeld Gardens checking the apartments for asbestos (Obama, 1995, p. 247).

Faced with extraordinary expenses to clean up the asbestos from Altgeld Gardens, the Chicago Housing Authority asked the U.S. Department of Housing and Urban Development for several million dollars in emergency cleanup funds. Barack had scored his first political victory. But that victory was short-lived, and Barack felt discouraged. The political struggles of black people were excruciating. For a while the black parents and their children had some hope, but they soon realized that the authorities would not follow up on their promises, that their housing and schools would remain as poor, neglected, and crime-ridden as before. The city officials worked with Barack's Developing Communities Project only reluctantly and, Barack thought, only out of loyalty to him. Some of the Altgeld Gardens residents who had worked with Barack dropped out. Mrs. Reece, the head of the Altgeld Gardens tenants' union, who saw Barack as a rival, would not speak to Barack and his aides anymore, publicly attacking them instead. The residents lost hope and became suspicious of both Barack and Mrs. Reece (Obama, 1995, p. 247).

Barack and his coworkers tried to get the U.S. Department of Housing and Urban Development to give the Chicago Housing Authority the millions of dollars it needed to remove the asbestos from the Altgeld Gardens project. This, again, resulted in failure, as the rigid federal bureaucrats would not grant the request. A white bureaucrat from the U.S. Department of Housing and Urban Development told the Chicago Housing Authority that they had to choose between having the asbestos removed from Altgeld

Gardens or having its plumbing and roofing repaired. Barack and his aides were sorely disappointed (Obama, 1995, p. 247).

After that, there were more losses and disappointments. Barack lost his volunteer Sadie Evans, whose husband had told her to look after herself and her own family rather than devote all her time to public service with little to show for it. Sadie told Barack that she and her family were going to try to leave Altgeld Gardens as fast as they could (Obama, 1995, p. 248). For Barack, this was quite discouraging. There are many black tragedies in his memoir: suicides, youngsters who called each other "nigger" and shot one another, a schizophrenic young lawyer, his own father's self-destruction. But Barack could thrive in the face of adversity. He never gave up, never ran away, never stopped working for the causes he had espoused, no matter how strong the opposition he encountered. He had lost his youthful innocence, his enthusiasm, and his idealism, but he gained political experience and wisdom. This was a process of emotional maturing.

Just as Napoleon's flight from Corsica to France in 1793 marked the turning point in his life, when he transformed himself from a Corsican rebel into a French nationalist (Falk, 2007), so did Barack's move from New York to Chicago in 1985 mark the turning point in his own life, his transition from aimless young black to community organizer and successful politician. His three years in Chicago from 1985 to 1988 saw his maturing into an outstanding politician who knew how to find relevant issues, how to get people involved, and how to outmaneuver his rivals. He would become a great leader, a great legislator, the first African American president of the United States of America, and one of the most remarkable presidents in U.S. history.

In Chicago, Barack had grown used to the sounds of gunfire, violence, killings, drugs, gang wars, young black hoodlums, young men crippled by violence—to every horror of black life in the slums. Yet in 1987 he sensed a more dangerous situation in Roseland. Barack, who did not himself live in Chicago's South Side, hired a deputy named "Johnnie." As in most other cases, for reasons of legal self-protection or confidentiality, Barack did not give "Johnnie's" full name in his memoir. His full name was Johnnie Owens, and he was a South Side resident (Lakshmanan, 2008). Barack liked Johnnie's curiosity, his feel for absurdities, and his psychological insight into depression (Obama, 1995, p. 249). Johnnie apprised Barack of the horrors of the South Side. Crime, drug addiction, violence, and desperation were on the increase. Parents were losing their authority over their children. Things were going from bad to worse. Fear and despair were gaining the upper hand over courage and hope (Obama, pp. 252–253).

Johnnie was a good teacher to Barack. Unlike Barack, he knew the black community intimately and understood its inner workings. Kids no longer listened to their parents, young people no longer listened to adults, and violence was rampant. It took only a couple of provocative words to set a black kid off and get him to kill another black kid. Adult blacks no longer dared to talk to those violent young boys or even go near them. They had as bad an image of those young black punks as white people did. Young black people who wanted to escape the circle of crime, drugs, and violence and make good had to fend for themselves (Obama, 1995, p. 253).

Unlike Johnnie, who feared the violent young black South Side punks, Barack's fears had to do with deeper emotional issues: the fears of not belonging, of being abandoned, of not being loved, of having no family (Obama, 1995, p. 253). And unlike Johnnie, who literally saw his world in black and white, dividing all black youngsters into "good kids" and "bad kids," Barack's view of reality was more nuanced. He did not know who was a good kid and who was a bad kid. Even when "Ruby Styles's" son "Kyle Jr." became violent on the basketball court after being called a punk, Barack still thought "Kyle" was basically a "good kid," but he was not sure that was enough to save him from a fate of crime and perhaps a violent death (Obama, pp. 255–256). Kyle's fate hung in the balance.

After some searching, Barack found a new issue to fight for that would both enhance his self-esteem and advance his career: the abysmal state of Chicago's public schools. His interest in the schools had begun with Collier's Carver Elementary School, but Barack's ambitions went much farther: he wanted a full reform of the city's public-school system. In his memoir, he described the sorry state of the run-down schools, neglected by the legislators and the bureaucrats, with chronic budget deficits, a chronic shortage of textbooks and toilet paper, and poor teachers. Barack developed a plan to reform the city's public schools and tried to sell it to the heads of the churches composing his Developing Communities Project (Obama, 1995, p. 256). A few years later, after becoming a lawyer, Barack would become the president of the Chicago Annenberg Challenge, a well-endowed nonprofit organization devoted to reforming the public schools.

In trying to reform the public schools, Barack suffered yet another reverse. The churches' response to his reform plan was underwhelming. Each of the eight churches that composed his Developing Communities Project was full of teachers, principals, and superintendents, who did not care much about the public schools, as they sent their own children to private schools, as well as parents who sent their children to Catholic schools and had no interest in changing the status quo. For Barack himself, the issue had become paramount. The plight of the public schools was horrendous, and, above all, it was a question of parents and children. The educational experts told Barack that while there might not be any bad children, there were a lot of bad parents (Obama, 1995, p. 257). The way

Barack saw it, the black American community had made "an unspoken settlement" with white America since the 1960s in which half the black children could advance while the other half fell behind. Barack was going to change all that, starting with Chicago's schools. He was going to create a "no child left behind" program decades before it became a reality.

Barack himself did not live in Chicago's South Side. He had a comfortable apartment in another part of the city. But his emotional involvement with the black communities of Roseland and Altgeld Gardens was no less strong than that of a South Sider. He began his public-school-reform campaign with Kyle Styles's high school, whose principal, Dr. Lonnie King, was eager to work with Barack's Developing Communities Project. King introduced Barack and his deputy Johnnie to a black man whom Barack called "Asante Moran," an enthusiast of Africa and one of his counselors, and Barack and Johnnie received an earful of African ideas and ideologies from him (Obama, 1995, p. 258).

"Asante Moran" believed that the public-school system was designed to control black people rather than educate them. American society paid attention to black kids only when they started making trouble. The need to belong is very powerful. Real education for black kids would mean giving them a true understanding of their African origins, their culture, their community, their world, and themselves. Had they received this kind of education, they would have had great motivation to learn because learning would make them belong to their community. Black kids learned about white European and American culture, not about their own. They were being taught a culture that rejected them and denied their humanity (Obama, 1995, p. 258).

Barack may have named "Asante Moran" after the black American educator Molefi Kete Asante (born 1942 as Arthur Lee Smith, Jr.), a scholar of African and African American studies who, like many other African Americans, had changed his given name to an African one because his original name was "a slave name;" he may have named himself after the Ashanti, a major African tribe in Ghana. "Asante Moran" had been to Kenya 15 years earlier, and he told Barack that his visit there had changed his life forever. On their way back, Johnnie asked Barack why he had never gone to Kenya himself. Barack admitted to Johnnie that he feared what he might find out about his father. Johnnie complained to Barack that his own father had come to his high-school graduation ceremony but had neither hugged nor kissed him. Barack envied Johnnie the fact that his father had been there for him at all: His own father had not (Obama, 1995, p. 261).

Dr. Collier's Carver Elementary School and "Asante Moran's" high school had helped Barack's Developing Communities Project devise a plan for providing Chicago's at-risk black teenagers with mentoring and tutoring services and involve their parents in long-term reform planning (Obama, 1995, p. 261). By 1987 Barack could not devote himself wholly to his Developing Communities Project. He was preoccupied with his African family in Kenya and with his future law studies. Barack first flew to Washington, D.C., where his half brother Roy Obama was living. Roy had married an American Peace Corps worker in Kenya and then moved with her to the United States. Barack had heard from their half sister Auma about Roy's conflicts with their father, Barak, and how he had left their father's Nairobi home in a rage. He and Auma had spoken to Roy on the telephone during Auma's visit. Roy had told them that everything in his life was just "lovely," that a visit from Barack would be "fantastic," and that staying with him and his wife would be "no problem." Barack was taken in by his half brother, but Auma knew better. She told Barack that Roy was as devious as their old man had been, that she had not seen Roy since their half brother David's funeral in Nairobi, and that Roy might be putting on a show for Barack (Obama, p. 262).

Indeed, Roy was more complicated and less honest than he seemed. He had been having serious marital trouble with his American wife. When Barack arrived in Washington, Roy asked him to stay in a hotel rather than at his home, as he had promised. Barack did not describe his disappointment with his brother nor his anger at him, saying only that he checked into a cheap hotel room and that his half brother showed up there an hour late. In the pictures Barack had seen of the young Roy, he was slender, had an Afro hairdo, a goatee, and a mustache, and was dressed in African clothes. Now he had become a big fat man who resembled the old man, their father, in a way that Barack found uncanny and unsettling (Obama, 1995, p. 263). Also, like their father, Roy had had a road accident: he drove very dangerously.

During their dinner together, Roy confessed to Barack that he did not like himself and that he blamed the old man for this (Obama, 1995, p. 264). When Roy told him about his traumas with their old man, Barack felt an admiration for Roy's emotional resilience, as he had for Auma's, but he thought that there was a big difference between them: Auma had put her painful past behind her, whereas Roy was still reliving it, as if it had just occurred. In the terms of the French Jewish psychoanalyst Boris Cyrulnik (1993, 2003), Auma was more resilient than Roy. Roy was a psychological captive of a past that he could not break with. He could never understand how a man as bright as his father could have fallen so low, how he could have destroyed his own life. But Roy himself was destroying his own life: he was drinking and overeating, and he was going to divorce his American wife. For some reason, Barack felt guilty. He could not help feeling that Roy was at risk, that he was driving himself toward a catastrophe, and that if he, Barack, were a better brother he would have acted to try to save Roy (Obama, p. 267). Barack may have been struggling with his unconscious feelings of fraternal rivalry and aggression toward Roy.

Upon his return to Chicago, he learned from his deputy, Johnnie, that Dr. Lonnie King, Kyle Styles's school principal, had asked for two jobs—one for his wife, one for his daughter—in the new program that Barack's Developing Communities Project was planning. Johnnie and Barack laughed their heart out, but the matter was serious: nepotism, favoritism, abuse of power. That night Barack was disturbed by four teenage black boys in a car that carried an ear-splitting "ghetto blaster" radio into his neighborhood. When he slipped on some shorts and went downstairs to ask them to stop disturbing people's sleep and go away, he realized from their angry reaction that these boys could easily become violent, that they had lost their capacity for empathy, that they were lacking a fundamental order in their lives that would treat them with respect rather than with fear or contempt. While he, Barack, had his place in this world, these poor black boys had no sense of belonging. They were totally adrift (Obama, 1995, pp. 269–271).

U.S. Senator Barack Obama thought that U.S. society suffered from insufficient empathy for its poor, weak, and sick members. This was why it tolerated atrocious housing for its poor black people, why it tolerated inadequate schools for its poor black children, why the boards of directors and the chief executive officers of American corporations gave themselves multimillion-dollar bonuses while cutting health-care coverage for their underpaid employees (Obama, 2006a, p. 82). During the subprime-mortgage financial crisis of 2008, the worst U.S. economic crisis since the Great Depression of the 1930s, the young Republican governor of South Carolina, Mark Sanford (born 1960), did not seem to have any empathy with his state's poor people. He was the first U.S. governor to reject a huge portion of the vast amount of federal stimulus money—$700 billion—earmarked by the U.S. Congress for South Carolina, saying "the fatal flaw of a lot of people in politics is that they want to be loved" (James, 2009). Sanford may have wanted to prove that he did not need to be loved to be an effective politician. On April 3, 2009, however, Governor Sanford reversed himself and accepted the federal stimulus funds.

Barack, the president, *does* need to be loved, to be accepted, and to belong, yet with him this was not a fatal flaw. Barack can also bear not to be loved, to do what he thinks was right even when people hate him for it, and to say "no" when necessary. In 2008 he withstood violent personal attacks on him and remained calm enough to win the U.S. presidency. In 2009 he pushed his health-care reform bill in the U.S. Congress—and got it passed—despite the terrible hate campaigns, rallies, and marches against him by his opponents, which portrayed him as a new Hitler or a new Stalin. During his entire three years organizing the Chicago South Side community (1985–1988), he was hated by many people in authority, yet he was loved by the black people that he organized through his Developing Communities Project.

In the fall of 1987, during his last year in Chicago as a community organizer, while meeting the black Protestant pastors and ministers in Chicago, Barack met the Reverend Jeremiah Alvesta Wright, Jr., the fire-brand Afrocentric black-liberation pastor of Trinity United Church of Christ on 95th Street at Parnell Street, in Southeast Chicago. Barack later recalled that this church sat in a residential neighborhood near the Frank Lowden Homes (Obama, 1995, p. 280), named after the Republican governor of Illinois from 1917 to 1921, Frank Orren Lowden (1861–1943).

Chicago's Trinity United Church of Christ is a predominantly black church with more than 8,500 members, the largest black church affiliated with the United Church of Christ, a predominantly white Christian denomination with roots in American Congregationalism, which had branched off from American Puritanism. Reverend Wright was a pro-African antiwhite preacher, who would later embarrass Barack and damage his 2008 presidential campaign when his racist antiwhite sermons came to light. Barack had been sent to Wright by an older churchman whom he called "Reverend Philips" in his memoir (Obama, 1995, pp. 272–280).

In the meantime, deciding to leave Chicago and pursue a professional career, Barack had applied to the top law schools in the United States, including Harvard—his father's graduate school—as well as Yale and Stanford. When he told his deputy Johnnie about this, the latter said that he had known it all along (Obama, 1995, p. 275). Barack's fierce political ambitions were only temporarily yielding to his academic ones. He was still searching for his identity—racial, ethnic, religious, political, academic, and personal. His Harvard biographer thinks that Barack had been planning to return to Chicago and to run for mayor after he graduated from law school (Niven, 2009, p. 16).

In late 1987, the skeptical and atheist Barack was agonizing over whether to become a Christian. His Developing Communities Project was an alliance of Catholic churches, and many of his fellow black community leaders in Chicago were devout Christians. Barack's mother had been secular, but she had "instilled" in him her spirituality, love, generosity, empathy, and kindness (Obama, 2006a, pp. 242–243). Barack later wrote that he was "finally able to walk down the aisle of Trinity one day and be baptized" (ibid., p. 246). He did not say when exactly he was baptized, or whether it was before or after his trip to Kenya in 1988. But it is almost certain that in 1988 he was baptized by the Reverend Wright at Chicago's Trinity United Church of Christ and was an active member there from 1988 to 2008 (Kantor, 2007a; Obama, 2006d, 2008).

Barack said that his mother's spirituality had to do with his decision to become a Christian, for "she had an unswerving instinct for kindness, charity, and love, and spent much of her life acting on that instinct, sometimes to her detriment" (Obama, 2006a, p. 242). Perhaps the fact that his mother had been so kind "to her detriment" made Barack fear becoming religious. Most of all, he feared making the same errors as his self-destructive parents had done. Being baptized was a major turning point for the reluctant, skeptical, and agnostic, if not atheist, Barack, who according to his own testimony had too many questions about God (such as why God had let his father abandon him and destroy his own life) to opt for a resolution of his inner conflicts through the mere formality and ritual of baptism (Obama, 1995, p. 287).

On Wednesday, November 25, 1987, Barack was shocked along with most of America when he learned that Harold Washington, the black mayor of Chicago, had suddenly died of a heart attack. In the United States, Thanksgiving Day is celebrated on the fourth Thursday in November, and that year it was November 26. Barack later recalled that Washington had died on the day before Thanksgiving (Obama, 1995, p. 287). Washington had just won reelection against his white rival. Barack did not reveal his feelings, but for him Washington's death was the loss of another "father."

Under these emotional circumstances, his looking to Pastor Jeremiah Wright as a new father figure was understandable. The mayor's immediate successor was David Duvall Orr (born 1944), who served briefly as interim mayor. He was in turn succeeded by Eugene Sawyer (1934–2008), who served from late 1987 to April 1989. Sawyer was then succeeded by the white politician Richard Michael Daley (born 1942), a son of the legendary former mayor Richard J. Daley (1902–1976). Barack felt that the Chicago political machine had killed Mayor Washington again by robbing his successors of power and by virtually annulling his achievements in favor of black people. He resumed his school-reform activities, trying hard to groom his deputy Johnnie as his successor at the Developing Communities Project as he prepared to leave Chicago for Harvard Law School.

Chapter 12

OUTDOING HIS FATHER

Synopsis: *In 1988, during his third year of black-community-organizing work in Chicago, the 26-year-old Barack Obama was accepted by Harvard Law School. Before going to Harvard, he spent five weeks in his dead father's homeland of Kenya, where he learned the full tragic story of his father, as part of his deep emotional struggle with his father's ghost and with his abandonment by that father. When he came back from Kenya he joined Chicago's Trinity United Church of Christ and was baptized (Kantor, 2007a). It was no accident that he had applied to the university where his father had received his master's degree. He would not only be as good as his father but also outdo his father. The highly intelligent Barack became an outstanding law student. He became an editor of the* Harvard Law Review *and later its first black president. During the summers he returned to Chicago to work as a summer associate at public-interest law firms, and this was where he met his future wife, Michelle, who had graduated from the same school the year he left for Harvard and who was his mentor at the first law firm he worked for. Barack was not only intelligent academically but also emotionally, having the equanimity and balance to settle conflicts, mediate, and conciliate. What he could not do between his parents—conciliate—he could do between the races and later between political antagonists. Black Chicago became his true home.*

In February 1988 the 26-year-old Barack was accepted by Harvard Law School for the school year that began in September. Harvard had been his father's alma mater. Deciding to go there, Barack met with some

20 Protestant ministers who had agreed to join his Developing Communities Project, along with his key aides, announcing that he was leaving Chicago in May and that Johnnie Owens would be taking his place as the director of the Developing Communities Project. Only one of Barack's aides, the white woman "Mary," was upset by this news. She asked Barack why he and "Will" were always unsatisfied, always in a hurry, always trying to do more. Barack, however, thought about "Mary's" fatherless daughters. Instead of trying to answer her unanswerable question, he walked "Mary" home and gave her a hug at he door (Obama, 1995, p. 290). Other than staying in Chicago and giving up his career, there was nothing he could do to ease her sadness about his leaving her. Barack's old associate, "Will," however, correctly predicted that Barack would be back in Chicago as soon as he had finished law school (Obama, p. 291).

AN ATHEIST BECOMES A CHRISTIAN

Before leaving Chicago, the atheist Barack made a Sunday visit to the Reverend Jeremiah Wright's Trinity United Church of Christ. There, he heard Wright deliver a sermon whose title he later recalled as "The Audacity of Hope," which later became the title of his keynote address at the Democratic National Convention of 2004, as well as the title of his second book. In fact, Wright's sermon was entitled "The Audacity to Hope" (Wright, 1990). Wright began this sermon by referring to another sermon that he had heard from a black colleague during the annual convocation of black ministers at Virginia Union University's School of Theology in Richmond, Virginia, a few years earlier. Wright's sermonizing colleague was the Reverend Frederick G. Sampson of Detroit, the minister of Detroit's Tabernacle Missionary Baptist Church from 1971 to 2001. In his sermon, he had described a painting titled *Hope* by the British symbolist painter George Frederic Watts (1817–1904), which the painter had donated to the newly created Tate Gallery in London. Wright, who erroneously called the painter "Watt," described this painting as follows:

> The painting's title is "Hope." It shows a woman sitting on top of the world, playing a harp. What more enviable position could one ever hope to achieve than being on top of the world with everyone dancing to your music? As you look closer, the illusion of power gives way to the reality of pain. The world on which this woman sits, our world, is torn by war, destroyed by hate, decimated by despair, and devastated by distrust. The world on which she sits seems on the brink of destruction. Famine ravages millions of inhabitants in one hemisphere, while feasting and gluttony are enjoyed by inhabitants of another hemisphere. This world is a ticking time bomb, with apartheid in one hemisphere and apathy in the other. Scientists tell us there are enough

nuclear warheads to wipe out all forms of life except cockroaches. That is the world on which the woman sits in Watt's painting. (Wright, 1990)

Wright went on to describe the horrors of the terrible world in which he and his flock lived, a world that was callous to human suffering:

Our world cares more about bombs for the enemy than about bread for the hungry. This world is still more concerned about the color of skin than it is about the content of character—a world more finicky about what's on the outside of your head than about the quality of your education or what's inside your head. That is the world on which this woman sits. You and I think of being on top of the world as being in heaven. When you look at the woman in Watt's painting, you discover this woman is in hell. She is wearing rags. Her tattered clothes look as if the woman herself has come through Hiroshima or Nagasaki. Her head is bandaged, and blood seeps through the bandages. Scars and cuts are visible on her face, her arms, and her legs. (Wright, 1990)

Later in the sermon, however, Wright skillfully manipulated the emotions of his audience from despair to hope. He talked about the biblical Hannah, her barrenness, her despair, and finally her happy pregnancy and her son, the prophet Samuel. Wright ended his sermon with the rousing words, "And that's why I say to you, hope is what saves us. Keep on hoping; keep on praying. God does hear and answer prayer" (Wright, 1990).

Barack's memory of Wright's sermon a few years later was more dramatic than its published version. He recalled the singing of the hymns, the African-dressed choir, the clapping and singing of the audience, the sound of the organ and the drums, the elation of the singers, their excited belief in being lifted by Jesus (Obama, 1995, pp. 291–292). This emotional chanting may have reverberated in Barack's mind with the image of being lifted by his father as a child: for even if Jesus was the Son of God, he could uplift the Christian believers.

Barack now recalled how Wright had appeared under a rugged large cross that hung from the church's rafters and remained silent while the devotions were being read, watching the faces of the audience and their reactions to the collection basket. After the collection, Wright mounted his pulpit and read the names of his congregants who had died that week, as well as those who were sick, with each name evoking murmurs or flutters among the congregants (Obama, 1995, p. 292).

As we have seen, Mayor Harold Washington's death the year before was a personal loss to Barack, who unconsciously sought a new father figure, and the Reverend Wright may have filled that void. Barack recalled how Wright made his congregants join hands, kneel, and pray at the foot of the rugged cross that hung from the rafters and thank the Lord for giving them Jesus, who bore their burden and shared their load, and for all that he had done for them (Obama, 1995, p. 292).

Wright's sermon "The Audacity to Hope" made such a deep impression on the young Barack that 16 years later, in 2004, he made it the title of his keynote address at the Democratic National Convention and the title of his second book (Obama, 2006a). Curiously, however, Barack recalled the title of Wright's sermon as "The Audacity of Hope" (Obama, 1995, p. 292). Changing "to" into "of" was only a change of preposition, but it thereby changed the verb *hope* into a noun, and this noun later became the motto of Obama's presidential campaign.

There was another little memory distortion in Barack's recollection of Wright's sermon. Barack remembered Wright as beginning his sermon with the biblical story of Hannah and her son Samuel, which in turn reminded Wright of Watts's painting *Hope* (Obama, 1995, p. 292). In the published version of the sermon, however, the order had been reversed. Wright had begun his sermon by describing the Reverend Frederick Sampson's sermon in Richmond about Watts' painting *Hope* and discussed the biblical Hannah and her son Samuel only later in his sermon (Wright, 1990). Did Barack's feelings about his own mother make him reverse the order in his memory?

The biblical image of the barren Hannah, who had finally become pregnant and given birth to the prophet Samuel, may have reverberated in Barack's unconscious mind with his emotions about his mother and himself. The way Barack remembered Wright's sermon, Wright had said that Watts' painting depicted a bruised and bloody harpist, wearing tattered rags, her harp containing only one frayed string, sitting atop a mountain. The valley below was full of the ravages of war and famine, strife, and deprivation (Obama, 1995, pp. 292–293). In Barack's recollection, at this point Wright began harping on his favorite theme—the cruelty, oppression, and deprivation inflicted on black people by white people.

Barack recalled that Wright had complained about the terrible waste of leftover food in the United States and on its luxurious cruise ships when Haiti's poor black people went hungry, about the greed of the white folks who ran the world, about apartheid in the southern hemisphere, and about apathy in the northern one, exclaiming, "That's the world! On which hope sits!" (Obama, 1995, p. 293). In the published version of Wright's sermon, however, no such sentence is to be found (Wright, 1990). Did Barack paraphrase or imagine some of Wright's emotional outbursts?

Curiously enough, the skeptical, atheistic or agnostic Barack was transported by Wright's religious sermon. He was deeply moved by the hope that Wright was trying to wring out of hopelessness and despair. While the black boys sitting next to Barack on the church bench seemed bored with Wright's sermon and doodled on their church bulletins, Barack listened intently as Wright carried on about the horrors of "Sharpsville" (the Sharpeville massacre in South Africa in 1960) and the nuclear bombing of Hiroshima in 1945, as if the two were comparable. In fact, fewer than 100 people had been killed in Sharpeville and hundreds of thousands in Hiroshima. Barack recalled that Wright had spoken about callous politicians and about black people's hardships, strife, and pain. The pastor carried on about the pain of middle-class women abused by their husbands and of children neglected by their wealthy parents (Obama, 1995, p. 293).

The emotional themes that Wright harped on, such as abused wives and abandoned children, were those that Barack knew too well and felt very painfully. The fiery Wright was good at playing the emotions of his congregants. The congregation began to shout, clap, cry out, sing, and dance. As Barack thought of all the misery that he had seen and heard in his three years in Chicago, of everything that he had been through, he began to cry. This was a major turning point for Barack. Shortly thereafter, before leaving Chicago for Harvard, after returning from his first trip to Kenya, he was baptized a Christian at Trinity United Church of Christ by its senior pastor, the Reverend Wright (Kantor, 2007a). Some journalists think that Barack was baptized "in the early 1990s," after he had met Michelle (Miller & Wolffe, 2008), but his memoir implies that this happened shortly after his return from Kenya in 1988 (Obama 1995, pp. 291–295; see also Obama, 2006a, p. 246).

Barack had found a new father figure in Wright and a new redeemer in Jesus Christ (Obama, 1995, pp. 294–295). Later, Barack himself would become a redeemer, a savior, a messiah, and a prophet in the eyes of millions of people all over the world (Abramsky, 2009, p. 6). Barack himself expressed it well in *The Audacity of Hope*. He believed that he owed his "fierce ambitions" to his internal image of his father and to his fervent wish to be loved by him but that his religious faith had come from his mother's values and that her faith had channeled his ambitions into organizing a poor black community "to cope with joblessness, drugs, and hopelessness" rather than into the pursuit of personal wealth (Obama, 2006a, pp. 243–244).

In other words, if Barack's fierce political ambitions had come from his identification with his idealized image of his father and from his impossible quest for his absent father's love, his religious faith came from his identification with his mother's values, however freethinking or atheistic she may have been. After his first meeting with Wright, however, it took Barack another year to resolve his inner conflict over his belief in God: he met the Reverend Wright in the fall of 1987, but not until 1988 did he let Wright baptize him a Christian.

IN SEARCH OF THE DEAD FATHER

Barack's decision to visit his father's homeland of Kenya and his father's grave had been slowly maturing in his mind ever since his half sister Auma visited him in 1987. In May 1988, Barack left Chicago and traveled to Europe for three weeks on his way to Africa. In white Europe he felt anxious, insecure, and mistrustful of strangers. Europe was beautiful, but it was not his: he, an African American, did not belong to it. He began to doubt himself, to suspect that his visit to Europe was a delaying tactic, that he was trying "to avoid coming to terms with the old man" (Obama, 1995, p. 301). After leaving Chicago, Barack felt a great emptiness inside himself: he was hoping that his trip to Kenya would help fill that void (ibid., p. 302). On the flight from London to Nairobi, he recalled an African from Senegal whom he had met in Spain and how akin he had felt to him. Barack's mind was still full of idealized images of Africa, Kenya, and his father, despite everything he had heard about them.

Barack flew to Kenya for the first time in the summer of 1988, before going to Harvard in the fall, and, as he later put it, for the first time in his life he felt he belonged, by virtue of his name, which was recognized at Nairobi's Kenyatta International Airport by a "strikingly beautiful" black British Airways stewardess, whom he called "Miss Omoro" (Obama, 1995, p. 305). Barack was obviously attracted to "Miss Omoro," for he returned to the airport later, hoping to see her again. His half sister Auma, who had returned from Germany to Kenya earlier that year, and his half aunt Zeituni Onyango came to greet Barack at the airport.

The woman whom Barack called "Aunt" Zeituni had been born in 1952. She was a half sister of Barack's father by his grandfather, Hussein Onyango Obama. She and her brothers, Omar, Yusuf, and Sayid, were the children of "Granny" Sarah, Onyango's third wife. Omar had left Kenya for the United States many years before, whereas Yusuf and Sayid remained in Kenya. At the age of 50 Zeituni would immigrate to the United States, claiming to seek asylum from racial persecution in Kenya. In 2008 she contributed money to Barack's presidential campaign. As it is illegal in the United States for foreign citizens, asylum seekers, and immigrants who have not received their green cards to make political donations, Zeituni was investigated by the Federal Election Commission and found herself fighting deportation by the U.S. Immigration Service as an illegal alien.

Auma and Barack dropped their 36-year-old Aunt Zeituni at Nairobi's Kenya Breweries, where she worked at that time. Auma, who had graduated from Heidelberg the year before and was teaching at the University of Nairobi, as well as holding another job, brought Barack to her apartment. Exhausted, he fell asleep as she went to work, and when he woke he met a troop of black-faced monkeys and a long-necked bird with huge green wings. Barack was getting nature's welcome to Africa (Obama, 1995, pp. 308–309).

Barack spent his first few days in Kenya with Auma, slowly getting to know Nairobi and Kenyan life and culture, everyday life, customs, and habits. Here, in Kenya, Barack felt at home. Everyone was black, and he could be himself. He did not have to pretend to be anything other than what he was and could find his true self (Obama, 1995, p. 311). Barack wished to fly away from Kenya with this feeling and this moment intact, without having to confront the painful truths about his dead father. But he knew that this was yet another subterfuge, another delay, another attempt to avoid coming to terms with his "old man" (Obama, p. 301).

Among other subjects, Auma and Barack discussed the Kenyan Mau Mau uprising, a bloody and popular insurgency by native Kenyan peasants against British colonialist rule from 1952 to 1960. The core of the Mau Mau revolt consisted of members of the Kikuyu tribe, who were joined by members of the Embu and Meru tribes. The uprising failed militarily, but it hastened Kenyan independence and motivated other Africans to fight against colonial rule. It created a rift between the white colonial community in Kenya and the British Home Office in London that set the stage for Kenyan independence in 1963. In official British documents, the Mau Mau uprising was called the Kenya Emergency. The name *Mau Mau* for the Kenyan rebel movement against the British was the colonial name: the rebels called themselves in Kikuyu *Muingi* ("The Movement"), *Muigwithania* ("The Understanding"), *Muma wa Uiguano* ("The Oath of Unity"), or the Kikuyu Central Association (KCA), as the Kikuyu had created the impetus for the insurgency. Veterans of the Mau Mau movement referred to themselves in English as the Land and Freedom Army.

Unfortunately, however, the bloody Mau Mau revolt against the British, which had brought about Kenyan independence, had not essentially changed Kenya: throughout Africa, white people could still live comfortably "on the backs of the darker races" (Obama, 1995, p. 314). Auma and Barack noted with displeasure that native Kenyan waiters and servants still acted in a servile manner toward white foreigners, while they treated their own black people in an undignified and rude manner, trying to withhold service from them as long as they could. Auma was very bitter about this. At a restaurant, the black waiters treated whites with deference, blacks with derision. Neocolonialism was in force, and Barack's entire being ached against it. He discovered to his dismay that the "free" black people of Africa were no more free than the poor black people of Chicago.

Barack remembered Isak Dinesen, the pseudonym of Baroness Karen von Blixen-Finecke (1885–1962), born Karen Christenze Dinesen, a Danish author who wrote both in Danish and in English. She is best known by English speakers for her novel *Out of Africa*, her account of living in Kenya, and for her story *Babette's Feast*, both of which were adapted into Academy Award–winning films. In Denmark she is best known for *The African Farm* (in Danish *Den afrikanske Farm*) and for her *Seven Gothic Tales* (in Danish *Syv fantastiske Fortællinger*).

Isak Dinesen's view of African life was obviously romanticized. Barack observed ruefully that in so-called independent Kenya, white people still continued their colonial traditions. A white man could still stroll through Isak Dinesen's home and indulge in fantasies of romance with a mysterious young baroness or visit "the Lord Delamare Hotel" to see portraits of Ernest Hemingway smiling after a successful game hunt, surrounded by grim-faced African coolies. Barack may have meant the Norfolk Hotel and its famous Lord Delamere Terrace, Nairobi's famous meeting place. He observed that white people were being served by black men without fear or guilt, that they marveled at the generous exchange rate for their currency and left a generous tip for their waiters. If a white man felt nauseated at the sight of leprous black beggars outside his hotel, he could always administer a ready tonic to himself. Black rule had come, after all, Kenya was their country, and white folks were only visitors (Obama, 1995, p. 314).

Slowly, gingerly, Barack began to approach the subject of his old man. He first got to know the members of his father's family. Barack met his Aunt Jane, a sister of his stepmother Kezia. Jane was the one who called to tell him about his father's death in 1982. He also met Kezia herself, who greeted him warmly, as if he were her own son, as well as Bernard, another "brother" who had been born to Kezia around 1970.

While Kezia was Bernard's mother, given her separation from her husband, Barack and the rest of his family doubted that Bernard and his brother Abo Samson were the sons of Barak Obama. The teenage Bernard had been an auto parts supplier in Nairobi. Later, as an adult, he had a child and converted to Islam, saying, "I'm a Muslim, I don't deny it. My father was raised a Muslim. But it's not an issue. I don't know what all the hullabaloo is about" (Harvey, 2008). He currently lives in England with his mother Kezia, as does Bernard.

One person that Barack badly needed to see was his Aunt Sarah, the sister of his dead father. This Sarah had the same first name as his paternal step-grandmother, Granny Sarah. Aunt Sarah had disputed Barack's father's will in court, seeking a part of his estate. She told people that Kezia's children, Auma, Roy, and Bernard, were not the Barak's children. Auma told Barack that Aunt Sarah was very bitter and that she kept telling everybody that Auma and her mother Kezia were to blame for her lowly state. Barak's estate was not worth much, but with his narcissistic pride and grandiosity he had made his entire family believe that it was. Auma thought that her brothers, sisters, aunts, and uncles were mired in endless arguments about Barak's estate, as if the dead Barak might somehow save them from their misery (Obama, 1995, p. 319). The family tragedy was going on. Many of the Obamas were abusive and self-destructive.

One of Barack's bags had got lost on his flight from London to Nairobi. The "strikingly beautiful Miss Omoro" had told him that it had gone to Johannesburg and promised him to track it down, but now the clerks at Kenyatta International Airport said they had no record of it. Despite the promises of "Miss Omoro," Barack learned that the only way to get anything done in Kenya was connections or bribes. This disheartened him, for his proud and rigid father had refused to learn this simple but unpleasant truth. Wherever he went in Nairobi, or all over Kenya, Barack felt his father's presence. It never left him (Obama, 1995, p. 323)—and not only in Kenya. Throughout his life, Hamlet-like, he would have to deal with his father's ghost, with the presence of his father in everything and everybody that touched his life. In fact, his entire memoir *Dreams from My Father* was the story of his struggle with that ghost.

Barack took his time before visiting his father's ancestral village and his father's sister, Aunt Sarah. At first, he tried to play good elder brother to his teenage half brother Bernard, taking him to play basketball on the University of Nairobi courts. Playing basketball was Barack's unconscious way of regaining his lost father, who had given him his first basketball during their one and only meeting when Barry was 10 years old. Barack tried to talk the do-nothing Bernard into doing something with his life, studying, working, and making something of himself. Bernard said he appreciated "having a big brother around" (Obama, 1995, p. 327).

Bernard had another elder brother named Abo Samson Obama, who had been born in 1968 to Kezia, his father's first wife and the mother of Roy and Auma. But Abo, with whom Barack did not even know for sure whether he shared a father, was not a good elder brother. Abo was a cell-phone shop manager in Kenya. Abo later moved to the United Kingdom, where he received a police caution for disturbance of the public order. In 2008 he was arrested in England and accused of sexual assault but not prosecuted for it. He had allegedly been living illegally in the United Kingdom for seven years. In 2009 he was denied entry into the United Kingdom while traveling from the United States back home to Kenya.

Barack, who came from a broken family, had been searching for his family, and for a good family, all his life. In Chicago, his Developing Communities Project had been a kind of good family to him. In Kenya, amid the problems of his family, he began to wonder about the nature of the human family. Was it a genetic, a social, or an economic entity? Was it "a store of shared memories, say? An ambit of love? A reach across a void?" (Obama, 1995, p. 327). Barack was trying to come to terms with his extensive and problematic Kenyan family, to understand where he came from, to fathom his family's psychological effect on him.

Barack missed having a good and healthy family. He tried to create an imaginary family for himself by imagining himself surrounded by three imaginary circles, which to some degree helped him conquer his painful feelings of helplessness and abandonment. The imaginary circles that Barack drew around himself in his mind gave him "an illusion of control" (Obama, 1995, p. 328) that he sorely needed, having been a child with no control over his abandonment by his father or over the immaturity of his mother. These imaginary circles gave him a feeling of security.

There was an inner circle "where love was constant and claims unquestioned," something that he had never really had, given the circumstances of his infancy and childhood. Outside this circle was a second one, which Barack called "a realm of negotiated love, commitments freely chosen," the circle of his community, work, and intimate relationships. Farther outside was a third circle, that of friends, colleagues, and acquaintances, including even Barack's supermarket cashier in Chicago. This third circle gradually expanded outward until it included the whole American nation and the entire "black African race," and even Barack's "moral course," and all the commitments that he had made to himself (Obama, 1995, pp. 327–328).

Psychologically, these imaginary circles in Barack's mind were a mighty intellectual effort to resolve an emotional conflict that could not be resolved, and his visit to Kenya proved it to him. The illusion of control that those imaginary circles gave him was shattered. The "astronomy" of his concentric circles collapsed because in Kenya everyone was family, and family was everywhere. In Nairobi's shops, offices, parks, and streets, everyone seemed to have known Barack's dead father. His half brothers, half sisters, aunts, stepaunts, and half aunts insisted on taking him to Nairobi's best bargain shops, no matter how far off. Fortunately, Barack's exquisite sense of humor helped him deal with this without becoming too upset (Obama, 1995, p. 328).

Barack received overwhelming attention from his Kenyan family. Auma took her half brother Barack to visit many of their relatives, half brothers, first cousins, uncles, aunts, and second cousins. At first he took to all this attention like a baby to his mother's breast, with infinite happiness and gratitude (Obama, 1995, p. 328). This was an emotional regression: Barack had temporarily become an infant again, his African family playing the role of a nourishing mother. But as time went by he recovered his reality-testing capacity and realized that the situation was "tough and getting tougher" (Obama, p. 329). He was now filled with tension, fear, and doubt.

Did he have to take care of this large family? In America he could use politics, organizing, and self-denial to feel good about himself. Here, in Kenya, he felt bad about not having enough money to take care of his extended family. They imagined him as a wealthy American lawyer or businessman, which he was not. His self-esteem was being imperiled.

Barack spoke little with his family members about his father while he was in Kenya. He had dealt with his father's ghost during his meeting with Auma in the United States, and now he deliberately avoided the subject. For many pages in his memoir, we are not told about a visit to his father's grave. But before he left Kenya, his Aunt Zeituni took him to meet his real aunt, Sarah Obama, his father's elder sister. Aunt Sarah had bitterly contested his father's will in court and was at odds with the rest of the Obama and Onyango families.

Aunt Sarah seemed angry, hurt, and suspicious. She told Barack that her other family members had been telling him lies about her and that it was she, not Granny, who had taken care of his father when he was a little boy. She said that her mother, Akumu, was Barack's grandmother, not Granny Sarah. Before Barack could answer, Aunt Zeituni and Aunt Sarah began an argument in Luo, in which both became angry and upset with one another. Aunt Sarah asked Barack for money, but all he could give her was $30 worth in Kenyan currency (Obama, 1995, pp. 331–334).

Aunt Zeituni dragged Barack away, visibly embarrassed about the argument she had had with Aunt Sarah. She told Barack that it was her own mother, Granny Sarah, who had raised his father, as his father's mother, Akumu, had left Barack's grandfather Onyango. Aunt Sarah was a tough cookie. She had married four times and had outlasted all her husbands. After Sarah's first husband died, she wanted Barack's father to support her and her child, and she feared that once her father died, she would be left with nothing. Aunt Zeituni told Barack that his father had made his first wife, Kezia, pregnant with Abo while he was still married to his third wife, Ruth. As Kezia was also living with another man at that time, no one could be sure who the true father of Abo and of his brother Bernard was. This was a pretty messy family situation (Obama, 1995, p. 335).

Barack had developed a lifelong capacity for displacing his personal issues onto public and political ones and rationalizing them in the name of the public good. For instance, rather than let himself be overwhelmed by his feelings of abandonment by his father, he organized the poor, fatherless families of Chicago's South Side. After his visit with his Aunt Sarah, Barack was filled with compassion for the poor people of Africa. A poor old woman had drawn his attention. He ran into a pregnant goat, an oncoming *matatu* (a shared taxicab), two cheerful little schoolgirls, and an old woman trying to sell some food, whom Barack imagined to be his paternal grandmother.

He wondered whether he should be kinder to his do-nothing half brother Bernard. A crowd of skinny young men that streamed out from a bus into the road seemed to him like so many Bernards, all of them hungry, striving, and desperate, all of them his brothers. In his mind, Barack had become the elder brother of all Africans. He had to take care of them all (Obama, 1995, pp. 335–336).

All of them were his brothers in his fantasy, but what could he possibly do for them? He learned that his Aunt Zeituni, whose husband, like Barack's father, was abusive and made her leave his house, had found shelter with none other than his father, Barak. Zeituni told Barack that his father had suffered greatly, that he had been very generous, that he had taken care of everybody when he could, that he did not bear anyone a grudge, and that after he recovered his position he was even nice to those family members who had refused to put him up during his long period of disgrace and poverty. But Zeituni could only see Barak's magnanimity, not his self-destructive narcissism, nor his abusiveness, which his son Barack understood intuitively. Zeituni warned Barack against being as generous as his father, telling him that if everyone was family, no one was family. Zeituni thought that Barack's father had never understood this (Obama, 1995, p. 337).

Barack did not say how he felt about his Aunt Sarah, nor about Aunt Zeituni. Years later, during his presidential campaign, Zeituni, who had entered the United States as an asylum seeker in 2002 and had contributed to his campaign, was found by the U.S. press living in a public-housing project in a poor section of Boston, illegally in the United States. The U.S. Immigration Service tried to deport her, but in 2009 a U.S. federal judge granted her a one-year stay to legalize her status. In 2010 Zeituni was granted asylum by the United States.

There were other embarrassing and painful stories in Barack's Kenyan family. Barak's third wife, Ruth, had had two sons by Barak, whom she named Mark and David, and David had been killed in a motorcycle accident. David had had a difficult relationship with his mother, who seems to be a difficult woman, and with his father. Barack's father's divorce from Ruth had been very bitter: she knew about his meetings with Kezia and about his fathering more children by her. Ruth supposedly married a Tanzanian named Ndesandjo, by whom she had a third son, Joseph, and whose last name she made her other sons take. Mark studied in America, and he later married a Chinese woman and became a businessman in China, cutting off his ties to the Obamas.

The psychologically minded Barack sensed intuitively that David's death had not been accidental, that he had had serious emotional problems before the accident, just like their father. He decided not to discuss David with Auma any longer, as these memories were too painful for her.

Then, suddenly, during Barack's visit, David's brother, Mark Ndesandjo, returned to Kenya from America, and his mother, Ruth Nidesand Obama Ndesandjo, invited Barack and Auma to her house for lunch with him.

Mark had graduated from Rhode Island's Brown University, an Ivy League school like Harvard and Columbia, and was studying physics at Stanford University (he later received an M.B.A. degree from Emory University). Auma was angry and disgusted with Ruth's invitation. She told Barack that Ruth had known for the past six months that she had returned from Germany, yet she did not care about Auma at all. Ruth only wanted to show off her son Mark, the Ivy League graduate, and to compare him to Barack. Yet Barack decided to accept Ruth's invitation, and Auma reluctantly agreed to go with him (Obama, 1995, p. 340).

When they met the domineering Ruth, she sent her husband away with their little boy Joey, so that the four of them, Ruth, Mark, Auma, and Barack, could remain by themselves (Obama, 1995, p. 341). Ruth then heaped praise on her son Mark and also told Barack that his father was "quite crazy" and that he was lucky he had only met him once. As could have been expected, Barack did not like Ruth. She spent the next hour alternately denigrating Barack's father and idealizing her son Mark. Ruth ignored Auma, concentrating on Barack, while an angry Auma sulked and tried to eat Ruth's food. Barack could not wait to leave, but Ruth insisted that Mark bring the family's photo album and show it to them while she served dessert (Obama, p. 342).

So Barack and Auma remained to see the family photographs. The pictures of family life with his father seemed so pretty to him that Barack was saddened by the thought of how badly his father's life had ended and had to look away lest they see him cry. Barack later told Auma that Ruth had never "gotten over" their father. Auma replied that neither had they (Obama, 1995, pp. 341–343). Indeed, Barack had not come to terms with his dead father. His preoccupation with his father's image was lifelong and had much to do with his career.

Still curious about his father, Barack sought out a separate face-to-face meeting with his half brother Mark, so that they could discuss their father without Ruth's interference. He invited Mark for lunch in one of Nairobi's Indian restaurants, and Mark ambivalently accepted. Like all of East and South Africa, Kenya has numerous Indian immigrants, many of whom consider themselves superior to Kenya's native black people. Mark spoke of his adoptive father, Mr. Ndesandjo, as if he were his real father. He wanted to have nothing to do with his biological father, Barak, whom Mark saw as a drunken father and an abusive husband. Mark wanted to cut himself off from his roots, to think of his father as dead even when he was alive (Obama, 1995, p. 344).

Barack had thought about the same things as Mark, but, unlike Mark, Barack was still angry at the old man for his abuse of his wives and for his abandonment of his children, including, of course, himself. Mark, however, sought to numb his rage at his father and to deny his African identity. Barack's conversation with Mark was brief and strained. Mark told Barack that he was moved by great music and poetry but not by their common father. He said he was not concerned with his racial identity. There was a moment in their conversation when Mark seemed to hesitate, to reconsider what he had just said, but he quickly came to and asked the waiter for the check. Mark told Barack that his life was hard enough without the added burden of self-questioning (Obama, 1995, p. 344).

When Barack and his half brother Mark parted, they exchanged addresses and promised each other to write, but Barack's heart ached at the obvious dishonesty of these promises (Obama, 1995, p. 345). When he returned to Auma's home and told her about his meeting with Mark, she laughed and told him that because Mark's mother Ruth had all the necessary documents, Mark's claim to their father's inheritance was the only one that was not contested. One might imagine from the extensive talk in Barack's memoir about his father's inheritance that it was quite large: in fact, it was next to nothing. His father had left no real estate or any other major fortune.

Barack put off visiting his father's grave as long as he could. After two weeks in Kenya, however, he talked a reluctant Auma into going on a safari with him. Barack had come to Kenya "thinking that I could somehow force my many worlds into a single, harmonious whole" (Obama, 1995, p. 347). Instead, he saw only more and more divisions, both within and outside his family. When his elder half brother Roy took the whole family out to dance at Nairobi's Garden Square Restaurant, which Barack called "Garden Square," they met Luo, Kikuyu, Kamba, Meru and Kalenjin people, drinking, dancing, shouting, and enjoying themselves (Obama, 1995, pp. 362–364). It may have been easier for Barack to think about Kenya's merry tribesmen than about his father's tragic fate.

Apparently, the people dancing at the Garden Square Restaurant did not include Maasai, Embu, and some 40 other black African tribes, nor the Asian Indians who treated black Africans haughtily. In neighboring Uganda, in 1972, Idi Amin Dada (1925–2003), the mentally disturbed president, had given Uganda's Asians 90 days to leave the country, following a dream in which, he claimed, God had told him to expel them from the country. The order for expulsion fit the Indophobic social climate of Uganda. The Ugandan government and people claimed that the Indians were hoarding wealth and goods to the detriment of indigenous Africans and sabotaging the Ugandan economy. Barack thought that this explained the Indians' behavior in Kenya, but his half sister Auma found them downright arrogant (Obama, 1995, p. 347).

In Kenya, Barack was still something of an idealist, hoping to bridge tribal and caste divisions, striving for a kind of third-world solidarity that his Kenyan family found naive. He wanted to break the stereotypes that his Luo "aunts" held about the various Kenyan tribes, or African nations, only to have them tell him that he was an idealist like his father. "Meaning he, too, was naive; he, too, liked to argue with history. Look what happened to him" (Obama, 1995, p. 348). And it was indeed one of Barack's deepest fears that he would end up like his father, destroying his own life. During the safari he admired the courage of their Maasai guardsmen, of his Kikuyu driver, of his half sister Auma, and of the British physicians from Malawi that joined them. Barack thought that Africa badly needed their kind of courage, that of realistic, decent, and honest people who will see their projects through (Obama, 1995, p. 358). He, too, needed that kind of courage and that determination, so as not to end up like his father.

Much of Barack's safari was spent at Maasai Mara, a large game reserve in southwestern Kenya, an extension of the Serengeti National Park game reserve in Tanzania. Named for Kenya's Maasai tribe, the traditional inhabitants of the area, and for the Mara River, which divides it, the Maasai Mara is famous for its exceptional population of game and for the annual migration of zebra and wildebeest from the Serengeti to Maasai Mara from July to October, a migration so immense that it is called the Great Migration. Barack later recalled enjoying his safari, and it also gave him additional time to prepare for his encounter with his father's ghost (Obama, 1995, pp. 346–358).

During Barack's third week in Kenya, when he got back to Nairobi from his safari, he and his half sister Auma received word through their half brother Bernard that Auma's brother Roy had returned from the United States earlier than planned, leaving his American wife in Washington. Roy had gone to the apartment of his Aunt Jane, the sister of his mother Kezia, and the whole extended family in Nairobi came there to see him. Auma told Roy that he had become fat, while Kezia, Roy's mother, told Barack that Roy was the head of the family now, being the eldest son. A Kenyan woman named Amy was also present, whom Roy announced he was going to marry. In keeping with the African tradition of ancestor worship and animism, Roy poured beer all over the floor to quench the thirst of their ancestors (Obama, 1995, p. 361).

Auma feared that Roy had inherited their father's hard-drinking ways. Some years later, however, Roy changed his ways and straightened out his life out by embracing Islam and his African heritage. He changed his first name to his Luo tribal name of Abongo, and by 1992, the time of

Barack's wedding, he had sworn off pork, smoking, and drinking. Barack was proud of many of his relatives at his wedding, but he was proudest of all of his elder half brother Roy, who had turned from a fat, self-destructive alcoholic into a thin, sober, princely African, like Barack's idealized image of their father in his youth (Obama, 1995, p. 441).

That evening at Nairobi's Garden Square Restaurant in 1988, however, Barack's half sister Auma was unhappy with her elder brother Roy. She obviously harbored bitter memories of her abusive father, and Roy reminded her of him. She complained that the Obama men always got away with anything, and she tried to dissuade Amy from marrying Roy. Both Roy and Amy seemed to have drunk too much, and Aunt Jane looked anxiously at Aunt Kezia. Aunt Zeituni boasted of being the best dancer in the family. Barack learned that his father had been an enthusiastic dancer and a good one, that his father's father had been an angry and stern disciplinarian, and that his father had defied his own father but that they finally wound up dancing together with their women. There had obviously been an oedipal conflict between the father and the grandfather. Everybody laughed heartily at the story of Barak and his father (Obama, 1995, pp. 363–364). In Barack's own mind, however, there was still a deep inner struggle between him and his father. He had to outdo him and not be self-destructive like him.

When Barack watched his half brother Roy dance with their half sister Auma, he immediately recognized the same look he had seen on his father's face in early 1972 in Hawai'i when the old man had first taught him how to dance. He felt tipsy and well, but his good feeling was marred by the sight of two men beating up a third one with billy clubs and cutting him up with a broken bottle. His half brother Roy told him that the two aggressors might be dangerous policemen. Roy also told him that he had spent a night in a Nairobi jail before their brother David died, that David had asked him for the keys to the motorcycle so he could get the papers to spring Roy from jail, and that he had given David the keys to the motorcycle that then killed him. Barack told Roy not to blame himself for David's death, but his description of the scene is heartrending (Obama, 1995, pp. 365–366).

It was no accident that Barack put off his visit to his father's grave for two weeks. He was trying to avoid the painful confrontation with his father's ghost. During the third week, at 5:30 P.M. one evening, he and the whole family—except Aunt Jane, Kezia's sister—took the night train from Nairobi heading west to Kisumu, on Lake Victoria, some 40 miles from his father's village. On his way there, Barack reflected on the British construction of this "great railway" from Mombasa on the Indian Ocean all the way to Lake Victoria and imagined the sensations of "some nameless British officer" on the train's maiden voyage.

Barack's thoughts returned to Mathare Valley, one of Nairobi's worst slums, which the train crossed on its way out of Nairobi. Would the imaginary British officer have felt triumphant because his train symbolized the victory of Western civilization over African "darkness"? Did he fear that the whole railway project was madness and that colonialism and imperialism would be defeated by black Africa? At the same time, Barack also tried to imagine the thoughts and feelings of a black African watching the new steel monster bellow black smoke as it snaked its way through his village. He wondered whether the African would have felt envious or would have feared the coming war between blacks and whites (such as Kenya's Mau Mau uprising must have been), but for some reason he could not imagine what the black African would have felt (Obama, 1995, p. 368).

Did Barack unconsciously refuse to identify with his black Kenyan father? Was he unconsciously projecting his own feelings on that imaginary nameless British officer whose thoughts he had tried to imagine? Did he feel that his own enterprise had been an act of folly and that his whole trip to Africa to deal with his father's ghost was pointless and fruitless? The person he most wanted to see in "Home Squared" was his Granny, Sarah Onyango Obama, the woman who had raised his father Barak as a child, after his father's mother Akumu had abandoned him.

As Barack tried to fall asleep in his rocking sleeping-car bunk bed, he kept thinking of his paternal grandfather, Onyango, whom Barack's half sister Auma blamed for their father's personal tragedy and for their family's misfortunes. Barack felt intuitively that Auma was right (Obama, 1995, pp. 371–372). Indeed, his father Barak had longed to be loved by his own father, Onyango, a man who could not love him, a man who had been abandoned by his wife Akumu and who had displaced his rage at her to her son. Rather than love his son by Akumu, Onyango had constantly attacked and criticized Barak.

Barack was trying to piece together his family's psychological puzzle in his mind, but it took his unconscious mind to do the emotional work for him, which was too painful for his conscious mind. This occurred in another dream. That night, while sleeping in the train, Barack had a nightmare, which he recalled in his memoir a few years later. Like the dream that he had had about his father five years earlier, this fascinating dream is worth trying to decipher. As before, however, without the dreamer's associations to the dream, this is no easy task. My dream-interpreter's task is made still more difficult by the stringent fair-use quotation limits and by Obama's publisher's denial of permission to exceed that limit. As with Barack's previous dream, discussed in chapter 10, I must paraphrase his inimitable account of this dream (Obama, 1995, p. 372).

Although he did not say so, it seems obvious that the scene of this night-mare was in Africa. In this dream, Barack was walking on a country road in a village with round huts when he ran into naked children who wore only bead strings. The children played, and old men waved to him. Suddenly, Barack realized that the villagers were looking behind him in fear and were running into their huts as he passed them. He heard a leopard growl and, fearing for his life, ran frantically into the nearby forest, where he stumbled all over the vegetation until he was exhausted and fell down on his knees. When he turned around toward the chasing leopard, night had fallen and he saw "a giant figure looming as tall as the trees, wearing only a loincloth and a ghostly mask" (Obama, 1995, p. 372).

The murderous leopard, then, had turned into a giant human ghost. Was it his dead father? When Barack was a child, his father had seemed a giant to him. In his nightmare, the ghost's dead eyes stared at him, and then Barack heard "a thunderous voice saying only that it was time." His whole body began to shake with fear. At this point in the dream the anxiety was too great for him to remain asleep. He woke up in a panic, banging his head against the lamp on his bunk wall. After that, he slowly began to calm down but could not fall asleep again (Obama, 1995, p. 372).

Could the leopard who turned into the giant ghostly figure in Barack's nightmare have stood for his dead father? He did not say whether the giant human figure in his dream was black, but he had come to Africa to search for his African father's ghost, and the giant figure in the dream wore a loincloth, symbolizing the African, and a ghostly mask. And what is the meaning of the thunderous voice that said that it was time Was it the voice of the giant figure in the ghostly mask or of someone else? Was it the voice of his father? Why did it frighten him to death? For what was it time? Was it time for him to face his father's ghost? Was it time for Barack to die, like his father?

After their train reached the port city of Kisumu, on Lake Victoria, the third-largest Kenyan city after Nairobi and Mombasa, Barack and Auma traveled by a primitive first-class bus toward their grandfather's estate at Kogelo, which is part of the greater Alego. They got off the bus at Ndori, a Kenyan mining town that is the closest town to the village. After a two-hour wait, they took a *matatu*, a shared taxicab, to the village. The word *matatu* comes from a Swahili phrase that means "for three." For three Kenyan shillings, one could travel on any route in colonial times. They finally arrived at their Home Squared in Kogelo, where they met two of their father's half brothers, Yusuf and Sayid, who were Zeituni's brothers and the children of Granny Sarah, as well as Sarah herself.

Barack later saw a photograph of his paternal grandfather, Onyango, with his wife Akumu and her children, Sarah and Barak, the latter being his father. Barack also discovered on the wall a picture of dreamy-eyed, dark-haired white woman and was told that she was the white woman whom Onyango had married in Burma during World War II (Obama, 1995, p. 375). His half brother Roy said mischievously that the woman did not look Burmese. The white woman reminded Barack of his mother. Yet Onyango had objected violently to his parents' marriage. The woman he called Granny—Sarah, who had raised his father—told him that she had only two problems: the leaking roof of her house and her poor son Omar in the United States, whom she had not heard from for over a year. Did Granny want Barack to solve her problems for her?

When Barack finally reached his father's grave, he found that it was next to that of his grandfather. Yet, while Onyango had a plaque with his name and the years of his birth and death on it, Barak's grave had only yellow bathroom tiles over it. Barack's half brother Roy complained to him that six years had passed since their father's death and there was still no plaque or inscription on his grave (Obama, 1995, p. 376). If Barack felt any anger or disappointment about the absence of an inscription on his father's grave, he did not say so in his memoir. Instead, he expressed his *joy* at all the events he had witnessed. Barack felt that everything he had done in Kenya had helped him find his true self, know who and what he was, give him a sense of closure about himself, and resolve his identity struggle (Obama, pp. 376–377).

Barack's elation about his newfound identity was broken, however, on their way back from the market, when his half sister Auma ran ahead to get her camera, leaving their Granny Sarah and him in the middle of the road. Barack, who spoke very little Luo or Swahili, and Granny, who spoke very little English, could hardly converse. They stood there embarrassed and rueful until Auma returned. Granny told Auma that it pained her not to be able to speak to her grandson and that he should not be too busy to know his own people and to learn Luo (Obama, 1995, p. 377). It may have pained Barack, too, even if she was not his biological grandmother.

Barack repeatedly called his step-grandmother his Granny and his half siblings his brothers and sisters in his memoir. Granny Sarah had raised Barack's father, Barak, when his father's mother, Akumu, had abandoned him, so Barack's paternal grandmother was Akumu, not Sarah. Many times in his life, Barack adopted people as his grandparents, parents, or siblings who were not really such. In the case of his Granny Sarah, she spoke only Luo and Swahili, and Barack spoke neither of these two languages. He was saddened, and as he looked at Granny, he knew that his current joy was transient, that there were more trials and tribulations to come, that he would still have to make many painful choices (Obama, 1995, p. 377).

For all his excitement about Africa, its people, and its way of life, Barack could not shake off his thoughts about his father. In the evening, the excitement wore off, the lamplight dimmed, and the family members became quiet and began to turn in. Barack's Granny brought out a twin-size cot and some blankets for him and Bernard, and he had to share his outdoor bed with his younger half brother. Barack was exhausted, his whole body was aching, but he could not fall asleep because he heard Granny and Auma talking inside, and he thought about his elder half brother Roy and about the yellow tiles on his dead father's grave (Obama, 1995, pp. 378–379). Did he not think that he himself could have placed a plaque or an inscription on his father's grave with his name and the dates of his birth and death? To the end of his memoir, there is no mention of Barack thinking of it. Did this omission express his tremendous ambivalence about his father?

In Kenya, Barack encountered a great deal of poverty, begging, misery, and discontent. After meeting people from the big cities, rural people began to think that they were really poor and that they were helpless to change their situation. Barack's half uncle Yusuf had done well for a while but then dropped out of the rat race and went back to his childlike dependence on his mother. Auma told Barack that Yusuf lived with his mother, Granny, doing daily chores for her, and that he was afraid to go out into the world and try to make it (Obama, 1995, p. 381). In fact, Yusuf's was yet another tragic case in Barack's Kenyan family.

In Barack's mind, the condition of the poor people of Africa was no different than that of the poor children of Altgeld Gardens in Chicago: both groups compared themselves with the wealthy people in their city or country, and both felt poor, deprived, and helpless by comparison. And as in Chicago, Barack thought that the poor people of Kenya needed to believe in themselves in order to improve their lot. Like his older brothers, his half uncle Sayid had not gone to a university, having no money. Sayid had spent three years working for Kenya's National Youth Corps and was now desperately hunting for a job in the Nairobi business community, getting rejected repeatedly. Yet, unlike Yusuf, Sayid persisted in his quest, courageous and undaunted (Obama, 1995, p. 381).

One remarkable thing about Barack's memoir is how quickly his thoughts repeatedly move back and forth, from the personal to the political and back again to the personal. For example, he gave himself little time to think about his father and about the absence of a plaque on his grave, yet he spent many hours, even days, thinking about the plight of Kenya's poor people. His half uncle Sayid mentioned the Nigerian writer Chinua Achebe (born 1930), best known for his first novel *Things Fall Apart*, perhaps the most widely read book in modern African literature. Achebe had written that "when two locusts fight, it is always the crow who feasts." Sayid told Barack that they had a similar expression in Luo and that Nigerians and Kenyans were the same (Obama, 1995, p. 382). But what was that to a black community organizer from Chicago on his way to Harvard Law School?

Before leaving Kenya, Barack traveled with his half brothers Roy and Bernard, their mother, Kezia, and his half uncle Sayid in the old jalopy of a local school principal from the Nyanza provincial capital of Kisumu to Kendu Bay, some 25 miles south of Kisumu, on the shore of Lake Victoria, to visit Barack's half brother Abo Samson and his family. The road from Kisumu to Kendu Bay, which passes through the Nyanza town of Ahero, is much longer, however, as it circumvents Winam Gulf, an extension of northeastern Lake Victoria into western Kenya. Barack's drive from Kisumu to Kendu Bay lasted several hours.

When Barack, Roy, Bernard, Kezia, and Sayid finally arrived in their family's home in Kendu Bay, after a long walk, Kezia took them to a pile of rocks and sticks, telling them that it was the grave of Barack's paternal great-grandfather Obama, the father of Onyango. The Luo name for the land around that grave was *K'Obama*, meaning "the land of Obama," and his family were called *Jok'Obama*, meaning "the people of Obama." Kezia also said that Barack's paternal grandfather, Onyango, had moved back to Alego from Kendu Bay because he did not get along with his brothers, one of whom was still alive and living in Kendu Bay (Obama, 1995, p. 383).

Barack's meeting with his half brother Abo was not a happy one. Abo demanded a present from his "rich American brother" and was complained that the cassette player Barack had given him was not a Sony. Abo's greed, selfishness, and ingratitude infuriated Barack, who, however, controlled his emotions by trying to focus on the resemblance between Abo and Bernard. One of the psychological processes by which Barack controls his emotions is unconscious displacement, the capacity to displace his painful feelings from the personal to the political. He thought about the striking resemblance between the no-good Bernard and the ungrateful Abo. The look in Abo's eyes made him think not only that Abo was a drug addict but also that he was much like the young Afro-American boys in Chicago, suspicious, guarded, calculating, feeling wronged, and seeking justice or revenge (Obama, 1995, p. 384).

In Kendu Bay, Barack discovered more members of his father's family. There was a tall, handsome woman named Salina, whose connection to the Obamas was unclear, and her strapping, mustachioed son, Billy, who worked at the Mombasa post office. They were not related to the Obama family, but Billy was a close friend of Roy Obama, and their fathers had been the same age (Obama, 1995, p. 385). The 27-year-old Barack was at an age in which marriage is a major preoccupation. Addressing him as "Bwana," Billy told Barack that his father had been "a very great man" but that he took better care of other men's children than of his own, because he did not want to look weak with his own (Obama, pp. 385–386). The East African term *bwana* is the Swahili form of the Arabic *abuna* ("our father"). It is a form of respect, like "Sir" in English. Billy told Barack of the blessings of marriage but also of its limitations. Marriage made Billy calm, made him feel like a man, but he had also taught his wife not to contradict him or oppose his wishes (Obama, p. 386).

Sayid, the son of Granny Sarah, was not married, but he thought that the practice of polygamy was the most serious African curse. The wives become jealous of one another, and their children become distant from their father (Obama, 1995, p. 386). Did Barack think of his father's many wives and of his own estrangement from his father? He later met his grandfather Onyango's brother, who looked like the oldest man he had ever seen. Barack was made to drink moonshine, an illegally distilled corn whiskey. Drinking it made him feel as if his chest exploded and as if it rained shrapnel down his stomach, and it made him drunk.

Barack's memory of what followed was dreamlike, and it was the third "dream" that he recalled in his memoir. This dreamlike memory, too, was about his father, and Barack related it in the present tense, as one does a dream. It began with a scene of drunkenness. The moon hangs low in the sky as he and Roy and the other people, whose figures "merge with the shadows of corn" (Obama, 1995, p. 388), enter a little house and find several more men there. There are more bottles of moonshine, which the men pour into glasses, at first with pomp and ceremony but then, as they become more drunk, in a sloppy and slovenly manner. While the others keep getting drunker, Barack stops drinking, though nobody notices him (Obama, pp. 388–389).

At this point in Barack's dreamlike memory, the image of his dead father became dominant, and all the other faces and voices of the people in his dream fused into those of his father. They were all drinking, laughing, and shouting, either too drunk to talk or else violently demanding to smoke or to drink, activities that had characterized his father. They alternately laughed and cried, became angry and happy, then calmed down, speaking in Luo and Swahili and English, stretching out their hands for money, clothing, or drink. Their voices reminded Barack of those of his "sodden" youth in New York and Chicago, the voices of his father (Obama, 1995, pp. 388–389).

This dreamlike memory is too obvious to require a psychoanalytic interpretation. Barack had come to Africa to search for his dead father, and the thoughts of his dead father never left him. In his drunken stupor, everybody became his father. Barack's half-uncle Sayid later told him more stories about his father, how his father gave everybody drinks, how he drove them in his Mercedes as if he were a *matatu* driver and then gave them back their fare, how people always flattered his father and called him a big man and a great man, and how his father was so happy at this. In fact, Barak had been self-destructive even through his own generosity. Sayid, however, who did not have the same mother as Barak (Sayid was Granny Sarah's son), called Barack's father "my brother" and praised his goodness, his generosity, his pride, and his independence. Sayid thought that Barak had feared that if he left the bar too early, people would speak ill of him and he would lose the company of his age mates (Obama, 1995, p. 390).

The following day, an ever-curious Barack asked his Granny Sarah to tell him the family story from the very beginning. She spoke in Luo, and Auma translated her words into English for Barack. Sarah began with the ancient Luo myths of the tribe's ancestry, until she finally reached Obama, her father-in-law, and Onyango, her husband. Barack considered Granny's story important enough to quote it in full. Granny was good storyteller, and Barack may have embellished her stories, which she told in Luo and which Barack's half sister Auma translated into English. The tragic story of his paternal grandfather Onyango is heartrending. As a young man, On-yango lived through the arrival of the white men in the provincial capital of Kisumu, and he was fascinated by them. The village elders had warned Onyango against going to Kisumu, but he was too curious and burned with desire to see the white men. When he returned home, instead of his loin-cloth, he wore the clothes of the white man. His family did not know what to make of him (Obama, 1995, pp. 397–398).

Reading Barack's memoir, one becomes entranced with Granny's story of his paternal grandfather, Onyango, whom Barack's half sister Auma had blamed for all the family's woes. When Onyango came home from Kisumu wearing the white men's clothes, his father Obama thought that his son was wearing those "strange skins" to hide the fact that he had been circumcised against Luo tradition and that Onyango's shirt was hiding a skin rash or sores. He warned his other sons not to go near Onyango, as he was unclean and they could be defiled by touching him. Onyango's brothers laughed at him and avoided him. Deeply humiliated, enraged with his father and with his brothers, Onyango returned to Kisumu and never wanted to see his father again (Obama, 1995, p. 398).

Abused children often become abusive spouses and parents. Onyango's emotional trauma was deep, and its effects lasted throughout his life. In reaction to his rejection and his humiliation by his father and brothers, Onyango became a narcissistic, hot-tempered, violent, and tyrannical man who became furious whenever people broke his rules. People called him "the Terror." Just as he had been abused by his father, wife and child abuse became part of his way of life, and, tragically, they later became part of his son's way of life. Onyango may have become a Muslim as an antidote to his feelings of helpless rage: As a Muslim he could boast four wives and deny his feelings of humiliation. Onyango worked for the white British colonialist rulers of Kenya and their army.

In his memoir, Barack recalled that at that point in the narrative, his feminist half sister Auma asked their Granny Sarah why African women put up with arranged marriages, wife beatings, and other humiliations by men. Having been beaten by Onyango herself, and having come to accept it as her husband's privilege and as her natural lot, Granny replied that women needed to be beaten so as to learn to do all that was required of them. The feminist Auma angrily told Barack that African women encouraged men to abuse them (Obama, 1995, p. 405). Granny, however, tried to justify and explain the behavior of the women of her generation. Barack, for his part, was preoccupied with his internal image of his paternal grandfather, Onyango Obama, which, like that of his father, was undergoing violent changes (Obama, p. 406).

Barack's emotions were mixed and turbulent as he heard the tragic story of his paternal grandfather. He understood his half sister Auma's frustration and rage at Onyango, but he also felt betrayed by Granny's story. Barack had imagined his paternal grandfather, however autocratic and cruel, as a man loyal to his own black people—the Obama, the Luo, and the Kenyan people in general. But now Barack had learned that Onyango had betrayed his own people by joining the white colonialists and by becoming a Muslim. In Barack's mind this evoked Louis Farrakhan's Nation of Islam in America. Just as his idealized image of his father had been shattered, so now his image of his grandfather had been broken, and he angrily thought of Onyango as a traitor, an "Uncle Tom," a collaborator with the white colonialists and a "house nigger" (Obama, 1995, p. 406).

Granny Sarah, however, who had no idea what her "grandson" was thinking, went on talking about her husband, Onyango, his son, Barak, and the tragic conflicts between father and son. In her home, Barack found the old British registry book describing his grandfather's service around 1930 and giving his name as Hussein II Onyango—without the name Obama. Onyango may have dropped his father's name due to his own tragic conflict with his father. Onyango was a 35-year-old Muslim at the time of this document. This British book, along with copies of Barak's letters to the U.S. universities when he was seeking admission in 1959, was all that Barack had inherited from his father. Barack returned to the house's backyard to revisit his father's and grandfather's graves, where he fell into a sort of daydream tinged with disappointment and anger with both his father and his grandfather. He felt as if the whole natural world was closing in on him, with nothing but his Granny's stories alive in his mind (Obama, 1995, p. 427).

Barack's Granny's stories about the lifelong conflict between his tyrannical grandfather and his self-destructive father had a profound emotional impact on him. Remembering Granny's story about his grandfather, he tried to imagine what it was like being Hussein Onyango Obama. In fact, as often happens in a three-generational situation, Barack seemed to take his grandfather's side against his father. He imagined his young grandfather in his hour of shame and humiliation, feeling the rage that Onyango must have felt. His grandfather's life was changed completely at that moment, and he had to make himself over, build a new life for himself, and forge his new identity through the force of his own will (Obama, 1995, p. 427). Had not Barack himself "reinvented himself" when he left New York for Chicago three years earlier?

Barack imagined how his grandfather must have felt impotent rage at his tormentors, whether they were his father, his brothers, or his British overlords (Obama, 1995, pp. 427–428). Barack was imagining his grandfather's feelings through projective identification. He, too, had to reinvent himself. He, too, was about to start a new life as a law student. He, too, through sheer force of will, would forge his new identity and make himself into a civil rights lawyer and a politician who would eventually attain the highest political office in this world. Yet he, too, could not escape the traumatic memories of his early life, his abandonment by his abusive, alcoholic, and self-destructive father. He, too, was full of impotent rage at his own dead father, and he, too, was a prisoner of his past.

Yet, despite Barack's projective identification with his paternal grandfather, his own father was more important to him than his grandfather. His quest for the ghost of his father had brought him to Africa. He now tried to imagine his father's predicament as a child. He imagined how his nine-year-old father had been abandoned by his own mother, how he began to cry, how he shook off his sister's hand, shouting that he wanted to go back home to his father's house. He imagined that his father had wanted to find a new mother, how he wanted to forget his predicament by gambling, and how he discovered the power of his intelligence (Obama, 1995, p. 428). Once again Barack's fantasies about his father were part reality, part unconscious projection.

Was Barack fearful that the slender emotional line that held him to his father would also snap when he wrote these words? His ability to identify and empathize with his abandoned father was amazing. In his memoir, Barack devoted entire pages to his fantasies about his young father. He imagined his father's panic as a clerk in a British colonial office, when he recalled his abandonment by his mother. He saw in his mind's eye how his father wrote all those letters to the American universities, trying desperately to get admitted to one with a scholarship. He thought that his father had sought to escape his own father's shame (Obama, 1995, p. 428), much as Barack himself sought to escape the shame of his own drunken, wife-abusing, child-abandoning, self-destructive father.

If the 27-year-old Barack wished to escape his father's "island of shame," he also identified with his father, however ambivalently. He imagined his father's joy when the letter of acceptance from the University of Hawai'i had arrived, "when the ship that would take him to America sailed in," and his father's pride in his degree, his expensive scarf, his American wife, his car, his verbal power, his figure, his money, his social skills, and his charm, which gave him such self-confidence that nothing could stop his ambitions. Yet despite all this, his father could not escape his past, as he was still trapped "on his father's island of shame," full of anger, doubt, and defeat, an abandoned child who forever longed for his mother (Obama, 1995, pp. 428–429).

Barack might as well have been talking about himself when he spoke of his father. He, too, could in no way escape his inner struggle with his father's image, no matter how far he went, no matter how many times he would visit his father's grave, no matter how far he outdid his father in every way. Barack, too, was still trapped in his father's "island of shame." He was ashamed of his alcoholic and abusive father, and he sought desperately to fight down and deny this painful feeling. Barack dropped to the ground next to his father's grave, ran his hand across the yellow tiles on top of it, and spoke to his dead father, telling him that there was no shame in his confusion, nor in his grandfather's before him. The only shame was in the silence that their fear had created, the fear of expressing their deepest thoughts and feelings (Obama, 1995, p. 429).

Like a good psychologist, Barack realized that his father's emotional problems had originated in those of his grandfather and that such problems were transmitted from one generation to the next, not through heredity but through the unhealthy father-son relationship. But Barack was writing this memoir in his early thirties, as a baptized Christian, and his faith loomed large in his feelings. He wished his father had told his own father that only through "faith born out of hardship" could all the modern amenities of the Western world be enjoyed and that faith did not depend on one's race or religion but was rather the faith in other people (Obama, 1995, p. 429).

Barack kept talking to his dead father. He thought that it was not his father's narcissism that had destroyed him but "the silence" and the lack of faith that kept him from saying what he felt and made him remain an atheist, bereft of faith, unable to love. If his father had been able to speak his feelings to his own father, he might not have lost his faith. And it was his father's lack of faith that made him cling to his unhappy past and miss out on all the happiness that could have been his had he had faith in others and loyalty to his origins. By abandoning his origins, his family, his loyalty, his faith, and his love, Barak had never been able to become whole (Obama, 1995, p. 429).

Barack was obviously reproaching his dead father for having abandoned him. He intuitively sensed his father's self-destructive narcissism, yet he was unable to express it in words. What he did express was his own pain at being abandoned by his father. He recalled sitting between the graves of his father and his grandfather and weeping for a long time. After that, he calmed down. He realized that he his entire life had sprung from this little Kenyan village, and he felt his father's emotional pain and the struggles of his brothers (Obama, 1995, p. 430).

Barack spent five weeks in Kenya, visiting his paternal family, their ancestral village, his grandfather's country, Nairobi, Kisumu, Kendu Bay, and Alego, and, above all, trying to grasp what kind of man his father had been. From his father's family, especially from his Granny, he again heard all the familiar stories about his father, including his self-destructive conflict with the Kenyan government, his alcoholism, his womanizing, his wife abuse, his road accidents, and his tragic death. But it was not only to find out the truth about his father that Barack had come to Kenya. It was also, like Shakespeare's Hamlet, to liberate himself from his father's ghost.

Sasha Abramsky thinks that in Barack's quest for "his father's legacy," he had found the bitter truth about his self-destructive, wife-abusive, child-abusive, alcoholic father who had died in "humiliating poverty" (2009, p. 81). Indeed, Barack's visits to his father's grave were among the most emotionally painful events in his life, but they also liberated him from the emotional shackles of his inner emotional conflict about his father. They inspired his memoir, *Dreams from My Father*, and they helped him resolve an inner conflict of identity that had troubled him all his life and become calm and settled in his racial and personal identity. While it is true that in the United States mulattoes are considered black, by opting to be black, Barack may have shown his preference for his black father over his white mother.

Before leaving Kenya, Barack and Auma became increasingly "melancholy," as if the Greek tragedy of their family had suddenly dawned on them. Fearing their upcoming loneliness, they decided to visit their youngest half brother, George Hussein Onyango Obama, the son of Barak Obama and his fourth wife, Jael Otieno. This visit brought them even more emotional pain. George, who also carried the name of his paternal grandfather, had been born in 1982, shortly before his father's death. He was now a six-year-old first-grade schoolboy at a Nairobi grade school. Barack's Aunt Zeituni drove him and Auma to the school without George's mother's knowledge, and George's reaction to him reminded Barack of his own reaction to his father when he was 10 years old. George was cold and diffident. Zeituni, Auma, and Barack had not sought Jael's permission before going to visit George, and the schoolmaster therefore asked them to leave. The unhappy scene reminded Barack powerfully of his painful meeting with his father when he was 10 years old, which had evoked fear and discomfort in him. To comfort himself, he imagined that some day, like him, George would look for his origins or his father, that he would come to him, and that he would then tell George their father's story (Obama, 1995, p. 432).

According to most sources, Barak and his fourth wife, Jael, had only one child: George Obama. Two Kenyan journalists, however, claim that they had two other sons, Rajab Obama and Hussein Obama, who are therefore also Barack's half brothers. Rajab has a college education and lives in one of Nairobi's better neighborhoods. These journalists have also discovered Barack's half niece, a girl named Mwanaisha (Ogosia & Mugwang'a, 2008). The Tanzanian capital of Dar-es-Salaam has a tailoring business named Obama Group, one of whose members is named Mwanaisha Hainad. Could she be Barack's half niece? Barack mentioned a Samson Otieno, though not as his relative, yet there is also a Reverend Samson Otieno in his Kenyan family (Obama, 1995, p. 304; *Saturday Nation* Correspondents, 2008). Is he related to Jael?

After the death of Barack's father, Barak, his widow Jael had married a French aid worker, who adopted her children and became their stepfather for about 10 years. George lived in South Korea for two years, while his French stepfather worked there and his mother resided there with her husband. According to the British journalist Michael Pflanz, the couple divorced, and, after returning to Kenya, George "slept rough for several years," until his aunt gave him a six-by-eight-foot corrugated metal shack in the Nairobi slum of Huruma Flats (Pflanz, 2008). After she divorced, Jael moved to the United States and settled in Atlanta, Georgia, keeping a low profile while sending money to her family in Kenya. The Kenyan journalists thought that her son Hussein Obama was quiet and spoke softly but that as he moved, from a distance, he resembled his half brother Barack (Ogosia & Mugwang'a, 2008).

Apparently, George rarely discusses his world-famous half brother. In 2008 George attended part-time vocational training in Buruburu, a large middle-class residential area in the Eastlands neighborhood of Nairobi, in the Makadara Division, near where he lived (Ogosia & Mugwang'a, 2008). George received little attention from the U.S. mass-communication media until an article in the Italian edition of *Vanity Fair* in August 2008 depicted him as living in poverty, shame, and obscurity in a Nairobi slum. George then spent much of his time angrily denying false reports that he had been abandoned by his famous half brother Barack.

Nonetheless, George's alleged poverty was seized on by Barack's archconservative enemies. The right-wing American columnist Dinesh D'Souza publicly solicited donations for George from his readers, while Jerome Corsi, the author of an anti-Obama book, publicly planned to give George a $1,000 check during his trip to Kenya. Their intention, of course, was to shame Barack for not helping his poor half brother. In 2008 Corsi and his young media consultant Tim Bueler were detained by the Kenyan immigration authorities while doing further research related to Corsi's book and were charged with lacking a work permit.

Corsi had scheduled a press conference in Nairobi to announce his research proving that, as a U.S. senator, Barack had raised a million dollars for the election campaign of the Kenyan Luo prime minister Raila Odinga and that Barack had helped run Odinga's campaign as a strategist, a tribal campaign against the Kikuyu that provoked the murderous violence and bloodshed by the Luo against the Kikuyu that had brought Odinga to power after a disputed election. However, the press conference was interrupted by Kenyan immigration officials, who detained Corsi for working in Kenya without a work permit. Corsi was later expelled from Kenya by its authorities. Corsi is only one of several anti-Obama "biographers" and hatemongers (Corsi, 2008; Freddoso, 2008; Goldberg, 2009; Malkin, 2009; Tarpley 2008a, 2008b).

After his half brother Barack became president of the United States, the 27-year-old George wrote a memoir with the help of the professional writer Damien Lewis (Obama, 2010). In this memoir, he related how he had found an identification model in his elder half brother Barack. The two met in 1988 during Barack's first visit to Kenya and again in 2006 when U.S. Senator Barack Obama returned to Nairobi. Like Barack, George had lost his father when he was baby, but in his case their father died, whereas Barry had seen his father at age 10.

George had also lost his stepfather when he and his mother, Jael, separated in 1997. George was 15 at that time. He was sent to a boarding school, where he did quite well at first, but after his parents' separation the adolescent George became angry and rebellious, dropped out of school, abused alcohol and drugs, and became a juvenile delinquent in the Nairobi slum of Huruma Flats. The young George and three of his friends were arrested by Nairobi's corrupt police, and he spent nine months in an infernal Nairobi prison for a crime he may never have committed. However, he refused legal representation and successfully represented himself and his friends at their trial. They were acquitted. George was free again.

After this harrowing experience, the young George underwent an identity crisis and had a change of heart. He transformed himself into a community organizer and activist like his elder half brother, whom he emulated, helping poor slum youth. When he met his 45-year-old half brother Barack in 2006, the 24-year-old George was greatly impressed by him; he claims that he knew Barack would run for the presidency of the United States. George very much wanted to become like Barack. In fact, he saw himself as Barack's Kenyan colleague. George has created a community group in his Nairobi slum to help its poor people. As his half brother has become the leader of the most powerful country in the world, so George wishes to lead the poorest people on the face of this earth.

Barack also met his dead father's old friend Dr. Rukia Odero, a female Kenyan historian. She told him and Auma how complicated African history and culture were and that nothing African was purely so, because elements of non-African cultures were absorbed by the local culture under colonial rule. Odero said that many U.S. blacks were disappointed in Africa because nothing African was really fully authentic. African Americans came to Africa searching for its authentic character, only to be disappointed (Obama, 1995, pp. 432–433). Similarly, Africans who wanted to study in America, like Barack's father, found that their education did not serve them very well. Odero thought that colonial rule had clouded Africans' view of their past and that it was up to her and her colleagues to clarify it. She said that Africans had to choose which of their customs—polygamy, female circumcision, collective land ownership, tribal loyalties, superstitions—they wished to preserve and which to modify or discard (Obama, pp. 433–434).

THE TURNING POINT: BARACK BECOMES A CHRISTIAN

Barack Obama returned to the United States in the summer of 1988 after a mighty inner struggle with his father's ghost in Kenya. Interestingly enough, he did not state the date of his baptism, saying only that it happened "one day" (Obama, 2006a, p. 246). While some journalists think that it happened "in the early 1990s" (Miller & Wolffe, 2008), after he had met his future wife Michelle, Jodi Kantor (2007a) believes that it happened earlier, after his return from Kenya in 1988. This point in time would fit with his memoir and with his other writings and statements and, as we shall see, would also make psychological sense.

Although he had been a lifelong secular agnostic or atheist, filled with doubt about religion and God (Obama, 1995, pp. 286–287), Jodi Kantor believes that it was before leaving Chicago for Harvard in 1988 that the 27-year-old Barack Hussein Obama had himself baptized a Christian by his new "father," Reverend Jeremiah Wright, Jr., the pastor of Trinity United Church of Christ in Chicago's South Side, who preached racist, antiwhite, anti-American, black-liberation sermons (Obama, 2006a, p. 246; see also

Kantor, 2007a). This was obviously a momentous event in Barack's life, yet, curiously, he made no mention of it in his memoir. Twenty years later the "good father" Wright damaged Obama's presidential campaign when his black-racist, antiwhite, and anti-American sermons came to light.

Like many other facts about Barack's life, his baptism and his Christianity, too, have been called into question by his rivals, opponents, critics, haters, and enemies. Some think that it was after his return from Kenya in 1988 that Barack was baptized a Christian by Wright (Kantor, 2007a). Barack himself wrote that after much soul-searching and new insights he "was finally able to walk down the aisle of Trinity one day and be baptized" (Obama, 2006a, p. 246). Was it an accident that he failed to mention the date of his baptism? Did he not wish to conceal its intimate emotional connection with his struggle with his father's ghost in Kenya? The conversion gave Barack a new family. Even though he was embracing his mother's spirituality, it was God the Father that he was seeking: "I felt God's spirit beckoning me. I submitted myself to His will, and dedicated myself to discovering His truth" (Obama, p. 246). Was Barack identifying with Jesus Christ, the fatherless Son of God?

It was thus no accident that Barack's baptism followed his visit to his father's grave in Kenya. By becoming a Christian, he was embracing his mother's ideas and feelings, but he was also adopting two new "fathers" in the Reverend Wright and in God the Father. The life-and-death struggle of Jesus with his father in the New Testament over drinking the bitter cup of God's wrath (Matthew 36:29) may have echoed Barack's own struggle with his father. In any event, this was a momentous event and a major turning point for the skeptical and atheist Obama. His quarrels with God may have been an unconscious displacement of his inner quarrels with his father. Later, Reverend Wright performed Barack's marriage ceremony in 1992 and baptized Barack's two daughters in 1998 and 2001. Later still, in 2008, Barack broke with Reverend Wright, who had embarrassed him and failed him as a good father.

The Chicago organization that Barack had been running, the Developing Communities Project, was initially based on Catholic churches, and many of the black people whom the young Barack was organizing in Chicago's South Side were Christian believers and churchgoers. They were not all Catholic, however: many of them were Baptists. The Baptist United Church of Christ had been formed in 1957 by the merger of the Congregational Christian churches and the Evangelical and Reformed Church. Chicago's Trinity United Church of Christ was a member of this Baptist denomination and organization.

The Reverend Wright's sermon "The Audacity to Hope" seems to have turned Barack from a religious skeptic into an enthusiastic Christian

(Kantor, 2007a). Wright was an idealized father figure for the young Barack. Like Joe Biden, Barack's vice president, he was old enough to be Barack's father. Wright was fiery and charismatic, and he easily swayed young people. He was black, and he loved Africa. Barack remained a member of Wright's church for 20 years. He was married there, and he had his two daughters baptized there by Wright. As a British weekly put it, "Trinity's Afrocentric bent, with its African visitors and women dressed in African robes, may have particularly appealed to the son of an African" (The Economist, 2008). But, unlike the racist, antiwhite Wright, Barack was an antiracist, postracial, and color-blind politician, opposing racial stereotypes, whereas Wright remained thoroughly racial, if not racist, hating white America for what it did to black people. In 2008, when Wright damaged Obama's presidential campaign when his "God Damn America" speech came to light, Obama had the wisdom and strength to repudiate his "bad father" and to resign from his church.

Barack has been compared—and has at times compared himself—to great Americans like Abraham Lincoln, Franklin D. Roosevelt, John F. Kennedy, and Dr. Martin Luther King, Jr. A now-well-known story about Roosevelt came to light on November 5, 2008, the day after Obama's presidential-election victory, when the black American singer Harry Belafonte was interviewed by the black American interviewer Tavis Smiley on the U.S. Public Broadcasting System television network about his reactions to that victory. Among other things, Belafonte recalled Roosevelt's wife, Eleanor Roosevelt, telling him that when she had introduced her husband to the black labor leader A. Philip Randolph, Roosevelt asked Randolph what he thought of the American nation, the plight of the Negro people, and where the nation was headed. Randolph eloquently told Roosevelt his ideas about what the president could do for the American Negroes. According to Eleanor, Roosevelt replied, "You know, Mr. Randolph, I've heard everything you've said tonight, and I couldn't agree with you more. I agree with everything that you've said, including my capacity to be able to right many of these wrongs and to use my power and the bully pulpit ... But I would ask one thing of you, Mr. Randolph, and that is, go out and make me do it" (Belafonte & Smiley, 2008).

Smiley's colleague, the American reporter Amy Goodman, who hosts the Public Broadcasting System radio show *Democracy Now*, told a meeting of journalists in Los Angeles on April 25, 2009, that Barack had echoed Roosevelt's "make me do it" reply at a Montclair, New Jersey, fund-raiser during his presidential campaign the year before. When a supporter asked him whether he could "carve a peace in the Middle East," Obama told the Roosevelt-Randolph story and said, "Make me do it" (Abramsky, 2009, pp. 73, 261n16; Goodman, 2009).

One problem with Goodman's story, however, is that Belafonte's "Make me do it" story about Roosevelt and Randolph came to light in Belafonte's interview only the day after Barack's campaign had ended. How could Barack have known of Roosevelt's classic line several months earlier? Abramsky thinks that "Obama has the ambition to change the world; but he knows, from everything he has studied of the past, that a president succeeds in bringing about transformations when his supporters keep up their pressure for change rather than sitting back quiescently and waiting for him to do it alone" (2009, p. 73).

The comparison of Barack to John F. Kennedy is intriguing. Theodore Chaikin Sorensen (born 1928), Kennedy's legendary speechwriter, wrote that "Kennedy liked to embellish his speeches with quotations from the widest possible variety of sources: Hemingway, Shaw, Aristotle, Socrates, Pericles, Demosthenes, Solon and Pindar" (2008, p. 140). Sorensen probably meant this as a tongue-in-cheek statement: he knew quite well that it was he who embellished Kennedy's speeches with those famous quotations. Barack, too, has his speechwriter, Jonathan Favreau, who plays Sorensen to Barack's Kennedy.

Indeed, like Kennedy, Barack appointed highly talented, well-educated, ambitious young people as his presidential-campaign advisers and later some of them to his White House staff. One of them is Samantha Power (born 1970), an Irish-born American journalist, writer, and scholar. In 2007 Barack named Power—who writes articles for *Time* magazine and had won the Pulitzer Prize for journalism—a senior foreign-policy adviser to his campaign. In March 2008, however, Power slipped up: in an off-the-record conversation with a Scottish reporter, she referred to Barack's rival Hillary Clinton as a "monster." Sensing a sensation, the reporter promptly published her epithet (Peev, 2008). The public firestorm sparked by the publication of Power's vicious attack on Clinton forced Barack to ask Power to resign from his campaign. Nonetheless, in November 2008, after his election as president of the United States, Obama invited Power to join his state department transition team. In January 2009, after naming Clinton his Secretary of State, Obama named Power the senior director for multilateral affairs on his National Security Council. At the same time, Power is also the Anna Lindh Professor of Practice of Global Leadership and Public Policy at the Carr Center for Human Rights Policy at Harvard University's Kennedy School of Government.

Jonathan Favreau (born 1981) is another example of Barack's brilliant appointments of bright young people to his staff. The Catholic Favreau was born in Massachusetts. From 1991 to 2003 he attended the College of the Holy Cross in Worcester, from which he graduated as his class valedictorian with a bachelor's degree in political science. He was the treasurer and debate-committee chairman for the College Democrats, studied classical piano, and directed the Welfare Solidarity Project. Favreau worked with Habitat for Humanity and with a University of Massachusetts program to bring visitors to cancer patients. He was the head of an initiative to help unemployed individuals improve their resumes and interview skills.

Favreau earned many honors in college, including the Primo Vannicelli Award, the Charles A. Dana Scholarship, a Harry S. Truman Scholarship, and memberships in the Political Science Honor Society, Alpha Kappa Delta, the College Honors Program, the Sociology Honor Society, and Pi Sigma Alpha. He was an editor of the college newspaper, and during the summers he earned his living selling newspapers as a telemarketer, while also interning in John Kerry's offices. It may be no accident that Barack hires people who are bright, young, well educated, ambitious, and talented like himself: they are a narcissistic mirror to him. His high-level narcissism is such that he gets his narcissistic pleasure from being around people who are on his own level.

Like Kennedy, too, Barack likes to embellish his speeches with famous quotations and title them after famous sermons or historical events. It was none other than Sorensen who recommended his talented young disciple Adam Frankel, a graduate of Princeton University, to Barack as his speechwriter. Barack appointed Frankel his second senior speechwriter, under Favreau. A president in his forties, surrounded by many young Ivy League–educated aides and advisers, Barack evokes memories of the youthful Kennedy (Abramsky, 2009, pp. 65–66).

Barack's prolonged struggle for his own identity had led him to a post-racial position, in which he would not let the issue of race divide his people. He himself is an African American. While some African Americans may not accept Barack as "black like me," to him, racial politics are a thing of the past. At the same time, he is himself a mixture of black and white, with a touch of foreignness about him—Kenya, Indonesia, and his numerous half siblings in many countries. The black American leader Andrew Young (2009) has said that Barack "isn't just black; he's an Afro-Asian-Latin European" [sic]. Foreignness and the fighting stance contribute to a leader's charisma. This charisma, which depends on our early-life perceptions of our mother's body during the separation-individuation phase (Schiffer, 1973, pp. 25–26, 58–60), may explain his great success and attraction.

Barack's father had studied economics at Harvard. In the fall of 1988, after his return from Kenya and after being baptized into Christianity in Chicago, Barack himself followed his dead father to Harvard. He attended Harvard Law School for three years (1988–1991). When he read the monumental trilogy about America in the years of Martin Luther King, Jr., by the white American historian Taylor Branch (born 1947), Barack felt it was his own story (Branch, 1988–2006; Niven, 2009, p. 13).

During his first year at Harvard Law School, Barack worked as an editor of the *Harvard Civil Rights-Civil Liberties Law Review,* America's leading progressive law journal. He impressed the law school faculty with his maturity and with his common sense as well as with the breadth of his knowledge. One of the teachers he impressed most was Laurence Henry Tribe (born 1941), a liberal professor of constitutional law and the Carl M. Loeb University Professor at Harvard. Tribe, who was Harvard Law School's preeminent expert on constitutional law, has described Barack as one of the most talented students he has ever taught, and he made him his research assistant on one of his *Harvard Law Review* articles (Niven, 2009, p. 16; Tribe, 1989). It was Tribe who recommended Barack to Senator John Kerry to deliver the keynote address at the Democratic National Convention in 2004.

Chapter 13

MICHELLE: MENTOR, LOVER, WIFE, AND MOTHER

Synopsis: *Michelle LaVaughn Robinson was born in early 1964 and was Barack Obama's junior by two and a half years. But emotionally and professionally she was his senior, as she was assigned to mentor him when he was still a law student and she was already a lawyer. Both of them were devoted to public-interest law and the defense of black people, and they fell in love with one another as each of them was an ideal mate for the other. Michelle was the descendant of black African slaves and therefore had full black credentials. She was publicly and politically active in Chicago's black community. She became Barack's lover and later, in 1992, his wife, after his grandfather, "Gramps," had died and Barack's mother got her Ph.D. in anthropology. A few years later Michelle became the mother of their first child, Malia Ann, and then of their second child, Natasha (Sasha). Michelle has fulfilled many different psychological roles in Barack's life and in some ways has been a mother to him, comforting him in his hours of distress. When her father died in 1991, Barack was in some ways a father to her too. Their relationship seems to be a very happy one, and their daughters, too, seem happy and well balanced.*

African Americans often trace their roots to black African slaves. Families are not trees, yet people think and speak of themselves as having roots in the places and times of their birth and of their parents and ancestors as being rooted or uprooted. During the late 1970s, Americans began to trace their roots back to Europe, Africa, Asia, or wherever their ancestors had come from. This was due, among other things, to the U.S. television series

Roots, which was based on the book *Roots: The Saga of an American Family* by Alex Haley (1921–1992), a black American writer who had successfully discovered the names and life histories of his African ancestors. *Roots* won many prestigious awards. It received unprecedented ratings by viewers, and its final episode was the third-highest-rated U.S. television program ever. *Roots* appealed to Americans of all ethnic groups. Not only black Americans but also many others began to search for their family histories.

The American Jewish journalist David Remnick (born 1958) discussed the generational issue in African American politics, calling Barack's generation "the Joshua generation." The young black leaders were to the preceding generation as the biblical Joshua was to Moses: they were the psychological sons and disciples of the leaders of the civil rights movement of the 1960s, such as Martin Luther King, Jr. (1929–1968), Andrew Jackson Young (born 1932), and Jesse Louis Jackson (born 1941). Barack and his fellow young black leaders had high expectations and fierce ambitions but also felt that they owed a great debt to their psychological "fathers" (Abramsky, 2009, p. 60; Remnick, 2008). Barack may have unconsciously transferred his ambivalent feelings about his own father to the political leaders who might have been his father.

Michelle was born in early 1964 and was a teenager when *Roots* was first broadcast in 1977. She had been born in Chicago's South Side to Fraser Robinson III (1935–1991), a city-water-plant employee and a Democratic Party precinct captain, and his wife, Marian Shields Robinson (born 1937), a secretary at Spiegel's catalog store, a leading direct-marketing company. Michelle's mother had taken good care of her, staying at home until Michelle entered high school. The Robinson family traced its roots to African slaves in the South before they were freed by the American Civil War (1861–1865).

In 2009 the American genealogist Megan Smolenyak discovered that Michelle Robinson Obama's mother, Marian Shields Robinson, was the great-great-granddaughter of Melvinia Shields, a Negro slave girl who had been raped by a white man (Smolenyak, 2010). Melvinia was born around 1844. Her South Carolina owner, David Patterson, died in 1852, and Melvinia was then sent to Mr. Patterson's daughter Christianne and her husband, Henry Shields, who lived in Georgia. The slave girl Melvinia was raped by a white man when she was 14 or 15. When her first son, Dolphus, was born around 1860, his mother gave him—and herself—the last name of her owners, Shields (Dolphus died in 1950). By 1870 Melvinia had had four children. Dolphus was the great-grandfather of Marian Shields Robinson (Smolenyak, 2010; Swarns & Kantor, 2009).

Michelle's ancestor Dolphus Shields was light-skinned. He moved his family to Birmingham, Alabama, and was very active in his community.

He cofounded the First Ebenezer Baptist Church and Trinity Baptist Church, which later became active in the civil rights movement, and he supervised Sunday schools at both churches (both of which still exist) and at Regular Missionary Baptist Church. Dolphus's wife, Alice Easley Shields, was Marian Shields Robinson's great-grandmother. Dolphus and Alice's son, Robert Lee Shields, was Marian's paternal grandfather. In 1906 Robert Lee married Annie Lawson, but he disappeared from the public records in 1932. Robert had a son named Pernell Shields, who moved to Chicago with his mother. Pernell was Marian's father (Smolenyak, 2010; Swarns & Kantor, 2009).

Smolenyak's discovery that Michelle Obama was the great-great-great-granddaughter of a black teenage slave girl who had been raped by a white man caused quite a stir in the U.S. mass-communication media. Whether or not Michelle was aware of this story, however, is not clear. While her maternal ancestor was a white rapist, Michelle's paternal ancestor, Jim Robinson, was a slave in South Carolina, where some of her family still reside. Some of the Robinsons had moved to Chicago as part of the great "Negro" migration from the South to the North after the Civil War. Michelle herself grew up in the South Shore area of Chicago and was raised in what she herself described as a conventional home, in which the father worked, the mother took care of the children at home, and the family had dinner together around the table in the evening (Bennetts, 2007).

During Michelle's childhood, the close-knit Robinson family kept together by playing games and by reading (Newton-Small, 2008). Michelle and her elder brother Craig (born 1962) were very bright: both skipped the second grade. By sixth grade, Michelle had joined a gifted-student class at the Bryn Mawr Elementary School, later renamed the Bouchet Academy (Ross, 2008). From 1977 on, the year of the first screening of *Roots*, she attended the Whitney Young High School in Chicago's Near West Side, Chicago's first magnet high school (a public school with specialized courses or curricula). Michelle did very well. She won many honors in school and was an outstanding student, (Bennetts, 2007; Bodden, 2010; Brill, 2009b; P. Brown, 2009b; Hudson, 2010; Weatherford, 2010b).

The round trip from Michelle's South Side home to her Near West Side high school took three hours every day. She was a classmate of Santita Jackson, a daughter of the Reverend Jesse Louis Jackson (born 1941), the black American civil rights activist and Baptist minister with long-lasting presidential aspirations. Michelle graduated from Whitney Young High School in 1981, when she was 17, as its class salutatorian—the second-highest honor in the graduating class, second only to the class valedictorian. These terms, like those of the Capitol and the Senate, are borrowed from the ancient Roman Empire, to which the United States often likes to compare itself (Bennetts, 2007; Bodden, 2010; Brill, 2009b; P. Brown, 2009b; Hudson, 2010; Weatherford, 2010b).

In 1981 Michelle went on to study sociology and African American studies at Princeton University, where she graduated cum laude with a bachelor of arts in 1985. Michelle followed her brother Craig to Princeton because he had shown her that it was possible for a black boy from Chicago's South Side to do this. He had enrolled in 1979 and graduated in 1983. At Princeton, Michelle challenged her French-language teachers on their teaching methods because she felt that they should have been more conversational. As part of her requirements for graduation, she wrote a thesis entitled, "Princeton-Educated Blacks and the Black Community" (Bennetts, 2007; Bodden, 2010; Brill, 2009b; P. Brown, 2009b; Hudson, 2010; Johnson, 2007; Ressner, 2008; Robinson, 1985; Weatherford, 2010b).

In 1985, the year Barack went to Chicago, Michelle was admitted to Harvard Law School. She obtained her J.D. degree in 1988, the same year Barack left Chicago to go to the same law school. Michelle thus preceded Barack by three years at the law school. She had not yet met Barack. While at Harvard, she took part in protests and demonstrations advocating the hiring of professors who were members of minorities, including those instigated by the African American law professor Derrick A. Bell, Jr. (born 1930). After Hillary Rodham Clinton and Laura Bush, Michelle Obama is the third U.S. first lady with a graduate-school degree (Connolly, 2008). Michelle is also a member of the black sorority Alpha Kappa Alpha, which had no active undergraduate chapter at Princeton when she attended that Ivy League school (Bogues, 2008).

Michelle was admitted to the Illinois Bar in May 1989. Barack and Michelle met for the first time that summer at the Chicago law firm of Sidley Austin. She was a civil rights lawyer there, he was a summer associate, and she was assigned to mentor him. Their relationship began with a business lunch and a community-organization meeting, where Barack impressed her, and quickly developed into a sexual and love courtship. The couple's first date was to see the Spike Lee movie *Do the Right Thing* in a movie theater. The courtship was a bit long: they became engaged in 1991 and did not marry until 1992, after Barack's grandfather had died and after his mother had received her PhD degree.

Barack said little about his courtship of Michelle in his memoir. He did write, though, that Michelle did not quite understand him, that she worried, like his father and his maternal grandfather, that he was a dreamer, and that her practicality and her Midwestern attitudes reminded him of his maternal grandmother, "Toot." When Barack first took Michelle to Hawai'i to meet his maternal grandparents, his grandfather, Gramps, told him that Michelle was very pretty, while his grandmother Toot found Michelle "very sensible," her highest form of praise (Obama, 1995, p. 439). He and Michelle now have two daughters, Malia Ann (born 1998) and Natasha, better known as Sasha (born 2001). After Barack's election to the U.S. Senate in 2004, the Obamas continued to live on Chicago's South Side, choosing to remain there rather than move to Washington, so as not to uproot their daughters from their schools and friends.

Throughout her husband's campaign for president of the United States, Michelle made a "commitment to be away [from her daughters] overnight only once a week—to campaign only two days a week and be home by the end of the second day" (Piasecki, 2008). The fact that Barack played basketball, which was his unconscious emotional tie to his father, made it easy for him to have a close friendship with Michelle's elder brother, Craig Robinson, a professional basketball player and men's basketball coach at Oregon State University. Michelle is also related to Rabbi Capers C. Funnye, Jr. (born 1952), one of the most prominent black rabbis in the United States, who heads a well-known black Jewish congregation in Chicago.

Why did Barack and Michelle not have children during the first five years of their marriage? Barack himself, in an open letter to his daughters published just two days before his inauguration as president of the United States, wrote that before they were born he had "thought that life was all about me—how I'd make my way in the world, become successful, and get the things I wanted" (Obama, 2009e). But, in view of his profound ambivalence about his own father, could his delayed parenthood also have been due to an initial ambivalence about being a father?

Barack and Michelle's first daughter was born on U.S. Independence Day, July 4, 1998. Her parents had been married for just under six years. They named her Malia Ann, her middle name being that of Barack's mother. Their second daughter, Natasha, whom they nicknamed Sasha, was born on August 10, 2001, six days after her father's 40th birthday. The Obama family seems well knit and happy, almost always smiling, at least in public photographs. It is a very different family from the unhappy ones that Barack's mother had created with her two husbands. Here, too, Barack was able to avoid his father's and his mother's errors and to give himself that loving family that he so badly missed as a child. He could repair the damage done to himself.

At the end of his first year at Harvard Law School, in 1989, Barack was made an editor of the prestigious *Harvard Law Review*. That summer he went back to Chicago as a summer associate at Newton Minow's law firm, Sidley Austin, where he met Michelle. At the age of 28 he was already showing enormous intellectual and emotional capabilities, let alone his public and political ones. In his senior year, 1990–1991, he was appointed the first

African American president of the *Harvard Law Review*. This was an extraordinary achievement. While the pioneering female black lawyer Clara Burrill Bruce (1882–1947) had presided over the *Boston University Law Review* in 1925, no black person had ever presided over the prestigious *Harvard Law Review*. Barack successfully used his impressive intellectual and emotional skills to mediate and resolve disputes among the fractious staff of the *Harvard Law Review* (Niven, 2009, p. 17).

The young law student Barack saw the law as an obsessive profession that applied rigid rules, regulations, and procedures to a disorganized world that did not conform to its conception of it. Yet the law was also the written record of the American nation's centuries-long argument with its own conscience (Obama, 1995, p. 437). Becoming a lawyer was another step in his road to becoming a politician, in being better able to help his African American brethren. Every summer from 1989 to 1991 he left Harvard for Chicago to work as a summer associate in a law firm and resume his connections with his African American community in this "black metropolis" (Drake & Cayton, 1945). He was still hoping to become Chicago's mayor, but his political career would take him first to the Illinois senate, then to the U.S. Senate, and finally to the White House.

According to the records of the Illinois Supreme Court's Attorney Registration and Disciplinary Commission, he passed his Illinois Bar examination and received his license to practice law in late 1991, retiring voluntarily in 2008. But his academic and professional achievements, and his civil rights and community work, however important to Barack, were not as important emotionally as meeting his future wife Michelle in 1989 and their marriage in 1992, which gave him the happy, well-knit family that he had never had and always yearned for.

Barack first met his future wife Michelle, herself a Harvard Law School graduate, in 1988, when he was working as a summer associate at the Chicago law firm of Sidley Austin. This was one of the oldest law firms in the world, the sixth-largest U.S.-based corporate law firm, with a staff of over 1,800 lawyers, annual revenues of over $1 billion, and offices in 16 cities worldwide. Michelle was assigned to mentor Barack, and she taught him patience, among other things, which was vital to his career (Obama, 1995, p. 439).

Barack introduced Michelle to his white mother, Ann, and to his grandparents, Gramps and Toot, in Hawai'i, who loved Michelle. They became engaged in 1991, and in 1992, on their trip to Kenya, he introduced her to his black family, who liked her as much as his white family in the United States did. He married Michelle in October 1992, the year of his grandfather's death and of his mother's getting her Ph.D. degree. They later had their daughters, Malia Ann and Natasha (Sasha).

The year before their wedding brought several losses to Barack and Michelle. Barack's cousin Billy, the son of Salina, whom he had met in Kenya in 1988, had contracted AIDS and died of it in 1991 (Obama, 1995, pp. 439–440). Then Barack's fiancée Michelle lost her father, Fraser Robinson III, whom Barack called "as good and decent a man as I've ever known" (Obama, p. 440). In early 1992, Barack himself lost his maternal grandfather, Gramps, who had become a shadow of himself years before. "Gramps" died on February 8, 1992, at the age of 73 and was buried at Punchbowl National Cemetery, on a hill overlooking Honolulu. Despite having to mourn their losses, Barack and Michelle decided to get married later that year. However, during their prenuptial trip to Kenya in 1992, Michelle learned some unpleasant truths about Africa:

> As an African American, Michelle was bursting with excitement about the idea of visiting the continent of her ancestors, and we had a wonderful time … But during our travels Michelle also heard—as I had heard during my first trip to Africa—the terrible sense on the part of most Kenyans that their fates were not their own. My cousins told her how difficult it was to find a job or start their own businesses without paying bribes. Activists told us about being jailed for expressing their opposition to government policies. Even within my own family, Michelle saw how suffocating the demands of family ties and tribal loyalties could be, with distant cousins constantly asking for favors, uncles and aunts showing up unannounced. On the flight back home to Chicago, Michelle admitted she was looking forward to getting home. "I never realized just how American I was," she said. She hadn't realized just how free she was—or how much she cherished that freedom. (Obama, 2006a, pp. 65–66)

Barack's election in 1990 as the first black president of the *Harvard Law Review* was a major academic and political event, not only in his own life but also nationally in the United States, and it was widely reported and followed by several long and detailed mass-communication-media profiles. He was suddenly catapulted into national prominence.

At about that time, the African American legal scholar Derrick A. Bell, Jr., who had organized antiracist protests at Harvard during Michelle's time as a law student, became the center of a racial drama at Harvard Law School when he temporarily resigned his professorship at the school. In 1980 Bell had become the dean of the University of Oregon Law School, the first African American to head a nonblack law school. He resigned from that university later, however, over a dispute about the faculty's racial diversity. Bell then taught law at Stanford University in California for a year and finally returned to Harvard Law School in 1986 as the tenured professor that he had been.

Back at Harvard Law School, Bell had staged a five-day sit-in inside his office to protest the school's failure to grant tenure to two legal scholars on the school staff, both of whom adhered to Bell's legal, political, and social ideology, namely that U.S. legal institutions helped maintain the dominance of the ruling class in society. The Harvard Law School administration claimed substandard scholarship and teaching on the part of the professors as the reason for its denial of tenure to them. The battle lines were drawn. Bell called the law school's refusal of tenure to his black colleagues an attack on their ideology. His sit-in mobilized black-student support but sharply divided the law school faculty (Bell, 1994; Niven, 2009, p. 17).

In 1990 Derrick Bell reentered the debate over hiring practices at Harvard Law School when he took an indefinite unpaid leave of absence from his tenured job until the school appointed a black female professor to its tenured faculty. At that time, of Harvard Law School's 60 tenured professors, 3 were black men and 5 were white women. None was a black woman. The school had never had a black woman on its tenured staff. The students held vigils and protests in solidarity with Bell, with the support of some of the faculty. Barack spoke up in favor of Bell, yet he was also accepted as an honest broker between the warring factions at the law school (Niven, 2009, p. 17). Bell's critics, including some of his colleagues, called his methods counterproductive, and Harvard officials insisted they had made enormous inroads in minority hiring. Four years later Bell published his view of the drama (Bell, 1994).

In the summer of 1990 Barack returned to Chicago again, this time as a summer associate at the law firm of Hopkins & Sutter, and, of course, to be with his beloved Michelle, who was still employed by the law firm of Sidley Austin. Hopkins & Sutter was an old Chicago law firm that would later merge with the Milwaukee law firm of Foley & Lardner. It had been founded in 1921 by Albert Hopkins and Harry Sutter. Hopkins had worked for two years at the Interstate Commerce Commission and for one year with the U.S. Bureau of Internal Revenue, the predecessor of the U.S. Internal Revenue Service, while Sutter was a tax counsel to the Guaranty Trust Company of New York. In 1923, the firm had opened an office in Washington, D.C. Hopkins & Sutter also operated an office in Detroit, Michigan. The firm was known for its expertise in tax, insurance, public policy, and transportation-finance work but not civil liberties law. Barack and Michelle were now on an almost-equal footing, as she was no longer his mentor, although she was a licensed lawyer and he was still a law student. In any event, they cemented their relationship. They would become engaged the following year.

In 1991 Barack graduated from Harvard Law School with a J.D. degree *magna cum laude,* outdoing both his father, who had obtained only a master's degree from Harvard (even though he had falsely represented himself as "Dr. Obama" in Kenya), and Michelle, who had not graduated with this distinction. Was it an oedipal victory over his father and a proof of his superiority to Michelle? In any event, the common career step for former editors of Ivy League law reviews was to clerk for a federal judge. Barack received several offers for such a clerkship, but he turned them all down. Instead, in the summer of 1991 Barack returned again to Chicago, where he had been a summer associate in the law firms of Sidley Austin and Hopkins & Sutter, and to his beloved Michelle. In August 1991 he turned 30 years old. It was time to plan his marriage to Michelle. Indeed, that year they became engaged to be married. On December 17, 1991, Dr. Barack Obama was admitted to the Illinois Bar, having passed his bar examination. Now both he and Michelle were licensed lawyers, on an equal footing professionally.

In 1991 and 1992 the new lawyer Barack worked for the Chicago office of Project Vote, also known as Voting for America, Inc., a nonpartisan, nonprofit, voter-registration organization that had been founded in 1982 by Sandy Newman, an American lawyer and civil rights activist. Newman later praised Barack highly, saying that he had done "one hell of a job" (Reynolds, 1993). Project Vote's great efforts to engage low-income and minority voters in the American political process included providing training, management, evaluation, and technical services to new voters. Project Vote succeeded in registering countless new voters.

In 1992 Barack organized the voter-registration efforts for the Democratic presidential candidate, Bill Clinton, another self-made man, who won the election (Gartner, 2008). Barack's was one of Project Vote's most successful voter-registration drives. Over 150,000 new African American voters were added to Chicago's rolls during this drive (Reynolds, 1993). Barack not only helped get Clinton elected president but also helped elect Carol Elizabeth Moseley Braun (born 1947) as a U.S. senator—the first black woman and first black Democrat ever elected to the U.S. Senate (Niven, 2009, p. 17). In 2004 Barack himself would take her seat in the same body.

Chapter 14

MARRIAGE: THE NEW FAMILY

Synopsis: *Barack Hussein Obama had come from a broken family, and he had lost his biological father at age 2 and his stepfather at age 10. Throughout his young life he was unconsciously looking for a good family to replace his bad one. For some time his maternal grandparents provided the parenting he needed, but the decline of his grandfather, "Gramps," in his later years made the search for a good father more pressing. The communities to which Barack belonged—the Punahou School in Hawai'i, Occidental College in Los Angeles, Columbia University in New York, the companies he worked for, Harvard University Law School and, above all, the black community of Chicago—were all substitute families. But Barack also needed to outdo his father and to create his own family. By marrying Michelle in 1992, on the 10th anniversary of his father's death, he created a good family to replace the bad one he had grown up in. He outdid his father in every way, not only with his JD degree, but also by never abandoning his children or his wife, being a good father to them. When he was forced to spend days away from them as a U.S. senator, he called home very frequently, missing his wife and children badly. By becoming president he could move his whole family with him into the White House. Barack's family is everything that his father's family was not.*

On October 3, 1992, Barack married Michelle in the sanctuary of Trinity United Church of Christ, in Southeast Chicago. The wedding was performed by the Reverend Jeremiah Wright, Jr., who had baptized Barack four years earlier. The wedding was a very happy event. It brought together the many members of Barack's Kenyan and American families, along with his former classmates from Hawai'i's Punahou School, Los Angeles's Occidental College, New York's Columbia University and Harvard Law School, his Chicago aides and associates, and his legal colleagues, all of whom were in good spirits (Obama, 1995, p. 440).

Barack was worried for a moment during his wedding ceremony when he saw his "wild" Kenyan half brothers and cousins make passes at his Indonesian half sister, Maya, fearing that they would embarrass and upset her. Maya handled herself quite gracefully, however, and Barack thought that his kid sister looked like a beautiful, wise Latin noblewoman (Obama, 1995, p. 440). His emotional expressions in his memoir make one feel that Barack loved Maya no less than he did Auma. Barack then turned his attention to his Kenyan half sister, Auma, whom he loved naturally, intensely, and deeply (Obama, p. 208). He was surprised when Auma cried during the wedding ceremony; she was the only guest who did (Obama, p. 440). Why did Auma cry? Did she feel that she was losing Barack to Michelle? Was she jealous? Did she feel abandoned?

When Barack watched Michelle's five- and six-year-old cousins, who were the official wedding-ring bearers, they seemed to him like "young African princes" (Obama, 1995, pp. 440–441). Barack was very proud of his elder half brother Roy, who had become a Muslim, changed his name to Malik Abongo Obama, sworn off pork, smoking, alcohol, and drugs, and become lean and clear-eyed. Roy's whole life had changed for the better, even though he still had his inner struggles and tensions. Barack did not overlook Roy's character defects and his dogmatic thinking but was enthralled with "the magic of his laughter," his generosity, his good humor, his gentleness, his readiness to forgive, and his quest for racial peace and harmony (Obama, pp. 441–442).

Before he met Michelle, the black community of Chicago had been Barack's substitute family. Now that he had his wife's family and was creating his own, he no longer needed that community to feel acceptance and belonging. His close friendship with Michelle's brother, Craig, around their mutual love of basketball, enhanced that feeling. Barack and Craig became as close as brothers. Sasha Abramsky (2009, p. 52) thinks that Michelle's family, which was stable, middle-class, and "structured in a way that his own family had never been," along with his two daughters by Michelle that came a few years later, filled the emotional void in Barack's soul that his community-organizing work had done earlier.

Barack ended his memoir on a very happy note. At his wedding, he felt incredibly lucky (Obama, 1995, p. 442). Indeed, his marriage to Michelle seems successful and happy. She is not only his wife but also his friend, his mate, his partner, his counselor, his teacher, his mentor, and the mother of his daughters. She and her family of origin have given Barack the family that he never had before and had always longed for. She is, you might say, his better half. Michelle has been the subject of almost as many studies as her husband (Andersen, 2009; Bodden, 2010; Brill, 2009b; Brophy, 2009; P. Brown, 2009b; Colbert, 2009; Dann, 2008; Edwards, 2009a; Fornek, 2007a; Graham Parker, 2009; Harris, 2009; Hopkinson, 2009; Hudson, 2010; Katirgis, 2009c; Kesselring, 2010b; Lindsay, 2009; Marcovitz, 2009; Mattern, 2010; Mundy, 2008; Nault, 2010; Norwood, 2009; Pickert, 2008; Uschan, 2010; R. Watson, 2009; Weatherford, 2010b; Wheeler, 2010; Willis & Bernard, 2009; J. C. Young, 2009; Zumbusch, 2010b).

Barack's first lady Michelle is his antidote to all the women who had broken his heart, beginning with his own mother. Obama's enemies, as well as the yellow press and the tabloids, have alleged a one-night extramarital "affair" between Barack Obama and his young campaign worker Vera Baker when he was running for the U.S. Senate in 2004. However, Ms. Baker has repeatedly and emphatically denied the rumor, and none of the serious U.S. mass-communication media (such as the *New York Times,* the *Wall Street Journal, USA Today, CNN, Fox News, ABC,* and *MSNBC*) has dignified this rumor by mentioning it. Moreover, even if there had been a one-night sexual affair between the two, it would only have made Barack Obama all too human, succumbing to sexual temptation during an extremely stressful time.

Chapter 15

FATHERHOOD AND POLITICS

Synopsis: *When Malia Ann Obama was born in 1998, six years after her parents married, Barack Obama became a proud father. Unlike his grandfather, "Gramps," who had been disappointed in not having a son and named his daughter Stanley after himself, Barack was happy with his daughter and named her Malia Ann, the middle name being his mother's. By that time he was an Illinois state senator. In 2000 he lost the Democratic primary race for the U.S. Congress to Bobby Rush, a more experienced and at that time more popular black politician, and he experienced it as a deeply humiliating and painful loss. In 2001, however, his second daughter, Natasha, nicknamed Sasha, was born, and his "fierce ambitions" were revived. His fatherhood seems to have reinforced his self-confidence and his determination to be a better father than his own father, and it also reinforced his empathy, his capacity for conciliation, and his ability to reform, repair, and improve his various communities, from black Chicago through the state of Illinois all the way to the United States of America. Despite his young age, he would become the father of his nation and take as good care of her as he could.*

At the time of his wedding in 1992, Barack's happiness was great: he had accomplished everything he had wished to achieve, and his life was full in every way. "I felt like the luckiest man alive," he wrote (Obama, 1995, p. 442). Barack's Harvard biographer thinks that his marriage to a black woman from Chicago's South Side cemented his black racial identity and gave him the sense of belonging to the black community that he had lacked

and longed for since his childhood, as well as important political connections (Niven, 2009, p. 18).

Indeed, from now on, Obama was clearly an African American politician, first in the Illinois senate and later in the U.S. Senate. For the rest of his
life, he would remain a black politician yet always try to remain a postracial one, as demonstrated by his apology to the white Cambridge police
officer in the unfortunate arrest of the black Harvard scholar Henry Louis
Gates, Jr., in July 2009. Gates had written the introduction to David
Niven's biography of Obama earlier that year. Obama at first criticized
Gates's unwarranted arrest by the white police in his own home as "stupid,"
but he apologized quickly thereafter, pointing out that race unfortunately
still played a part in American life. He invited both the arresting officer
and the arrested man to share a beer with him at the White House.

At the time of Barack's wedding, his community-organizing career and
his law school studies were behind him, but his political career, during
which he would, as in his favorite sport of basketball, suffer many "sharp
elbows and blindside hits," was still ahead of him (Obama, 2006a, p. 22).
You will remember that Barack not only loves to play basketball but that
it is also one of his primary unconscious links to his father. In 1991 and
1992 he worked again for the black Chicago community, this time as a
civil rights lawyer. From 1993 to 1996 he was a civil rights lawyer at Davis,
Miner, Barnhill & Galland, a small Chicago law firm specializing in civil
rights litigation and neighborhood economic development. At the same
time, he also taught constitutional law as a lecturer at the University of
Chicago. He later spent eight years in the Illinois senate (1997–2004), and
four years in the U.S. Senate (2005–2008), before being elected president
of the United States. By that time, the world's expectations of him were so
great that he was bound to disappoint many people all over the world who
looked on him as a kind of savior or messiah. The Nobel Peace Prize that
U.S. President Obama was awarded in 2009 for his nuclear-disarmament
work, even though he was waging wars in Iraq and Afghanistan, was a
measure of those expectations.

On July 4, 1998, after a few years' delay due to their careers, the
37-year-old Barack and his 34-year-old wife Michelle had their first child,
a daughter they named Malia Ann. On August 10, 2001, her sister, Natasha
(Sasha) was born. However much Barack may have wanted a son, he was
not about to do what his maternal grandfather Gramps had done to his
daughter, naming her Stanley Ann after himself. Barack and Michelle were
delighted with their daughters. Barack loves being a father: unlike his own
father, he would never abandon his children. Yet some of the great trials
and tribulations of his life were still ahead of him. They would come after
he became a U.S. senator and then the president of the United States.

Barack's marriage to Michelle not only rooted him in the African American community but also brought him new political connections in Illinois, such as the presidential aspirant Reverend Jesse Louis Jackson (born 1941) and his son, the U.S. Representative Jesse Louis Jackson, Jr. (born 1965), as well as many Democratic Party friends in Chicago and elsewhere. Jesse Jackson was an important ally. The civil rights activist and Baptist minister had been a candidate for the U.S. Democratic presidential nomination in 1984 and 1988 and served as the Democratic shadow senator for the District of Columbia from 1991 to 1997. He was the founder of the National Rainbow Coalition and of the Project to Save Humanity.

On the night of November 4, 2008, when Obama won the presidency of the United States, he addressed a huge crowd of supporters in Chicago's Grant Park (Abramsky, 2009, p. 69). The television cameras focused on Jackson standing in the crowd in Grant Park with tears streaming down his cheeks (Niven, 2009, p. 42). Cheryl Johnson, a black Chicago activist, told the journalist Karen Springen that Jackson was crying "not because there's finally a black President, but because it's not him" (Springen, 2008). But Jackson might also have been crying out of joy, because his lifelong civil rights struggle had succeeded and an African American had finally become president of the United States.

For a few years Barack and Michelle had pursued their careers, children being deferred. After leaving the law firm of Sidley Austin, Michelle worked as an aide to Mayor Richard Michael Daley, the white politician who became the mayor of Chicago in 1989. The popular Daley was a member of the national and local Democratic Party and was repeatedly reelected, becoming the longest-serving mayor in Chicago's history. When Barack understood that his ambition of becoming mayor of Chicago was unrealistic, he decided to pursue another political avenue by running for the Illinois senate. From 1992 to 1996 he worked as a lawyer and taught constitutional law, while contemplating his political future.

In 1993 Michelle Robinson Obama became the executive director for the Chicago office of Public Allies, a nonprofit American organization encouraging young people to work on social issues in nonprofit non-governmental organizations and in U.S. government agencies. Public Allies was a largely taxpayer-funded organization, dedicated to youth-leadership development. Founded in 1992 by the social activists Vanessa Kirsch and Katrina Browne in Washington, D.C., Public Allies soon had other offices in major U.S. cities. The founders recruited Michelle to run their Chicago office. She worked there for nearly four years and set fund-raising records for the organization.

In 1995, as his mother was dying of cancer, Barack published his touching memoir, *Dreams from My Father*, which won good reviews in the press but did not enjoy great sales. Above all else, writing this book helped Barack free himself from his father's ghost and from his ambivalent identification with his father and to forge his mature identity as a black American politician. Only after Obama broke into the U.S. national scene with his election victories in Illinois and with his keynote address "The Audacity of Hope" at the Democratic National Convention in 2004 did the book become a best seller (Niven, 2009, p. 18).

The year 1992 had been pivotal in Barack's life: his beloved grandfather Gramps died, his mother got her PhD in anthropology, and he married Michelle LaVaughn Robinson, "the love of my life," as he called her in his presidential-nomination acceptance speech at the Democratic National Convention in 2008. They seem to love one another deeply and have two lovely, healthy, and lively daughters, whom they love and who love them. Moreover, during his early thirties, Barack's meteoric political career progressed rapidly. Barack was also given a lectureship at the prestigious University of Chicago Law School, and he continued his law firm work for the black community. In 1994 he became a senior lecturer at the law school, but he declined a full-time tenured position at the university to be able to continue his public work. Politics was more important to him than academia.

Barack passed the Illinois Bar examination in late 1991 and could have practiced law right away. However, he did not actually practice law in 1992. Instead, he taught constitutional law at the University of Chicago Law School, as a lecturer from 1992 to 1996 and as a senior lecturer from 1996 to 2004. In 1993, after working for Bill Clinton's campaign in the U.S. election of 1992, in which Clinton was elected president, Barack began to work as a civil rights attorney in the Chicago law firm of Davis, Miner, Barnhill & Galland. There, he was an associate from 1993 to 1996 and then, after he became an Illinois state senator, an "of counsel"—an attorney who is employed by a law firm but is not an associate or a partner of his employer—from 1996 to 2004. The records of the Illinois Supreme Court's Attorney Registration and Disciplinary Commission show his lawyer's license and registration as active until he voluntarily retired in 2008.

While working as a civil rights lawyer and constitutional-law lecturer from 1993 to 1996, Barack contemplated his political career, which in 1997 took him to the Illinois senate. In 1995, the year his mother died, he published his poignant memoir, *Dreams from My Father*, which he had been writing for some time and which can be seen as his meditation on his loneliness and on his racial identity. At the same time, his quest for a political career was not meant only to better the lot of his fellow black people: It was also a quest for an antidote to his early feelings of helplessness and to a conciliation between the races, which as a child he had wanted to create between his father's black African family and his mother's white American one.

Why was politics so important to Barack? Politics is about power and control, manipulation and power struggles, no less than it is about ideals and progress. When asked why he wanted to go into "something dirty and nasty like politics," Barack had a ready speech in reply: politics was not only about "dirty" backbiting, intrigues, and power struggles but also about civil rights, about uniting people, and about improving society (Obama, 2006a, pp. 3–4). This seems like an idealized view of politics. Consciously, Barack must have believed in his speech, as well as considering it a good answer to journalists and to the public. Unconsciously, politics may have attracted him not only because it enabled him to help poor people but also because it gave him a sense of power that assuaged his early feelings of helplessness and abandonment. There is no contradiction here. Human action is overdetermined. It has conscious and unconscious motives. The unconscious needs do not have to agree logically with the conscious ideals. In fact, the conscious ideals may be an ideological superstructure or an intellectualization of the unconscious needs.

THE CONSTITUTION AS A GOOD MOTHER

The young Illinois state senator Obama was something of an idealist. He believed in that noble "other tradition of politics" as a means of healing society and in acting on his belief. When he gave his pep talk about this noble tradition of politics to journalists, supporters, and other people, it sounded convincing to him (Obama, 2006a, p. 4). The junior legislator delivered his speech to the Illinois General Assembly with "an earnestness and youthful swagger" (ibid.). The U.S. Constitution was Barack's favorite subject. As we have seen, it had unconscious maternal connotations for him: It protected him—and all Americans—from the abuse of their rights by their government, and it was up to him to protect it, too, just as he felt with his mother as a child in Indonesia.

Americans call the people who drafted the U.S. Constitution the founding fathers of the American nation, and Barack idealized those founding fathers no less than he had his own father. Like his father, the founding fathers were dead, but their Constitution abided (Obama, 2006a, pp. 85–120). The Constitutional Convention of 1787 in Philadelphia (also known as the Philadelphia Convention, the Constitutional Congress, the Federal Convention, and the Grand Convention at Philadelphia) had explicitly sought "a more perfect union" for America. This convention is one of Barack's favorite moments in American history, and the "more perfect union" is one of his favorite themes, often repeated in his books and speeches.

In 2005 U.S. Senator Barack Obama delivered a commencement speech to the graduating seniors at Knox College in Illinois, saying that America was "a journey to be shared and shaped and remade by people who had the gall, the temerity to believe that, against all odds, they could form 'a more perfect union' on this new frontier" (Obama, 2006c, p. 144; see also Abramsky, 2009, p. 73). Barack's mother had used the phrase "against all odds" in the title of her doctoral dissertation (Dunham, 1992). Whether consciously or not, Barack was using his mother's words and was talking about his own success "against all odds."

In 2008 Senator Obama delivered a major presidential-campaign speech on race relations in America, entitled "A More Perfect Union," at Philadelphia's National Constitutional Center, designed to enhance interracial conciliation. Sasha Abramsky thinks that Obama wrote that speech himself, even though he had very good speechwriters (2009, p. 66). As in the case of Lincoln's quest for union (Strozier, 1982), Obama's quest for "a more perfect union" may be due to the very imperfect union between his parents that affected his entire life.

Barack taught U.S. constitutional law at the University of Chicago Law School from 1994 until 2004, when he ran for the U.S. Senate. He continued teaching while he was a state senator (1997–2004), although he always put his political career ahead of his academic one. It was no accident that he taught U.S. constitutional law rather than any other aspect of the law. Barack was more interested in people than in God, and, he thought that, unlike the Christian New Testament, which purports to convey God's own word, the U.S. Constitution was written by human beings.

Barack felt that the U.S. Constitution was still very relevant to American life, more than two centuries after it was written, and that it and the other founding documents—the Declaration of Independence and the Federalist Papers—were a fascinating record of the intense political struggles of the founding fathers. By deciphering these founding documents one could not always guess what the founding fathers had felt, but one could understand what they thought and their ideals (Obama, 2006a, p. 102). Was not this exactly what Barack had done when he went to Kenya and struggled to figure out his real father's feelings and thoughts when he was alive?

To Barack, a strict construction of the U.S. Constitution was inadequate: the Constitution taught you *how* to think, not *what* to think. The judiciary needed to interpret it and to update it to the needs of our time (Obama, 2006a, pp. 106–107). This became quite important to him in 2009, when he named the Latino judge Sonia Sotomayor to the U.S. Supreme Court. He did not want rigid, strict constructionists on the Court. He wanted a free, liberal, and progressive interpretation of the Constitution. Obama's other political battles as president have been in the same vein.

OBAMA AND LINCOLN

The most important values and ideals that U.S. Senator Obama believed were enshrined in the U.S. Constitution were individual liberties. He has fought for civil rights, liberty, and freedom in all their aspects and varieties, for the U.S. Bill of Rights (the first 10 amendments to the U.S. Constitution), for the freedom to do anything that does not hurt or damage others, for the freedom from having hurtful or damaging things done to you, and for the freedom to have education and health care, which are among his top priorities (Obama, 2006a, p. 103). Barack had seen many of those rights and freedoms trampled underfoot in Chicago and elsewhere. Such ideals may have prompted him, when he became president of the United States, to order the closure of the infamous Guantánamo incarceration camp for Islamic terrorists in Cuba by the end of 2010.

Unfortunately, Barack's idealization of the founding fathers and of their founding documents ran up against the unpleasant reality that the white founding fathers had not given any rights or liberties to their black African slaves, who were treated as the chattel of their masters and owners. Barack cited the infamous case of the freed African American slave Dred Scott (1799–1858), who, before the American Civil War, "walked into the U.S. Supreme Court a free man, but left a slave" (Obama, 2006a, p. 114). Barack was referring to the notorious U.S. Supreme Court ruling of 1857 in the *Dred Scott vs. Sandford* case, namely, that Africans imported into the United States and held as slaves, and their descendants—whether or not they were slaves—were neither "legal persons" nor U.S. citizens. The Court ruled that the U.S. Congress had no authority to prohibit slavery in its federal territories. The Supreme Court also ruled that slaves could not sue anyone in court and that they could not be taken away from their owners without due process.

Some slaves had run away from their masters, but in its *Dred Scott vs. Sandford* ruling of 1857, the U.S. Supreme Court dehumanized black people. It made slaves legal nonentities and made it illegal to assist fugitive slaves. Dred Scott himself became a slave again. It took the American Civil War (1861–1865) to give the African American slaves their liberty. That war was the deadliest one in American history: 620,000 soldiers were killed, and a huge number of civilians suffered casualties on both sides. The war pitted the southern slave-owning states against the northern "free states." The Southern Confederacy was defeated by the "Yankees" under U.S. President Abraham Lincoln (1809–1865), the Illinois lawyer and leader of the

Republican party, to whom many Americans—including, at times, Barack himself—like to compare Barack Obama (Obama, 2005).

In 1858 Lincoln delivered a famous speech at the Illinois Republican Convention, entitled "A House Divided" (Strozier, 1982). Over 1,000 Republican delegates had met in the Illinois statehouse in Springfield for the convention. They had chosen Lincoln as their candidate for the U.S. Senate, to run against the Democratic candidate Stephen A. Douglas. The title of Lincoln's address came from a sentence in his speech's introduction, "A house divided against itself cannot stand," which in turn came from the Christian New Testament: "How can Satan cast out Satan? And if a kingdom be divided against itself, that kingdom cannot stand. And if a house be divided against itself, that house cannot stand. And if Satan rise up against himself, and be divided, he cannot stand, but hath an end" (Mark 3:23–25).

Some of Lincoln's friends believed that his "House Divided" speech was much too radical for the occasion. Lincoln's law partner, William Herndon (1818–1891), thought that Lincoln was morally courageous but politically unwise. Herndon said that Lincoln told him he was looking for a universally known figure of speech that would rouse people to the peril of the times. Another lawyer friend, Leonard Swett (1825–1889), who advised and assisted Lincoln throughout his political career, believed that the "House Divided" speech had lost Lincoln his U.S. Senate campaign to the Democratic candidate Stephen Douglas. Lincoln beat Douglas in the presidential election of 1860, but was assassinated in 1865, after the end of the American Civil War. In 1866 Swett wrote to Herndon about Lincoln's speech, complaining that "Nothing could have been more unfortunate or inappropriate" (Herndon & Weik, 1888, p. 529).

The American historian and psychoanalyst Charles Strozier (1982) thought that Lincoln's "House Divided" speech derived from his own emotions within his family. Strozier gave us the most profound account possible of Lincoln's inner life—from the time he was a young man in Illinois, going through his adolescent identity struggles, to his ascent to the presidency, when he guided the nation through the American Civil War. With the skills of an open-minded historian and a trained psychoanalyst, Strozier examined Lincoln's relationships with his mother, his stepmother, his two young loves, and his wife, Mary Todd. He also considered Lincoln's feelings toward his father and male friends and colleagues. In the second edition of his book, Strozier used the writings of Herndon, Lincoln's long-time law partner, to update and expand his psychological portrait of the 16th U.S. president (Strozier, 2001; see also Herndon & Weik, 1888).

Strozier's analysis of Lincoln's relationships with his parents and his wife, and their connections to his political action, annoyed the historian Herman Belz, who, like many conservative historians, dislikes psychoanalysis. The more open-minded historian Jean Baker, however, whose biography of Mary Todd Lincoln presented Lincoln's wife as a prototype of Victorian womanhood, was more sympathetic to psychoanalysis, except when it came to Lincoln's marriage: Baker saw Mary as a far more stable woman than Strozier did. Strozier's response to their criticisms of his book demonstrated the necessity for informed psychoanalytic interpretation by biographers drawing connections between private and public life but also the perils of reductionism and of reading too much into too little, such as Lincoln's striking juxtaposition of a story about killing a turkey and a mention of the death of his mother in a brief autobiographical essay (Boritt & Forness, 1988).

One of the tragic ironies of the infamous *Dred Scott vs. Sandford* case was the fate of John Sandford, the brother of the slave owner's widow, Irene Sandford Emerson, who had become Dred Scott's owner after the early death of her husband in 1843. The respondent's name was actually Sanford, but a Court clerk misspelled it "Sandford" and the Court retained the error. Sandford had become the executor of the Emerson estate and was therefore the party sued by Dred Scott. This same Sandford became psychotic during the trial and was committed to an insane asylum. Scott was returned as property to Irene Emerson. However, in 1850, Irene had married the abolitionist Calvin Clifford Chaffee (1811–1896), a New York physician who had settled in Massachusetts. In 1854 Chaffee was elected on the Know Nothing Party ticket to the 34th U.S. Congress as part of the party's sweep of the Massachusetts congressional delegation that year.

The Know Nothing Party had originated in New York in 1843 as the American Republican Party. It spread to other states as the Native American Party and became a national party in 1845. In 1855 it renamed itself the American Party. The *Know Nothing* term originated in the secret organization of the party: when a member was asked about it, he was supposed to reply, "I know nothing." The Know Nothing Party was a nativist American political movement of the 1840s and 1850s. It was fueled by Protestant fears that the country was being taken over by Irish Catholic immigrants, who were regarded as hostile to U.S. libertarian values and controlled by the pope in Rome. Mainly active from 1854 to 1856, the Know Nothing Party strove to curb further immigration and naturalization, but its efforts met with little success. The party had few prominent leaders, and the largely middle-class and Protestant membership was fragmented over the issue of slavery. Most of them ended up joining the antislavery Republican Party by the time of the 1860 presidential election, in which Lincoln was elected president of the United States.

It is not clear whether Chaffee was aware that his wife owned the most prominent slave in America until a month before the Supreme Court decision. Too late to intervene, Chaffee had his wife Irene return Scott to his original owners, the Blow family of Missouri. Missouri was a free state, as opposed to the southern slave-holding states, so the Blow family could emancipate Scott. He was in fact freed on May 26, 1857, and worked as a porter in St. Louis for less than a year before dying from tuberculosis in 1858. He was survived by his wife, Harriet Scott, and by his daughter, Eliza Scott. Dred Scott was buried in Calvary Cemetery, St. Louis, Missouri. His widow Harriet was long thought to be buried near her husband, but it was recently proved that she was buried in Greenwood Cemetery in Hillsdale, Missouri. She outlived her husband by 18 years, dying in 1876. In 1997, Dred and Harriet Scott were inducted into the St. Louis Walk of Fame.

Barack was acutely aware of the infamous Dred Scott case, but he would not take sides in the great dispute between those who saw the founding fathers, who owned slaves and ignored them in their Constitution, as hypocrites and those who saw the U.S. Constitution as a necessary instrument for the formation of the United States, which only "sought to postpone what they were certain would be slavery's ultimate demise" (Obama, 2006a, p. 115). Barack was too ambivalent to be able to take sides in this argument. He loved America too much, her founding documents and her institutions, everything about her, to dwell on "the circumstances of its birth" (ibid.). Yet he obviously could not forget or brush aside the terrible abuse of black people in America over many generations, which was still an open sore in the American soul (ibid.).

Just as he had tried to understand and to forgive his parents' defects and the psychic damage they had done to him, including his father's abandonment of him, Barack was trying to understand and forgive the gross injustice done by America's founding fathers to their black "children" and to emphasize their noble intentions and their defense of individual liberties. America had become Barack's great good mother. The name *America* has maternal connotations (Niederland, 1989). America and its Constitution seem to have taken the place of his idealized mother in Barack's unconscious mind, whereas the founding fathers had taken the place of his biological father. As with his mother, he adored the Constitution but also realized its defects. And, as with his father, he idealized the founding fathers but also realized their faults.

Barack strove to reconcile his positive feelings about the U.S. constitution, which he greatly admired, with his ambivalent feelings about its framers, who had held slaves ands unpheld slavery. Wavering between idealism and realism, Barack remembered that the unbending idealist William Lloyd Garrison (1805–1879) had first called for the abolition of slavery and that the African American slaves Denmark Vesey (Telemaque Vesey, 1767–1822), Frederick Douglass (Frederick Augustus Washington Bailey, 1818–1895), and Harriet Tubman (1822–1913) had been the first to recognize that they had to fight for their liberty because "power would concede nothing without a fight" (Obama, 2006a, p. 116).

Like other men who are greatly preoccupied with their origins and with how they came to be what they are, Barack has a keen sense of history (Abramsky, 2009, pp. 59–82). He has read many historical books, especially about African American history, black slavery, Lincoln, the American Civil War, and the U.S. civil rights movement. William Lloyd Garrison was a prominent white American abolitionist and social reformer. He edited the radical abolitionist newspaper *The Liberator* and was a founder of the American Anti-Slavery Society, which, as early as 1831, called for the abolition of slavery. It took another 34 years for the American Civil War to bring this about. In his newspaper Garrison promoted the immediate emancipation of the slaves in the United States. Garrison was also a prominent voice for the women's suffrage movement and a fierce critic of the prevailing conservative religious orthodoxy in America that supported slavery and opposed suffrage for women. It had indeed taken a rigid and unbending idealist like Garrison to help abolish slavery and give women the vote in the United States.

Barack's choice of historical heroes was fascinating. Vesey was an African American slave who was brought to the United States from the Caribbean. Inspired by the revolutionary actions of slaves during the Haitian revolution of 1791, and furious at the closing of the African Church in America, Vesey, after purchasing his freedom from his owner, planned what would have been one of the largest slave rebellions in the United States. Word of the revolt plans was leaked, however, and the authorities of Charleston, South Carolina, arrested the plot's leaders before the uprising could begin. Vesey and his coplotters were tried, convicted of treason, and executed. Many antislavery activists regarded Vesey as a hero.

During the American Civil War the African American abolitionist Frederick Douglass used Vesey's name as a battle cry to raise African American regiments like the 54th Massachusetts Volunteer Infantry to the Union cause. Douglass was an African American abolitionist, women's suffragist, editor, orator, author, statesman, and reformer. Douglass was one of the most prominent figures in African American and U.S. history. When he lived in Anacostia, a historic neighborhood in the mostly black Southeast Washington, D.C., he was known as "the Sage of Anacostia" and "the Lion of Anacostia." He was a firm believer in the equality of all people, black and white, male and female, Native American and immigrant. Harriet Tubman was an African American abolitionist, humanitarian, and Union spy during the American Civil War. Born a slave, she escaped from her owner and then made 13 missions back to the South to rescue more than 70 other slaves, using the network of antislavery activists and safe houses known as the Underground Railroad. She also helped the radical white abolitionist John Brown (1800–1859) recruit 21 men for his armed raid on the U.S. armory and arsenal at Harpers Ferry, Virginia, in 1859 (for which he was hanged). After the Civil War, when women still did not have the right to vote, she struggled for women's suffrage. Such were the people who inspired Barack.

Along with Barack's realism and his willingness to see opposing views of the same issue, his values and ideals have always been a key aspect of his psychological makeup, and they go hand-in-hand with his practicality, his ambition, and his determination. This became evident in June 1995 when the black state senator Alice Palmer (born 1939) announced that she was vacating her Illinois senate seat to run in the Democratic primary for the U.S. Congress against Jesse Jackson, Jr., and Emil Jones. A week after Palmer made her announcement, the newspapers reported that she would support Obama, who had been appointed the new chairman of the Chicago Annenberg Challenge and whose *Dreams from My Father* would be published the following month, for her vacant senate seat.

The fiercely ambitious Obama seized the opportunity. In July 1995 he launched a campaign committee to run for the Illinois state senate. In September Palmer introduced and endorsed Obama for her former state senate seat. Obama's mother Ann died on November 7. Did he have the time and emotional space to mourn his loss of her? It seems that Obama's emotions had by now unconsciously turned to another mother figure, Palmer, who was 22 years his senior and who had endorsed him for her vacant seat.

In December 1995 there was high drama between the 56-year-old Palmer and the 34-year-old Obama. After Palmer lost her U.S. congressional race, she desperately tried to regain her Illinois senate seat. Very late in the race, on the last day to file nominating petitions, she filed one with 1,580 hastily gathered signatures. Obama, whose mother had just died, had the emotional, intellectual, and political wherewithal to challenge Palmer's petition and those of the three other prospective candidates in court. Nearly two-thirds of the signatures on Palmer's petition were found invalid, leaving her only about 550 valid ones, some 200 short of the required 757 signatures of registered voters residing in the 13th District of Illinois.

The 13th District of Illinois spanned Chicago's South Side neighborhoods, from Hyde Park and Kenwood in the north down south to the South Shore, then west to Chicago Lawn. Barack's Harvard biographer has pointed out that Illinois's 13th District included Barack's two worlds: that of the university teacher and lawyer, the liberal, wealthy, racially integrated. and cosmopolitan Hyde Park neighborhood, and that of the black community organizer, the poor, black, South Side neighborhoods (Niven, 2009, p. 19).

Since none of the prospective candidates running against Obama had the minimum number of valid signatures, this left Obama, who had filed a nominating petition with over 3,000 signatures on the very first filing day, the only candidate on the March 1996 Democratic Party primary-election ballot for the Illinois state senate. Naturally, he won the race and was elected to the state senate. When questioned about his motives for challenging his rivals' nominating petitions, Obama replied that his challenges were necessitated by the obvious legal flaws in their nomination-petition-signature sheets. "To my mind, we were just abiding by the rules that had been set up," he said 11 years later, and when asked if the voters had not been done a disservice by a ballot with no opposing candidates, he replied with self-confidence—some say with arrogance—"I think they ended up with a very good state senator" (Jackson & Long, 2007a). The psychodrama was fascinating. In 2008 a bitter and vengeful Palmer endorsed Hillary Clinton over Obama for the Democratic presidential nomination, but Hillary lost the race to Obama.

Obama's Harvard biographer thinks that his initial achievements in the Illinois General Assembly were modest (Niven, 2009, p. 19). Nonetheless, Obama repeatedly showed his talent for empathy, conciliation, mediation, and bipartisanship. Successfully working with his Republican colleagues in the Illinois General Assembly, Obama gained bipartisan support for his legislation reforming political ethics and health-care laws. He sponsored or cosponsored laws that banned the personal use of campaign money by state legislators and their accepting gifts from political lobbyists. He sponsored a law increasing tax credits for low-income workers, negotiated state-welfare reform, and promoted increased child-care subsidies. His progressive agenda in his state was in line with that of the Clinton administration's agenda on the national level. He was one of the most progressive of the Illinois state senators, but he was also flexible, willing to compromise with his conservative opponents to achieve his aims.

When Obama arrived in the Illinois state capital of Springfield in early 1997 as a freshman state senator, he ran into an older colleague, Dennis Jacobs, a "hard-drinking, fast-talking, wheeler-dealing feisty Irish-American" from rural Illinois (Abramsky, 2009, p. 83). Jacobs said to Obama provocatively, "You don't belong in Springfield" (Abramsky, p. 83). A shocked and angry Obama asked Jacobs whether he was trying to insult him or to pick a fight with him. Jacobs replied that the reverse was true: he had meant that Obama was too smart to be in the Illinois General Assembly, that the petty politicians in Springfield would not appreciate his talents, and that Obama was destined for bigger things. Jacobs's flattery satisfied Obama's narcissism, and the two men became close friends. Abramsky thinks that Jacobs's compliment helped shore up Obama's self-confidence (ibid.).

Obama's self-confidence was also boosted when as a freshman state senator he was admitted to a group of poker-playing state senators who met in the home of Terry Link, another freshman state senator. State Senator Jacobs told Abramsky that

> Barack has that easy little laugh, that easy little smile. Let's call it his winning smile. He's an easygoing guy who isn't afraid to say, "Hey, I understand you play a little poker. Let's get together and play a little poker." He gives you that little smile and says, "Yeah, I'm on." And they say, "Yeah, you're on," and include him in. The guy, he's just a guy; and coming from my vernacular and my area, where I was born and raised, to me that's number one. If you're just a good old guy or a good old gal, that's what you are. And that's what President Obama is, he's just a good guy. (Abramsky, 2009, p. 84).

After two years of active social legislation, State Senator Obama was reelected to the Illinois senate in 1998, defeating his Republican Jewish opponent, Yesse Yehudah, in the general election. He continued to pursue his liberal and progressive agenda. However, his first years in the Illinois General Assembly were hardly a garden of roses. He described them realistically, if not bitterly, some 10 years later: "When I moved to Illinois [in 1985] to work as a community organizer, I had no money in my pockets and didn't know a single soul. During my first six years in the state legislature [1997–2002], Democrats were in the minority, and I couldn't get a bill heard, much less passed" (Obama, 2005). Most of Obama's legislative achievements in the Illinois senate came after the Democrats took control, in 2003–2004.

Still, Obama may have been exaggerating. Even during his first years in the Illinois senate, he was able to pass some important legislation. For instance, in 2001, as cochair of the bipartisan Joint Committee on Administrative Rules, Obama supported Illinois Republican Governor George Ryan's regulations on payday-loan and predatory-mortgage lending, aimed at saving poor people from having their homes foreclosed by greedy lenders. Almost always self-controlled, Obama was cool, stable, cerebral, and almost unemotional, while his black colleagues in Springfield, the veterans of the civil rights battles, were more given to emotional and dramatic outbursts. They felt that he was too ambitious and that he had to pay his dues and await his turn. He, however, worked with progressive Republicans and moderate Democrats, showing an outstanding ability to work with different political viewpoints without losing his own liberalism.

In his two books, Barack displayed surprising psychological insight and sophistication for a politician. Whereas most politicians rely on the unconscious defenses of splitting, projection, and externalization, and many of them are paranoid (Hofstadter, 1965; Robins & Post, 1997), Obama has the ability for introspection and for courageously facing his true feel-ings. In 1999–2000 Obama continued his social-legislation activity in the Illinois senate, working with colleagues across the political spectrum. He sought to balance the interests of his constituents, the well-to-do in Chi-cago's Hyde Park neighborhood with those of the poor in Chicago's South Side. In this he was following the dictum of the well-known Democratic House Speaker Thomas (Tip) O'Neill (1912–1994) that all politics was local (Niven, 2009, p. 20).

Chapter 16

A HUMILIATING DEFEAT

Synopsis: *In 2000 Barack Obama mounted an impulsive challenge to Bobby Rush, the four-term black incumbent of the U.S. congressional seat from the First Congressional District of Illinois. As Obama himself later wrote, it was an ill-considered race. Rush said publicly that "Barack Obama went to Harvard and became an educated fool. Barack is a person who read about the civil-rights protests and thinks he knows all about it" (Scott, 2007d). Obama was also hurt by his relationship with Tony Rezko, a controversial white Chicago developer, and his endorsement by the Republican* Chicago Tribune, *which wanted to unseat Rush. In their single televised debate, the streetwise Rush drubbed Obama badly, making him look like a brash young upstart. Rush defeated Obama by a wide margin. Obama later revealed in* The Audacity of Hope *that he felt terribly humiliated by this defeat and that even today he still burns "with the thought of my one loss in politics" (2006a, p. 126). He made his humiliation into a general theory of what motivates politicians: the fear of humiliation by defeat. Yet his self-esteem, his self-confidence, and his fierce ambitions were such that within a year he was planning his race for governor or U.S. senator. He had the support of his family, which was vital for a man who ardently wished to be a good husband and father.*

In 1999 Obama's "chronic restlessness" and his "fierce ambitions" (Obama, 2006a, pp. 5, 243) led him to inflict on himself a humiliating political defeat, the only one in his career at that time. His ambitions and his grandiose self could not settle for membership in a state legislature. His ideal self-image demanded more. Like Alice Palmer in 1996, he decided to challenge the black Democratic incumbent, Bobby Lee Rush (born 1946), for his U.S. congressional seat from the First Congressional District of Illinois, which Rush had held since 1993.

The 38-year-old Obama's challenge to the 53-year-old Rush enraged some older black American politicians. Donne E. Trotter (born 1950), the ranking Democrat on the Illinois senate appropriations committee and one of Obama's rivals, called him "not black enough" and went so far as to attack Obama in the alternative black weekly *Chicago Reader* as "a white man in black face" (Mendell, 2007, p. 131). This was a derogatory reference to the "black face" that white American actors had put on when playing black people, at a time when black actors were excluded from the American stage and screen.

Rush himself, a fiery former Black Panther leader, derided Obama as a highbrow idealist: "Barack Obama went to Harvard and became an educated fool. Barack is a person who read about the civil-rights protests and thinks he knows all about it" (Scott, 2007d). President Bill Clinton backed Rush, and Obama was also hurt by his relationship with Tony Rezko, a controversial white Chicago property developer, and by his endorsement by the Republican *Chicago Tribune*. In their single televised debate, the streetwise Rush drubbed Obama badly. Rezko had attracted much negative public attention because of his indictment (and subsequent conviction) on political corruption charges that were, however, unrelated to Obama.

Obama described this humiliating loss in the prologue of his *Audacity of Hope*. He attributed his foolhardy challenge of Rush to his "restlessness," called it "ill-considered," and admitted that he had lost badly. He also, however, credited this humbling experience with teaching him the vital lesson "that life is not obliged to work out as you'd planned" (Obama, 2006a, p. 5). This was a healthy psychological reaction, one that would stand him in good stead as his political life went on. Yet he had felt invincible, superior, and unique, and it was a big blow to his self-esteem. Later in the same book, Obama revealed that he felt terribly humiliated by this defeat, and that even as he was writing his book the memory of his defeat still burned him inside (Obama, 2006a, p. 126). In fact, he turned his humiliation into a general theory of what motivates politicians: the fear of humiliation by defeat. After his humiliating and painful loss to Rush in 2000, Obama briefly considered abandoning politics altogether and going back to his law practice and law teaching.

Barack's love of basketball playing is not only his major unconscious tie to his father but also his conscious link to his brother-in-law, Craig Malcolm Robinson, a successful basketball coach and a former Ivy League Basketball Player of the Year. Craig, who is six-foot-six-inches tall, is 5 inches taller than Barack. However, Craig is one year Barack's junior. He had been a basketball player and coach when he first met Barack in 1991 and is now the head men's basketball coach at Oregon State University. In 2007 Craig told a reporter that in their very first meeting Barack declared his ambition of becoming president of the United States:

> In the early 1990s, when his sister [Michelle] brought her new boyfriend [Barack] home for the first time, Craig Robinson was understandably wary. Even though Michelle Robinson was 5-foot-11 and a Harvard law graduate, [to him] she was still his little sister. And while her suitor was 6-1, good-looking, ambitious and intelligent, her brother was looking for something more. "Then this guy said he liked basketball," the Brown basketball coach recalled during an interview this week. "And that was a very good sign" ... "We play a lot of pickup ball," said Robinson ... As for his brother-in-law, Robinson still shakes his head when he remembers that initial meeting. "We were talking about a variety of things and he said, 'I'm thinking about running for president one day,'" Robinson said. "I said, 'President? President of what?'" (Fitzpatrick, 2007).

Obama saw no way of unseating either of the black Congressmen from his district, Daniel Davis and Jesse Jackson, Jr. However, almost every U.S. president before him had been a state governor, a U.S. senator, or a vice president. As each state had only one governor and two U.S. senators, attaining such an office was a major achievement. Barack sought to be either the governor of Illinois or a U.S. senator from Illinois.

Only three black politicians had achieved statewide office before: Edward Brooke of Massachusetts (born 1919) as a U.S. senator, Douglas Wilder of Virginia (born 1931) as the governor of his state, and Carol Moseley Braun of Illinois (born 1947) as a U.S. senator. Obama now tried to understand the motives of people who became U.S. senators. He thought that becoming a senator required "a certain megalomania," great ambition, and "an almost fanatical single-mindedness"—and "the fear of total, complete humiliation" (Obama, 2006a, pp. 125–126, 243).

In his stand-up comedy act at the White House Correspondents Association's dinner on May 9, 2009, upon completing his first 100 days in office, Obama jokingly said that he planned to complete his next 100 days in office in 72 days "and on the 73rd day I will rest," an obvious allusion to God's creation of the world (Genesis 2:2). Obama's well-controlled megalomania is part of his high-level narcissistic grandiose self. In *The Audacity of Hope* he repeatedly recalled his humiliating loss to Rush in the Democratic Congressional primary race in 2000 (Obama, 2006a, pp. 5, 126–128). Obviously, the humiliation that he had felt then was deep, and it was a profound narcissistic injury to him. Obama is a high-level narcissistic leader, however, one who gets his narcissistic satisfaction by bringing others up to his own level rather than by putting them down. He sublimates his aggression quite well. At the previously mentioned dinner he put down many of his subordinates, friends and colleagues in a joking manner. His sense of humor is highly developed and exquisite.

THE AUDACITY OF AMBITION

In September 2001, shortly after the tragic 9/11 Islamic terrorist attacks on the United States, Obama met with a political consultant to discuss his plans for statewide office—as the governor of Illinois or a U.S. senator from Illinois. According to his own description of the meeting, in which his middle name of Hussein became a major political issue that would keep dogging him, the media consultant told Obama that his Arabic middle name had become a political liability. Obama was momentarily devastated (Obama, 2006a, pp. 5–6).

A lesser man might have given up his "fierce ambitions" (Obama, 2006a, p. 243) right then and there. Obama himself later wrote that he had realized that the media consultant was right and that this was very painful for him (Obama, 2006a, p. 7). He envied his successful colleagues who did not bear such a name, though he thought that he had begun to realize that he would have to accept that his political dream would never happen. Likening the bad news to a patient being informed of his terminal illness, he wondered whether he had gone through the stages of denial, anger, bargaining, and despair that "the experts" thought he needed to go through in such a situation, but he believed that he had "accepted his limits and his mortality" (Obama, p. 7). Obama was referring to the theories of the Swiss-American psychiatrist Elisabeth Kübler-Ross (1926–2004) about the emotional stages that dying and grieving people must go through, the last of which was acceptance (Kübler-Ross, 1969; Kübler-Ross & Kessler, 2005). The implication in his phrasing is that he had considered himself immortal.

Yet, incredibly, Obama also thought that it was this very acceptance of himself, his limits and his mortality, that made him run for the U.S. Senate. He told his wife that it was an "up-or-out" strategy, his last shot at the job (Obama, 2006a, p. 7). Even more incredibly, Obama's wife Michelle, who had been getting tired of raising their children on her own (Obama, p. 6), supported him in what he later called his "thoroughly cockeyed idea" of running for the U.S. Senate (Obama, p. 7). Obama later wrote wryly that Michelle had given him her consent out of pity for him, "though she also suggested that given the orderly life she preferred for our family, I shouldn't necessarily count on her vote" (Obama, pp. 7–8). Did he know or feel that it was *not* to be his last race and that within six years he would be running for president of the United States—and be elected? Certain it is that his humiliating defeat in 2000 only strengthened his fierce ambitions.

Sasha Abramsky thinks that Obama had a perfect sense of timing when he ran for the U.S. Senate in 2004, that he had honed his political skills to such a degree that he could "read the electorate's mood flawlessly" (2009, p. 74). The Reverend Robert C. Jones, Jr., of Miami, Florida, a friend of Obama's, told Abramsky that Obama knew how to seize the historical moment when that moment seized him. Jones thought that Obama also knew how to transcend the polarization between Democrats, Republicans, Independents, liberals and conservatives, to "step up and bring these people together and move forward" (Abramsky, 2009, pp. 74–75).

Indeed, some of Obama's most remarkable skills have been mediation and conciliation. Yet in the Arab-Israeli conflict those skills have so far proven insufficient. In March 2010, after repeated breaches of Israel's promises to halt its settlement activities in the Palestinian West Bank, an angry U.S. President Obama had a private meeting with the Israeli prime minister Benjamin Netanyahu, in which Obama demanded that Netanyahu give him a written statement of his plans for peace with the Palestinian Arabs. Perhaps Obama is still waiting for his supporters to "make him do it," as Amy Goodman (2009) recalled him saying to the supporter who asked him whether he could "carve a peace in the Middle East." The British-born American journalist Kai Bird has urged Obama to go to Jerusalem in an all-out effort to finally achieve a peaceful solution to the intractable Arab-Israeli conflict (Bird, 2010).

Chapter 17

FIERCE AMBITIONS

Synopsis: *From 1997 to 2004 Barack Obama served in the Illinois state senate, where he honed his extraordinary skills of empathy, conciliation, and bipartisanship to achieve his goals. Among the moves he sponsored and led was the unanimous, bipartisan passage of legislation to monitor and control racial profiling by requiring police to record the race of drivers they detained and legislation making Illinois the first state to mandate the videotaping of homicide interrogations. Obama thus fought not only racism but also attempts to hide the truth and subvert justice—unlike his own father, who had passed himself off as a great hero and turned out to be a self-destructive, narcissistic alcoholic. Obama's narcissism is of the constructive, high-level type. The "fierce ambitions" that Obama describes in* The Audacity of Hope *(Obama, 2006a, p. 243) joined with his need to outdo his father and to repair his "mother," America, by making it less racist, more tolerant, and kinder to its children. In 2004 he mounted a very successful campaign for the U.S. Senate seat from Illinois, winning the Democratic Party's nomination for that office, delivering the keynote address at the Democratic National Convention, and defeating his Republican opponent, the rigid, ultraconservative, and self-righteous Alan Lee Keyes, by a very wide margin.*

Already in May 2002, Obama commissioned a public-opinion poll to assess his prospects in a U.S. Senate race two years later. He created a campaign committee, began raising funds, and by August had lined up the outstanding political consultant David Axelrod (born 1955), a politically savvy move that showed Obama's excellent capacity to appraise people's character. In 2002 Obama was reelected to the Illinois senate. Obama formally announced his candidacy for the U.S. Senate in January 2003. At about the same time he became the chairman of the Illinois senate's Health and Human Services Committee when the Democrats, after a decade in the minority, regained a majority in the senate. Obama sponsored and led the unanimous, bipartisan passage of legislation to monitor racial profiling by requiring police to record the race of drivers they detained and legislation making Illinois the first American state to mandate videotaping of homicide interrogations.

While he made money from the sale of his memoir, Obama's campaign for the U.S. Senate seat in 2004 went well, and he still believed in the noble tradition of politics (Obama, 2006a, p. 2). In 2004, during Obama's election campaign for the U.S. Senate, police representatives credited him for his active engagement with the Illinois police organizations in enacting his death-penalty reforms. The Republican U.S. Senate incumbent, Peter Fitzgerald (born 1960), and his Democratic predecessor, Carol Elizabeth Moseley Braun (born 1947), whom Fitzgerald had unseated and who now sought to unseat Fitzgerald in her turn, could make no such claims. For personal reasons of their own, both Fitzgerald and Moseley Braun decided not to contest the U.S. Senate race, launching wide-open Democratic and Republican primary contests involving 15 candidates—7 Democrats and 8 Republicans. Obama's candidacy was boosted by Axelrod's excellent advertising campaign featuring images of the late Chicago Democratic Mayor Harold Washington and by an endorsement from the daughter of the late Paul Martin Simon (1928–2003), a white former Democratic U.S. Senator from Illinois.

Obama's defeat in 2000 by Bobby Rush had taught him the need to mend fences and seek alliances with key black leaders like the Illinois state senator Emil Jones (born 1935), the Democratic minority leader in the Illinois General Assembly and later the president of the Illinois senate, and his younger colleague Donne Trotter (born 1950). In *Dreams from My Father*, Obama dismissed Jones—without mentioning him by name—as "an old ward heeler who'd made the mistake of backing one of the white candidates in the last mayoral election" (Obama, 1995, p. 223). Did he unconsciously displace his contempt for his "old man" to the "old ward heeler"? Obama's Harvard biographer thinks that Jones had either not read Obama's memoir or paid little heed to it (Niven, 2009, p. 23). Did Jones know that Obama had referred to him as "an old ward heeler"? Jones gave the hardworking Obama several key assignments and "adopted" him as a son, whereas Obama was still unconsciously searching for a father figure.

In 2002 the Democrats won the Illinois state election and became the majority party in the Illinois senate. Jones was elected the first African

American majority leader in the Illinois General Assembly. By that time Obama was already contemplating his U.S. Senate race, and he asked Jones for his backing. Jones made Obama the chairman of the Illinois senate's Health and Human Services Committee and also encouraged him to lead the passage of the bill requiring the videotaping of all police interrogations and confessions in homicide cases. Using his best interpersonal skills, Obama did so with bipartisan support as well as support from death-penalty opponents and the police itself, thus ensuring the bill's passage by the legislature.

With most of Jones's endorsement and his own hard work in reaching out to his colleagues, Obama began his police-reform campaign on the right foot, with much more support and goodwill from the African American community than he had had in 2000. He was supported by the black U.S. congressmen Daniel Davis and Jesse Jackson, Jr., by the black radio station WVON, and by Michelle's friends in the black community. WVON serves the greater Chicago area, airing an African American talk-show format. The Reverend Al Sharpton and Santita Jackson, the daughter of civil rights leader Jesse Jackson, as well as Jesse Jackson himself, hosted talk shows on the station. Obama had become "black enough" for the African American community to adopt him as one of its own.

With most of the black community behind him, State Senator Barack Obama received the support of his white colleagues in the Illinois senate, of Newton Norman Minow, the former Federal Communications Commission chairman and owner of the Sidley Austin law firm, and of Paul Simon, the former U.S. senator from Illinois, who brought Obama the support of southern Illinois conservatives. Minow liked Obama greatly, declaring that he had a first-class intellect as well as a first-class temperament (Mundy, 2007; Niven, 2009, p. 24). By the time Simon died on December 9, 2003, both he and his daughter had endorsed Obama for Simon's seat in the Senate. An American journalist thought that "Barack Obama needed more than talent and ambition to rocket from obscure state senator to presidential contender in three years. He needed serious luck" (Mundy, 2007). In fact, it was not only luck but also Obama's character strengths and virtues. Obama's stability, equanimity, flexibility, and emotional intelligence were his chief assets. His choice of Axelrod as his consultant was also quite fortuitous.

Obama's campaign in 2003–2004 to win the Democratic Party's nomination for the U.S. Senate seat from Illinois ran into a very serious snag in the shape of two heavyweight rivals. One was Marson Blair Hull, Jr. (born 1942), a billionaire businessman-turned-politician who wanted that nomination for himself. The other was Daniel W. Hynes (born 1968), a young state comptroller with excellent political connections and statewide support.

Hull was the founder and chief executive officer of the Hull Group, an equity-option market-making firm that he sold to the then highly successful financial firm of Goldman Sachs. By January 2004 Hull was leading Obama in the public-opinion polls. In all the polls leading up to the March 16 Democratic primary, Hull enjoyed a substantial lead over Obama and also had widespread name recognition resulting from a well-financed television advertisement effort. He spent over $28 million of his personal fortune on this campaign, whereas Obama had barely $500,000 and could raise only another $250,000. Obama was desperate, because television advertising costs hundreds of thousands of dollars per minute and without television ads he had no chance of winning in America.

It is touching to read Obama's description of his own predicament in *The Audacity of Hope*. He knew that he was the better candidate yet felt impotent to outdo his rival. He told his supporters that he had no money to match Hull, that even under the best of circumstances he could raise no more money than would suffice for four weeks of publicity, and that they should not waste all their budget in August. He asked them to be patient, calm, and confident. But wherever he looked he could see Hull's recreational vehicle traveling around Illinois, as big and luxurious as a cruise ship. Obama had a hard time taking his own advice (Obama, 2006a, p. 135).

However, Obama did not panic or despair. He doggedly kept up his campaign, driven, as he later admitted, by his fierce ambitions, his megalomania, his fanatical single-mindedness, and his fear of public humiliation by losing the race (Obama, 2006a, pp. 125–126, 243). His future Republican presidential-campaign rival, U.S. Senator John McCain, had helped pass a campaign-finance law in the Senate that allowed rivals of millionaires like Hull to raise $12,000 per donor rather than the normal $2,000. Obama was the only candidate who had opposed the U.S. war in Iraq from the outset, a courageous stand that he had made at an antiwar rally in Chicago in October 2002. He was no pacifist and did support some wars, such as the war against Al-Qaeda and the Taliban in Afghanistan and Pakistan, but not the Iraq one, which he called "a dumb war. A rash war. A war based not on reason but on passion, not on principle but on politics" (Crowley, 2008, p. 14). This was a prescient view, which by 2004 was shared by many Democrats and the U.S. public, and by the time Obama became president, U.S. troops were being withdrawn from Iraqi cities.

Fortunately for Obama, shortly before election day in the 2004 U.S. senatorial campaign, some journalists got hold of Hull's divorce papers and court records, and allegations that Hull had abused his ex-wife began to surface in the mass-communication media. Hull's ex-wife had alleged that during a physical fight between them he had threatened to kill her. This had led the police to arrest Hull for battery, though no charges had been filed against him. However, due to his bad press, Hull's poll numbers began to drop, and Obama gained the lead in the race.

Hull's voters began to switch to Obama. Barack later recalled his extraordinary stroke of good luck as owing to the "mysterious" momentum that his campaign had generated, which made rich people as well as small donors contribute to it. The pace of the contributions grew rapidly. Using a horse-race metaphor, and alluding to his skin color, Obama recalled that his "dark-horse status" saved him from "the more dangerous pitfalls of fund-raising," such as owing political favors to his donors (Obama, 2006a, p. 135). Because most of the corporate political-action committees gave him nothing, he did not owe them anything. The few political-action committees that supported him also agreed with his liberal and progressive views. Hull spent six times as much on his campaign ads as Obama, but he never attacked Obama personally, which Obama thought was to Hull's credit, though Hull may have regretted not doing so. It was a close race. Obama wisely ran his television ads toward the end of the campaign, and then the media published Hull's wife's allegations against him, which "imploded" his campaign (Obama, 2006a, pp. 135–136).

I believe that the "mysterious" reason for Obama's campaign gaining momentum "at some point" (Obama, 2006a, p. 135) was not only the television ads that his campaign manager Axelrod carefully crafted for him but also Obama's personal charisma. The personal charisma of a political leader is an elusive psychological quality. It is not one of the strengths and virtues in the positive-psychology handbook. To the ancient Greeks charisma was a gift or grace of the gods. To the German sociologist Max Weber it was a personality trait or quality that set the leader apart from others and caused him to be treated as special, unique, and endowed with exceptional qualities and powers. The Canadian Jewish psychoanalyst Irvine Schiffer (1973, pp. 57–86) studied what he called the psychological ingredients of charisma: part-foreignness, imperfection, the calling, the fighting stance, the social station, the sexual mystique, the hoax, and the innovative lifestyle. Each one of these ingredients of charisma derives its power from the unconscious emotional life of the leader's followers, which harks back to their early-life experiences with their parents.

Obama has several, though not all, of the emotional ingredients of charisma delineated by Schiffer. Contrary to conventional wisdom and to Max Weber, these ingredients are not inherent in the leader's personality but rather depend on the early emotional life of the followers, who unconsciously attribute charisma to their leader, who in the followers' unconscious minds reincarnates their early mothers. The more the followers are stuck in their early fusional relationship with their mother, the more likely they are to attribute charisma to their leader. Obama is a unique mixture of the familiar and the foreign: part Hawai'ian, part African, part American, part Indonesian, part white, part black. He was also seen as the heir to both the black mayor Harold Washington and to the white U.S. senator Paul Simon (Niven, 2009, p. 26).

Hull was not Obama's only rival for the U.S. Senate seat from Illinois: there were six of them. The other Democratic heavyweight was Daniel W. Hynes, a brilliant young man who had graduated *magna cum laude* from the University of Notre Dame in 1990 with a B.Sc. degree in economics and computer science. Hynes had also received a J.D. degree with honors from Loyola University Law School in 1993 and was a lawyer like Obama. Hynes had also served as a health-care attorney at an important Chicago law firm. Moreover, Hynes was the son of Tom Hynes, a former Illinois senate president, Cook County assessor, Democratic ward committeeman, and member of the U.S. Democratic National Committee. Obama was confronted with a formidable opponent who had the support of 85 out of 102 Democratic county chairmen in Illinois before he even entered the U.S. Senate race with Hull and Obama (Obama, 2006a, pp. 140–141).

Driven by his "fierce ambitions," his grandiose self, his single-mindedness, and his fear of humiliation, Obama did not recoil from Hynes any more than he did from Hull. Obama doggedly sought and obtained the endorsements of several service-workers unions and did not feel that this made him in any way inappropriately indebted to them. He realized that he owed political favors to the unions that supported him. He did not feel sullied by such debts, because the people he owed them to did hard work for little pay and cared about their fellow citizens. Obama felt that he had gone into politics to fight for such people and was glad that there was a union to remind him of his obligation to their struggles (Obama, 2006a, p. 142).

In the March 2004 Democratic primary election for the U.S. Senate seat from Illinois, Obama won an unexpected landslide victory, with 53 percent of the vote in a seven-candidate field, 29 percent ahead of his nearest rival, Hynes. This unprecedented victory made him overnight a rising star in the Democratic Party and started well-justified speculation about a presidential future. In July 2004 Obama was chosen by the Democratic presidential nominee, John Kerry, to deliver the keynote address at the Democratic National Convention in Boston, at the height of Obama's campaign for the U.S. Senate seat.

Sasha Abramsky (2009, pp. 77–79) thinks that the U.S. administration of President George W. Bush was seen by the rest of the world as an arrogant, narcissistic, and swaggering empire and that Obama sought to repair this bad image of America. In his keynote address, entitled "The Audacity of Hope," Obama urged the U.S. government of George W. Bush to change its economic, social, and military priorities, while criticizing the Bush administration's mismanagement of the Iraq War and speaking about their obligations to American soldiers. The speech was inspired by the sermon "The Audacity to Hope" of his mentor and father figure, the Reverend Jeremiah Wright, Jr. He criticized the partisan views of the electorate and urged all Americans to find unity, saying, "There is not a liberal America and a conservative America; there's the United States of America." Some nine million viewers watched Obama's speech on television. It was the highlight of the convention, and it instantly elevated his status as a rising star in the Democratic Party.

Having won the Democratic primary election for the U.S. Senate seat from Illinois in March 2004 and having delivered the keynote address at the Democratic National Convention in late July, Barack Obama became a national sensation. He won his U.S. Senate seat in November, after his white Republican opponent, Jack Ryan (born 1959), had dropped out of the race due to a sex scandal involving his ex-wife. Ryan's black replacement, the Harvard-educated Alan Lee Keyes (born 1950), was a rigid, self-righteous, ultraconservative, and unfortunate candidate. Obama won both the Democratic primary election and the U.S. Senatorial race by sizable margins but, rather than attribute these successes and victories to his own hard work and charisma, he thought they were due to an inexplicable stroke of good luck (Obama, 2006a, p. 23).

Obama later marveled at how well his U.S. Senate campaign had gone in 2004 due to a "stroke of good luck." He and the other six Democratic candidates had never attacked each other personally. His richest rival, Hull, flamed out near the end of the campaign as his divorce scandal and charges of wife abuse came to light. Obama's Republican rival Ryan was felled by a divorce scandal. Obama had traveled throughout Illinois without being attacked. He was chosen to deliver the keynote address at the Democratic National Convention, which gave him "seventeen minutes of unfiltered, uninterrupted airtime on national television" (Obama, 2006a, p. 23). Finally, after Ryan's fall, the Illinois Republicans chose the worst possible candidate, the pompous, archconservative, and self-righteous Keyes, as their candidate for the U.S. Senate seat.

With his self-esteem secure, Obama did not shrink from the emotional blows that his political opponents were bound to inflict on him. Having played basketball since childhood, he saw politics as a full-contact sport and thought of its blows, knocks, and hits as part of the game: they came with the territory (Obama, 2006a, p. 22). Basketball playing is one of his chief passions, his unconscious link to his father. Obama thought that modern politics often rewarded scandalous behavior: fabricating stories, distorting meanings, insulting and questioning motives, and "poking through their personal affairs in search of damaging information" (ibid., pp. 77–78).

He also thought that modern politicians were overly swayed by the in-credible forces of money, organized people, and the mass-communication media, which affect their entire behavior (ibid., pp. 130–131).

Obama's white Republican opponent for the U.S. Senate seat from Illi-nois, Jack Ryan, had not only run an aggressive and negative campaign, at-tacking Obama personally, but also tried to discredit Obama in every way he could by digging up dirt on his personal life. Ryan had hired a young man named Justin Warfel to track Obama everywhere with a handheld video camera and to film his every word and action, so that Ryan might use them against him whenever possible. After a couple of days the tracking turned into stalking. Obama's attempts to reason with Justin were fruitless. Like a soldier captured by the enemy, all Justin would give was "his name, rank and phone number" (Obama, 2006a, p. 79). After two or three days of this an angry Obama publicly shamed Justin by exposing him before a group of reporters (ibid., 2006a, pp. 78–79). Obama received an apology from Ryan's campaign, and Justin henceforth kept his distance from him.

The Republicans' choice of the rigid, conservative, and self-righteous black politician Keyes as their nominee for the U.S. Senate seat from Illinois was indeed the greatest blessing that Obama could have expected. Keyes had twice sought the Republican nomination for president of the United States (in 1996 and in 2000) and lost each time. The Republicans chose Keyes to run against Obama on August 8, 2004—86 days before election day—after their previous nominee, Ryan, had withdrawn due to a sex scandal with his ex-wife and after all the other potential Republi-can nominees had declined to run. The *Washington Post* called Keyes a "carpetbagger" since he had never lived in Illinois.

In U.S. history, *carpetbagger* was the derogatory name Southerners gave to northern white Republicans who moved into the South during the Reconstruction era (1865–1877) that followed the American Civil War, because their travel bags were made of carpet. In the Republican Party, the carpetbaggers formed a coalition with black freedmen (freed slaves) and with white scalawags (Southerners supporting the Reconstruction govern-ments after the American Civil War, often for private gain). Together they politically controlled the former Confederate states for varying periods (1867–1877). The Southerners thought that the carpetbaggers wanted to loot and plunder the defeated South. The term *carpetbagger* is still an insult in common American usage. The term is used derisively to refer to a politi-cian who runs for public office in an area he or she is not originally from or in which he or she has lived for only a very short time.

When asked by the National Public Radio show host Tavis Smiley to answer charges of carpetbagging in view of his criticism of Hillary Clinton running for the U.S. Senate from New York, Keyes denounced Clinton's campaign as "pure and planned selfish ambition" while claiming that his own campaign was waged out of "a moral obligation to run" after being asked to run by the Republican state committee—and because he believed that it was God's will (Keyes & Smiley, 2004). Keyes was an ultraconservative fundamentalist Christian with no real ties to Illinois. Alluding to an ultraconservative U.S. pundit, Obama called Keyes "a cross between a Pentecostal preacher and William F. Buckley" (2006a, p. 249).

Pentecostalism is an American Christian renewal movement that emphasizes the direct personal experience of God through the baptism in the Holy Spirit as evidenced by speaking in tongues. Pentecostal preachers are known for their religious fervor. William Frank Buckley, Jr. (1925–2008), was an ultraconservative American intellectual, author and commentator. He founded the right-wing U.S. political magazine *National Review* in 1955, hosted the Public Broadcasting Service's television show *Firing Line* from 1966 until 1999, and was a nationally syndicated newspaper columnist. His speaking and writing style was famed for its erudition, wit, and use of uncommon words, as well as for Buckley's mannerisms.

Keyes was not only ultraconservative but also a self-righteous preacher by nature. Keyes was convinced that he knew perfectly well what God and Jesus Christ thought and felt, and he pronounced Obama unfit to run for the U.S. Senate. "Jesus Christ would not vote for Barack Obama," Keyes said angrily and publicly, because of the votes that Obama had, as a member of the Illinois General Assembly, had cast in 2001 against a package of three antiabortion bills that Obama found too broad and unconstitutional. Keyes accused Obama of supporting anti-Christian behavior. Keyes had come from Maryland, had never lived in Illinois, and was hated by many of his colleagues in the Republican National Committee. Despite all this, the Illinois Republican committee had chosen him as its candidate for the U.S. Senate. One of Obama's Republican colleagues in the Illinois legislature told him that the Illinois Republicans had wanted a Harvard-educated black conservative to challenge the Harvard-educated black liberal Obama. "He may not win, but at least he can knock that halo off your head" (Obama, 2006a, pp. 247–248).

Keyes was an obsessional and narcissistic man with rigid, self-righteous, and ultraconservative views on every political and religious issue, including abortion, homosexuality, and gay marriage. As many politicians do unconsciously, including President George W. Bush, he split his world into black and white, the forces of conservative good against those of liberal evil. As Obama ironically put it, "Mr. Keyes could deliver a grammatically flawless disquisition on virtually any topic" (Obama, 2006a, p. 248). Like a Pentecostal preacher, Obama recalled, with obvious pleasure and heavy irony, Keyes worked himself into a holy frenzy, rocking his body, sweating profusely, jabbing the air with his finger, "his high-pitched voice trembling with emotion as he called the faithful to do battle against the forces of evil" (ibid., p. 248).

In contrast to Obama's high-level constructive narcissism, Keyes, like Obama's father, was undone by his own self-destructive grandiosity, by his saying whatever came into his mind with no self-censorship, and by alienating "just about everybody" (Obama, 2006a, pp. 248–249). Keyes made Obama so angry that Obama had to suppress his natural urge to wring his rival's neck whenever they met. Obama did not know why Keyes was able to upset him so badly. "I found him getting under my skin in a way that few people ever have" (Obama, p. 250).

Obama's murderous rage at Keyes was so great that during one of his televised debates with Keyes before the U.S. Senate election, the usually calm and self-confident Obama became tongue-tied, irritable, and uncharacteristically tense. When his supporters asked Obama why he was letting Keyes drive him out of his mind, Obama did not have a good answer for them (Obama, 2006a, p. 250). He did not know that his rage at Keyes had been unconsciously displaced from his dead father, who had pontificated to his son about moral behavior and high ideals while he himself abused his wives and children, became an alcoholic, and destroyed his own life.

Obama thought that he had to take Keyes seriously because he claimed to speak for Obama's Christian religion and because some of his extremist views had many adherents within the Christian church. This may have been an unconscious rationalization on Obama's part. What really got under his skin may have been his unconscious reaction to Keyes as a reincarnation of his father, who had been just as grandiose, narcissistic, offensive, self-righteous, and self-destructive as Keyes himself. The rigid, obsessional, grandiose, and religious Keyes may well have reminded Obama of his self-destructive, grandiose father, who had always thought of himself as superior to everybody else and had misrepresented himself as a doctor, a wealthy man, and an important person, even when he was jobless and destitute and had no doctorate.

Obama thought that Keyes epitomized right-wing fundamental American Christianity. Keyes spoke like a fiery biblical prophet. Obama had no trouble countering his opponent's political and constitutional arguments, but he found it hard to deal with Keyes's religious orations. Keyes accused Obama of supporting the "abominations" of homosexuality and abortion. Obama wanted to tell Keyes that it was folly to read the Bible literally and that the pope was not infallible, but that would have offended millions of American Catholics. Instead, Obama replied that America was a pluralistic society, that one could not impose one's religious views on others, and that he was running for the U.S. Senate, not the Catholic Church. Yet within himself Obama still had doubts about the purity and sincerity of his Christian faith (Obama, 2006a, pp. 251–252).

Obama was mindful of his opponent's implicit accusations against him because his Christian faith was not as solid as he wished it to be. Abramsky (2009, p. 57) thinks that pluralism and diversity were a crucial and vital part of Obama's existence. Due to his unconscious transference from his father to Keyes, Obama let Keyes do to him what his father had done to him earlier: put him in the box of the accused. Fortunately for Obama, however, the self-righteous Keyes antagonized just about everybody, and his personal attacks on Obama failed to dent the latter's public support. Obama would defeat Keyes by a landslide.

In July 2004 Obama's former teacher at Harvard Law School, Professor Laurence Henry Tribe, spoke highly of him to Bob Shrum, the top adviser to U.S. Senator John Kerry, the Democratic presidential nominee. Thanks to the efforts of Obama's consultant David Axelrod and to Tribe's recommendation, Kerry chose Obama to deliver the keynote address at the Democratic National Convention in Boston. This was a major achievement. The black congresswoman Barbara Charline Jordan (1936–1996) had given a highly esteemed keynote address at the Democratic National Convention 28 years earlier, in 1976, but Obama's speech outdid hers.

Obama's historic speech took place in Boston's Fleet Center, across the Charles River from Harvard University, his *alma mater* and that of his father. He began his speech by invoking his dead father: "My father was a foreign student, born and raised in a small village in Kenya. He grew up herding goats, went to school in a tin-roof shack. His father, my grandfather, was a cook, a domestic servant to the British." Obama added that "through hard work and perseverance" his father had been admitted to a university in that "magical place" called America "that shone as a beacon of freedom and opportunity to so many who had come before" (Obama, 2004).

Obama's Harvard biographer thinks that Obama described his father as an immigrant (Niven, 2009, p. 28). This is an error. The word *immigrant* occurred only once in the speech, in a rousing sentence: "It's the hope of slaves sitting around a fire singing freedom songs; the hope of immigrants setting out for distant shores; the hope of a young naval lieutenant bravely patrolling the Mekong Delta; the hope of a millworker's son who dares to defy the odds; the hope of a skinny kid with a funny name who believes that America has a place for him, too. Hope in the face of difficulty. Hope in the face of uncertainty. The audacity of hope!" (Obama, 2004).

Obama skillfully used his keynote address to appeal to the various ethnic, social, and religious groups composing the Democratic Party's voters and to rally as many diverse American groups as possible to the Democratic cause. He invoked the names of a well-known black American and a well-known white American. The black man was Booker T. Washington (1856–1915), an educator, orator, author, and the dominant leader of the African American community from the 1890s to his death. The white man was Horatio Alger, Jr. (1832–1899), a prolific author of novels about boot-blacks, newsboys, peddlers, buskers, and other poor children in their rise from humble backgrounds to middle-class security and comfort; Alger's novels were hugely popular in their day.

Obama spoke for 17 minutes and was interrupted 33 times by applause, an average of one applause every 30 seconds. He skillfully packed plenty of punch into a speech that comprised less than 2,300 words. Obama's Harvard biographer thinks that in his brief address Obama not only appealed to colored people and immigrants but also compared his father and himself to the heroes Washington and Alger. Nor did he forget to appeal to rural Midwesterners by invoking his Kansan mother and her hardworking father, mentioning his grandfather's military career as well. Obama "staked a family claim to the dignity of their labor—in both senses of that word" (Niven, 2009, pp. 28–29).

In his keynote address, Barack Obama compared himself with Franklin D. Roosevelt and with Harry Truman, two popular Democratic U.S. presidents. He related his grandparents' story, his mother's, and his own, saying that America had given such a uniquely diverse person as himself the opportunity to make it. He mentioned his grandfather's postwar college study under the G.I. Bill. Obama failed to mention, however, that his grandfather had dropped out of college shortly after enrolling at the University of California at Berkeley. Was he still ashamed of Gramps? Obama's praise for America was sky-high. He said that in no other country in the world would his saga have been possible. Niven thinks that "Obama returned to situate himself in a no less profoundly American tradition, that of American exceptionalism" (2009, p. 29).

As he had done in the Illinois legislature, Obama went beyond partisanship. He opposed America's division into liberal and conservative, white and black, Latino and Asian, and insisted that there was just one United States of America. Unconsciously, this was like a child saying that he had only one mother. He castigated the Bush administration's Patriot Act, which eroded the civil liberties of Americans in the name of national security, and the U.S. Supreme Court's decision to halt the Florida presidential-vote recount in November 2000, which had given the U.S. presidency to Bush when it rightfully belonged to Al Gore. He depicted the voters' choice as between the politics of hope and the politics of cynicism. In rousing tones, he invoked Martin Luther King, Jr., and Jesse Jackson. The extraordinary speech, whose title came from the Reverend Wright's sermon, was followed by the singing of a gospel choir, urging everyone to "keep on pushing." Overnight, Obama became a national political sensation (Archibold, 2004; Niven, 2009, p. 31).

As could have been expected, in the November 2004 election for the U.S. Senate seat from Illinois, the Democrat Obama defeated the Republican Keyes by a landslide. The popular Obama won 70 percent of the statewide vote, while the impossible Keyes won only 27 percent. It was the largest victory margin for a statewide political race in Illinois history. The U.S. mass-communication media played a major role in this victory. Obama knew it, yet he felt that they often distorted the facts, to the point that at times it was impossible to determine what really happened (Obama, 2006a, pp. 144–146). He was right, as the false claims by Keyes that Obama was a Marxist, a Communist, an atheist, and "not really black" because his ancestors had not been African slaves would continue to dog Obama during his presidential campaign of 2008 (Niven, 2009, p. 27).

When Barack Obama became a U.S. senator, there had been only two African American U.S. senators in the modern era: Edward William Brooke (born 1919), a Republican from Massachusetts, and Carol Moseley Braun (born 1947), a Democrat from Illinois. Brooke's term had ended in 1979, and Moseley Braun's in 1999, which now made Obama the only African American U.S. senator. After John Kerry lost the presidential election to the incumbent George W. Bush, Obama became the new star of the Democratic Party. From 2004 he was considered a likely contender for his party's next presidential nomination in 2008.

After Obama became a Democratic U.S. Senator from Illinois, he also became a millionaire. Barack and Michelle Obama used the proceeds from his 1995 book *Dreams from My Father*, which was reissued in 2004, to move from their nice Hyde Park condominium apartment in Chicago's South Side to a private home in neighboring Kenwood, which was worth $1.6 million at that time. Kenwood is one of the most elite neighborhoods in Chicago. The famous homosexual murderers Nathan Freudenthal Leopold, Jr. (1904–1971), and Richard Albert Loeb (1905–1936) had lived in Kenwood, as had their teenage victim, Bobby Franks (1909–1924). Kenwood includes two Chicago Landmark districts (Kenwood District and North Kenwood District). A number of prominent organizations in the area, like the Hyde Park-Kenwood Community Conference, refer to the community as Hyde Park-Kenwood or Hyde Park-South Kenwood.

The Obamas did not leave Chicago's South Side but were now living in the affluent neighborhood of Kenwood. However, from early 2001 Obama spent most of his time in Washington, away from his wife and children, which was not an abandonment as his father had done with him and his mother yet was painful for him. He missed his wife and daughters and often called home several times daily. In 2006 U.S. senator Obama won the Grammy Award for the Best Spoken Word Album for his audio recording of himself reading his *Dreams from My Father*. He also published his second book, *The Audacity of Hope*, whose title was that of his keynote address at the Democratic National Convention in 2004 and which he had borrowed from his mentor, the Reverend Wright.

The Syrian-born Antoin (Tony) Rezko was a Chicago developer whose real-estate deals were considered shady or not quite legal. In June 2005, U.S. Senator Obama and Rezko purchased adjoining land parcels in the Chicago neighborhood of Kenwood. At the same time Obama paid $1.65 million for a Georgian revival mansion, while Rezko paid $625,000 for an adjacent lot, as yet undeveloped. Both men closed the deals on their properties on the same day. In January 2006, in order to increase the size of his yard, Obama bought a small part of Rezko's land for $104,500 which was $60,000 above the assessed value of the small parcel bought by Obama.

Unfortunately for Obama, soon after his land purchase from Rezko, the latter was indicted and later convicted on political-corruption charges, which, however, were unrelated to Obama. In November 2006, to avoid guilt by association, Obama wisely and publicly regretted the mistake he had made in buying the small piece of land from Rezko (McKinney & Fusco, 2006). In 2007, after U.S. Senator Obama announced his presidential candidacy, *Money* magazine estimated the Obama family's net worth at $1.3 million. Their 2007 U.S. tax return showed a household income of $4.2 million—up from about $1 million in 2006 and $1.6 million in 2005—mostly from the sale of his popular books.

When Obama launched his second book, *The Audacity of Hope*, as he spoke of his work as a U.S. senator in Washington and of the heavy price that his wife and daughters were paying for it, due to his absence from home, he began to cry silently. Was he crying because of their pain, his own guilt feelings, or his loneliness in Washington? His wife Michelle calmed him down. One of the key subjects of the book was the bad effect of America's mass-communication media on its political culture (Obama, 2006a, pp. 144–146). Obama was not upset by right-wingers like the radio talk-show host Rush Limbaugh, who coarsely called him "Osama Obama," or by Glenn Beck of the ultraconservative Fox News television network, whose attacks on him were a knee-jerk reflex to his name, but he did fear more sophisticated right-wing critics, like Margaret Ellen Noonan (born 1950), better known as Peggy Noonan, an intelligent conservative columnist of the William F. Buckley ilk.

In 2005 U.S. Senator Barack Obama took part in the dedication ceremony of the new Lincoln Presidential Library in Springfield, Illinois, and his five-minute speech there was later published as an essay in *Time* magazine under the title of "What I See in Lincoln's Eyes" (Obama, 2005). Not surprisingly, in that essay Obama identified himself with Lincoln: "*In Lincoln's rise from poverty, his ultimate mastery of language and law, his capacity to overcome personal loss and remain determined in the face of repeated defeat—in all this he reminded me not just of my own struggles.* He also reminded me of a larger, fundamental element of American life—the enduring belief that we can constantly remake ourselves to fit our larger dreams" (Obama, 2005; italics added).

Obama's right-wing foes pounced on the italicized sentence. Three days later, Obama was publicly savaged by Peggy Noonan in the *Wall Street Journal* (Noonan, 2005). She was the author of seven conservative books on politics, religion, and culture, a weekly columnist for the *Wall Street Journal*, and a former speechwriter and special assistant to U.S. President Ronald Reagan. Five of Noonan's seven books had been *New York Times* best sellers. Quoting the single "incriminating" sentence from Obama's piece, Noonan used scathing irony to attack him:

> *Oh. So that's what Lincoln's for. Actually Lincoln's life is a lot like Mr. Obama's.* Lincoln came from a lean-to in the backwoods. His mother died when he was 9. The Lincolns had no money, no standing. Lincoln educated himself, reading law on his own, working as a field hand, a store clerk and a raft hand on the Mississippi. He also split some rails. He entered politics, knew more defeat than victory, and went on to lead the nation through its greatest trauma, the [American] Civil War, and past its greatest sin, slavery. *Barack Obama, the son of two University of Hawaii students, went to Columbia and Harvard Law after attending a private academy that taught the children of the Hawaiian royal family.* He made his name in politics as an aggressive Chicago vote hustler in Bill Clinton's first campaign for the presidency. (Noonan, 2005; italics added)

Noonan had unfairly attacked Obama for his Ivy League education, which, naturally, had not been available to Lincoln. Obama was truly pained by Noonan's attack on him. The very title of her piece, "Conceit of Government," offended him. Noonan had compared Obama to an arrogant peacock, "flapping his wings" in *Time* magazine, comparing himself to Lincoln and implying that he outdid Lincoln. Unlike Lincoln, she had written, Obama had never seen a log cabin and had never even approached Lincoln's greatness. And if he kept comparing himself to Lincoln, she wrote sarcastically, he never would. "Ouch!" wrote Obama later (2006a, p. 147).

Noonan's piece, which called Obama an egomaniac, hurt Obama, and he admitted it. Here again we see Obama's capacity for emotional honesty, his emotional intelligence, his ability to own up to his true feelings. He even admitted in his book that the public beating he had received from Noonan was partly deserved (Obama, 2006a, p. 147). But he also learned from this affair how important it is for a politician to weigh his words carefully, because "a single ill-considered remark can generate more bad publicity than years of ill-considered policies" (Obama, 2006a, p. 147).

Before coming to Washington, Illinois state senator Obama, who, as one could clearly see from his stand-up comedy acts at the White House Correspondents Association's dinner and at the Kennedy Center Honors dinner in 2009, has an excellent sense of humor, including the ability to laugh at himself, had been emotionally open, free, spontaneous, humorous, passionate, and honest. After becoming a U.S. senator and coming to Washington, however, U.S. Senator Obama discovered that on Washington's Capitol Hill, jokes, irony and spontaneity, and especially passion, could be politically dangerous (Obama, 2006a, pp. 147–148). In order to survive politically, this consummate politician had to learn to temper his natural spontaneity and to control his emotions. He became "no-drama Obama," as General Tony McPeak called him.

Obama learned a very important lesson from Noonan's public attack on him. The single sentence that Noonan had quoted from his *Time* magazine essay made him look bad. Like every important piece of journalism, Noonan's piece raced through the World Wide Web. Every right-wing website posted the piece to paint Obama as a megalomaniac fool (Obama, 2006a, p. 148). Although he had clearly added in his next sentence that Lincoln reminded him not only of his own struggles but also of the struggles of America, Noonan had left out his second sentence in her attack. This was selective quotation at its most damaging. Obama learned that a single ill-considered sentence could make him look arrogant or megalomaniac and that his political enemies could take it out of context and make this distortion look like the truth once it had been copied and circulated endlessly in the mass-communication media. Henceforth he would try to be very careful what he said and wrote.

THE SECOND BOOK

In 2005 U.S. Senator Obama, the author of the 1995 memoir *Dreams from My Father*, was commissioned by his publisher Random House to write *The Audacity of Hope*, whose title was derived from his keynote address at the Democratic National Convention in 2004, which in turn came from the sermon entitled "The Audacity to Hope" by his former pastor, Reverend Wright. Noonan's attack on him that year may have been one reason Obama accepted the offer to write this second book. In this book he related his personal and political career from 1996 to 2006. Unlike his previous book, which had much to do with his father, this one was inspired by his mother and his maternal grandmother.

In what might look like a feminist spirit, Obama dedicated *The Audacity of Hope* "To the women who raised me—MY MATERNAL GRAND-MOTHER, TUTU, who's been a rock of stability throughout my life, and MY MOTHER, whose loving spirit sustains me still" (Obama, 2006a, dedication page). This dedication begs some questions. Why did he put his grandmother before his mother? Why did he call her Tutu—also the last name of the black South African clergyman and Nobel-Peace-Prize-winner Desmond Tutu—and not Toot, as he had called her in *Dreams from My Father*? Why did he mention his grandmother's name but not his mother's name? Why did he did not dedicate the book to his dead grandfather, Gramps? Was it because Gramps had so deeply disappointed Barry during his adolescence?

During 2006 U.S. Senator Obama agonized over whether to run for president of the United States. His "fierce ambitions" (Obama, 2006a, p. 243) drove him to do so, but his fear of humiliation, the kind he had suffered in his 2000 defeat to Bobby Rush, and his concern for his wife and daughters, whom he would have to subject to grueling public scrutiny, gave him pause. In late 2006 his wife and daughters finally gave their consent to his bid for the presidency. Obama's wife, Michelle, later told a *Glamour* magazine interviewer that she feared that her husband's presidential campaign would disrupt their family, that she worried about how her children would handle all the attention from the mass-communication media, and that when she imagined her husband being elected, she had goose pimples (Abramsky, 2009, p. 53; Lewis Lee, 2007, 2008).

Michelle does not idealize Barack. She told her black interviewer, Tonya Lewis Lee, that her husband was "snorey and stinky … very much human, so let's not deify him" (Lewis Lee, 2007). Michelle and her daughters also made similar critical remarks about Barack in their televised interview with Maria Menounos of *Access Hollywood* the following year (Hoffecker, 2008). Abramsky thinks that Michelle was "gently trying to deflate" her husband's "bubble of effortlessness," the amazing ease with which he walked the hallways of power, his incredible self-confidence, and his extraordinary calm. Yet Michelle also told the same interviewer that Obama had something special to offer the voters (Abramsky, 2009, pp. 85–86; Lewis Lee, 2007, 2008). Despite her ever-present fear that Barack might be assassinated, Michelle agreed to let him run for president, and she seems to have handled her husband's campaign, his election, and her role as first lady quite well. By contrast, Alma Powell had vetoed a presidential race by her husband, Colin Powell, out of the very same fear.

As he launched his presidential bid in February 2007 at the state house in Springfield, Illinois, the issues of Obama's name, race, identity, and "blackness" came back to the public forefront. Debra Dickerson (born 1959), a prolific African American writer, now repeated the old-hat charge made by Keyes in 2004 that Obama was "not really black" because his forefathers had not been African slaves (Dickerson, 2007). Most African Americans, however, did not share her feelings. They agreed with the black writer George Samuel Schuyler (1895–1977) that black people all over America, no matter their descent, no matter how light or dark their skin, learned very early in their lives that their black skin color was a disadvantage in a white world (Schuyler, 1966, p. 1).

Chapter 18

THE AUDACITY OF AMBITION

Synopsis: *At the time Barack Obama became a U.S. Senator in 2005 there had been only two African American U.S. senators in the modern era: Edward William Brooke (born 1919), a Massachusetts Republican, and Carol Elizabeth Moseley Braun (born 1947), an Illinois Democrat. Brooke's term had ended in 1979 and Moseley Braun's in 1999, which made Obama the only African American U.S. senator. He engaged in a vigorous legislative program in the areas of race relations, the environment, education, nuclear nonproliferation, health, and other public-interest legislation. His mentor and "father" in the Senate was the Republican Senator Richard Lugar, his senior by almost 30 years, who worked with Obama to sponsor important environmental and public-interest legislation. Obama, however, could not rest until he reached the very top: the U.S. presidency. His ideal self, his grandiose image of himself, his need to repair his motherland, demanded that he attain the pinnacle of power and, unlike his father, use that power to take care of America like a good father. Obama ran an unprecedented campaign using the power of the Internet, in which he defeated a pack of Democratic rivals, including his most formidable one, U.S. Senator Hillary Clinton of New York, who had the support of her husband, the former president. Some political analysts thought that Bill Clinton actually hurt his wife's campaign. In any event Obama's well-balanced and almost imperturbable personality, and his extraordinary charisma, due to his being so special and different from any other candidate, helped him win the nomination of the Democratic Party and the presidency of the United States, in which his Republican rival John McCain made many errors and was roundly defeated.*

U.S. Senator Barack Obama, whose wife, Michelle, was a descendant of African slaves and whose father was an African, identified himself with the African American community. He was a member of the new generation of African American political leaders like Deval Laurdine Patrick (born 1956), the black governor of Massachusetts, and Artur Genestre Davis (born 1967), the black congressman from Alabama, who, unlike the black leaders of the previous generation, were educated in Ivy League law schools, were less partisan and more pragmatic, flexible, and practical, and were ready to compromise with whites, Republicans and conservatives. Some of these black leaders had adopted less liberal and even conservative positions to win statewide office. They were willing to compromise with conservatives to achieve their aims.

In the November 2006 elections, the Democrats gained control of the U.S. House of Representatives and of the U.S. Senate. In February 2007, after his wife and children had given their assent, U.S. Senator Obama announced his candidacy for U.S. president outside the Illinois state capitol in Springfield. The previous Illinois politician to win the U.S. presidency had been Abraham Lincoln, a native son of Illinois, and Barack was a native of Hawai'i, with no executive experience. He was also a junior U.S. senator. Obama used his formidable talent for forging alliances with people of all political colors, including Republican conservatives. He worked with the Republican Senator Tom Coburn for transparency and accountability in the U.S. government. The Republican Senator Richard Lugar of Indiana (born 1932) became his mentor and his new "father figure." Like father and son, the elder and the younger senators worked together to eliminate nuclear stockpiles in the former Soviet republics, where they traveled. In 2009 Obama received the Nobel Peace Prize for his work to eliminate nuclear weapons as well as for his efforts to create a peaceful dialogue between the United States and the Muslim world.

Unlike his Senate colleagues, Senator Obama disliked the interminable Senate committee and subcommittee meetings (Niven, 2009, p. 34). Instead, he attended numerous town-hall meetings in Illinois and raised funds for his fellow Democrats. He badly missed his wife and children, who were in Chicago, while he was in Washington. In 2005 and 2006 he called home every day and returned home almost every week. After he entered the U.S. presidential race in February 2007, his campaign activities strained his family life. Alma Powell, the wife of General Colin Powell, had vetoed her husband's U.S. presidential bids in 1996 and 2000 for fear of his being assassinated, and Michelle feared the same fate for Barack. Nonetheless, she and their two daughters ultimately consented to his presidential candidacy, and in November 2007, in a speech in South Carolina, Barack cited "the fierce urgency of now," a phrase of Martin Luther King, Jr., as a justification for his "precocious" bid for the presidency (Dickinson, 2007). His Democratic rivals, however, shared his fierce ambitions and fierce sense of urgency.

Though Obama's presidential-primary rivals were all centrist Democrats on domestic issues and all of them agreed on foreign issues, his rivals were more experienced and more senior than he was. They were a formidable array of U.S. politicians: Senators Chris Dodd of Connecticut, Joe Biden of Delaware, and Hillary Clinton of New York, and Governor John Edwards of North Carolina who had been John Kerry's running mate in the 2004 presidential election. There was one major difference between Obama and the others, however: in 2002 the others had voted for a Senate resolution supporting the U.S. war in Iraq, while Obama had opposed it. Though the antiwar Democratic nominee John Kerry had narrowly lost to George W. Bush in 2004, the following years made more and more Americans opposed to the Iraq war. It began to dawn on Americans that Obama had been the only statesman with the correct insight about the tragic U.S. war in Iraq, which had cost the United States endless losses of blood and treasure. From February 2007 to January 2008 Obama's presidential campaign raised $140 million, much of it from small donors over the Internet (Niven, 2009, p. 35).

In January 2008 Obama won the Iowa caucuses, the first race of the U.S. presidential campaign, with the overwhelming support of young white voters and antiwar activists. In the Iowa caucuses, Iowans gather all over the state to elect delegates to their county conventions, which in turn elect delegates to statewide conventions, which finally elect the delegates to the national Democratic and Republican conventions, which choose their presidential nominees.

Every four years, during presidential-election years, the Iowa caucuses receive tremendous attention from the U.S. mass-communication media. Each candidate tries hard to win them. They are considered the earliest indication of where the candidates are headed. A quarter of a million Iowans had turned up to caucus in Iowa, twice the normal turnout. In late January 2008 Obama also won the South Carolina primary election, defeating Clinton and Edwards. He became a mainstream and leading candidate (Niven, 2009, p. 36).

After her losses in Iowa and South Carolina, Obama's chief rival, Hillary Clinton, mobilized all her forces, money, and support to win the first U.S. presidential primary election, that of New Hampshire. In the presidential election, each state has a certain number of delegates to the Electoral College, and each state holds primary elections for the Democratic and Republican candidates. Each candidate tries to win as many primary elections as possible, so as to increase his or her delegate count. New Hampshire holds its primary election before all the other states, and therefore winning it is very important to all the candidates. U.S. elections are held on Tuesdays, and the New Hampshire primary falls on the third Tuesday in March. The people of New Hampshire hold town-hall meetings and municipal elections. Clinton defeated Obama in the March 2008 Democratic primary election in New Hampshire.

By the spring of 2008 it was Clinton versus Obama for the Democratic Party's presidential nomination, as the other candidates gradually dropped out of the race. Clinton had the endorsements of important black Democratic leaders like Congressman Charles Rangel of New York (born 1930) and Congressman John Lewis of Georgia (born 1940), but Obama had the support of many others. He also raised more money than Clinton by wisely using the Internet. In March 2008, after his loss in New Hampshire, Senator Obama enlisted some very prominent people to support his presidential campaign. The retired general Merrill Anthony McPeak (born 1936), a former chief of staff of the U.S. Air Force, citing Obama's emotional balance, called him "no drama Obama" and "no shock Barack" (McCormick, 2008). These epithets were picked up by political commentators like Andrew Sullivan (2008) and Arianna Huffington (2008). President Obama has retained his reputation for keeping his cool even under provocation. His self-esteem and self-confidence help him take lightly what others see as unbearable insults and defamations.

Chapter 19

ABANDONING ANOTHER "BAD FATHER"

Synopsis: *The Reverend Jeremiah Wright, Jr., the fiery anti-white leader of Chicago's Trinity United Church of Christ, had baptized Barack Obama a Christian in 1988, after he had gone to Kenya and wrestled with his father's ghost (Kantor, 2007a). Wright had also married Obama and baptized his two daughters. Wright felt a deep rage at "white America" for all the wrongs it had done to the African blacks, from the old slavery to modern discrimination. During the presidential campaign of 2008 the U.S. mass-communication media unearthed racist sermons that Wright had given in 2001 and 2003 against white America in which he blamed America itself for the 9/11 tragedy and accused it of genocide against the black people. Obama gave a speech entitled "A More Perfect Union" invoking the Constitutional Convention of 1787 and trying to conciliate the Reverend Wright, who had been a father figure to him. But Wright made yet another inflammatory speech to the National Press Club in which he once more repeated his wild and racist anti-white accusations. To salvage his campaign, Obama was forced to break with Wright and denounce his racism. This meant losing yet another father figure, but it gave Obama new emotional vigor and reinforced his conciliatory character.*

In early 2008, the 66-year-old Reverend Jeremiah Alvesta Wright retired from his post after 36 years as the senior pastor of his Trinity United Church of Christ congregation, and he no longer had daily responsibilities at the church. Following his retirement, the Reverend Wright's beliefs and manner of preaching were scrutinized by investigative journalists when segments from his sermons were publicized in connection with Obama's presidential campaign. Naturally, Obama's foes sought to use his preacher's sermons to discredit him.

In March 2008 Obama's presidential campaign was dealt a serious blow by the publication by ABC News of two incendiary racist sermons by his firebrand pastor, the Reverend Wright. The first sermon, entitled *The Day of Jerusalem's Fall*, had been given on September 16, 2001, just five days after Al-Qaeda's terrorist attacks on the United States, which felled the Twin Towers of New York's World Trade Center, killing thousands of innocent people. These attacks had also downed a passenger plane in Pennsylvania, killing hundreds more, and had hit the Pentagon. Wright's second sermon, entitled *Confusing God and Government*, had been delivered on April 13, 2003. In inflammatory anti-white and anti-American terms, Wright had blamed white America for its own troubles and accused the U.S. government of committing genocide against the black people. One could hardly imagine a worse anti-white and anti-American sermon (Wright, 2003, 2008).

In *The Day of Jerusalem's Fall*, the sermon delivered by Wright on September 16, 2001, Reverend Wright at first cited Psalm 137 from the Bible. This psalm is about the exile of the Jews from Judah to Babylon (in 586 B.C.E.), their grief, and their wish for revenge on the Babylonians. The psalm's text moves from grief to rage, revenge, and violence. Here is the Authorized Version of this psalm, the one most likely known to Wright:

> By the rivers of Babylon, there we sat down, yea, we wept, when we remembered Zion. We hanged our harps upon the willows in the midst thereof. For there they that carried us away captive required of us a song; and they that wasted us required of us mirth, saying, Sing us one of the songs of Zion. How shall we sing the LORD's song in a strange land? If I forget thee, O Jerusalem, let my right hand forget her cunning. If I do not remember thee, let my tongue cleave to the roof of my mouth; if I prefer not Jerusalem above my chief joy. Remember, O LORD, the children of Edom in the day of Jerusalem; who said, Rase it, rase it, even to the foundation thereof. O daughter of Babylon, who art to be destroyed; happy shall he be, that rewardeth thee as thou hast served us. Happy shall he be, that taketh and dasheth thy little ones against the stones.

This last verse is horrifying, although it may not have been so to those who wrote it: modern biblical scholars attribute the Psalms to various Jewish authors from different time periods in Israel's history, ranging from the time of King David (ca. 1000 B.C.E.) to the intertestamental period (ca. 420–20 B.C.E.). In those days murderous violence in war, including the murder of children and babies, was common. At the beginning of his sermon, however, Wright seemed to oppose the wish for revenge. He talked about the "insane" cycle of violence and hatred:

> There's a move in Psalm 137 from thoughts of paying tithes to thoughts of paying back—a move, if you will, from worship to war, a move in other words from the worship of the God of creation to war against those whom God created. And I want you to notice very carefully this next move. One of the reasons this Psalm is rarely read in its entirety [is] because it is a move that spotlights the insanity of the cycle of violence and the cycle of hatred. (Wright, 2008).

Soon thereafter in his sermon, however, Wright had commented on an interview with the former U.S. ambassador Edward Peck that he had seen on the conservative Fox News television network the day before. Peck was a retired U.S. career diplomat who had served for 32 years in the U.S. Foreign Service. Wright himself seemed to move from "the insanity of the cycle of violence and the cycle of hatred" to the preaching of violence and revenge. Here are Wright's inflammatory comments:

> I heard Ambassador Peck on an interview yesterday. Did anybody else see him or hear him? He was on Fox News. This is a white man, and he was upsetting the Fox News commentators to no end. He pointed out—did you see him, John?—a white man, he pointed out, ambassador, that what Malcolm X said when he got silenced by Elijah Muhammad was in fact true—America's chickens are coming home to roost. We took this country by terror, away from the Sioux, the Apache, the Aroawak, the Comanche, the Arapajo, the Navajo. Terrorism! We took Africans from their country to build our way of ease and kept them enslaved and living in fear. Terrorism! We bombed Grenada and killed innocent civilians, babies, non-military personnel. We bombed the black civilian community of Panama with stealth bombers and killed unarmed teenagers, and toddlers, pregnant mothers and hard working fathers. We bombed Gaddhafi, his home, and killed his child. Blessed be they who bash your children's head [sic] against the rocks. (Wright, 2008)

This horrifying last sentence was a paraphrase of the last verse of Psalm 137, which Wright had just cited at the outset of his sermon. The U.S. television networks broadcast video clips from this sermon in which Wright said, "We bombed Hiroshima, we bombed Nagasaki, and we nuked far more than the thousands in New York and the Pentagon, and we never batted an eye … and now we are indignant, because the stuff we have done overseas is now brought back into our own front yards. America's chickens are coming home to roost" (Wright, 2008). This last comment, quoting Malcolm X, was interpreted by the U.S. mass-communication media as meaning that America had brought the September 11, 2001, attacks on itself.

Wright continued his sermon: "Violence begets violence. Hatred begets hatred. And terrorism begets terrorism. A white ambassador said that, y'all, not a black militant. Not a reverend who preaches about racism. An ambassador whose eyes are wide open and who is trying to get us to wake up and move away from this dangerous precipice upon which we are now poised. The ambassador said the people that we have wounded don't have the military capability we have. But they do have individuals who are willing to die and take thousands with them. And we need to come to grips with that" (Wright, 2008). Incredibly, in this sermon Wright seemed to have justified Al-Qaeda's horrific attack on the United States in which thousands of people were killed.

In his other controversial sermon, *Confusing God and Government* of April 13, 2003, the so-called "God Damn America" sermon (Wright, 2003), Wright had said that the U.S. government had repeatedly lied to the people, abused black people, and committed genocide against them. Wright had said, "The government gives them the drugs, builds bigger prisons, passes a three strike law and then wants us to sing God Bless America. Naw, naw, naw! Not God Bless America. God Damn America! That's in the Bible. For killing innocent people. God Damn America for treating us citizens as less than human. God Damn America as long as she tries to act like she is God and she is Supreme." ABC News and the other U.S. mass-communication media publicized this sermon as well, calling it Wright's "God Damn America" sermon (R. Martin, 2008).

This was too much for Obama. The shocking revelations about the bad "father" were actively hurting his "son." The American mass-communication media went into a frenzy, demanding that Obama dissociate himself from his racist pastor. Obama's response was to make another memorable anti-racist speech, a desperate attempt to keep his ties to this father figure who had baptized him, married him, and baptized his children. He would use Wright's antiwhite racism as a platform for teaching America antiracism and racial harmony. On March 18, 2008, at the National Constitutional Center in Philadelphia, Obama delivered a major campaign speech that he entitled "A More Perfect Union" (Niven, 2009, pp. 51–65; Obama, 2009c). The title was borrowed from the famous *Essay to Form a More Perfect Union* made by the U.S. Constitutional Convention in the same place in 1787.

In some ways Obama's "More Perfect Union" speech was reminiscent of Lincoln's "House Divided" speech. It was a speech about slavery, racism, bigotry, the American Civil War, and racial persecution—and racial reconciliation. Obama referred to his own life story. As in his 2004 address, he mentioned his black Kenyan father and his white Kansan mother, his grandfather's work during the Great Depression and military service during World War II, and his grandmother's wartime work in a bomber factory. He talked about his life in Indonesia and his studies at Harvard.

To appeal to the black electorate, Obama said, "I am married to a black American who carries within her the blood of slaves and slaveowners—an inheritance we pass on to our two precious daughters" (Obama 2009c; see also Niven, 2009, pp. 54–55).

Obama said that he had "brothers, sisters, nieces, nephews, uncles and cousins, of every race and every hue, scattered across three continents, and for as long as I live, I will never forget that in no other country on Earth is my story even possible." He added that the American nation was more than just a collection of ethnic, racial and religious identities: "out of many, we are truly one" (Obama, 2009c; see also Niven, 2009, p. 55). While this expressed a worthy sentiment of unity, it was also the English translation of the Latin phrase *E pluribus unum* on the seal of the president of the United States. Obama himself would be the one out of many. The U.S. television talk-show hostess Oprah Winfrey would call him "the One."

Like his 2004 keynote address, Obama's "More Perfect Union" speech of 2008 revealed his identification with the United States of America and his idealization of "her." This idealization of America as a great, good mother comes through in many acts and speeches of President Obama. But, while idealizing America, he also feels that it is his task and his mission to re-pair her, to make her more just, more compassionate, a better place, and "a more perfect union." And, as Noonan had put it, however viciously, Obama does compare himself to Lincoln, to the founding fathers of the United States, and to the members of the Constitutional Convention. This is part of his high-level constructive and reparative narcissism—the opposite of his father's self-destructive narcissism.

"A More Perfect Union" was a serious emotional and intellectual speech. The American journalist Hendrick Hertzberg (born 1943) thinks that Obama took the risk in this speech of treating the American people as adults capable of complex thinking, which, Hertzberg (2008) implied, they were not. In-deed, Obama does not think in black-and-white, divisive terms but rather tries to see the differences and the shades of gray and color while trying to unite, to mediate, and to conciliate. He rejected Wright's black-and-white racism yet stated that he could no more disown the pastor than he could disown the black American community itself, or his white grandmother with her racial prejudices, for that matter (Niven, 2009, p. 38).

In his Philadelphia speech, Obama encouraged white Americans, His-panic Americans, and other nonblack Americans to try to understand the history of slavery and racism in America. One could not wish away Wright's anger, Obama said, one could not condemn it, without understanding its roots. Likewise, he said, black people ought to try to understand the roots of white fears and their opposition to schoolchild busing or affirmative action, which were not necessarily racism. Obama urged American not to view race as a spectacle or a tragedy but to move beyond the racial stalemate and pursue racial harmony and collaboration.

Obama had tried to save his presidential campaign and to achieve racial conciliation without losing his fiery "father" in Chicago. But Wright would not leave his adopted "son" in peace. In April 2008 Wright gave a speech to the National Press Club in Washington, which had invited him to clarify his sermons. Once again he blamed Al-Qaeda's terror attacks of September 11, 2001, on America's foreign policy and praised the Nation of Islam and its extremist, antiwhite, racist leader, Louis Farrakhan. Wright also said that the United States had invented the AIDS virus as a genocidal weapon against the black minority, as in the infamous Tuskegee experiment, a clinical study conducted between 1932 and 1972 in Tuskegee, Alabama, by the U.S. Public Health Service. In that study hundreds of poor, mostly illiterate "Negro" sharecroppers with syphilis were used as a "control group" without treatment for research related to the natural progression of the untreated disease, in the hopes of justifying treatment programs for blacks. In short, rather than douse the flames, Wright fanned them.

Wright's outrageous racist speech left Obama no choice: he publicly condemned Wright's speech and broke off his 20-year relationship with the pastor who had baptized him into Christianity, married him, and baptized his daughters (Fowler, 2008). Now the "son" was abandoning his bad "father." It was a painful decision but an inevitable one, if he wished to preserve his integrity and his campaign. Yet another "father" had let him down, hurt him in his fervent quest for the presidency. The son had no choice but to abandon his bad father. This meant losing yet another father figure, but it gave Obama new emotional vigor and reinforced his conciliatory character.

Shortly thereafter, Barack Obama lost the Pennsylvania Democratic presidential-primary election to his chief rival, Hillary Clinton, who, according to Obama's Harvard biographer, had succeeded in portraying herself as a regular whisky-drinking, gun-swinging girl from her grandfather's home town in Pennsylvania (Niven, 2009, p. 39). Clinton portrayed Obama as an elitist black leader who had a serious problem understanding white working-class voters, and she won the West Virginia and Kentucky Democratic primaries as well. Obama, however, began to show his mettle: He won the Democratic primaries in North Carolina and Montana, losing narrowly in Indiana. He remained calm under Clinton's fire.

The U.S. president is chosen by an electoral college, whose delegates from each state are elected by the voters in a complex, indirect process based on the party primaries, in which voters choose among candidates for the party's presidential nomination. Obama kept his lead over Clinton in the total electoral-college pledged-delegate count and in the superdelegates, an informal term used for some of the delegates to the Democratic National Convention who are not selected by the party primaries and caucuses in each state but are rather seated automatically, based solely on their status as current or former party leaders and elected officials. Others are chosen during the primary season. The superdelegates are free to support any candidate for the presidential nomination.

Despite Hillary Clinton's fight to the bitter end and her furious "Shame on you, Barack Obama" speech of February 3, 2008, in which she accused Obama of using false information about her in a campaign mailer and of dirty tricks "out of Karl Rove's play book," Obama remained calm under fire. By June 3, Obama had secured the presidential nomination of his party, the first African American ever to do so. Four days later Clinton conceded defeat. She later endorsed her bitter rival and became President Obama's secretary of state. When the highly contagious and mortally dangerous H1N1 influenza, or swine flu, broke out in Mexico in 2009 and Clinton returned from a state visit to that country, Obama publicly joked that when they met she had embraced him and had urged him to go to Mexico, which was a beautiful country. The joke betrayed his deeper sense that Clinton had wished him dead.

Barack Obama's Harvard biographer thinks that his subject's six-month presidential-primary race against "Hilary [sic] Clinton" was "the longest, closest, most exciting, and first truly national, party campaign in American political history" (Niven, 2009, p. 39). In August 2008, during the Democratic National Convention in Denver, Colorado, Hillary Clinton and her husband, the former U.S. president Bill Clinton, both endorsed Obama, who chose the white, older, and more experienced U.S. Senator Joe Biden as his running mate, a choice that got a rave review from Bill Clinton himself. Obama gave a rousing acceptance speech before some 80 thousand ecstatic admirers at Denver's Invesco Field at Mile High (which had replaced the old Mile High Stadium), and polls gave him an eight-point lead over his Republican rival, John McCain. He defeated McCain roundly in the final election. The audacity of his ambition had succeeded beyond his wildest dreams.

Chapter 20

OBAMA'S CHARISMA

Synopsis: *In his classic book* Charisma: A Psychoanalytic Look at Mass Society *(1973), the Canadian Jewish psychoanalyst Irvine Schiffer pointed out that political leaders who are different in subtle ways from their followers and who are "partly foreign" have greater charisma than ordinary members of the national group. This has to do with the incomplete infantile process of separation and individuation, in which we emerge from a fusional relationship with our mother into a separate and individual psychological existence. In many people this process is only partially completed, and this immature part of ourselves attributes the charisma to the part foreigner, just as our mother's body had seemed partly familiar and partly foreign during the separation-individuation process. Barack Hussein Obama, who is seen as part white, part black, part American, part foreign, thus acquired a great amount of psychological charisma in the eyes of his followers. To this was added the charisma of the calling, of the fighting stance, and of the social station, other psychological ingredients of charisma that have their roots in our childhood development. The unconscious mind thus played no less a role in Obama's followers than it did in Obama himself.*

Obama's Harvard biographer attributes his presidential victory in 2008 to "four key factors": first, he ran a flawless campaign unmatched for sophistication and political acumen by any Democrat in recent memory; second, he forewent federal matching campaign funds to raise a record $640 million by October 15, half of it from small individual contributions; third, the American voters preferred his economic policies; and fourth, his campaign combined great Internet savvy with an extensive grassroots network of admirers and supporters and field organizers trained at "Camp Obamas" around the United States (Niven, 2009, p. 41).

The U.S. presidential candidate Barack Obama had indeed had an outstanding team of political advisers and campaign managers, such as David Axelrod, Rahm Emanuel, Eric Holder, Jonathan Favreau, and Tim Geithner, many of whom later became members of his cabinet and his chief aides. Obama had skillfully picked very capable advisers who helped him organize an unprecedented campaign that won him the presidency. He had also campaigned actively in every state, not only in the Democratic-majority "blue" states but also in the Republican-majority "red" ones. His Harvard biographer thinks that Obama was a "quintessentially American candidate" who had "built one of the most broad-based, diverse, and national coalitions of voters since World War II" (Niven, 2009, p. 43). Niven actually thinks that the U.S. subprime economic crisis of 2008 was a godsend to Obama, as it helped shape his presidential-election victory (pp. 44–45).

There was, however, a fifth, psychological, factor, in Obama's stunning and unprecedented victory, which Niven did not consider but which was no less important than the others. Obama's personal charisma, which he owed in large part to his being special, extraordinary, partly foreign and different from any other American who had ever sought the office, played a major role in his victory. Barack Hussein Obama not only has foreign-sounding names but is also a left-handed mulatto, has lived in Indonesia, and is different in many subtle ways from most Americans, both white and black. It was the charisma of the outsider, of the foreigner, of a man who is part white, part black, part American, part foreign, left-handed, different in some way from every other American, which derives from our unconscious early feelings about our mother: during that early phase of infantile separation and individuation, the mother seems at once familiar and foreign to us (Schiffer, 1973, pp. 25–26, 58–60).

The fact that Obama's presidential tally of 67 million votes was larger than any total won in any direct, free, and democratic election for a head of government anywhere in the world was due not only to an extraordinary campaign but also to his extraordinary appearance, personality, and character. This combination of the "quintessentially American candidate" with the part stranger, outsider, and foreigner gave Obama (and still gives him) his enormous charisma. In addition, he had the charisma of the fighting stance, which also derives from our childhood development, from the oedipal stage, which in many people remains unresolved (Schiffer, 1973, pp. 37–39). Even when he received the Nobel Peace Prize in Norway in late

2009, Obama told the world about "necessary and justified wars" to defeat evil and terror that will not yield to any suasion.

Not only did Obama win the presidency of the United States, but his Democratic Party also gained control of both houses of the U.S. Congress in the 2008 election. His Harvard biographer thinks that Obama received "the clearest mandate of any Democratic president since Lyndon Johnson" (Niven, 2009, p. 45). Since becoming president of the United States of America in January 2009, Obama has used this mandate to issue many executive orders and help enact numerous social reforms in the U.S. Congress to improve the lot of poor Americans and America's social order, as well as its relations with the rest of the world.

But the world expects too much of Obama. Given his extraordinary personal charisma and his intellectual and emotional gifts, many people around the world want Obama to be a messiah, redeemer, savior, or prophet who will save them from nuclear and environmental catastrophe, bring peace to nations involved in perennial conflict, and end genocide, terror, famine, disease, corruption, and all the other plagues and problems of this world (Abramsky, 2009, p. 6). Naturally, Obama is not superhuman, and he cannot fulfill all these expectations. Naturally, too, all these people around the world are bound to be disappointed. It is no wonder that his popularity has dropped from about two-thirds of the American people to about one-half. At the same time, he has enacted far-reaching reforms, such as the U.S. health-care revolution that has given medical care to over 30 million previously uninsured Americans.

In the tragic Arab-Israeli conflict (Falk, 2004), of all the nations around the world, the Palestinian Arabs seem to expect less of Obama than any other people that have been polled or surveyed (Niven, 2009, pp. 45–46). Almost three-quarters of Palestinians thought that it did not matter who won the U.S. election, that the United States would always support Israel against them, and that their daily lives would not improve. Ironically, and tragically, many Israelis also distrust Obama, thinking that he plans to put undue pressure on Israel to dismantle its settlements in the West Bank and to make territorial and other concessions to the Palestinian Arabs. The British-born American journalist Kai Bird has called upon Obama to visit Jerusalem in order to resolve the conflict (Bird, 2010).

Obama's Harvard biographer thinks that the success of his presidency will be measured by his ability to bring peace to the Palestinian Arabs and Israeli Jews, to Iraq, Afghanistan, Sudan, Congo, and other nations, to give "nations beset by war and genocide, poverty and disease, the audacity to hope" (Niven, 2009, p. 46). This may be true, and Obama has indeed succeeded in getting his health-care-reform bill passed in the U.S. Congress, but the success of his presidency will also be measured by his ability to save America from its economic crisis, by the international effects of U.S.

foreign policy, and by his actions in many other areas. Obama won the 2009 Nobel Peace Prize, and yet, as I write this, the United States wages terrible wars in Iraq and in Afghanistan, and another bitter war is being fought in Pakistan between government forces and Al-Qaeda and Taliban fanatics.

Even President Barack Obama cannot solve all the world's problems. The Arab-Israeli conflict is as persistent and intractable as ever (Falk, 2004) and, as we can see in Afghanistan, Pakistan, and India, the war against Islamic terror is far from being won (Falk, 2008). Iran is developing nuclear weapons and threatening Israel with extinction. Obama has tried to stop Israel from attacking Iran's nuclear installations, suggesting instead the use of sanctions, diplomatic alternatives, and even a blockade of Iran. But Israel's national security adviser is a hawk named Uzi Arad (born 1947), a disciple of Herman Kahn (1922–1983), better known as "Dr. Strangelove," and Arad is "thinking about the unthinkable" (Kahn, 1962, 1984). With right-winger Benjamin Netanyahu as Israel's prime minister, it is hard to say what Israel will do if it considers its existence threatened. If Israel does bomb Iran, tens of thousands of missiles may rain on it from Gaza, Syria, and Lebanon, and Israel's missile-defense system is not yet effective and in place. Can Obama, who has his hands full with fighting the Taliban and Al-Qaeda in Afghanistan and Pakistan, let alone the host of other domestic and foreign issues on his plate, prevent or deal effectively with such a terrible scenario?

THE BILL AYERS CONTROVERSY

During the U.S. presidential campaign of 2008, along with the Jeremiah Wright controversy and numerous other controversies concerning Obama's birth, origins, name, religion, and beliefs, which dogged him during his presidential campaign, there was yet another controversy, over the authorship of his memoir, *Dreams from My Father.* In May 2008 the American journalist Janny Scott came up with the following story:

> Mr. Obama's story first surfaced publicly in February 1990, when he was elected as the first black president of The Harvard Law Review. An initial wire service report described him simply as a 28-year-old, second-year [law] student from Hawaii who had "not ruled out a future in politics"; but in the days that followed, newspaper reporters grew interested and produced long, detailed profiles of Mr. Obama. The coverage prompted a call to him from Jane Dystel, a gravelly voiced [New York] literary agent described by Peter Osnos, then the publisher of Times Books, as "a good journeyman with a hard edge." The home page of her firm's Web site currently features clients'

best sellers including "Lies at the Altar: The Truth About Great Marriages."
Ms. Dystel suggested Mr. Obama write a book proposal. Then she got him a
contract with Poseidon Press, a now-defunct imprint of Simon & Schuster.
When he missed his deadline, she got him another contract and a $40,000
advance from Times Books. (Scott 2008b)

Scott, who had published several favorable articles about Obama in the
New York Times, went on to relate the story of the publication of his memoir *Dreams from My Father*:

> By the time Mr. Obama landed at Times Books, he had a partial manuscript.
> He required minimal editing, said Henry Ferris, his editor, who is now a
> vice president and executive editor at William Morrow. He simply needed
> guidance in paring and shaping the sections already written and keeping
> the rest from becoming too long. The writing, Mr. Ferris said, "is very much
> his own." The two worked mostly by telephone and by manuscripts sent by
> Federal Express between New York and Chicago. Mr. Obama, an inveterate
> journal writer who had published poems in a college literary magazine but
> had never attempted a book, struggled to finish. *His* [Indonesian-American]
> *half-sister, Maya Soetoro-Ng, said he eventually retreated to* [the Indonesian
> island of] *Bali for several months with his wife, Michelle, "to find a peaceful
> sanctuary where there were no phones."* He showed drafts to a few close rela-
> tives including his grandmother, of whom Ms. Soetoro-Ng said, "It probably
> made her a little nervous, having the family written about, just because you
> don't do that in Kansas." (Scott 2008b; italics added)

Barack himself, however, never mentioned writing his memoir in Bali or
anywhere else in Indonesia. Moreover, the Balinese episode supposedly
took place after Obama's graduation from law school in 1991, but at that
time he was not yet married to Michelle.

Not content with Scott's story, her anti-Obama neoconservative colleague Jack Cashill claimed that the former Weatherman activist William
Charles Ayers (born 1944) had helped Obama write his memoir, *Dreams
from My Father* (Cashill, 2008a, 2008b). Weatherman, also known as the
Weathermen and later as the Weather Underground Organization, was
an American radical-left organization. It originated in 1969 as a fac-
tion of Students for a Democratic Society (SDS) that was composed
of the national leadership of SDS and their supporters. With a charismatic and articulate leadership whose radical positions were characterized by anti-imperialist, feminist, and black-liberationist rhetoric, the
Weatherman group conducted a violent campaign of bombings through
the mid-1970s. The "Days of Rage," their first public demonstration on
October 8, 1969, was a riot in Chicago timed to coincide with the trial of

"the Chicago Seven." In 1970 the group issued a "Declaration of a State of War" against the U.S. government, under the name Weather Underground Organization.

Associating Obama with Ayers, therefore, was an act of aggression on Cashill's part, designed to damage Obama's presidential prospects. Citing spurious reports in the British tabloids and yellow press, Cashill claimed that Ayers had helped Obama write his memoir:

> [Obama's] agent hustled him a new, smaller contract. Ayers published his book *To Teach* in 1993. Between 1993 and 1996, [Ayers] had no other formal authorial assignment than to co-edit a collection of essays [Ayers & Ford, 1996]. This was an unusual hole in his very busy publishing career. Obama's memoir was published in June 1995. Earlier that year, Ayers helped Obama, then a junior lawyer at a minor law firm, get appointed chairman of the multi-million dollar Chicago Annenberg Challenge grant. In the fall of that same year, 1995, Ayers and his wife, Weatherwoman Bernardine Dohrn, helped blaze Obama's path to political power with a fundraiser in their Chicago home. In short, *Ayers had the means, the motive, the time, the place and the literary ability to jumpstart Obama's career*. And, as Ayers had to know, a lovely memoir under Obama's belt made for a much better resume than an unfulfilled contract over his head. (Cashill, 2008a; italics added)

Cashill's story was inaccurate. Ayers, the formerly violent Weatherman leader, had become a respectable university teacher and author. He and his former colleague Ann Hallett had become education reformers. The American philanthropist Walter Annenberg (1908–2002) had laid down a challenge to America's big cities to come up with double the money he would give them for education reform and for improving their public schools. In 1993 Ayers, Hallett, and Warren Chapman of the Joyce Foundation drafted a proposal to this effect and sent it to Annenberg's office. Annenberg accepted their proposal and offered them $50 million if they could raise $100 million to match his grant. Ayers and Hallett then approached the MacArthur Foundation, the Joyce Foundation, and the Spencer Foundation for this money. The three foundations created the Annenberg Challenge Board to handle Annenberg's grants. It was then that Obama's name came up as the candidate to chair the Chicago Annenberg Challenge.

Cashill's statement was also inaccurate in other ways. Ayers did publish other books during the time in question (Ayers, 1993, 1995), and Obama's law firm of Davis, Miner, Barnhill & Galland was not a minor law firm but rather a respectable Chicago law firm founded in 1971 by Allison Davis, a well-known Chicago lawyer and real-estate developer. This law firm was involved in civil rights litigation and neighborhood economic-development work but also provided legal services to private individual and corporate clients. Finally, Obama's appointment as the chairman of the Chicago Annenberg Challenge was not proposed by Ayers but by Deborah Leff, the president of the Joyce Foundation, and by Patricia Graham, the head of the Spencer Foundation.

Obama's extraordinary self-confidence was a key factor in his appointment as the chairman of the Chicago Annenberg Challenge and is also the key to his incredible political success. George Galland, the junior partner in the law firm of Davis, Miner, Barnhill & Galland, where Obama had worked, thought that Obama's self-confidence and self-esteem were natural to him and in no way arrogant. "I don't think anyone who ever dealt with Barack ever had any doubt that he was plenty confident that he was an unusually talented person and would go plenty far ... I never saw an insecure bone in his body, to tell you the truth," Galland told Sasha Abramsky in his colloquial English (Abramsky, 2009, p. 86). We have already seen what Obama's mentors, teachers, and colleagues, such as Larry Tribe and Geoff Stone, thought of his self-confidence.

The Annenberg Challenge began in 1993 when Walter Annenberg, a former U.S. ambassador to the United Kingdom and the most generous living American philanthropist, gave $500 million over five years to support public-school reform in America's big cities, challenging his fellow donors and the big-city community to match his gifts with double the amount. The Chicago Annenberg Challenge was only 1 of 18 local public-school-reform projects that between them received $387 million over those five years. The Chicago Annenberg Challenge was created in 1995, the year Obama's memoir was published, and lasted until 2001. It worked with half of Chicago's public schools and was funded by a $49.2 million grant over five years. The grant was contingent on being matched by double that amount from the Chicago school reformers—$98.4 million—of which $49.2 million came from private donations and $49.2 million from public money. Contrary to Cashill's statements, Ayers was one of the three people who coauthored the initial grant proposal, but he had nothing to do with the naming of the chairman.

The Chicago Annenberg Challenge had an eight-member board of directors representing foundations, universities, and other organizations that had no vested interest in Annenberg money. It approved grants, hired an executive director and project staff, and decided which money could count toward the required $98.4 million matching funds required by the Annenberg grant. The board was handpicked by Adele Smith Simmons, the president of the MacArthur Foundation, who had been asked by Vartan Gregorian—the president of Brown University, the president of the Carnegie Corporation, a former president of the New York Public Library, and a former professor of Southwest Asian history, a dean, and a provost of the University of Pennsylvania—to create a diverse board of directors from the community, business interests, and civic leaders, a board that would include no more than nine directors.

Obama's appointment as the chairman of the Chicago Annenberg Challenge was decided at a meeting of the presidents of the three largest independent foundations active in Chicago public-school reform—Adele Simmons, the president of the MacArthur Foundation; Patricia Graham, the president of the Spencer Foundation; and Deborah Leff, the president of the Joyce Foundation. The latter suggested Obama for the office of chairman of the board. After meeting Obama and being impressed by him, Graham told him that she wanted him to be the chairman of the board of directors. Obama said that he would agree to serve as chairman if Graham would be his vice chairman, to which Graham agreed.

Ian Mosley, a racist friend of Cashill, went on to embellish his story in a mean fashion meant to discredit and damage Obama:

> So Obama had a year to write a book. He received a $125,000 advance, and all he was able to do was take a vacation in Bali. *Sounds like a typical Black work ethic. It also sounds like Obama just flat out lacks any writing talent.* Bill Ayers however was a prolific writer—except for a period of time in '94 and '95 when Obama miraculously turned out the book he had failed to write in 1990, before he knew Bill Ayers. Liberals could argue that this is merely a coincidence. Still, if you received a $125,000 advance, this sort of money should have motivated anyone (with writing talent) to make a very serious effort to put together their best possible work. Obama never produced anything by his first deadline most probably because he has no writing talent. (Mosley, 2009; italics added)

In fact, as we know, Obama has extraordinary writing talent, and Cashill and Mosley were engaging in yellow journalism. Many serious people have disputed their story, not the least of them Ayers himself. The British tabloids had been the first to raise the Ayers authorship theory, but the connection was picked up by various Internet blogs and newspapers in the United States. The matter was raised by John McCain in the spring of 2008, and later in one of the televised debates between Obama and his Republican rival McCain by the moderator, George Stephanopoulos. It later became an issue for the McCain presidential campaign.

During the 2008 U.S. presidential-election campaign, however, intensive journalistic investigations by the *New York Times*, Cable News Network, and other U.S. news organizations and mass-communication media, however, concluded that Obama did not have any close relationship with Ayers and, in fact, that Obama had condemned Ayers's violent tactics. In an op-ed piece after the election, Ayers himself, now a distinguished professor of education and senior university scholar at the University of Illinois at Chicago, denied any close association with Obama and castigated the Republican campaign for its use of guilt-by-association tactics.

In a new edition of his memoir, Bill Ayers also described his relationship with Barack Obama as that of "neighbors and family friends" (afterword in Ayers, 2008). However, in a television interview on the American Broadcasting Corporation's *Good Morning America* talk show, Ayers later said, "I'm describing [in the afterword] how the blogosphere characterized the relationship. I would really say that we knew each other in a professional way, again on the same level as say thousands of other people" (Associated Press, 2008).

In fact, after his contract with Simon and Schuster fell through, Obama was commissioned by Random House to write a book about race relations. After much inner turmoil and several changes of plans, this led to his fascinating memoir, *Dreams from My Father*, which he probably wrote with his wife Michelle around 1993–1994. It was first published in 1995, the year his mother died of cancer. The main psychological theme of the book is not race relations, however, but rather Obama's struggle with his father's ghost and his ambivalent identification with him. This book was without question inspired by his lifelong struggle with his father's image within himself. The book ended with his wedding in 1992, at which he "felt like the luckiest man alive" (Obama, 1995, p. 442). The book was reissued in 2004 and has sold millions of copies.

Chapter 21

REPAIRING "MOTHER AMERICA"

Synopsis: *Barry Obama's need as a child to protect his vulnerable mother and to repair his broken family was unconsciously translated in his adult life into the need to protect his community, whether it was black Chicago, the state of Illinois, or the United States of America. It was no accident that his political career began as his mother was dying of cancer and he could do nothing to save her. Since then, he has used his power and done his utmost to give protection, love, and guidance to his adopted mother figures, above all his motherland. He has tried to improve the life of black people and of all Americans. He has mediated and conciliated to resolve many disputes in politics. As president, he has succeeded in forging a new health-care plan for all Americans, including the minority that has no health insurance at all. He has acted to protect the environment, to save the lives of U.S. soldiers in Iraq, and to stop nuclear proliferation. Barack has tried to be the protective and loving father that his own father could not be, not only to his daughters but to all of America.*

Barack Obama likes to think of his native and beloved United States as a free country whose people share a fundamental decency, a common set of positive values, and "a running thread of hope" that inspires "pride, duty and sacrifice" (Obama, 2006a, p. 11). Barack's list (or wish list) of common American values includes liberty, optimism, community, family, patriotism, citizenship, faith, honesty, fairness, humility, kindness, courtesy, good manners, competence, and compassion. Yet he also knows that there are serious tensions between the values of individualism and communality, autonomy and solidarity, liberty and public obligations (Obama). Barack thinks, however, that the vast size of the United States and its abundant resources have allowed it to negotiate these tensions without recourse to violent revolutions, as in Europe (Obama, p. 68).

Barack is not a wide-eyed idealist. He is a realist who is aware of America's flaws. He understands the fragility of the peace between America's contradictory values. Human beings tend to distort their common values and to adapt them to their needs and views. They can change the positive values of self-reliance and independence into selfishness and license, and transform "ambition into greed and a frantic desire to succeed at any cost" (Obama, 2006a, p. 68). Patriotism can become nationalism, jingoism, xenophobia, or McCarthyism. Religious faith, as in the case of Alan Keyes, can become rigid self-righteousness, closed-mindedness, and cruelty toward people of other faiths. Generosity and charity can degenerate into a paternalism in which one will not accept that others can decide and act for themselves (Abramsky, 2009, p. 64; Obama, 2006a, p. 68).

For Barack, unconsciously, America is a great, good mother that is, however, seriously flawed and needs to be repaired, just as his own mother had been when he was a child. It is his task to protect and repair America, just as he felt that he had to protect his mother in Indonesia when he was a child and as he wished to repair his broken family. He could not save his mother from dying, but he can save America and make it a wonderful mother again. He has been trying to repair and to improve her ever since he became a U.S. senator, whether by reforming her health-care system, improving her environment, saving the economy, and improving the Supreme Court and justice system, or by his executive orders, proposed legislation, diplomatic efforts, or his pursuit of the war on the Taliban and Al-Qaeda in Afghanistan and Pakistan. He is now in the role of the father, America is in the role of the mother, and he will take good care of it.

In 1996, Barack went into politics, which had become a natural calling for him. Here, he aimed to give America what his father had not given him but what his maternal grandfather had tried to give him: protection, love, and guidance. Barack won a seat in the Illinois senate and won it again in 1998 and in 2002. His wife, Michelle, became pregnant in the fall of 1997 and gave birth to their first daughter, whom they named Malia Ann, on U.S. Independence Day, July 4, 1998. Barack became a father, and he was not going to be the self-centered, arrogant father that his own father had been. He was going to be a good, giving, caring, empathic, and loving father, spending as much time with his daughter as he could. Her sister Natasha (better known as Sasha) was born on June 10, 2001. She was a comfort to her father after his painful loss to Bobby Rush in the primary race for the U.S. Congress the year before.

While living in Chicago, after first going to kindergarten, Malia and Sasha Obama attended the private and prestigious University of Chicago Laboratory School. The Obama girls also had many extracurricular activities, including soccer, dance, and drama for Malia, gymnastics and tap dancing for Sasha, and piano and tennis lessons for both girls. Having been hurt by his own father, Barack tried to protect his daughters from harm. However, during the presidential campaign, on U.S. Independence Day, July 4, 2008, in Butte, Montana, on the occasion of Malia's 10th birthday, he and his wife Michelle consented to give an exclusive family interview on the televised gossip show *Access Hollywood* (Hoffecker, 2008).

In the *Access Hollywood* interview, the interviewer was Maria Menounos, a pretty, pleasant, and empathic young white woman, and the Obama family ambience was loving, easygoing, and relaxed. Nonetheless, the 10-year-old Malia and the 7-year-old Sasha spilled the beans about some of their parents' habits and their family problems, as young children are wont to do, unwittingly embarrassing to their parents. Among other things, Malia mentioned her father's annoying habit of leaving his heavy bag near the front door, which causes her to trip over it, and Michelle mentioned Barack's old pants and shoes. Barack said, "I'm baffled by this whole thing myself, because I hate to shop." Despite the pleasant atmosphere, there was some embarrassment (Hoffecker, 2008).

Barack and Michelle had for the most part kept their daughters away from photographers' lenses and reporters' tape recorders, but, perhaps thinking that their happy-family image would enhance Barack's presidential prospects, they agreed to the girls' on-camera appearance. The interview was broadcast by *Access Hollywood* on July 8, 9, and 10, 2008. Meanwhile, on the CBS morning *Early Show*, Barack had second thoughts about letting his daughters be interviewed:

> **Russ Mitchell,** an *Early Show* cohost: Senator, on another note, we're seeing your kids out on the campaign trail more, we've seen them on television as well. Will we see them more as the campaign moves forward?
>
> **Barack Obama:** No, I don't think so. You know, we had a unique situation in Montana where it was Malia's birthday, and all of us, I think, got caught up in the festivities, and so they had a chance to be their adorable selves on TV, but generally, we've been very protective of them. You know, in retrospect, I think, you know, if you'd asked me, we probably wouldn't have done it then, we wouldn't do it again.

Sasha had revealed, when told that they would be getting ice cream after the interview, that her father did not like sweets, to which Barack replied, "I like pie!" Since apple pie is as basic an American value as motherhood, an American journalist thought that Barack was "mindful, perhaps, of not alienating a vast majority of the American public" (Hoffecker, 2008).

The topic of his daughters came up again when Barack was interviewed on the morning shows of the three major U.S. television networks (ABC, CBS, and NBC). Asked by Diane Sawyer on ABC's *Good Morning America* (she has since left the network) whether he was sorry that he and his wife had agreed to the *Access Hollywood* interview, Barack replied he had "a little bit of pause" when he watched the televised interview, "particularly given the way that it sort of went around the cable stations. I don't think it's healthy, and it's something that we'll be avoiding in the future." On NBC's *Today* show, which has the same corporate parent as *Access Hollywood*, Barack told the host, Matt Lauer, "We wouldn't do it again, and we won't be doing it again" (Hoffecker, 2008).

On January 18, 2009, two days before his inauguration as president of the United States, hundreds of thousands of people gathered at Washington's Lincoln Memorial to hear some of the world's best musicians perform a preinauguration concert organized by Emmett Beliveau, Barack's inauguration-committee director (Abramsky, 2009, pp. 2, 69). On that same day Barack published an open letter to his daughters in *Parade* magazine, describing what he wants for them and for every child in America: "to grow up in a world with no limits on your dreams and no achievements beyond your reach, and to grow into compassionate, committed women who will help build that world" (Obama, 2009e). Barack publicly told his daughters how he moved from selfishness to altruism. He said that as a young man he was self-centered, thinking only about his career, but when he became a father he discovered that the joy he saw in his daughters was greater than any joy he had in himself. Because of all the great things he wanted for his daughters, he had decided to run for president of the United States (Obama, 2009e).

Was Barack being disingenuous? After all, he knew that he had not sought the presidency of the United States just because of what he wanted for his daughters but also because of his own ambitions, his megalomania, his fanatical single-mindedness, and his fear of public humiliation (Obama, 2006a, pp. 125–126, 243). However, by the time Barack published those words, he may have convinced himself that he had done it all for the sake of his daughters. Malia and Sasha now attend the private Sidwell Friends School in Washington, the same Quaker school that has been attended by America's first children Chelsea Clinton, Tricia Nixon Cox, and Archibald Roosevelt, and currently also by the grandchildren of Vice President Joe Biden.

Barack's political career often forced him away from his wife and daughters, especially after he won the U.S. Senate seat from Illinois in 2004 and had to live in Washington from early 2005. In 2000 Barack had lost the Democratic primary race for the U.S. House of Representatives from Illinois to the four-term incumbent, Bobby Rush, by a margin of two to one. It was his one major loss, and he experienced it as a painful and humiliating defeat, but he gained name recognition from this lost race. Barack served in the Illinois senate from 1997 to 2004. He used his power with wisdom as he went about reforming Illinois's political ethics and health-care laws. The last two years, when the Democrats controlled the Illinois General Assembly, were especially fortuitous.

Barack sponsored a law increasing tax credits for low-income workers, negotiated welfare reform, and promoted increased subsidies for child care. In 2001, as co-chairman of the Joint Committee on Administrative Rules in the Illinois General Assembly, Barack supported the Republican governor George Ryan's payday-loan and predatory-mortgage regulations aimed at averting home foreclosures. Michelle had become pregnant again in the fall of 2000, and on June 10, 2001, their second daughter was born, whom they named Natasha and nicknamed Sasha. Sasha also happens to be a male name, the Russian nickname for Alexander. Was Barack disappointed at not having a son, as his maternal grandfather had been when Barack's mother was born?

Barack sees himself as a great reformer, like Lincoln. In 2003, when the Democrats controlled the Illinois General Assembly, he sponsored and led in the Illinois senate the unanimous, bipartisan passage of legislation to monitor racial profiling—the inclusion of racial and ethnic characteristics in determining whether a person is considered likely to commit a particular type of crime or an illegal act—making Illinois the first state in the United States to mandate the videotaping of homicide interrogations and confessions. Since Lincoln is one of the presidents with whom Barack is often compared and with whom he identifies, it is fascinating to note what Barack has to say about Lincoln.

There is little doubt that Barack identifies with Lincoln. Barack admires what he sees as Lincoln's extraordinary grasp of the "deliberative function of our democracy" (Obama, 2006a, p. 116), his courage, the strength of his convictions, his unwavering struggle against the pernicious evil of slavery while preserving the American union. Barack feels that he himself has many of these qualities or wishes to have them. Yet, at the same time, he also sees the "distressful" aspects of Lincoln's practicality, those that led him to strike unsavory deals with the slaveholding Confederacy in order to avoid civil war. Also, once war had broken out, he appointed many able generals only to fire them, to keep changing his strategies, and "to stretch the Constitution to the breaking point in order to see the war through to a successful conclusion" (Obama, 2006a, pp. 116–117).

Idealizing Lincoln, Barack believed that Lincoln had never betrayed his principles, never abandoned his convictions to achieve his goals of ending slavery and preserving the union. He believed that Lincoln had been able to maintain in himself the balance between two conflicting values: the ideal of talking and negotiating common ground with one's adversaries and the occasional necessity to act forcefully on his convictions as if he were infallible (Obama, 2006a, p. 117). Was Barack reading his own thoughts and feelings into Lincoln's mind and actions?

In the language of positive psychology, Barack sees many strengths and virtues in Lincoln that he also sees in himself: self-awareness, humility, empathy, compassion, realism, and idealism. Barack believes that Lincoln's humility gave him empathy for his Confederate enemies and enabled him to see the horrors of the war that he was himself conducting (Obama, 2006a, p. 117). Does he feel the same way about the wars that he is waging in Afghanistan and Pakistan? It is true that Lincoln did not see the world in black and white, as did George W. Bush, but was rather able to understand the feelings of his adversaries and enemies. Did Lincoln intuitively sense that there may not be any absolute truth when he added that "we should pursue our own absolute truths only if we acknowledge that there may be a terrible price to pay" (Obama, 2006a, p. 117)?

Barack does believe in some absolute truths, though what they are is not always clear (Obama, 2006a, p. 116). Does he believe in the absolute justice of his war on the Afghan and Pakistani Taliban and of the ongoing U.S. war on Al-Qaeda in Iraq? How can there be such a thing as an absolute truth for a leader who, unlike his predecessor, does not believe in black-and-white thinking? This is a psychological puzzle that is not easy to solve. It seems that Barack wavers between his deep convictions and strongly held values and his awareness that "there is nothing either good or bad but thinking makes it so" (Shakespeare, *Hamlet, The Prince of Denmark*, act II, scene 2, lines 250–251).

President Obama knows how to say "no" when necessary. Unlike many incompetent generals, he is not afraid of not being loved (Dixon, 1976). One impressive example occurred toward the end of his presidential campaign, in the fall of 2008, when Senator Obama visited Iraq, where the United States was waging war against local "insurgents" and "terrorists," along with two of his colleagues, Charles Hagel and Jack Reed. Obama was the front-runner in the race for president of the United States. When he met General David Petraeus, the commander of the multinational military force in Iraq (now the commander of the U.S. Central Command), the latter pleaded vigorously with Senator Obama for additional troops to win the war in Iraq. Petraeus screened an impressive PowerPoint presentation to reinforce his plea.

Senator Obama, who had opposed the U.S. war in Iraq from the outset, listened to Petraeus carefully, watched his presentation, and then calmly replied, "You know, General, if I were in your shoes, I would be making the exact same argument. Your job is to succeed in Iraq on as favorable terms as we can get. But my job as a potential Commander in Chief is to view your counsel and interests through the prism of our overall national security" (J. Klein, 2008). The other two senators who accompanied Obama told Petraeus they agreed with Obama. It was a vintage Obama reply, combining empathy with firmness and decisiveness.

President Obama also knows how to say "yes" when necessary. In the fall of 2009, U.S. General Stanley McChrystal, the commander of U.S. and NATO forces in Afghanistan, publicly asked President Obama for an additional 40,000 troops to enable him to successfully defeat Al-Qaeda and the Taliban in Afghanistan. A brilliant Special Forces officer and strategist, McChrystal knew how to manipulate the mass-communication media to achieve his goals. To bring public pressure to bear on his commander-in-chief, he publicly warned Obama that the U.S. campaign in Afghanistan would fail without these additional troops. Obama was caught in a bind: he had replaced the previous U.S. commander with the talented and flexible McChrystal earlier that year. Should he accede to the general's request or fire McChrystal for his public insubordination?

Faced with a tough decision, Obama carefully weighed his options for over two months. The Afghan presidential election of 2009 had been rigged by the incumbent, Hamid Karzai. Obama asked U.S. Senator John Kerry, the chairman of the Senate Foreign Relations Committee (who had also been Obama's predecessor as the Democratic presidential nominee in 2004 and one of his sponsors for that nomination in 2008), to fly to Afghanistan and assess the political and military situation there. Upon Kerry's return, Obama's White House chief of staff, Rahm Emanuel, and Senator Kerry announced publicly that Afghanistan must have a legitimate government before the United States sends any more troops to that country. Obama continued to consider his options that fall, even as he walked atop the Great Wall of China and bowed deeply to Emperor Akihito of Japan.

By December 2009, President Obama had made up his mind. He announced at West Point Military Academy in West Point, New York, that he had decided, as the commander-in-chief of U.S. armed forces, that protecting U.S. security required him to send an additional 30,000 troops to Afghanistan: not the 40,000 men that General McChrystal had demanded, but a considerable force nonetheless. In his West Point speech, however, Obama carefully added that when the Afghan armed forces could handle the insurgency on their own, hopefully by 2011, the United States would withdraw its forces from Afghanistan.

Shortly thereafter, U.S. Ambassador Richard Holbrooke, the special U.S. envoy to Afghanistan and Pakistan, went on Fareed Zakaria's CNN television show *Global Public Square* and said that U.S. troops should never have entered Afghanistan's Korangal Valley, where there was no insurgency, and also made it clear that the United States was after Al-Qaeda, the terrorist group that had destroyed America's World Trade Center, rather than after the Afghan Taliban insurgents. Obama had thus balanced his antiwar stand with the political and military reality, and General McChrystal's demands for more troops with Vice President Biden's counsel to withdraw U.S. forces from Afghanistan. But when General McChrystal publicly and repeatedly derogated his civilian superiors, an angry President Obama did not hesitate to first call him on the carpet and then to fire him.

OBAMA AND THE FILIBUSTER

In U.S. politics, the word *filibuster*, or "talking out a bill," is used to designate a form of obstruction in a legislature or other decision-making body whereby one attempts to delay or entirely prevent a vote on a proposal by extending a debate on that proposal, talking endlessly to prevent the bill from being brought to a vote. The term *filibuster* was first used in 1851. It was derived from the Spanish word *filibustero* (a pirate or a freebooter), which in turn had evolved from the French word *flibustier* (a pirate or a buccaneer), which derived from the Dutch word *vrijbuiter* (freebooter). This term *filibuster* at first designated American adventurers, mostly from the southern states, who tried to overthrow the governments of Central American states, and was later applied to the use of the filibuster as a tactic for pirating or hijacking a debate.

In 2005, at the beginning of the second term of President George W. Bush's administration, to defeat the Democrats' filibusters, the Republican-dominated U.S. Senate invented and passed the "nuclear option," a new Senate procedural rule by which the Senate's presiding officer, Vice President Dick Cheney, could bypass the Senate parliamentarian, ignore two centuries of precedent, and end the filibuster by banging his gavel and declaring that the Senate rules no longer allowed it in the case of judicial nominations (Obama, 2006a, p. 98). To Obama, an inveterate basketball player (it is his chief unconscious link to his father), the Republicans were unfairly "changing the rules in the middle of the game" (ibid.). The Republicans themselves had used the filibuster often but were now trying to rob the Democrats of that privilege. The Republican threat of the nuclear option was enough to deter their Democratic opponents from filibustering. It was exactly in the crucial matter of judicial nominations that the use of the filibuster was so important.

When Barack Obama was a U.S. senator (2005–2008), the political wars in the Senate over George W. Bush's archconservative nominees to the

Supreme Court often led to compromises between the Democratic and Republican senators over the use of the filibuster. The Republicans threatened that if the Democrats overused the filibuster, the Republican Vice President Cheney, who presided over the Senate, would use the nuclear option to end it. At one point, 14 senators, 7 Democrats and 7 Republicans, struck a deal to reserve the filibuster for unspecified "extraordinary circumstances." Obama refused to join that "Gang of Fourteen." Bush's Supreme Court nominees were way too bad for him, beyond any circumstances, extraordinary or otherwise. Even then, Obama could see his colleagues' viewpoint. He felt that he could not blame his Democratic colleagues for striking the deal because, without it, the nuclear option would have occurred, and the Republicans would have had absolute control (Obama, 2006a, p. 118).

The nonagenarian Democratic U.S. Senator Robert Byrd of West Virginia (1917–2010), a mentor and friend of Obama's, was so ecstatic about the filibuster deal with the Republicans that he marched through the halls of the Capitol in tandem with his Republican colleague, Senator John Warner of Virginia, announcing to reporters that they had saved the republic (Obama, 2006a, p. 118). Watching them with amusement, Obama smiled to himself and recalled his private visit with Senator Byrd, in which the old political warrior had given him an autographed copy of his book on the history of the Senate (Byrd, 1988–1994). Robert Byrd came to the Senate to vote for Obama's health-care reform bill but also criticized Obama's use of his appointed public-policy czars as an inordinate extension of White House powers (Abramsky, 2009, pp. 223–224).

EMPATHY IN THE SERVICE OF POLITICS

The way Illinois state senator Barack Obama was able to pass his legislation about the videotaping of interrogations and confessions in homicide cases was characteristic of his approach to politics, which was to achieve consensus rather than to win arguments and battles. The purpose of that legislation was to prevent innocent people from being executed and to put an end to police brutality and torture, while making sure that those who committed heinous crimes were punished. Obama thinks that in today's political climate, no compromise would have been possible. Death-penalty opponents would cite racism and police brutality while its proponents would denounce Obama's bill as encouraging violent crime. To avoid the public clash between the two camps, which would be seized on by the predatory mass-communication media, and to reconcile their conflicting views, Obama held private meetings with prosecutors, public defenders, police organizations, and death-penalty opponents, avoiding the press like the plague (Obama, 2006a, p. 71).

Instead of fighting duels with his opponents, Obama collaborated with his conservative colleagues in the Illinois General Assembly, including the notorious Edward Petka (born 1943), a former Illinois state's attorney who later became a legislator and then a 12th Circuit judge, a man who had obtained murder conviction and death sentences for numerous people, to achieve a compromise bill that nonetheless preserved the essence of his reform. Obama held early Monday morning meetings with all the parties involved, including the police, in which he asked tough questions, kept his sense of humor, and made friends of potential enemies. Their former Republican colleague Kirk Dillard had high praise for Obama's character and negotiating skills (Abramsky, 2009, p. 54).

The secrecy imposed by State Senator Obama on the negotiations about the death-penalty issue and the videotaping of homicide interrogations was not designed to limit the transparency of the political process but rather to prevent the press from destroying the consensus that he achieved. Obama talked about common American values, modified the bill to accommodate police objections, and finally got the bill passed unanimously in the Illinois senate and signed into law by Governor George Ryan. In 2004 Illinois state senator Obama won the race for the U.S. Senate seat from Illinois. He was sworn in on January 4, 2005, and continued to work hard to protect mother America.

In 2005 U.S. Senator Obama found a new "adoptive" father figure in the Senate—and it was a Republican, a member of the rival party. As one American journalist put it, "old-school realist Richard Lugar, the five-term Republican senator from Indiana, has embraced new-school realist and rising star Barack Obama, the junior Democratic senator from Illinois. The relationship is admiring. 'I very much feel like the novice and pupil,' Obama has said of Lugar. And it's warm. Lugar praises Obama's 'strong voice and creativity' and calls him 'my good friend.' In short, the two agree on much and seem to genuinely like each other. Rather unusual in hyper-partisan Washington, these days" (Larson, 2006).

U.S. Senator Lugar (born 1932) is no ordinary politician. He has received numerous awards, including the Guardian of Small Business, the Spirit of Enterprise, the Watchdog of the Treasury, and 34 honorary doctorates from U.S. and other universities. In 2008 Lugar and Joe Biden, his Democratic partner in the Senate Committee on Foreign Relations, who later became Obama's running mate and vice president, received the *Hilal-i-Pakistan* (Crescent of Pakistan) award from the government of Pakistan for their continued support of that country. Lugar and Biden had introduced a plan in July 2008 that would give $1.5 billion in aid per year to support economic development in Pakistan.

Senator Lugar is also an active campaigner for nuclear disarmament and a member of the board of the Nuclear Threat Initiative, chaired by Ted Turner and Sam Nunn. U.S. Senator Obama, too, was interested in nuclear-threat reduction. Lugar and Obama became a true father-and-son team, and they were serious about reducing the threat of a nuclear holocaust that would destroy all life on our planet. During the Senate's summer recess in 2005, Lugar and Obama visited Russia, Azerbaijan, and Ukraine to inspect the nuclear facilities there. Due to a Russian bureaucrat's fears, Lugar was detained for three hours at a Russian airport in Perm, near the Ural Mountains, whence the two senators were due to depart for a meeting with the president of Ukraine and with the speaker of its parliament. Senator Lugar was released after a brief discussion between U.S. and Russian officials, and the Russian government apologized for this incident.

In April 2006 *Time* magazine selected Lugar as one of America's 10 best senators. In January 2007 U.S. President Bush signed the Lugar-Obama Nuclear Non-Proliferation and Conventional Weapons Threat Reduction Initiative into law. Their initiative furthered Lugar's previous work with the Democratic Senator Sam Nunn of Georgia (born 1938) in de-activating weapons in the countries of the former Soviet Union, which led to the Lugar-Nunn Cooperative Proliferation Detection, Interdiction Assistance, and Conventional Threat Reduction Act of 2006. The Lugar-Obama program focuses on terrorists and their use of multiple types of weapons.

On October 15, 2008, the day of the final presidential debate between Obama and McCain, Lugar gave a speech at the National Defense University praising Obama's foreign-policy approach and warning against the dangers of the isolationist, and reactive policies espoused by McCain. At that debate, Obama listed Lugar among the individuals who had shaped his ideas and who would help him run the government. There were rumors that Obama or McCain (whoever won the presidency) would name Lugar to be secretary of state but that he would rather keep his Senate seat. In 2009 President Obama won the Nobel Peace Prize. Senator Lugar had contributed in no small measure to this achievement of his younger friend.

The Democrat Obama had no trouble adopting the Republican Lugar as his mentor and father figure in 2005 because he did not fall prey to the unconscious splitting and conscious black-and-white thinking that so deeply divide and polarize U.S. politics. In fact, he devoted the entire first chapter of his book *The Audacity of Hope*, which he published the following year, to explaining why the old liberal-conservative divisions did no work, why strict, one-sided, rigid partisanship was a big mistake, how human problems were too complex and difficult to be solved with simple black-and-white, either-or ideas. When he was younger, his rebellion against his grandfather's authority had led him to self-indulgence and self-destructiveness (Obama, 2006a, p. 38), but as an adult he had learned to avoid black-and-white, us-versus-them attitudes.

This was no mean achievement. Politics is an endeavor in which the temptation to see things in black and white and to take the adversary approach is very great. Unconscious splitting, projection, and externalization are common psychological processes in politics. The politician tends to see himself and his party as the good guys and his opponents and the other party as the bad guys. For the 43-year-old Obama to be able to transcend such black-and-white thinking, to embrace bipartisanship and complex solutions, and "to balance idealism and realism" (Obama, 2006a, p. 51) was a great psychological accomplishment. In fact, he had already been able to do so in the Illinois senate, and his U.S. Senate campaign was won primarily thanks to this empathetic, humane, compassionate attitude that did not fall into the either-or trap.

Obama was so flexible and open-minded that he could even see the pleasant aspects of the rigid and ultraconservative Republican president George W. Bush, whom Obama's fellow Democrats reviled. Bush had twice invited Obama to meet him in the White House. Obama found Bush likable, shrewd, and disciplined "with the same straightforward manner that helped him win two elections" (Obama, 2006a, p. 55). He intuitively liked Bush and found him to be a pleasant man in their private relations.

Yet, during their second meeting, a White House breakfast that President Bush held in early 2005 with the incoming U.S. Senators, Obama discovered another, unpleasant side of Bush, the rigid, black-and-white side. When Bush discussed his second-term agenda, he became a different man. It was almost like Dr. Jekyll turning into Mr. Hyde: "The President's eyes became fixed; his voice took on the agitated, rapid tone of someone neither accustomed to nor welcoming interruption; his easy affability was replaced by an almost messianic certainty" (Obama, 2006a, p. 56). While the Republican senators admired Bush's "decisiveness," Obama saw that Bush's power had placed him in dangerous isolation, which made Obama grateful to America's founding fathers for the wonderful system of checks and balances they had devised to protect its democracy and freedom (Obama, 2006a, p. 56).

Nevertheless, after the breakfast meeting, when Obama met Bush face to face, the latter was relaxed and affable again: Mr. Hyde had become Dr. Jekyll once more. The two men hit it off so well that Obama put his arm over Bush's shoulder as they talked, a gesture that he later thought might well have made many of his friends and the Secret Service agents uneasy (Obama, 2006a, p. 58). When discussing empathy, Obama said that it forced us to see the world through the other person's eyes. He had to try to see the world through Bush's eyes, no matter how strongly he disagreed with him. Otherwise, no bipartisan, joint political action was possible. With this capacity for empathy, Obama could understand his opponents and reach an accommodation with them that furthered his goal, values, and ideals. Rather than adopt a confrontational style, as many politicians do, he was able to take a collaborative one (Obama, p. 82).

In the U.S. Senate, collaborating with his colleagues on both sides of the aisle in a bipartisan effort, Senator Obama helped enact the Energy Policy Act of 2005. He also supported the Secure America and Orderly Immigration Act introduced by his Republican colleague John McCain and by his Democratic colleague Ted Kennedy (1932–2009), which was meant to curb illegal immigration from Mexico and the rest of Latin America, even though he himself had fierce presidential ambitions (Obama, 2006a, p. 243) and knew that he might lose Hispanic votes due to this. Perhaps fortunately for him, this bill was never voted on in the Senate. The Comprehensive Immigration Reform Acts of 2006 and 2007 were compromises based on the original McCain-Kennedy bill.

U.S. Senator Obama also supported the Secure Fence Act of 2006, which created a huge fence between the United States and Mexico to stop illegal drug trafficking and gun running. Obama hoped that this act would help stop the drug traffickers that go back and forth across the U.S.-Mexican border bringing deadly drugs into the United States and deadly weapons into Mexico. Indeed, with thousands of people murdered by Mexican drug cartels in Ciudad Juárez and other cities, this is a major issue for both the U.S. and Mexican governments.

Senator Obama was deeply concerned with making America a better place in terms of life, politics, immigration, defense, and everything else. Working with his Republican colleagues, and especially with his mentor and father figure Lugar, Obama cointroduced the Lugar-Obama bill to halt the spread of dangerous and illicit conventional weapons (Lugar & Obama, 2005). With his Republican physician colleague Dr. Tom Coburn, he introduced the Coburn-Obama Federal Funding Accountability and Transparency Act, which authorized the establishment of an Internet search engine that would easily uncover and reveal all U.S. government spending. Obama sponsored legislation requiring nuclear-plant owners to notify state and local authorities of radioactive leaks from their plants. He also introduced a bill to criminalize deceptive practices in federal elections. Obama fought against AIDS and for abortion rights.

Despite his deep concern for the welfare of poor Americans, U.S. Senator Obama did not shy away from foreign-policy issues. Ambivalently identifying with his tragic African father and empathizing with the poor victims of tribal wars in Africa, Obama initiated legislation to help the victims of the Congo war. In late 2006, President Bush signed into law the Democratic Republic of the Congo Relief, Security, and Democracy Promotion Act, the first piece of U.S. federal legislation enacted with Obama as its primary sponsor.

Senator Obama personally introduced or sponsored no fewer than 137 bills in the U.S. Senate. Two of these became law. The number 137 does not include bills that Obama supported or cosponsored, such as the Coburn-Obama Federal Funding Accountability and Transparency Act of 2006 or the Lugar-Nunn Cooperative Proliferation Detection and Interdiction Assistance Act of 2006. Nor does it include amendments to other bills, although in the U.S. Senate these are not required to be germane to the parent bill and can therefore effectively be bills in their own right. During the same time period (2005–2008), Obama cosponsored 689 bills in total, 408 of which had secured his support by the day they were originally introduced in the Senate.

Chapter 22

A HAPPY CONCLUSION

Synopsis: *As we have seen, this psychoanalytic study of Barack Obama's unconscious motivations is complemented by a study of his personality in the terms of the positive-psychology school's* Character Strengths and Virtues *handbook. These strengths and virtues are classed in six categories, namely* wisdom and knowledge *(creativity, curiosity, open-mindedness, love of learning, perspective),* courage *(bravery, persistence, integrity, vitality),* humanity *(love, kindness, social intelligence),* justice *(citizenship, fairness, leadership),* temperance *(forgiveness and mercy, humility, prudence, self-control), and* transcendence *(appreciation of beauty and excellence, gratitude, hope, humor, spirituality). Interestingly enough, empathy is not listed among these strengths and virtues. It is obvious, however, that Obama has many of these strengths and values. Obama himself thinks that his many battles in the U.S. Senate were not only political but rather battles over human values. He devoted an entire chapter of* The Audacity of Hope *to those values. Barack's list of "common American values" includes not only liberty but also optimism, community, family, patriotism, citizenship, faith, honesty, fairness, humility, kindness, courtesy, good manners, competence, and compassion. Despite the all-too-human mistakes he has made, he has been able to maintain most of his values and his integrity in the dirty game and contact sport of politics that he plays so well, seeking to achieve his high-minded goals.*

In a town-hall meeting at the University of New Orleans in the fall of 2009, a nine-year-old black fourth-grade schoolboy named Tyren Scott said to

President Obama, "I have to say, why do people hate you? They supposed to love you! God is love." Obama tried to reassure the boy that things were not as bad as they seemed. "First of all," he said "I did get elected President, so not everybody hates me, now." But he conceded that "if you're watching TV lately, it seems like everybody's just getting mad all the time. You've got to take it with a grain of salt. Some of it is just what's called politics." It is not clear whether the little black schoolboy understood the phrase "take it with a grain of salt." Struggling for words to explain the situation, Obama added, "Once one party wins then the other party kind of gets ... feels like it needs to poke you a little bit to keep you on your toes." Before giving the boy a reassuring hug, Obama told him half-humorously, "I'm a pretty tough guy. Are you a tough guy?" (Thompson, 2009).

Indeed he is. While this is a psychoanalytic study, it does not focus on Obama's psychopathology but rather on the opposite—on his enormous psychological strength and health. The positive-psychology school has something to contribute to our understanding of Obama. We have seen at the beginning of this book that Obama has many psychological strengths and virtues. The *Character Strengths and Virtues* handbook of the positive-psychology school (Peterson & Seligman, 2004) lists the following virtues and strengths:

1. *Wisdom and knowledge:* creativity, curiosity, open-mindedness, love of learning, perspective
2. *Courage:* bravery, persistence, integrity, vitality
3. *Humanity:* love, kindness, social intelligence
4. *Justice:* citizenship, fairness, leadership
5. *Temperance:* forgiveness and mercy, humility, prudence, self-control
6. *Transcendence:* appreciation of beauty and excellence, gratitude, hope, humor, spirituality.

Obama clearly has many of these strengths and virtues. Obama himself thinks that his battles in the U.S. Senate were not merely political but rather battles over values. He devoted an entire chapter of *The Audacity of Hope* to those values (Obama, 2006a, pp. 53–84). Obama has said that while his "fierce ambitions" may have been fueled by his father, he received his values—and his faith—from his "spiritually awakened" mother (Obama, pp. 242–244). Those values included kindness, generosity, empathy, and compassion but also honesty, fairness, straight talk, and independent judgment. Let us recall the positive-psychology list of character strengths and virtues on which, as we said at the outset of this book, Obama would score quite high, even though empathy, one of his chief strengths, is not listed among them. Obama thinks that discussing one's values is essential in political life. "It is the language of values that people use to map their world" (Obama, p. 64).

While thinking about his own values, Obama asked himself what were the core values that all Americans held in common (Obama, 2006a, p. 63). To him, values were of the utmost importance. The key American value was liberty, the freedom from oppression by an arbitrary government. This made him think of the Bill of Rights, the first 10 amendments to the U.S. Constitution. The Bill of Rights gives Americans many rights and freedoms that are not enjoyed by people in most other countries. Its 10 amendments were introduced by James Madison to the First U.S. Congress in 1789 as a series of articles and came into effect in 1791, after being ratified by three-fourths of the states then in the Union. Obama thinks that much of his admiration for America's Bill of Rights came from his Indonesian childhood and from his Kenyan family, as these two countries constantly trampled individual rights under the boot of army generals and the whims of corrupt officials (Obama, p. 65).

To Obama, the Bill of Rights symbolizes American values. It is indeed an extraordinary document. The Bill of Rights gave Americans freedom of speech; freedom of the press; freedom of religion; freedom of assembly; the right to petition the government for a redress of grievances; the right to form militias and to bear arms; protection from quartering of troops in one's house; protection from unreasonable search and seizure; the right to due process; protection against double jeopardy, self-incrimination, and eminent domain; the right to trial by jury; the right of the accused to confront his accusers, to have compulsory process for obtaining witnesses in his favor, and to have the assistance of a lawyer for his defense; the right to civil trial by jury; the prohibition of excessive bail and cruel and unusual punishment—as well as additional rights not specifically enumerated in the Bill of Rights, and the delegation to the states and people of all powers that are not delegated to the Union by the Constitution.

In his discussion of his values, Obama recalled the famous second sentence of the U.S. Declaration of Independence of 1776: "We hold these truths to be self-evident, that all men are created equal, that they are endowed by their Creator with certain unalienable Rights, that among these are Life, Liberty and the pursuit of Happiness." He thinks that all Americans believe in liberty, with all its aspects (Obama, 2006a, pp. 64–66). To him, liberty is more important than any other value. This longing for liberty made his wife Michelle want to leave Kenya and return to America when they visited Kenya in 1992. Ostensibly, Obama's love of liberty and his abhorrence of despotic regimes that robbed their people of their freedom, such as Kenya's, made him visit the West African country of Ghana rather than his father's country of Kenya in his first visit to black Africa as president of the United States in July 2009.

In fact, Ghana is not as free and democratic as Obama would believe. The former British colony of the Gold Coast, in which masses of black African slaves were seized, imprisoned, and shipped to America, had become a nominal parliamentary democracy at its independence in 1957, but several military and civilian regimes then followed. After the presidential and parliamentary elections and the drafting of the Ghanaian constitution in 1992, the last military government gave way to the Fourth Republic of Ghana. The constitution divided political powers among the president, the parliament, the cabinet, the council of state, and an independent judiciary. The Ghanaians come from six major tribes: the Akan (the Ashanti and the Fanti), the Ewe, the Ga-Adangbe, the Mole-Dagbani, the Guan, and the Gurma. Because of the dominance of the Akan, the people's representation in the legislature is flawed, with some low-population districts having more representatives per person than high-population ones (Berry, 1994).

The more important reason for Obama's choice of Ghana over Kenya was to visit Cape Coast Castle, one of several slave castles in Ghana where the black African slaves were kept in dungeons and lived in sweltering heat with only tiny vents to let in some fresh air before being shipped off to slavery in America. Obama's visit to Cape Coast Castle, where he compared the slave castle to the German concentration camp of Buchenwald, which he had visited the month before, received worldwide publicity. Obama spoke eloquently about liberty and the evils of slavery.

At the same time, Obama knows the grave danger posed by political ideologies. They are rigid, trapped in black-and-white, either-or, us-and-them thinking, and he must steer clear of any ideology, whether all-liberal or all-conservative. Values, in contrast, are flexible, and they adapt themselves to people's real needs and feelings. He believes that the difference between values and ideologies was crucial: values were applied to facts, whereas ideology ignores facts that call it into question (Obama, 2006a, p. 72). Indeed, had the world's great powers that fought the Cold War, the United States and the Soviet Union, those that adopted the capitalist and Communist ideologies, understood this psychological difference between values and ideologies, the Cold War might perhaps have been averted, and so might the terrible "hot wars" of the twentieth century. Nazi ideology, too, which brought about the destruction of tens of millions of innocent people, was a highly distorted, black-and-white view of humanity.

Obama's values have guided his political action. In January 2007, for instance, Senator Barack Obama cosponsored a bill with his Democratic colleague Senator Russell Feingold that would set new ethical standards for the U.S. government. Their bill sought to establish a gold standard for reform. Among the provisions of the Obama-Feingold bill that were adopted by the Senate and by the House were bans on receiving gifts and meals from lobbyists; new rules to slow the revolving door between public-sector and private-sector service; and an end to the subsidized use of corporate jets. The Republican-dominated Senate finally approved a watered-down version of this bill, the Honest Leadership and Open Government Act of 2007, which was signed into law by President George W. Bush in September. In 2008 both presidential candidates, Senators Barack Obama and John McCain, offered amendments to this act, although neither were official cosponsors of it. The uncontroversial bill was passed in the Senate by an 83–14 margin, with Obama voting for it and McCain voting against.

Honesty is a vital matter for Obama. He himself had felt dishonest as an adolescent, and his father had not been honest: he had presented himself as that which he was not. Obama would make America honest. Being honest about the error of the U.S. war in Iraq was a major goal for him. In January 2007 U.S. Senator Obama introduced the Iraq War De-Escalation Act, which would have stopped the U.S. troop surge of 21,500 men in Iraq and would have begun a phased withdrawal of U.S. troops from Iraq, removing all combat forces by March 31, 2008. The Republicans obstructed Obama's bill, which was referred to a Senate committee and died there. Later in 2007, Obama sponsored an amendment to the Defense Authorization Act, adding safeguards for personality-disorder military discharges, so that traumatized U.S. soldiers returning from Iraq would get treated fairly back at home. He also cosponsored a bill to reduce global poverty. He sponsored the Iran Sanctions Enabling Act, which called for divestment of American state pension funds from Iran's oil and gas industry, and cosponsored legislation to reduce the threat of nuclear terror.

Although, as we have seen, Obama tries to suit his actions to his words, his words to his actions, some philosophers have discussed Obama's rhetoric. Writing in the fall of 2008, at the height of Obama's presidential campaign, the Slovenian sociologist, philosopher, and Lacanian psychoanalyst Slavoj Žižek (born 1949) pointed out that Obama's greatest political achievement was his "subtle rhetoric" and that "he has, in his refined and non-provocative way, introduced into the public speech topics that were once unsayable: the continuing importance of race in politics, the positive role of atheists in public life, the necessity to talk with 'enemies' like Iran." Žižek also thought that "the danger for Sen. Barack Obama is that he is already doing to himself what later historical censorship did to [Martin Luther] King: he's cleansing his program of contentious topics in order to assure his electability" (Žižek, 2008).

This was inaccurate. The presidential candidate Barack Obama had not cleansed his program of contentious issues such as the Iraq War, healthcare reform, homosexual marriage, abortion, and other controversial issues in the United States. Žižek called Obama's rhetoric hypocritical but added that "one should not blame Obama for his hypocrisy. Given the complex situation of the United States in today's world, how far can a new [U.S.] president go in imposing actual change without triggering economic meltdown or political backlash?" (Žižek, 2008). In fact, the reverse seems true. Obama sounds sincere in his expressions of empathy and compassion, and a comparison between his speeches and his actions shows that his rhetoric expresses his true feelings. In fact, Obama himself has wondered why politicians could not talk about values "in ways that don't appear calculated or phony" (Obama, 2006a, p. 77). He thinks that because political action and gestures have become so crafted and scripted by speechwriters and media consultants, it is increasingly hard for the public to tell honest sentiment from political stagecraft (Obama, 2006a, p. 77).

One of the issues that irked Obama when he was a U.S. senator was the incredible "ethic of greed" among the chief executive officers of U.S. corporations. While in 1980 an average CEO in the United States made 42 times the pay of an average hourly worker, by 2005 it was 262 times as much. At the same time, "the explosion in CEO pay has had little to do with improved performance. In fact, some of the country's most highly compensated CEOs over the past decade have presided over huge drops in earnings, losses in shareholder value, massive layoffs, and the underfunding of their workers' pension funds" (Obama, 2006a, p. 75). Obama saw this as a cultural problem: America's CEOs had lost any sense of shame in their ethic of greed. Their lack of empathy for others made it possible for the CEOs to deny the feelings and needs of their employees. In a U.S. public-opinion poll, most Americans ranked corruption, greed, and materialism, after "raising kids with the right values," as America's most important moral challenges (Obama, 2006a, pp. 75, 82). Indeed, the global economic crisis of 2008–2009, which he had to face after being elected president, proved the correctness of his assessment.

Having been a child from a broken family himself and a restless adolescent rebel, Obama believed in good parental guidance above everything. He thought that no amount of money would improve scholastic performance if the students' parents did not instill the values of hard work and delaying gratification in their children. American society was lying to its children and to itself, and betraying its own values, when it pretended that its children could realize their potential in dangerous, badly built, and badly equipped schools with poorly trained teachers (Obama, 2006a, p. 76). As a state and federal legislator, Obama sponsored numerous bills to improve the public schools in which America's poor children were educated. He also became the chairman of the Chicago Annenberg Challenge to improve those schools. Obama believed that the U.S. government should embody in its behavior the communal values that bind Americans together. Culture was very important, but government can help shape that culture (Obama, p. 77).

BARACK OBAMA AND THE U.S. CONSTITUTION

Obama's attitude of reverence and love for the Constitution of the United States is so intense that one might be tempted to think that, unconsciously, the Constitution is his idealized mother. It protects the American nation, and he, in turn, wants to protect it at all costs. In fact, after America herself, the Constitution is his most prized and idealized political object.

U.S. Senator Obama devoted an entire chapter of *The Audacity of Hope* to the importance of the U.S. Constitution and how the Bush administration was trying to use its majority in Congress to flout constitutional rights, abuse its power, nominate judges that would do its bidding, rob the other branches of government of their power, legalize torture and eavesdropping on citizens, rob people of their legal rights by calling them enemy combatants, and engage in other actions that would normally have been considered illegal and unconstitutional (Obama, 2006a, pp. 85–120). He often recalled his old and venerable colleague Senator Robert Byrd of West Virginia and his admonitions to his fellow senators to fight for the rights specified in the Constitution and to resist the executive's attempts to subvert the Constitution (Obama, pp. 118–120).

As we have seen, U.S. Senator Obama was very concerned with the legislative institution of the filibuster and its abuse by both Republicans and Democrats, especially when trying to advance or block the nomination of federal judges (Obama, 2006a, pp. 95–100). To him, those fights over judicial nominations mattered personally: they involved the protection of basic human dignity, and he had seen too much of it trampled under foot in Chicago—and in Kenya. The arcane and esoteric procedural rules of the Senate, the constitutional separation of powers, judicial nominations, all of these mattered greatly because they determined the way Americans lived together and defined American democracy no less than elections. Obama believed that the American political system was quite complicated but that it was only by working through that system that Americans could shape their values and commitments (Obama, pp. 100–101).

The State Children's Health Insurance Program, administered by the U.S. Department of Health and Human Services, provides matching funds to states for health insurance to families with children. The program was designed by the U.S. Congress with the intent of covering uninsured children in families with incomes that are modest but not low enough to qualify for Medicaid. Already when he was a U.S. Senator, Obama, who later, as president, forged a new health-care plan for America so that no American was left without health insurance and medical care, sponsored a Senate amendment to the State Children's Health Insurance Program providing job protection for family members of soldiers with combat-related injuries who must care for those soldiers.

In February 2007 U.S. Senator Obama announced his candidacy for the Democratic presidential nomination. During the presidential campaign, in addition to his slogans of "Yes, We Can" and "Change We Need," protection, guidance, and love were his key words, rather than honor, as was the case with his Republican opponent, Senator McCain. In his presidential-nomination acceptance speech at the Democratic National Convention in Denver in 2008, Obama said that government programs could not replace parents and that "*fathers must take more responsibility to provide love and guidance to their children*" (Obama, 2008). Did he have his own father in mind? Certainly he is one father who has provided love and guidance to his two daughters, which his father had not done for him. He now aims to give that same fatherly protection, love, and guidance to America—his symbolic mother and family—and to heal its wounds, as, in some ways, he had to do with his real mother during his earlier life.

THE CHIEF JUSTICE AND THE PRESIDENT

In 2005 U.S. President Bush nominated the 50-year-old conservative Republican judge John Glover Roberts, Jr., to justice of the U.S. Supreme Court and, later that year, during Roberts' confirmation hearings, after the death of former Chief Justice William Rehnquist (1924–2005), to chief justice. During the confirmation hearings in the U.S. Congress, U.S. Senator Obama was one of the 22 Democratic senators who opposed Roberts' confirmation. Nonetheless, on September 22, 2005, the U.S. Senate Judiciary Committee, with its then-Republican majority, approved Roberts's nomination by a vote of 13 to 5. The Democratic senators Ted Kennedy, Richard Durbin, Charles Schumer, Joe Biden, and Dianne Feinstein cast the dissenting votes.

In January 2009 it fell to Chief Justice Roberts to swear in Senator Obama as president of the United States. Article 2, section 1 of the U.S. Constitution, drafted by the Constitutional Convention in 1787 and entitled "The President," says, "Before he enter on the Execution of his Office, he shall take the following Oath or Affirmation: *I do solemnly swear (or affirm) that I will faithfully execute the Office of President of the United States, and will to the best of my ability, preserve, protect and defend the Constitution of the United States.*" The new president can choose between the word *swear* with its religious connotation and the word *affirm* with its secular one.

While the Constitution does not mandate that anyone *administer* the oath to the new president, by tradition the oath is administered by the chief justice of the Supreme Court (sometimes by another federal or state judge). The first president, George Washington, was sworn in by Robert Livingston, the chancellor of the State of New York in 1789, while President Calvin Coolidge was sworn in by his father, a Justice of the Peace and Vermont notary public who lived in a home without electricity, phone, or running water, in 1923. Again, by American tradition and convention, incoming presidents raise their right hand and place their left one on a Christian Bible while taking the oath of office. For the left-handed Obama, this was an unusual undertaking.

On Tuesday, January 20, 2009, the white U.S. Chief Justice John G. Roberts swore in the black Barack H. Obama as the 44th president of the United States of America. This was the first time in U.S. history that a Supreme Court justice swore in a president who had voted against his confirmation. Roberts may well have harbored feelings of hurt or anger toward Obama. It is therefore not surprising that during Obama's swearing-in ceremony, the two antagonists spoke at the same time, interrupting one another, and that Roberts made a slip of the tongue while administering the oath to Obama. Traditionally, the official who swears in the new president reads out the text of the oath, in short parts, which the new president repeats after him, one part after another. While the oath reads "I do solemnly swear that I will faithfully execute the office of President of the United States," the chief justice read out, "I, Barack Hussein Obama, do solemnly swear, *that I will execute the office to President to the United States faithfully ...*"

Obama had taught U.S. constitutional law at the University of Chicago for 10 years. Realizing that Roberts had made a mistake, Obama, who knew the text of the oath by heart, paused for a moment and then slowly and deliberately began to repeat the wrong words that Roberts had said, trying to let the chief justice correct himself. Roberts did so, saying "faithfully the office of President of the United States." Due to Roberts's mistake, however, the swearing in was ruled invalid, and Obama had to take the oath of office again the next day, January 21, with Roberts once more administering the oath, this time without errors.

On the surface of things, this was a haphazard lapse on the chief justice's part. If one looks a little deeper, however, it was no accident. The two men were bitter antagonists. Roberts had not forgotten Obama's opposition to him during his Senate confirmation hearings. Six years Obama's senior, Roberts had been the managing editor of the *Harvard Law Review*, of which Obama later became the president. Justice Roberts was a conservative Republican, Senator Obama a liberal Democrat. Did Roberts unconsciously wish to botch Obama's swearing-in ceremony—as he in fact did?

Obama took the mishap in stride and was sworn in again by Roberts on January 21, 2009. Roberts and Obama, however, did not forget their rivalry and enmity. On January 21, 2010, a year to the day after Obama's second swearing-in ceremony, the U.S. Supreme Court removed the limit on corporate political spending by a five-to-four vote. The ban had been confirmed by two earlier Supreme Court decisions. The majority that voted to overturn the ban, led by Roberts, argued that the First Amendment to the U.S. Constitution guaranteed the right of free speech and that the ban had violated that right. The dissenters who voted to retain the limit argued that unlimited corporate donations to political campaigns would corrupt U.S. politics and its democracy.

Two days later, on January 23, 2010, when President Obama delivered his weekly radio and Internet address, he said that the Supreme Court decision had "handed a huge victory" to special interests who would dominate and corrupt U.S. politics if the ruling were to stand (Johnston, 2010). Obama vowed to work with the U.S. Congress to amend the law on this issue. In his first State of the Union address on January 27, 2010, delivered to a joint session of the U.S. House of Representatives and Senate, President Obama once more criticized the Supreme Court's ruling. By U.S. tradition, Chief Justice Roberts was in the audience, along with his Supreme Court colleagues. Later, Roberts publicly complained that he was forced to sit "expressionless" while Obama's congressional friends cheered his address, that the State of the Union address had degenerated into "a political pep rally," and that he was not sure why he was there (Time, 2010).

President Obama quickly moved to make important appointments to the White House and to his Cabinet and key advisers, most of which were easily confirmed by the U.S. Congress: Rahm Emanuel (born 1959) as White House chief of staff, David Axelrod (born 1955) as his senior adviser, Jonathan Favreau as his chief speechwriter, Robert Gates (born 1943) as his secretary of defense, and Timothy Geithner (born 1961) as his secretary of the treasury. Obama's only serious error was the naming the former U.S. Senator Thomas Andrew Daschle (born 1947) for his secretary of health and human services. The vigilant U.S. press quickly discovered that Daschle had avoided paying certain obligatory taxes and had also received favors that could be construed as bribes. Daschle had to withdraw his name from nomination.

We have observed Obama's fascination with America's founding fathers and its unconscious relation to his ambivalent feelings about his own father. In his inauguration speech on January 20, 2009, Obama once more invoked the founding fathers, his own father, and "the father of our nation" (George Washington):

> As for our common defense, we reject as false the choice between our safety and our ideals. *Our Founding Fathers*, faced with perils we can scarcely

imagine, drafted a charter to assure the rule of law and the rights of man, a charter expanded by the blood of generations ... And so to all other peoples and governments who are watching today, *from the grandest capitals to the small village where my father was born:* Know that America is a friend of each nation and every man, woman and child who seeks a future of peace and dignity, and that we are ready to lead once more ... This is ... why *a man whose father less than 60 years ago might not have been served at a local restaurant can now stand before you to take a most sacred oath* ... At a moment when the outcome of our revolution was most in doubt, *the father of our nation* ordered these words be read to the people. (Obama, 2009f, italics added)

With a father who had abandoned him and let him down so severely, for Obama, the founding fathers and the father of our nation were idealized replacements. During his inauguration festivities, the African American poetess and Yale literature professor Elizabeth Alexander (born 1962) read a poem entitled "Praise Song for the Day" that Obama had invited her to compose for his inauguration. The poem was about the daily life of Americans. The poetess sang the praises of human work and human love, the everyday wonders and pleasures of life, concluding with the words: "In today's sharp sparkle, this winter air, anything can be made, any sentence begun. On the brink, on the brim, on the cusp—praise song for walking forward in that light."

Some readers of the poem were critical. Erica Wagner (born 1967), an American writer living in Great Britain, called Alexander's poem unmemorable, repetitious, pedestrian, and dull (Wagner, 2009). Whatever the merits or demerits of Alexander's poem, Sasha Abramsky thinks that it was a rare honor for her to be invited to read her poem at Obama's inauguration, as only three other poets had been given such an honor before. Abramsky thinks that Alexander's poem fit the central theme of Obama's inauguration, "that this was a new America, an administration that would listen to the voices of ordinary men, women, and children" (2009, pp. 70–71).

Indeed, Obama wanted his presidency to primarily serve ordinary people and poor people. Harry Boyte, the director of the Humphrey Institute of Public Affairs at the University of Minnesota, and Carmen Sirianni, the research director for new citizenship at Brandeis University in Massachusetts, had written a policy paper for the Obama campaign about the role of ordinary people in the new American citizenship, and Obama had adopted it (Abramsky, 2009, pp. 71–72).

With his self-esteem and self-confidence intact, Obama has little trouble acknowledging his own mistakes. At the time of the unfortunate arrest of the black Harvard professor Henry Gates in July 2009, Obama at first called the arresting police officer stupid, then apologized and invited the police officer and the professor to have beer with him at the White House. Similarly, Obama had made a mistake by nominating Daschle, and he was quick to own up to it (Walsh, 2009). He saw it as a minor error on his way to bigger and better things.

Obama's fierce ambitions made him want to make enormous changes during his first 100 days in office. In his first few days in office Obama issued numerous executive orders and presidential memoranda reversing many of President Bush's policies, including Bush's ban on U.S. federal funding to foreign establishments that allow abortions (known as the Mexico City Policy or the Global Gag Rule). Obama facilitated the disclosure of government information under the Freedom of Information Act, directed his defense secretary Bob Gates to develop plans to withdraw U.S. troops from Iraq, and reduced the secrecy of presidential records. He also issued a presidential order to close the notorious Guantánamo Bay detention camp in Cuba by January 2010.

The first month of Obama's presidency saw his signing into law a $787 billion economic-stimulus package, aimed at helping the economy recover from the deepening recession that had begun with the great economic crisis of 2008. The bill included greatly increased federal spending for health care, infrastructure, and education, as well as various tax breaks and incentives and direct assistance to individuals. Obama also made a high-profile visit to Capitol Hill to engage with congressional Republicans, but the health-care-reform bill ultimately passed largely on a party-line vote. Even within his own Democratic Party, some legislators opposed some parts of his bill for fear of alienating their constituencies (Scherer, 2009). The significant differences between the House and Senate versions of Obama's health-care-reform bill were later ironed out in the House-Senate conference committee and signed by the president.

Barack Obama firmly believed that the U.S. war in Iraq was an error and that the war in Afghanistan and Pakistan was justified. On February 18, 2009, U.S. President Obama announced that the U.S. troop strength in Afghanistan would be boosted by 17,000 men to help fight the Taliban and Al-Qaeda terrorists in Afghanistan and Pakistan. In the announcement, Obama asserted that the increase was necessary to stabilize a deteriorating political and military situation in Afghanistan, which had not received the attention, direction, and resources that it urgently required. On February 27, Obama declared that U.S. combat operations in Iraq would end by the summer of 2010. Obama stated in his remarks to the Marines who were about to deploy to Afghanistan, telling them plainly that their combat mission in Iraq would end by August 31, 2010.

The list of Obama's presidential actions during the first months of his presidency is mind-boggling. Besides the numerous bills that he submitted to Congress, it includes a staggering number of executive orders, presidential memoranda, and presidential proclamations. The executive orders alone included those on the presidential records; ethics commitments by executive-branch personnel; the closure of the notorious Guantánamo detention center in Cuba; a review of detention-policy options, ensuring lawful interrogations; the nondisplacement of qualified workers under federal service contracts; economy in government contracting; and notification of employee rights under federal labor laws.

Obama's first flurry of executive orders also included the revocation of Bush's executive orders concerning regulatory planning and review, the establishment of the President's Advisory Council for Faith-Based and Neighborhood Partnerships, amendments to Clinton's executive orders on the National Economic Council and the Domestic Policy Council, an order establishing the President's Economic Recovery Advisory Board, the establishment of the White House Office of Urban Affairs, an amendment to Bush's executive order on stem-cell research to remove barriers to responsible scientific research involving human stem cells, creation of the White House Council on Women and Girls, and establishment of the White House Office of Health Reform and the Chesapeake Bay Protection and Restoration Agency. Together with Obama's numerous presidential memoranda and proclamations, and his legislative bills, all this amounts to an enormous if quiet revolution in U.S. politics. No wonder he joked at the White House Correspondents Association's dinner after his first 100 days in office that he hoped to complete his next 100 days in 72 days and that on the 73rd day he would rest.

Obama's greatest success during the first year of his presidency was his health-care reform. His mother had died of cancer without proper medical care due to her lack of adequate insurance or due to her insurers refusing to pay for her care. His maternal grandmother had died just before his election victory after having had expensive hip-replacement surgery while she was dying of cancer. There can be little doubt that Barack's feelings about health reform in America are connected to his personal feelings about the fate of his mother and grandmother—to whom he dedicated his *Audacity of Hope*. Did he have conscious or unconscious guilt feelings about being unable to save his dying mother? Certain it is that he devoted an extraordinary amount of emotional and intellectual energy to reforming America's health-care system and that his tenacity, persistence, and patience paid off in the long run, however many conservative enemies he may have made along the way.

Obama's "fierce ambitions" (Obama, 2006a, p. 243) extend to reforming, repairing, and ameliorating not only health care but also every aspect of American life. He wants to right the wrongs and to fix the injustices of his motherland. On May 22, 2009, he signed into law a bill designed to protect debt-ridden consumers from excessive and unwarranted charges by greedy credit card companies. The White House staged a bill-signing ceremony in the Rose Garden, an indication of the legislation's importance to Obama. Though opposed by financial companies, the bill had cleared the U.S. Congress with broad bipartisan support. Obama made it clear that he did not champion the changes with the intention of helping those who buy more than they can afford through reckless spending or wishful thinking. "Some get in [debt] over their heads by not using their heads," the president said. "I want to be clear: we do not excuse or condone folks who've acted irresponsibly." And yet, he said, for many millions of Americans, "trying to get out of debt has been made difficult and bewildering by their credit-card companies" (Elliott, 2009). His new law was designed to protect them (Elliott, 2009).

Obama's relations with the mass-communication media are deeply ambivalent. He enjoyed their support and even their adulation for three years, and they helped him win the presidency of the United States, yet he fears their tremendous influence. While he had no reason to complain personally about his treatment by the media, he still had to watch them carefully: they had idealized him and made him the object of tremendous hopes and expectations. It was impossible for him to live up to all these expectations, and he knew that the same media, if they became disappointed in him, could turn around and attack him (Obama, 2006a, p. 144).

This was a very insightful statement. The mass-communication media built up so many expectations for President Obama that he is bound to disappoint numerous people. No man alive can live up to all these expectations, can fix everything that is wrong with our planet, not even a president of the United States with all his power and goodwill. In 2008 *Time* magazine backed Obama passionately for the presidency. Since then, the magazine's political commentator Joe Klein has changed from a great admirer of Obama to one of his frequent critics.

STAND-UP COMIC: OBAMA'S SENSE OF HUMOR

In his stand-up comedy act at the White House Correspondents Association's dinner on the completion of his first 100 days in office, on May 9, 2009, President Obama jokingly said that he hoped to finish his second 100 days in 72 days and that on the 73rd day he would rest (cf. Genesis 2:2). In every joke there is a kernel of truth. Why did he choose the number 72? Did it have anything to do with the 72 *houris*, or virgins, that according to Islamic belief await the *shaheed* in heaven? What would Barack Hussein Obama, who fights Islamic fanatics and terrorists, have in common with a Muslim *shaheed*? Is there still something of the Muslim in him, as his enemies believe? And why did he compare himself to God? Was this the megalomania of politicians that he himself had written about? (Obama, 2006a, p. 125). It is well known that megalomania and paranoia are fairly common among politicians (Robins & Post, 1997).

Were Obama's true feelings about Islam expressed in his speech in Cairo, Egypt, on June 4, 2009, entitled "A New Beginning"? In that speech at Cairo University, Obama sought to place the relations between his country and the Muslim world on a new footing, in contrast to his predecessor George W. Bush, who in the aftermath of the September 11, 2001, tragedy had described himself as a "crusader" against the "terror of Islam."

Obama's Cairo speech abounded with flattering references to Islam. He first spoke about Cairo University's rival, Al-Azhar University, founded in 970–972, which is the chief center of Arabic literature and Sunni Muslim learning in the world, and the world's second-oldest degree-granting university. The university had been founded by the Fatimid dynasty of Egypt, who fancied themselves the descendants of Fatimah, a daughter of the Prophet Muhammad. Fatimah was called *az-zahra* (the brilliant), and the university was named after her. Here are some of the things Obama said at Cairo University:

> I am honored to be in the timeless city of Cairo, and to be hosted by two remarkable institutions. For over a thousand years, Al-Azhar has stood as a beacon of Islamic learning; and for over a century, Cairo University has been a source of Egypt's advancement. And together, you represent the harmony between tradition and progress. I'm grateful for your hospitality, and the hospitality of the people of Egypt. And I'm also proud to carry with me the goodwill of the American people, and a greeting of peace from Muslim communities in my country: *as-salaam alaykum* [peace be upon you]. (Obama, 2009d)

Obama went on to praise Al-Azhar University, Islamic learning, and the achievements of the Muslim world in medicine, science, mathematics, and human affairs:

> For over a thousand years, Al-Azhar has stood as a beacon of Islamic learning … America and Islam … overlap, and share common principles—principles of justice and progress; tolerance and the dignity of all human beings … I also know civilization's debt to Islam. It was Islam—at places like Al-Azhar—that carried the light of learning through so many centuries, paving the way for Europe's Renaissance and Enlightenment. It was innovation in Muslim communities—it was innovation in Muslim communities that developed the order of algebra; our magnetic compass and tools of navigation; our mastery of pens and printing; our understanding of how disease spreads and how it can be healed. Islamic culture has given

us majestic arches and soaring spires; timeless poetry and cherished music; elegant calligraphy and places of peaceful contemplation. And throughout history, Islam has demonstrated through words and deeds the possibilities of religious tolerance and racial equality. (Obama, 2009d)

Did Obama mean every word he said in Cairo? After all, all this praise for Islam came from an African American Christian who in his youth had been an agnostic or an atheist and who had a Swahili first name and an Arabic middle name. Obama had written at length about his religious faith in *The Audacity of Hope* (Obama, 2006a, pp. 231–268). He believed that his work in Chicago as a young community organizer had helped him mature and that he had been drawn to Christianity by the black American Christian religious tradition's "power to spur social change," until he "was finally able to walk down the aisle of Trinity United Church of Christ one day and be baptized" (Obama, pp. 244–246).

Obama's Christian faith, however, had neither saved him from doubt nor weakened his grip on reality. It did not make him give up his critical thinking, his social commitments, his values, or his political career (Obama, 2006a, p. 246). What did he feel about his grandfather's Muslim religion, which Obama's father had rejected in his youth? Obama's spiritual journey into the Christian faith had involved some of the key people in his life—his mother Ann, his father Barak, his wife Michelle, and his adoptive father figure, the Reverend Jeremiah Wright, Jr.

The way Obama saw it, his mother's fundamental faith in people's goodness and in the value of human life had channeled his fierce ambitions into religious faith. He had studied political philosophy, he wrote, because he had sought to confirm his mother's values. Obama sought "both a language and systems of action that could help build community and make justice real" (Obama, 2006a, p. 244). This was why he had gone to work as a community organizer in Chicago to fight drugs, unemployment, and despair (pp. 243–244). His abandonment by his father and his father's tragic fate had been unjust, and he could do nothing to change them. In politics, he was not helpless. In fact, he may have gone into politics for this reason.

When the 77-year-old U.S. Senator Edward Kennedy of Massachusetts died on August 25, 2009, the 48-year-old President Obama lost one of his father figures. The Kennedys had filled the psychological role of royalty in Massachusetts. After Ted Kennedy's death, his coffin was transported from the Kennedy Compound in Hyannis Port, Martha's Vineyard, Massachusetts, past numerous landmarks named after the Kennedys, to Boston's John F. Kennedy Library, where tens of thousands of people paid their respects to the dead leader.

As the Kennedys were Irish American Catholics, on August 29, 2009, a funeral procession carrying Ted Kennedy's coffin departed from the

John F. Kennedy library to Boston's Our Lady of Perpetual Help Basilica for a Roman Catholic funeral mass. President Obama and the former U.S. presidents Jimmy Carter, Bill Clinton, and George W. Bush attended the funeral service, along with Vice President Joe Biden, three former U.S. vice presidents, 58 U.S. senators, 21 former U.S. senators, many members of the U.S. House of Representatives, and several foreign dignitaries (Weir, 2009). Bush's father, the 85-year-old former president George H. W. Bush, declined to attend without stating his reason, saying only that his son would represent him. President Obama delivered the eulogy. Here is one typical and memorable passage:

> [Edward Kennedy] told us [that] … "individual faults and frailties are no excuse to give in—and no exemption from the common obligation to give of ourselves." Indeed, Ted was the "Happy Warrior" that the poet Wordsworth spoke of when he wrote:
>
> *As tempted more; more able to endure,*
> *As more exposed to suffering and distress;*
> *Thence, also, more alive to tenderness.*
>
> Through his own suffering, Ted Kennedy became more alive to the plight and the suffering of others—the sick child who could not see a doctor; the young soldier denied her rights because of what she looks like or who she loves or where she comes from. The landmark laws that he championed— the Civil Rights Act, the Americans with Disabilities Act, immigration reform, children's health insurance, the Family and Medical Leave Act—all have a running thread. Ted Kennedy's life work was not to champion the causes of those with wealth or power or special connections. It was to give a voice to those who were not heard; to add a rung to the ladder of opportunity; to make real the dream of our founding. He was given the gift of time that his brothers were not, and he used that gift to touch as many lives and right as many wrongs as the years would allow. (Obama, 2009b)

Obama might as well have said the same things about himself. Yet these were also the words of a son eulogizing his father. Obama had loved Ted Kennedy as much as he did his father, without the anger that he harbored at his abusive father.

While in late 2009 U.S. President Obama was the laureate of the 2009 Nobel Peace Prize, he has some very difficult war-and-peace issues to deal with. While striving to achieve peace all over the world, he must fight nasty wars in Iraq, Afghanistan, Pakistan, Yemen, Somalia, and other countries against the Al-Qaeda and Taliban Islamic terrorists who consider themselves Allah's freedom fighters and want to be holy martyrs and who see the Americans as vile infidels or filthy crusaders. He needs to plug the holes in America's homeland-security system against suicide-bombing attacks such as the one attempted on Christmas Day 2009 by the Nigerian Muslim fanatic Umar Farouk Abdulmutallab, the son of one of Africa's wealthiest men and former Nigerian cabinet minister. Curiously, the highly intelligent and articulate Obama misplaced the accent on Abdulmutallab's last name during his televised statement to the press on January 5, 2010.

After the failed bomb attack on Christmas day 2009, the former vice president under George W. Bush, Richard Cheney, an archconservative and implacable foe of Obama, attacked President Obama for his "weak" response to the botched terrorist attack. Obama responded forcefully: "It is telling that Vice President Cheney and others seem to be more focused on criticizing the Administration than condemning the attackers," his communications director Dan Pfeiffer wrote on the official White House Internet blog. "Unfortunately too many [politicians] are engaged in the typical Washington game of pointing fingers and making political hay, instead of working together to find solutions to make our country safer."

During his first term of office Obama ambitiously seeks to bring peace to the Middle East, a region in which the psychological obstacles to peace between the Palestinian Arabs and the Israeli Jews are immense (Falk, 2004). In his first State of the Union address on January 20, 2010, the first anniversary of his presidency, he admitted publicly that his Middle East peace initiative had failed, blaming this failure on the intransigence of both the Israeli and the Palestinian leaders, each because of his own internal political considerations. Nonetheless, Obama did not give up, directing his secretary of state, Hillary Clinton, and his special envoy to the Middle East, George Mitchell, to pursue their peacemaking efforts, which they have been doing.

In January 2010, five months after the death of U.S. Senator Edward Kennedy, a special election was held in Massachusetts for his successor. This election was won by the 50-year-old conservative Republican candidate, Scott Philip Brown, whose victory upset the absolute Democratic majority in the U.S. Senate and threatened to derail Obama's health-care reform. With his popularity down to about 50 percent of the American people and his political agenda under fire, U.S. President Barack Obama agreed to be interviewed by Diane Sawyer on ABC Television News.

Sawyer asked Obama whether one presidential term was not enough for him in view of the very difficult issues he had to deal with (the heavy opposition to his health-care-reform initiative, the wars in Iraq and Afghanistan, and the Arab-Israeli conflict). The self-confident Obama laughed and told Sawyer that his job was not to get reelected but to help his people. He said that he would rather be a really good one-term president than a mediocre two-term one and that he would not sacrifice his ambitious political goals to win a second term in the White House. Obama added, "I don't want to look back on my time here and say to myself all I was interested in was nurturing my own popularity" (Obama, 2010).

President Obama made those statements shortly after unveiling a new package of financial initiatives aimed at easing the economic burden of the American lower and middle class, prior to his State of the Union address. The Democrats' loss of the U.S. Senate election in Massachusetts had cost the president's party its filibuster-proof majority in the Senate and forced Obama to reassess his political moves in the face of solid Republican opposition and public unrest. Nonetheless, he doggedly pursued his health-care reform, which, thanks to his signing of an executive order outlawing federal funds for abortions, was passed by the U.S. House of Representatives on March 21, 2010.

By February 2010 President Obama had significantly escalated the nine-year-old war on the Al-Qaeda terrorists and their Taliban allies with a large-scale assault on the terrorists in Afghanistan's Helmand province by U.S. and NATO forces under General Stanley McChrystal. Ironically, the Nobel Peace Prize winner was waging all-out war. George W. Bush's former vice president, Richard Cheney, publicly declared to a meeting of the Conservative Political Action Conference that Obama was "a one-term president" and that he would not be reelected in 2012. Soon thereafter, Bush's top political adviser, Karl Rove, published a memoir in which he portrayed Obama as a dangerous socialist (Rove, 2010).

Cheney had accompanied his elder daughter, Liz Cheney Perry, to the conservative conference as "arm candy," the American term for an especially attractive date, escort, or companion to a special event. He had not been expected to speak at the conference. Nonetheless, when invited to speak, he could not resist the temptation. Cheney told the American conservatives that the year 2010 would be "a big year for Republicans," citing the Republican victories in New Jersey's and Virginia's gubernatorial races and in the Massachusetts Senate race as "enormously encouraging" for the Republican party's prospects in the midterm fall election. As usual, he attacked Obama's policies and his legislative actions.

On top of his troubles at home, Obama had to deal with a fanatical Islamic government in Iran that sought to acquire nuclear weapons and that had threatened to annihilate Israel, with a nationalist right-wing Israeli government that often broke its promises to him, as well as with Islamic terrorists and fanatics in Iraq, Yemen, Somalia, Afghanistan, and Pakistan. He has had to fight desperate pirates from Somalia and murderous drug traffickers from Mexico. With the American public deeply divided about his health-care reform, his popularity in January 2010 hovered around 50 percent of the U.S. public, 17 percent lower than a year earlier.

A lesser man would have changed course to increase his popularity and his chances for a second term as president of the United States. The self-confident Obama, however, was not afraid to take on the U.S. bankers who were trying to foil his financial-sector-reform bill, designed to prevent another economic crisis, and to pursue his battle for U.S. health-care reform, which was passed by the U.S. Congress in March 2010. Thirty-two million Americans who had not had any health insurance would henceforth receive health care. The American public remained divided about Obama, but this did not deter him from doing what he believed in, namely, helping poor people extricate themselves from their vicious circle of poverty, drugs, crime, and unemployment.

It will take all of Obama's character strengths and virtues, his self-confidence, his empathy, his patience, his integrity, his sense of humor, his gift for mediation and conciliation, his persistence, and his optimism to deal with all his difficulties and to achieve all these seemingly impossible tasks. I believe that he will prove equal to his awesome task. If he loses the 2012 presidential election despite being a good president during his first term of office, I do not believe that he will regret it deeply. There will always be important things for Barack Obama to do.

REFERENCES

Abramsky, Sasha (2009). *Inside Obama's brain*. New York: Penguin Portfolio.

Abramson, Jill & Keller, Bill (2009). *Obama: The historic journey*. New York: The New York Times.

Alinsky, Saul David (1971). *Rules for radicals: A pragmatic primer for realistic radicals*. New York: Random House.

Andersen, Christopher (2009). *Barack and Michelle: Portrait of an American marriage*. New York: William Morrow.

Anderson, Benedict Richard O'Gorman (1983). *Imagined communities: Reflections on the origin and spread of nationalism*. London: Verso.

Anderson, Veronica (1993, September 27–October 3). 40 under forty: Barack Obama, director, Illinois Project Vote. *Crain's Chicago Business, 16*(39), 43.

Archibold, Randal C. (2004, July 29). The Illinois candidate: Day after, keynote speaker finds admirers everywhere. *The New York Times.*

Ayers, William (1993). *To teach: The journey of a teacher* (Foreword by Herbert Kohl). New York: Teachers College Press.

Ayers, William (Ed.) (1995). *To become a teacher: Making a difference in children's lives* (Foreword by Jonathan Kozol). New York: Teachers College Press.

Ayers, William (2001). *Fugitive days: A memoir*. Boston: Beacon Press.

Ayers, William (2008a, November 14). Ayers says he's not friends with Obama: Former radical says relationship is more of a professional one. *MSNBC. com.* http://www.msnbc.msn.com/id/27721538/

Ayers, William (2008b). *Fugitive days: Memoirs of an anti-war activist*. New edition. Boston: Beacon Press.

Ayers, William & Ford, Patricia (Eds.) (1996). *City kids, city teachers: Reports from the front row*. New York: New Press.

Baldwin, Tom (2007, December 21). Stay-at-home Barack Obama comes under fire for a lack of foreign experience. *The Sunday Times.*

Barker, Kim (2007, March 25). History of schooling distorted. *Chicago Tribune.*

Baron, Samuel H. & Pletsch, Carl (Eds.) (1985). *Introspection in biography: The biographer's quest for self-awareness.* Hillsdale, NJ: Analytic Press.

Bashir, Halima (with Lewis Damien) (2008). *Tears of the desert: A memoir of survival in Darfur.* New York: One World Ballantine Books.

Becker, Jo & Drew, Christopher (2008, May 11). Pragmatic politics, forged on the South Side. *The New York Times.*

Belafonte, Harry & Smiley, Tavis (2008, November 5). Transcript of Tavis Smiley's interview with Harry Belafonte, the *Tavis Smiley Show,* PBS television station KCET. http://www.pbs.org/kcet/tavissmiley/archive/201001/20100118_belafonte.html

Bell, Derrick A. (1994). *Confronting authority: Reflections of an ardent protester.* Boston: Beacon Press.

Bennetts, Leslie (2007, December 27). First lady in waiting. *Vanity Fair.*

Bernstein, David (2007). The speech: When Barack Obama launched into his keynote address at the 2004 Democratic National Convention, he was still an obscure state senator from Illinois. *Chicago Magazine.* http://www.chicagomag.com/Chicago-Magazine/June-2007/The-Speech/

Berry, LaVerle Bennette (Ed.) (1994). *Government and politics, a country study: Ghana.* Washington, DC: Library of Congress Federal Research Division.

Binion, Rudolph (1976). *Hitler among the Germans.* New York: Elsevier.

Bird, Kai (2010, June 28). Next Week in Jerusalem? *The Nation.* Online version at http://www.thenation.com/article/next-week-jerusalem

Black, Allida Mae (2009). *The first ladies of the United States of America.* Foreword by Michelle Obama. 12th ed. Washington, DC: White House Historical Association.

Blos, Peter (1979). *The adolescent passage: Developmental issues.* New York: International Universities Press.

Blos, Peter (1998). The second individuation process of adolescence. In Maja Perret-Catipovic & François Ladame (Eds.), *Adolescence and psychoanalysis: The story and the history* (chap. 5). London: Karnac Books. (Reprinted from *The Psychoanalytic Study of the Child, 22,* 162–186, 1967)

Bodden, Valerie (2010). *Michelle Obama: First lady and role model.* Edina, MN: ABDO Publishing.

Bogues, Austin (2008, July 14). Sorority celebrates Michelle Obama's acceptance. *The New York Times.*

Bone, James, Crilly, Rob & Macintyre, Ben (2008, October 30). Found in a run-down Boston estate: Barack Obama's aunt Zeituni Onyango. *The Times.*

Boritt, Gabor S. & Forness, Norman O. (Eds.) (1988). *The historian's Lincoln: Pseudohistory, psychohistory, and history.* Urbana: University of Illinois Press.

Bosman, Julie (2006, November 9). Obama's new book is a surprise best seller. *The New York Times.*

Boss-Bicak, Shira (2005, January). Barack Obama '83: Is he the new face of the Democratic Party? *Columbia College Today.*

Bourcier, Cammy S. (2008). *Barack Obama.* Philadelphia: Mason Crest.

Boylan, Peter (2008, December 24). Obama tries to escape in Hawaii. *Time.*

Branch, Taylor (1988–2006). *America in the King years* (Vols. 1–3). New York: Simon and Schuster.

Brill, Marlene Targ (2006). *Barack Obama: Working to make a difference.* Minneapolis, MN: Millbrook Press.

Brill, Marlene Targ (2009a). *Barack Obama: President for a new era* (Rev. ed.). Minneapolis, MN: Lerner Publishing.

Brill, Marlene Targ (2009b). *Michelle Obama: From Chicago's South Side to the White House.* Minneapolis, MN: Lerner Publishing.

Brodeur, Nicole (2008, February 5). Memories of Obama's mother. *Seattle Times,* p. B1.

Brody, David (2007, July 30). Obama to CBN News: We're no longer just a Christian nation [television broadcast]. *Christian Broadcasting Network.*

Brophy, David Bergen (2009). *Michelle Obama: Meet the first lady.* New York: Collins.

Brown, Floyd (2008). *Obama unmasked: Did slick Hollywood handlers create the perfect candidate?* Bellevue, WA: Merril Press.

Brown, Patty (2009a). *Barack Obama.* Kansas City, MO: Andrews McMeel.

Brown, Patty (2009b). *Michelle Obama.* Kansas City, MO: Andrews McMeel.

Brown, Sarah (2005, December 7). Obama '85 masters balancing act. *The Daily Princetonian.*

Burgan, Michael (2010). *Barack Obama.* Chicago, IL: Heinemann Library.

Butterfield, Fox (1990, February 6). First black elected to head Harvard's Law Review. *The New York Times,* p. A20.

Byrd, Robert C. (1988–1994). *The Senate, 1789–1989* (Mary Sharon Hall, Ed.). Washington: U.S. Government Printing Office.

Calmes, Jackie (2007, February 23). Statehouse yields clues to Obama. *Wall Street Journal.*

Calmes, Jackie (2009, January 3). On campus, Obama and memories. *The New York Times.*

Camp, Lee (2008, July 28). Obama's wailing wall note leaked to press. *The Huffington Post.*

Carson, Clayborne (1981). *In Struggle: SNCC and the black awakening of the 1960s.* Cambridge, MA: Harvard University Press.

Cashill, Jack (2008a, October 9). Who wrote *Dreams from My Father? American Thinker.*

Cashill, Jack (2008b, October 17). Evidence mounts: Ayers co-wrote Obama's *Dreams. American Thinker.*

Chappell, David L. (2004). *A stone of hope: Prophetic religion and the death of Jim Crow.* Chapel Hill: University of North Carolina Press.

Chassie, Karen (Ed.) (2007). *Who's who in America, 2008.* New Providence, NJ: Marquis Who's Who.

Chipman, Kim (2008, February 11). Obama drive gets inspiration from his white mom born in Kansas. *Bloomberg.com.*

Colbert, David (2009). *Michelle Obama: An American story.* Boston: Houghton Mifflin.

Connolly, Katie (2008, November 29). Very little in common but that "O." *Newsweek.*

Cooke, Jennifer G. & Morrison, J. Stephen (Eds.) (2009). *U.S. Africa policy beyond the Bush years: Critical challenges for the Obama administration.* Washington, DC: Center for Strategic and International Studies Press.

Corey, Shana (2009). *Barack Obama: Out of many, one* (James Bernardin, Illustrator). New York: Random House Children's Books.

Corr, John (1990, February 27). From mean streets to hallowed halls. *Philadelphia Inquirer,* p. C01.

Corsi, Jerome R. (2008). *The Obama nation: Leftist politics and the cult of personality.* New York: Simon & Schuster.

Corsi, Jerome R. (2009a, August 4). World Net daily exclusive: Born in the USA? Obama "Mama": 15 days from birth to Seattle class. Dunham signed up for assignments just 2 weeks out of delivery room. *World Net Daily.*

Corsi, Jerome R. (2009b, July 28). World Net daily exclusive: News analysis. New doubts revealed in Obama's nativity story. School documents show mother left father within weeks of birth. *World Net Daily.*

Couric, Katie (2009, October 28). Michelle Obama: Your first lady (special recognition). *Glamour.*

Crouch, Stanley (2006, November 2). What Obama isn't: black like me. *New York Daily News.*

Crowley, Michael (2008, February 27). Cinderella story: Is Obama's Iraq record really a fairy tale? *The New Republic.*

Cummins, Joseph (2009). *President Obama and a new birth of freedom: Obama's and Lincoln's inaugural addresses and much more.* New York: Collins.

Cyrulnik, Boris (1993). *The dawn of meaning.* New York: McGraw-Hill.

Cyrulnik, Boris (2003). *The whispering of ghosts: Trauma and resilience* (Susan Fairfield, Trans.). New York: Other Press.

Dajani, Lana (2009). *My letter to president Barack Obama.* Washington, DC: Twenty Stories.

Dann, Carrie (2008, July 10). Michelle Obama talks fatherhood. *MSNBC First Read.*

Davey, Monica (2004a, March 7). Closely watched Illinois Senate race attracts 7 candidates in millionaire range. *The New York Times.*

Davey, Monica (2004b, May 17). From crowded field, Democrats choose state legislator to seek Senate seat. *The New York Times.*

Davis, Frank Marshall (1992). *Livin' the blues: Memoirs of a black journalist and poet* (John Edgar Tidwell, Ed.). Madison: University of Wisconsin Press.

Davis, William (2008). *Barack Obama: The politics of hope.* Stockton, NJ: OTTN Publishing.

De Medeiros, Michael (2009). *Barack Obama*. New York: Weigl.

De Zutter, Hank (1995, December 8). What makes Obama run? *Chicago Reader*.

Devaney, Sherri, Devaney, Mark & Uschan, Michael V. (2007). *Barack Obama*. Detroit: Lucent Books.

Dickerson, Debra J. (2007, January 22). Colorblind: Barack Obama would be the great black hope in the next presidential race—if he were actually black. *Salon.com*.

Dickinson, Tim (2007, November 3). "The fierce urgency of now": When Obama's good, he's muy damn bueno. Read the speech he's delivering today in South Carolina. *Rolling Stone*.

Dickinson, Tim (2008, March 20). The machinery of hope. *Rolling Stone*.

Dixon, Norman F. (1976). *The psychology of military incompetence*. London: Jonathan Cape; New York: Basic Books.

Dobbs, Michael (2008, March 30). Obama overstated Kennedy's role in helping his father. *Washington Post*.

Dorning, Mike (2007a, September 17). Obama's policy team loaded with all-stars. *Chicago Tribune*.

Dorning, Mike (2007b, October 4). Obama reaches across decades to JFK. *Chicago Tribune*.

Dorning, Mike & Parsons, Christi (2007, June 12). Carefully crafting the Obama "brand." *Chicago Tribune*.

Dougherty, Phil (2009, February 7). Stanley Ann Dunham, mother of Barack Obama, graduates from Mercer Island High School in 1960. *HistoryLink.org* http://www.historylink.org/index.cfm?DisplayPage=pf_output.cfm&file_id=8897

Dougherty, Steve (2007). *Hopes and dreams: The story of Barack Obama*. New York: Black Dog & Leventhal.

Drake, St. Clair & Cayton, Horace R. (1945). *Black metropolis: A study of Negro life in a northern city* (Introduction by Richard Wright). New York: Harcourt, Brace and Co.

Drucker, Peter Ferdinand (1999). *Management challenges for the 21st century*. New York: HarperBusiness.

Drummond, Tammerlin (1990, March 12). Barack Obama's law personality: Harvard Law Review's first black president plans a life of public service. *Los Angeles Times*, p. E1.

Dunham, Stanley Ann (1992). *Peasant blacksmithing in Indonesia: Surviving and thriving against all odds* (2 vols.). Honolulu: University of Hawai'i at Manoa. Published as *Surviving against the Odds: Village Industry in Indonesia*. (2009). Ed. Alice G. Dewey and Nancy I. Cooper. Foreword by Maya Soetoro-Ng, afterword by Robert W. Hefner. Durham, NC: Duke University Press.

Dupuis, Martin & Boeckelman, Keith (2008). *Barack Obama: The new face of American politics*. Westport, CT: Praeger.

Edwards, Roberta (2008). *Barack Obama: An American story* (Ken Call, Illustrator). New York: Grosset & Dunlap.

Edwards, Roberta (2009a). *Michelle Obama: Mom-in-chief* (Ken Call, Illustrator). New York: Grosset & Dunlap.

Edwards, Roberta (2009b). *Who is Barack Obama?* (John O'Brien, Illustrator). New York: Grosset & Dunlap.

Ehrenstein, David (2007, March 19). Obama the "magic Negro." *Los Angeles Times.*

Elliott, Philip (2009, May 22). Obama signs law curbing surprise credit card fees. *The Huffington Post.* http://www.huffingtonpost.com/2009/05/22/obama-signs-law-curbing-s_n_206944.html

Elovitz, Paul H. (2008). A comparative psychohistory of McCain and Obama. *The Journal of Psychohistory, 36,* 98–143.

Epstein, Brad M. (2009). *Barack Obama 101: My first presidential-board-book* (Large format ed.). Los Angeles, CA: Michaelson Entertainment.

Erikson, Erik H. (1959). *Identity and the life cycle: Selected papers* (with a historical introduction by David Rapaport). New York: International Universities Press.

Erikson, Erik H. (1968). *Identity: Youth and crisis.* New York: Norton.

Essoyan, Susan (2008, July 27). A teacher's hefty influence. *Honolulu Star-Bulletin.*

Falcone, Michael (2007, December 21). Obama's "one thing." *The New York Times.*

Falk, Avner (1975–1976). Identity and name changes. *Psychoanalytic Review, 62,* 647–657.

Falk, Avner (1985). Aspects of political psychobiography. *Political Psychology, 6,* 605–619.

Falk, Avner (1989a). Border symbolism. In H. F. Stein & W. G. Niederland (Eds.), *Maps from the mind: Readings in psychogeography.* Norman: University of Oklahoma Press. (Reprinted from *The Psychoanalytic Quarterly, 43,* 650–660, 1974)

Falk, Avner (1989b). Border symbolism revisited. In H. F. Stein & W. G. Niederland (Eds.), *Maps from the mind: Readings in psychogeography.* Norman: University of Oklahoma Press. (Reprinted from *International Review of Psycho-Analysis, 10,* 215–220, 1983)

Falk, Avner (2004). *Fratricide in the Holy Land: A psychoanalytic view of the Arab-Israeli conflict.* Madison: University of Wisconsin Press.

Falk, Avner (2007). *Napoleon against himself: A psychobiography.* Charlottesville, VA: Pitchstone.

Falk, Avner (2008). *Islamic terror: Conscious and unconscious motives.* Westport, CT: Praeger Security International.

Falk, Laine (2009). *Meet President Barack Obama.* New York: Children's Press.

Feinstein, Stephen (2008). *Barack Obama.* Berkeley Heights, NJ: Enslow.

Fitzpatrick, Frank (2007, March 2). Barack Obama's closest opponent: Brown coach Craig Robinson plays pickup basketball with his famous brother-in-law. *Philadelphia Inquirer.* http://www.encyclopedia.com/doc/1G1-160039193.html

Foer, Franklin, et al. (2007). *Election 2008: A voter's guide* (David Cowles, Illustrator). New Haven, CT: Yale University Press.

Fornek, Scott (2004, October 3). "I've got a competitive nature": Beneath the rock star fame is a politician who plays hard to win, whether it be in Scrabble or a race to topple an incumbent. *Chicago Sun-Times.*

Fornek, Scott (2007a, October 3). Michelle Obama: "He swept me off my feet." *Chicago Sun-Times.*

Fornek, Scott (2007b, September 9). Son of presidents and tribal chiefs: In a special report, Sun-Times political editor Scott Fornek reveals Barack Obama's remarkably far-flung family tree. *Chicago Sun-Times.*

Fowler, Mayhill (2008, April 11). Obama: No surprise that hard-pressed Pennsylvanians turn bitter. *The Huffington Post.*

Franklin, Ben A. (2005, June 1). The fifth black senator in U.S. history makes F.D.R. his icon. *Washington Spectator.*

Freddoso, David (2008). *The case against Barack Obama: The unlikely rise and unexamined agenda of the media's favorite candidate.* Washington, DC: Regnery Publishing.

Freud, Sigmund (1953). The horror of incest. First part of *Totem and Taboo.* In James Strachey (Ed.), *The complete psychological works of Sigmund Freud* (Vol. 13, pp. 1–17). London: Hogarth Press and the Institute of Psycho-Analysis.

Friel, Brian, Cohen, Richard E. & Kirk, Victor (2007, January 31). Obama: Most liberal senator in 2007. *National Journal.*

Galbraith, Peter W. (2009, October 19). How to rig an election: A former top U.N. official recounts the fraud he witnessed during Afghanistan's presidential vote—and why he lost his job for speaking up. *Time, 174*(15).

Gartner, John D. (2008). *In search of Bill Clinton: A psychological biography.* New York: St. Martin's Press.

Gates, Henry Louis, Jr. (2008, November 5). In our lifetime: From toiling as White House slaves to President-elect Barack Obama, we have crossed the ultimate color line. *Theroot.com.* http://www.theroot.com/views/our-lifetime

Gitaa, Moraa (2008, October 30). Barack Obama: A story of race and inheritance. *The African.* http://www.africanmag.com/FORUM-735-design004

Glauberman, Stuart & Burris, Jerry (2008). *Barry: How Hawaii shaped Barack Obama.* Honolulu: Watermark.

Gnecchi, Nico (2006, August 27). Obama receives hero's welcome at his family's ancestral village in Kenya. *Voice of America.*

Goldberg, Bernard (2009). *A slobbering love affair: The true (and pathetic) story of the torrid romance between Barack Obama and the mainstream media.* Washington, DC: Regnery Publishing.

Goldman, Adam & Tanner, Robert (2008, May 15). Old friends recall Obama's years in LA, NY. *The Huffington Post.*

Goleman, Daniel (2006). *Emotional intelligence.* New York: Bantam Books.

Gonyea, Don (2007, September 19). Obama's loss may have aided White House bid. *National Public Radio.*

Goodman, Amy (2009, January 22). Push Obama to follow through on peace vows. *Capital Times* (Wisconsin). http://www.commondreams.org/view/ 2009/01/22-10

Gordon, Michael R. & Zeleny, Jeff (2007, November 2). Obama pledges "aggressive" Iran diplomacy. *The New York Times.*

Gormley, Beatrice (2008). *Barack Obama: Our 44th president.* New York: Simon & Schuster Children's Publishing and Aladdin Paperbacks.

Graham Parker & Thelma, Margina (2009). *I am Michelle Obama: The first lady.* Tucker, GA: Tumaini.

Gray, Kevin Alexander (2008). *The decline of black politics: From Malcolm X to Barack Obama.* London and New York: Verso Books.

Greenstein, Fred I. (2009). *The presidential difference: Leadership style from FDR to Barack Obama* (3rd ed.). Princeton, NJ: Princeton University Press.

Grimes, Nikki (2008). *Barack Obama: Son of promise, child of hope* (Bryan Collier, Illustrator). New York: Simon & Schuster Books for Young Readers.

Gross, Dan (2008, March 20). Obama on WIP: My grandmother's a "typical white person." *Philadelphia Daily News.*

Grossman, James R. (1989). *Land of hope: Chicago, black Southerners, and the great migration.* Chicago: University of Chicago Press.

Harris, Bill (2009). *The first ladies fact book: The stories of the women of the White House from Martha Washington to Michelle Obama.* New York: Black Dog and Leventhal.

Hart, Gary (2006, December 24). American idol: Review of *The Audacity of Hope* by Barack Obama. *The New York Times.*

Harvey, Oliver (2008, July 26). Obama's brother is in Bracknell. *The Sun.* http:// www.thesun.co.uk/sol/homepage/news/the_real_american_idol/article 1472877.ece

Haugen, David M. (Ed.) (2008). *Health care.* Detroit: Greenhaven Press/Gale.

Heilemann, John (2007, October 22). When they were young. *New York Magazine, 40*(37), 32–37, 132–133.

Helman, Scott (2007a, September 23). In Illinois, Obama dealt with lobbyists. *The Boston Globe.*

Helman, Scott (2007b, October 12). Early defeat launched a rapid political climb. *The Boston Globe.*

Helman, Scott (2008, August 25). Small college awakened future senator to service. *The Boston Globe.*

Hendon, Rickey (2008). *Black enough/white enough: The Obama dilemma.* Chicago: Third World Press.

Herndon, William Henry & Weik, Jesse William (1888). *Lincoln: The true story of a great life, the history and personal recollections of Abraham Lincoln.* Springfield, IL: Herndon's Lincoln Pub.

Hertzberg, Hendrik (2008, November 17). Obama wins. *The New Yorker.*

Hill, Johnny Bernard (2009). *The first black president: Barack Obama, race, politics, and the American dream.* New York: Palgrave Macmillan.

Hoffecker, Leslie (2008, July 9). Top of the ticket: The Obama girls' first TV interview may well be their last. *Los Angeles Times.*

Hofstadter, Richard (1965). *The paranoid style in American politics, and other essays.* New York: Alfred A. Knopf.

Honan, Mathew (2008). *Barack Obama is your new bicycle: 366 ways he really cares.* New York: Penguin Group.

Hoover, Will (2007, February 11). Obama's declaration stirs thrills at Punahou. *The Honolulu Advertiser.*

Hopkins, Linda B. (2006). *False self: The life of Masud Khan.* New York: Other Press.

Hopkinson, Deborah (2009). *Michelle* (A. G. Ford, Illustrator). New York: HarperCollins Katherine Tegen Books.

Horn, Geoffrey M. (2009). *Barack Obama.* Pleasantville, NY: Gareth Stevens.

Horne, Gerald (2007a, March 28). Rethinking the history and future of the Communist Party. *Political Affairs Magazine.* http://www.politicalaffairs.net/article/articleview/5047/

Horne, Gerald (2007b). *The white Pacific: U.S. imperialism and black slavery in the South Seas after the Civil War.* Honolulu: University of Hawai'i Press.

Horwitt, Sanford D. (1989). *Let them call me rebel: Saul Alinsky, His life and legacy.* New York: Alfred A. Knopf.

Hudson, Amanda (2010). *Michelle Obama.* Pleasantville, NY: Gareth Stevens.

Hudson-Weems, Clenora (2008). *Africana womanism and race and gender in the presidential candidacy of Barack Obama.* Bloomington, IN: AuthorHouse.

Huffington, Arianna (2008, November 24). Hillary + Obama = High drama. *The Huffington Post.*

Hughes, Libby (2009). *Barack Obama: Voice of unity, hope, and change.* Bloomington, IN: iUniverse.

Ifill, Gwen (2009). *The breakthrough: Politics and race in the age of Obama.* New York: Doubleday.

Jackson, David (2008, March 15). Barack Obama: I trusted Rezko. Senator says friend raised more money than previously known. *Chicago Tribune.*

Jackson, David & Long, Ray (2007a, April 3). Obama knows his way around a ballot. *Chicago Tribune.*

Jackson, David & Long, Ray (2007b, April 4). Barack Obama: Showing his bare knuckles. *Chicago Tribune.*

Jackson, John S. (2006). *The making of a senator: Barack Obama and the 2004 Illinois Senate race.* Carbondale: Occasional Paper of the Paul Simon Public Policy Institute, Southern Illinois University.

Jackson, Phil & Delenhanty, Hugh (1995). *Sacred hoops: Spiritual lessons of a hardwood warrior.* New York: Hyperion.

James, Randy (2009, June 25). Straying Governor Mark Sanford. *Time.* http://www.time.com/time/nation/article/0,8599,1907022,00.html#ixzz0nkvA7Wvy

Janken, Kenneth R. (2003). *White: The biography of Walter White, Mr. NAACP.* New York: New Press.

Jarrett, Vernon (1992, August 11). "Project Vote" brings power to the people. *Chicago Sun-Times*, p. 23.

Johnson, Rebecca (2007, September). The natural: To the role of would-be First Lady, Michelle Obama brings modesty, dedication—and a reputation for truth-telling. Rebecca Johnson meets the candidate's wife. *Vogue*. http://www.vogue.com/feature/2007_Sept_Michelle_Obama/

Johnston, Nicholas (2010, January 24). Obama Criticizes Supreme Court Ruling on Campaign Spending. *Bloomberg Businessweek*. http://www.businessweek.com/news/2010-01-24/obama-criticizes-supreme-court-ruling-on-campaign-spending.html

Jones, Tim (2007, March 27). Obama's mom: Not just a girl from Kansas. Strong personalities shaped a future senator. *Chicago Tribune*.

Jorgensen, Laurel (2006, December 28). Illinois barber shop of Ali, Obama must move: Hyde Park Hair Salon will have to relocate after 80 years of business. *Charleston Daily Mail*.

Joseph, Peniel E. (2010). *Dark days, bright nights: From black power to Barack Obama*. New York: BasicCivitas.

Kahn, Herman (1962). *Thinking about the unthinkable*. New York: Horizon Press.

Kahn, Herman (1984). *Thinking about the unthinkable in the 1980s*. New York: Simon and Schuster.

Kantor, Jodi (2007a, April 30). Barack Obama's search for faith. *The New York Times*.

Kantor, Jodi (2007b, January 28). In law school, Obama found political voice. *The New York Times*, p. 1.

Kantor, Jodi (2007c, June 1). One place where Obama goes elbow to elbow. *The New York Times*.

Kantor, Jodi (2008a, March 18). An effort to bridge a divide. *The New York Times*.

Kantor, Jodi (2008b, August 28). The mystery and constancy of Barack Obama. *International Herald Tribune*.

Katirgis, Jane (2009a). *Celebrating first lady Michelle Obama in pictures*. Berkeley Heights, NJ: Enslow Publishers.

Katirgis, Jane (2009b). *Celebrating President Barack Obama in pictures*. Berkeley Heights, NJ: Enslow Publishers.

Katirgis, Jane (2009c). *Celebrating the inauguration of Barack Obama in pictures*. Berkeley Heights, NJ: Enslow Publishers.

Kellman, Jerry (2008, September 2). Entry in *Barackopedia*. http://www.barackopedia.org/page/Jerry+Kellman

Kennedy-Shaffer, Alan (2009). *The Obama revolution*. Beverly Hills, CA: Phoenix Books.

Kesselring, Susan (2010a). *Barack Obama*. Mankato, MN: Child's World.

Keyes, Alan Lee & Smiley, Tavis (2004). Interview on the *Tavis Smiley Show*. National Public Radio, Public Broadcasting System.

Kesselring, Susan (2010b). *Michelle Obama*. Mankato, MN: Child's World.

King, Oona T. (2007, September 15). Oona King on Barack Obama's *Dreams from My Father*: The poignant story of how Barack Obama struggled to define his identity as a black man in the US. Life story. *The Times*.

King, Richard H. (1992). *Civil rights and the idea of freedom*. New York: Oxford University Press.

Klatell, James M. (2006, August 28). Obama urges Kenya to stop corruption: Illinois Senator tells Kenyans to oppose ethnic divisions in government. *USA Today*. http://www.usatoday.com/news/world/2006-08-28-obama-africa_x.htm

Klein, Aaron (2009, October 27). BORN IN THE USA? Michelle contradicts Obama nativity story. Divulges Ann Dunham was "very young and very single" at birth of U.S. president. *World Net Daily*. http://www.wnd.com/index.php?fa=PAGE.view&pageId=114259

Klein, Joe (2008, October 22). Why Barack Obama is winning. *Time*. http://www.time.com/time/nation/article/0,8599,1853025-1,00.html

Knoepfle, Peg (Ed.) (1990). *After Alinsky: Community organizing in Illinois*. Springfield, IL: Sangamon State University.

Kodama, Marie C. (2007, January 19). Obama left mark on HLS: Profs fondly recall Law School alum as he launches presidential bid. *Harvard Crimson*.

Kovaleski, Serge (2008, July 7). The long run: Obama's organizing years, guiding others and finding himself. *The New York Times*.

Kübler-Ross, Elisabeth (1969). *On death and dying*. New York: Macmillan.

Kübler-Ross, Elisabeth & Kessler, David (2005). *On grief and grieving: Finding the meaning of grief through the five stages of loss*. New York: Scribner.

Lakshmanan, Indira A. R. (2008, July 3). Obama draws on lessons from Chicago streets to propel campaign. *Bloomberg.com*. http://www.bloomberg.com/apps/news?sid=aGhxb4MGMqXo&pid=20601070

Larson, Christina (2006, September). Hoosier daddy: What rising Democratic star Barack Obama can learn from an old lion of the GOP. *Washington Monthly*. http://www.washingtonmonthly.com/features/2006/0609.larson.html

Lasswell, Harold D. (1930). *Psychopathology and politics*. Chicago: University of Chicago Press.

LeFevre, Charlette (2009, January 6). From Capitol Hill to Capitol Hill: Confirmation that Barack Obama lived on Capitol Hill—Seattle. *Seattle Museum of the Mysteries*. http://www.seattlechatclub.org/museum.html

LeFevre, Charlette & Lipson, Philip (2009, January 28). Baby sitting Barack Obama on Seattle's Capitol Hill. *Seattle Museum of the Mysteries*. http://www.seattlechatclub.org/museum.html

Lemann, Nicholas (1992). *The promised land: The great black migration and how it changed America*. New York: Vintage Books.

Lerner, Michael (2006, July 3). U.S. senator Barack Obama critiques Democrats' religiophobia. *Tikkun*.

Levenson, Michael & Jonathan Saltzman (2007, January 28). At Harvard Law, a unifying voice: Classmates recall Obama as even-handed leader. *The Boston Globe*. http://www.boston.com/news/local/articles/2007/01/28/at_harvard_law_a_unifying_voice/

Lewis Lee, Tonya (2007, September 3). Your next first lady? *Glamour* Magazine interview with Michelle Obama. *Glamour.*

Lewis Lee, Tonya (2008, October 3). Michelle Obama looks back (and ahead!). The political superstar and mom of two talks to Tonya Lewis Lee about politics, marriage and what she wants for young women. *Glamour.*

Libert, Barry & Faulk, Rick (2009). *Barack, Inc.: Winning business lessons of the Obama campaign.* Upper Saddle River, NJ: Pearson Education.

Lindsay, Rae (2009). *America's first ladies: Power players from Martha Washington to Michelle Obama.* Warwick, NY: Gilmour House.

Little, Malcolm (with Alex Haley) (1965). *The autobiography of Malcolm X.* New York: Grove Press.

Littwin, Mike (2007, August 29). Obama's "change" could be more than a coined phrase. *Rocky Mountain News.*

Lizza, Ryan (2007, March 19). The agitator: Barack Obama's unlikely political education. *The New Republic.*

Lizza, Ryan (2008, July 21). Making it: How Chicago shaped Obama. *The New Yorker.*

Luce, Lila F. L. (2009). *Barack Obama: Yes, we can!* Nairobi: Sasa Sema.

Lugar, Richard G. & Obama, Barack H. (2005, December 3). Junkyard dogs of war. *The Washington Post*, p. A23.

Mack, John Edward (2002). Looking beyond terrorism: Transcending the mind of enmity. In Chris E. Stout (Ed.), *The psychology of terrorism* (Vol. 1, pp. 173–184). Westport, CT: Praeger.

Mack, Kenneth & Chen, Jim (2004, October 21). Barack Obama before he was a rising political star. *Journal of Blacks in Higher Education, 45,* 98–101.

Malkin, Michelle (2009). *Culture of corruption: Obama and his team of tax cheats, crooks, and cronies.* Washington, DC: Regnery Publishing.

Mann, Fred (2008, February 2). Kansas roots show in Obama. *Wichita Eagle.*

Mansfield, Stephen (2008). *The faith of Barack Obama.* Nashville, TN: Thomas Nelson.

Marables, Manning & Clarke, Kristen (Eds.) (2009). *Barack Obama and African-American empowerment: The rise of black America's new leadership.* New York: Palgrave Macmillan.

Maraniss, David (2008, August 22). Though Obama had to leave to find himself, it is Hawaii that made his rise possible. *The Washington Post.* http://www.washingtonpost.com/wp-dyn/content/article/2008/08/22/AR2008082201679.html

Marcovitz, Hal (2009). *Michelle.* Broomall, PA: Mason Crest.

Marks, Jennifer L. (2009). *President Barack Obama.* Mankato, MN: Capstone Press.

Marsh, Michael (2007). *The NIBA guide to Barack Obama: The political history, the record, the facts.* Evanston, IL: NIBA Media Group.

Martin, Jonathan (2008, April 8). Obama's mother known here as "uncommon": Stanley Ann Dunham loved this area but moved to attend college in Hawaii, marrying Obama's father. *Seattle Times*, p. A1.

Martin, Roland S. (2008, March 21). The full story behind Wright's "God Damn America" sermon. *Anderson Cooper 360°*, Cable News Network.

Matchan, Linda (1990, February 15). A Law Review breakthrough. *Boston Globe*, p. 29.

Mattern, Joanne (2010). *What's so great about Michelle Obama.* Hockessin, DE: Mitchell Lane.

Matthews, Gerald, Zeidner, Moshe & Roberts, Richard D. (2002). *Emotional intelligence: Science and myth.* Cambridge, MA: MIT Press.

Mazzetti, Mark (2007, July 8). Rumsfeld called off 2005 plan to capture top Qaeda figures. *International Herald Tribune.*

McClelland, Edward (2007, February 12). How Obama learned to be a natural. *Salon.com.*

McCormick, John (2007, September 21). Obama's mother in new ad. *Chicago Tribune.*

McCormick, John (2008, March 13). Obama enlists ex-commanders: "No shock Barack" fires back at rivals. *Chicago Tribune.*

McIntire, Mike (2008, February 3). Nuclear leaks and response tested Obama in Senate. *The New York Times.*

McKinney, David & Fusco, Chris (2006, November 5). Obama on Rezko deal: It was a mistake. *Chicago Sun-Times.*

McMickle, Marvin A. (Ed.) (2009). *The audacity of faith: Christian leaders reflect on the election of Barack Obama.* Valley Forge, PA: Judson Press.

Meacham, Jon (2008, August 23). On his own: Cerebral and cool, Obama is also steely, and his strength comes from the absence of a father. The making of a self-reliant man. *Newsweek.* http://www.newsweek.com/id/155173

Mendell, David (2004, September 25). Obama would consider missile strikes on Iran. *Chicago Tribune.*

Mendell, David (2007). *Obama: From promise to power.* New York: Harper-Collins

Merida, Kevin (2007, December 14). The ghost of a father. *Washington Post*, p. A12. http://www.washingtonpost.com/wp-dyn/content/article/2007/12/13/AR2007121301784.html

Michael, Saul (2007, December 23). I'm no Muslim, says Barack Obama. *New York Daily News.*

Miller, Lisa & Wolffe, Richard L. (2008, July 12). Finding His Faith: So much has been made about Barack Obama's religion. But what does he believe, and how did he arrive at those beliefs? *Newsweek.* http://www.newsweek.com/id/145971

Mish, Frederick C. (Ed.) (2009). *Merriam-Webster's dictionary of basic English.* Springfield, MA: Merriam-Webster.

Moberg, David (2007, April 16). Obama's community roots. *The Nation.*

Montgomery, Rick (2008, May 26). Barack Obama's mother wasn't just a girl from Kansas. *The Kansas City Star.*

Moracha, Vincent & Mosota, Mangoa (2006, September 4). Leaders support Obama on graft claims. *The Standard* (Nairobi).

Moraitis, George (1985). A psychoanalyst's journey into a historian's world: An experiment in collaboration. In Samuel H. Baron & Carl Pletsch (Eds.), *Introspection in biography: The biographer's quest for self-awareness.* Hillsdale, NJ: Analytic Press.

Morris, Dick & McGann, Eileen (2008). *Fleeced: How Barack Obama, media mockery of terrorist threats, liberals who want to kill talk radio, the do-nothing Congress, companies that help Iran, and Washington lobbyists for foreign governments are scamming us—and what to do about it.* New York: Harper Books.

Mosley, Ian (2009, April 20). Did Bill Ayers write Obama's books? *Altermedia News USA.*

Mucha, Peter (2008, March 22). Obama's "typical white person" makes waves. *The Philadelphia Inquirer.*

Mullen, Bill V. (1999). *Popular fronts: Chicago and African-American cultural politics, 1935–1946.* Urbana: University of Illinois Press.

Mundy, Liza (2007, August 12). A series of fortunate events: Barack Obama needed more than talent and ambition to rocket from obscure state senator to presidential contender in three years. He needed serious luck. *The Washington Post,* p. W10.

Mundy, Liza (2008). *Michelle: A biography.* New York: Simon & Schuster.

Nardo, Don (2009). *Barack Obama.* Minneapolis, MN: Compass Point Books.

Nather, David (2008, January 14). The space between Clinton and Obama. *CQ Weekly.*

Nault, Jennifer (2010). *Michelle Obama.* New York: Weigl Publishers.

Nazer, Mende (with Damien Lewis) (2003). *Slave.* New York: Public Affairs.

Nairobi Star (2008, November 6). Kenya: Leaders "forget" attacks on Obama. *Nairobi Star.* http://allafrica.com/stories/200811070023.html

Nevergold, Barbara A. Seals & Brooks-Bertram, Peggy (Eds.) (2009). *Go, tell Michelle: African American women write to the new first lady.* Albany: State University of New York Press.

Newsweek (2008, November 17). How he did it: A team of *Newsweek* reporters reveals the secret battles and private fears behind an epic election. *Newsweek.* http://www.newsweek.com/id/167582

Newton-Small, Jay (2008, August 25). Michelle Obama's savvy sacrifice. *Time.*

Neyman, Jenny (2009, January 20). Obama baby sitter awaits new era—Soldotna woman eager for former charge's reign. *Redoubt Reporter.*

Nichols, Catherine (2009). *Barack Obama.* Mankato, MN: Child's World.

Niederland, William G. (1989). The naming of America. In Howard F. Stein & William G. Niederland (Eds.), *Maps from the mind: Readings in psychogeography* (pp. 82–96). Norman: University of Oklahoma Press. (Reprinted from *The unconscious today: Essays in honor of Max Schur,* Mark Kanzer (Ed.), 1971, New York: International Universities Press).

Nitkin, David & Merritt, Harry (2007, March 2). A new twist to an intriguing family history. *Baltimore Sun.*

Niven, Steven J. (2008, November 5). Another tremor in the iceberg: Barack Obama's candidacy and the modern civil rights movement. *Oxford African American Studies Center.* http://www.oxfordaasc.com/public/featureded/guest_1.jsp

Niven, Steven J. (2009). *Barack Obama: A pocket biography of our 44th president.* New York: Oxford University Press.

Noonan, Peggy (2005, June 29). Conceit of government: Why are our politicians so full of themselves? *The Wall Street Journal.*

Noonan, Peggy (2006, December 15). The man from nowhere. *The Wall Street Journal.*

Noonan, Peggy (2008, January 4). Out with the old, in with the new. *The Wall Street Journal.*

Norwood, Mandi (2009). *Michelle style: Celebrating the first lady of fashion.* New York: William Morrow.

O'Hanlon, Michael E. (2009). *Budgeting for hard power: Defense and security spending under Barack Obama.* Washington, DC: Brookings Institution Press.

Obama, Barack H. (1988). Why organize? Problems and promise in the inner city. *Illinois Issues, 14* (8–9), 40–42.

Obama, Barack H. (1995). *Dreams from my father: A story of race and inheritance.* New York: Times Books.

Obama, Barack H. (2002, October 2). Remarks of Illinois State Sen. Barack Obama against going to war with Iraq. *BarackObama.com.* http://www.barackobama.com/2002/10/02/remarks_of_illinois_state_sen.php

Obama, Barack H. (2004, July 27). Keynote address to the Democratic National Convention: Transcript. *The Washington Post.*

Obama, Barack H. (2005, June 26). What I see in Lincoln's eyes. *Time.* http://www.time.com/time/magazine/article/0,9171,1077287,00.html

Obama, Barack H. (2006a). *The audacity of hope: Thoughts on reclaiming the American dream.* New York: Crown Publishers.

Obama, Barack H. (2006b, June 28). "Call to renewal" keynote address. Barack Obama U.S. Senate Office.

Obama, Barack H. (2006c). Commencement address at Knox College June 4, 2005. In James Daley (Ed.), *Great speeches by African Americans: Frederick Douglass, Sojourner Truth, Dr. Martin Luther King, Jr., Barack Obama, Jr., and others,* pp. 143–150. Mineola, NY: Dover Publications. http://www.americanrhetoric.com/speeches/barackobamaknoxcollege.htm

Obama, Barack H. (2006d, October 23). My spiritual journey. *Time.* http://www.time.com/time/magazine/article/0,9171,1546579,00.html

Obama, Barack H. (2006e, December 1). Race against time—World AIDS Day speech. Obama U.S. Senate Office.

Obama, Barack H. (2006f, November 20). A way forward in Iraq. *Chicago Council on Global Affairs.*

Obama, Barack H. (2007a, March 2). AIPAC Policy Forum remarks. Barack Obama U.S. Senate Office.

Obama, Barack H. (2007b, August 30). Hit Iran where it hurts. *New York Daily News.*

Obama, Barack H. (2007c, August 1). Policy address on terrorism by the Honorable Barack Obama, United States Senator from Illinois. *Woodrow Wilson International Center for Scholars.*

Obama, Barack H. (2007d, July–August). Renewing American leadership. *Foreign Affairs.*

Obama, Barack H. (2008, August 28). Presidential nomination acceptance speech at the Democratic Natioanl Convention. http://uspolitics.about.com/od/speeches/a/obama_accept.htm

Obama, Barack H. (2009a). *Barack Obama in his own words* (Lisa Rogak, Ed.; miniature ed.). Philadelphia and London: Running Press.

Obama, Barack H. (2009b, August 29). *Eulogy at the funeral of Edward M. Kennedy.* The White House Office of the Press Secretary.

Obama, Barack H. (2009c). A more perfect union: Presidential campaign speech. In Steven J. Niven, *Barack Obama: A pocket biography of our 44th president* (pp. 51–65). New York: Oxford University Press. (Original speech given March 18, 2008).

Obama, Barack H. (2009d, June 4). *Remarks by the president on a new beginning.* Speech at the University of Cairo, Egypt. Office of the Press Secretary, The White House.

Obama, Barack H. (2009e, January 18). What I want for you—and every child in America: An open letter to his two daughters. *Parade Magazine.*

Obama, Barack H. (2009f, January 20). Barack Obama's inaugural address. *The New York Times.* http://www.nytimes.com/2009/01/20/us/politics/20text-obama.html

Obama, Barack H. (2010, January 25). Transcript: Diane Sawyer interviews Obama. *ABC News.* http://abcnews.go.com/WN/Obama/abc-world-news-diane-sawyer-diane-sawyer-interviews/story?id=9659064

Obama, Barack H. & Brownback, Sam (2005, December 27). Policy adrift on Darfur. *The Washington Post.*

Obama, Barak H. (1965, July). Problems facing our socialism. *East Africa Journal*, *2*, 26–33.

Obama, George Hussein (with Damien Lewis) (2010). *Homeland: An extraordinary story of hope and survival.* New York: Simon & Schuster.

Ochieng, Philip (2004, November 1). From home squared to the U.S. Senate: How Barack Obama was lost and found. *The East African.*

Ochieng, Philip (2009, January 17). The pride of a people: Barack Obama, the Luo. *Daily Nation* (Nairobi).

Ogosia, Kenneth & Mugwang'a, Michael (2008, August 25). New links in dreams from Obama's father. *Saturday Nation* (Nairobi).

Okrent, Daniel (2009, October 5). Notown: Hubris, racial tension, myopic politicians and the woeful auto industry brought this iconic American city to its knees. Here's how the Motor City can rise again. The first installment of a yearlong look inside the once and future Detroit. *Time.*

Olopade, Dayo (2008, August 25). Barack's big night? *New Republic.*

Oywa, John (2008, November 4). Tracing Obama Senior's steps as a student at Maseno School. *The Standard* (Nairobi).

Page, Clarence (2007, February 25). Is Barack black enough? Now that's a silly question. *Houston Chronicle.*

Pallasch, Abdon M. (2007, December 17). As lawyer, Obama was strong, silent type; He was "smart, innovative, relentless," and he mostly let other lawyers do the talking. *Chicago Sun-Times*, p. 4. http://www.suntimes.com/news/politics/obama/700499,CST-NWS-Obama-law17.article

Parsons, Christi (2007, February 6). Obama launches an '07 campaign—to quit smoking. *Chicago Tribune.*

Pastan, Amy (2009). *First ladies* (Rev. ed.). In association with the Smithsonian Institution. New York: Dorling Kindersley.

Payne, Charles (1995). *I've got the light of freedom: The organizing tradition and the Mississippi freedom struggles.* Berkeley: University of California Press.

Payne, Charles W. (2009, May 26). *Spiegel* interview with Obama's great-uncle: "I was horrified by lengths men will go to mistreat other men." *Der Spiegel.*

Pearson, Rick & Long, Ray (2007, May 3). Barack Obama: Careful steps, looking ahead. *Chicago Tribune.*

Peev, Gerri (2008, March 7). Hillary Clinton's a monster: Obama aide blurts out attack in Scotsman interview. *The Scotsman.*

Peterson, Christopher, Maier, Steven F. & Seligman, Martin E. P. (1993). *Learned helplessness: A theory for the age of personal control.* New York: Oxford University Press.

Peterson, Christopher & Seligman, Martin E. P. (2004). *Character strengths and virtues: A handbook and classification.* Oxford and New York: Oxford University Press.

Pflanz, Mike (2008, August 31). Barack Obama is my inspiration, says lost brother: Senator Barack Obama's "lost" half-brother has said his famous relative was the inspiration who helped him turn his life around. *The Daily Telegraph.*

Piasecki, Joe (2008, June 5). Mother, wife, superstar: Michelle Obama "hits a home run" at Pasadena fundraiser. *Pasadena Weekly.*

Pickert, Kate (2008, October 13). Michelle Obama, a life. *Time.*

Powell, Michael (2008, January 5). Embracing his moment, Obama preaches hope in New Hampshire. *The New York Times.*

Price, Joann F. (2008). *Barack Obama: A biography.* Westport, CT: Greenwood Press.

Price, Joann F. (2009). *Barack Obama: The voice of an American leader.* Westport, CT: Greenwood Press.

Pugh, Allison J. (1990, April 18). Law Review's first black president aims to help poor. *The Miami Herald*, p. C1.

Ralph, James R., Jr. (1993). *Northern protest: Martin Luther King, Jr., Chicago, and the civil rights movement.* Cambridge, MA: Harvard University Press.

Ramos, Constance F. (Ed.) (2008). *Our friend Barry: Classmates' recollections of Barack Obama and Punahou School.* Raleigh, NC: Lulu e-books.

Remnick, David (2008, November 17). The Joshua generation: Race and the campaign of Barack Obama. *The New Yorker*.

Remnick, David (2010). *The bridge: The life and rise of Barack Obama*. New York: Alfred A. Knopf.

Ressner, Jeffrey (2008, February 22). Michelle Obama thesis was on racial divide. *Politico.com*.

Reynolds, Gretchen (1993). Vote of confidence: A huge black turnout in November 1992 altered Chicago's electoral landscape—and raised a new political star: a 31-year-old lawyer named Barack Obama. *Chicago Magazine, 42*(1), 53–54.

Rice, Xan (2008, June 6). "Barack's voice was just like his father's—I thought he had come back from the dead." Interview with Sarah Obama. *Guardian*.

Ripley, Amanda (2008, April 9). The story of Barack Obama's mother. *Time*.

Roach, Ronald (2004, October 7). Obama rising. *Black Issues in Higher Education*.

Robins, Robert S. & Post, Jerrold M. (1997). *Political paranoia: The psychopolitics of hatred*. New Haven, CT: Yale University Press.

Robinson, Michelle LaVaughn (1985). *Princeton educated blacks and the black community*. Seeley G. Mudd Manuscript Library, Princeton University.

Robinson, Mike (2007, February 10). Obama got start in civil rights practice. *The Boston Globe*.

Robinson, Tom (2009). *Barack Obama: 44th U.S. president*. Edina, MN: ABDO Publishing.

Rohter, Larry (2008, April 10). Obama says real-life experience trumps rivals' foreign policy credits. *The New York Times*.

Ross, Rosalind (2008, November 10). Kids at Michelle Obama's old school see reflection. *Chicago Sun-Times*.

Rove, Karl (2010). *Courage and consequence: My life as a conservative in the fight*. New York: Threshold Editions.

Sabar, Ariel (2007, July 16). Barack Obama: Putting faith out front. *Christian Science Monitor*.

Samuels, David (2008, October 22). Invisible man: How Ralph Ellison explains Barack Obama. *The New Republic*.

Sanderson, Elizabeth (2008, January 6). Barack Obama's stepmother living in Bracknell reveals the close bond with him … and his mother. *Daily Mail*.

Sapet, Kerrily (2008). *Political profiles: Barack Obama*. Greensboro, NC: Morgan Reynolds.

Saturday Nation Correspondents (2008, November 1). Bull awaits Obama win in Kogelo village. *Saturday Nation* (Nairobi).

Savory, Tanya (2010). *A dream fulfilled: The story of Barack Obama*. West Berlin, NJ: Townsend Press.

Scharnberg, Kirsten & Barker, Kim (2007, March 25). The not-so-simple story of Barack Obama's youth. *Chicago Tribune*. http://www.chicagotribune.com/news/politics/obama/chi-070325obama-youth-story-archive,0,3864722.story

Scherer, Michael (2009, May 25). What is Obama's biggest problem? *Time*.

Schiffer, Irvine (1973). *Charisma: A psychoanalytic look at mass society*. Toronto: University of Toronto Press.

Schneider, Dorothy & Schneider, Carl (2010). *First ladies: A biographical dictionary* (3rd ed.). New York: Facts on File.

Schoenberg, Shira (2007, November 21). Obama shares school plan. *Concord Monitor*.

Schuman, Michael A. (2008). *Barack Obama: "We are one people."* Berkeley Heights, NJ: Enslow Publishers.

Schuyler, George S. (1966). *Black and conservative: The autobiography of George S. Schuyler*. New York: Arlington House.

Scott, Janny (2007a, July 30). In Illinois, Obama proved pragmatic and shrewd. *The New York Times*.

Scott, Janny (2007b, December 28). A member of a new generation, Obama walks a fine line. *International Herald Tribune*.

Scott, Janny (2007c, October 30). Obama's account of New York years often differs from what others say. *The New York Times*.

Scott, Janny (2007d, September 9). In 2000, a streetwise veteran schooled a bold young Obama. *The New York Times*.

Scott, Janny (2008a, March 14). A free-spirited wanderer who set Obama's path. *The New York Times*.

Scott, Janny (2008b, May 18). The long run: The story of Obama, written by Obama. *The New York Times*, p. 1.

Secter, Bob & McCormick, John (2007, March 30). Barack Obama: Portrait of a pragmatist. *Chicago Tribune*, p. 1.

Seligman, Martin E. P. (1975). *Helplessness: On depression, development, and death*. San Francisco: W. H. Freeman; New York: Scribner.

Seligman, Martin E. P. (1991). *Learned optimism*. New York: Alfred A. Knopf.

Seligman, Martin E. P. (2002). *Authentic happiness: Using the new positive psychology to realize your potential for lasting fulfillment*. New York: Free Press.

Shachtman, Tom (2010). *Airlift to America: How Barack Obama, Sr., John F. Kennedy, Tom Mboya, and 800 East African students changed their world and ours*. New York: St. Martin's Press.

Sharma, Dinesh (2010). *Islam, multiculturalism, and the making of a global president*. Westport, CT: Praeger.

Sheridan, Michael & Baxter, Sarah (2007, January 28). Secrets of Obama family unlocked. *The Sunday Times*.

Sirvaitis, Karen (2010). *Barack Obama: A leader in a time of change*. Minneapolis, MN: Twenty-First Century Books.

Slevin, Peter (2006, December 17). Obama says he regrets land deal with fundraiser. *The Washington Post*.

Slevin, Peter (2007a, November 13). For Obama, a handsome payoff in political gambles. *The Washington Post*.

Slevin, Peter (2007b, February 9). Obama forged political mettle in Illinois capitol. *The Washington Post*.

Smith, Ben (2008, July 25). Israeli paper publishes Obama's wall note. *Politico.com.* http://www.politico.com/blogs/bensmith/0708/Obamas_note.html

Smith, David James (2008, March 23). The ascent of Barack Obama, Mr. Charisma: He has burst out of obscurity to make a bid for the White House. David James Smith traces the roots of Barack Obama's ambition. *The Sunday Times.*

Smolenyak, Megan (2010, February 20). Michelle Obama's roots: "Colored persons cohabiting . . . on 27th February, 1866." *The Huffington Post.*

Solomon, Deborah (2008, January 20). Questions for Maya Soetoro-Ng: All in the family. *The New York Times.*

Sorensen, Ted (2008). *Counselor: A life at the edge of history.* New York: Harper.

Souza, Peter (2008). *The rise of Barack Obama.* New York: Triumph Publishing.

Springen, Karen (2008, November 5). The view from Altgeld Gardens: At the Chicago apartment block where Obama worked as a community organizer, remembering a "God-sent" young man. *Newsweek.* http://www.newsweek.com/id/167634

Stern, Seth (2007, January 31). Obama-Schumer bill proposal would criminalize voter intimidation. *The New York Times.*

Stone, Geoffrey R. (2004). *Perilous times: Free speech in wartime from the Sedition Act of 1798 to the War on Terrorism.* New York: W. W. Norton.

Stone, Geoffrey R. (Ed.) (2006–2012). *Inalienable rights* (15 vols.). Oxford and New York: Oxford University Press.

Stone, Geoffrey R. (2007a). *Top secret: When our government keeps us in the dark.* Lanham, MD: Rowman & Littlefield.

Stone, Geoffrey R. (2007b). *War and liberty: An American dilemma.* New York: W. W. Norton.

Stone, Geoffrey R., Seidman, Louis M., Sunstein, Cass R., Tushnet, Mark V. & Karlan, Pamela S. (1986). *Constitutional law.* Boston: Little, Brown.

Street, Paul Louis (2009). *Barack Obama and the future of American politics.* Boulder, CO: Paradigm Publishers.

Strozier, Charles B. (1982). *Lincoln's quest for union: Public and private meanings.* New York: Basic Books.

Strozier, Charles B. (2001). *Lincoln's quest for union: A psychological portrait* (Philadelphia: Paul Dry Books.

Sugrue, Thomas J. (2010). *Not even past: Barack Obama and the burden of race.* The Lawrence Stone Lectures. Princeton, NJ: Princeton University Press.

Sullivan, Andrew (2008, June 5). No drama Obama. The daily dish. *Atlantic Monthly.*

Suryakusuma, Julia (2006, November 29). Obama for president . . . of Indonesia. *The Jakarta Post.*

Sutcliffe, Jane (2010). *Barack Obama.* Minneapolis, MN: Lerner Publishing.

Swarns, Rachel L. & Kantor, Jodi (2009, October 7). In first lady's roots, a complex path from slavery. *The New York Times.*

Sweet, Lynn (2007, February 20). Obama's research memo—on himself. *Chicago Sun-Times.*

Tani, Carlyn (2007). *A kid called Barry: Barack Obama '79*. Honolulu: Punahou School. http://www.punahou.edu/page.cfm?p=1715

Tapper, Jack (2007, March 30). Life of Obama's childhood friend takes drastically different path: Story of Keith Kakugawa provides interesting window into life of Obama. *ABC News*. http://abcnews.go.com/GMA/story?id= 2989722&page=1

Tarpley, Webster Griffin (2008a). *Barack H. Obama: The unauthorized biography* (Joseph Azar, Illustrator). Joshua Tree, CA: Progressive Press.

Tarpley, Webster Griffin (2008b). *Obama: The postmodern coup. Making of a Manchurian candidate*. Joshua Tree, CA: Progressive Press.

Tayler, Letta & Herbert, Keith (2008, March 2). Obama forged path as Chicago community organizer. *Newsday*, p. A6.

Thanawala, Sudhin (2008, August 3). Advice dissent. *Chicago Sun-Times*.

The Economist (2008, August 21). Barack Obama: Explaining the riddle. The man who has called himself "a blank screen" is about to take centre-stage. *The Economist*.

The Irish Times (2009, January 1). Facing the reality of deprivation. *The Irish Times*.

Thomas, Evan (2009). *A long time coming: The inspiring, combative 2008 campaign and the historic election of Barack Obama*. New York: PublicAffairs.

Thomas, Garen (2008). *Yes we can: A biography of Barack Obama*. New York: Feiwel and Friends.

Thompson, Paul (2009, October 16). Why do people hate you? Barack Obama stumped by 10-year-old's unsettling question. *London Evening Standard*. http://www.thisislondon.co.uk/standard/article-23757441-why-do-peo ple-hate-you-barack-obama-stumped-by-10-year-olds-unsettling-ques tion.do

Time (1966, October 28). Essay: What the Negro has—and has not—gained. *Time* http://www.time.com/time/magazine/article/0,9171,899347-1,00.html

Time (2010, March 22). Verbatim: John Roberts. *Time*.

Todd, Chuck & Sheldon Gawiser (with Ana Maria Arumi and G. Evans Witt) (2009). *How Barack Obama won: A state-by-state guide to the historic 2008 presidential election*. New York: Vintage Books.

Tomasky, Michael (2006, November 30). The phenomenon: Review of *The Audacity of Hope* by Barack Obama. *The New York Review of Books, 53*(19).

Tribe, Laurence Henry (1989, November). The curvature of constitutional space: What lawyers can learn from modern physics. *Harvard Law Review, 103*(1).

Tucker, Eric (2007, March 1). Family ties: Brown coach, Barack Obama. *ABC News*.

Tumulty, Karen (2007, May 29). Obama's campaign published a detailed health care reform plan in May 2007. Obama channels Hillary on health care. *Time*.

Tuttle, Kate (2003, January–February). Tribute: author, editor, activist Philippe Wamba, 1971–2002 [obituary]. *Black Issues Book Review*. http://findarti cles.com/p/articles/mi_m0HST/is_1_5/ai_96125997/

Uschan, Michael V. (2010). *Michelle Obama*. Detroit: Lucent Books.

Vogel, Joseph (2007). *The Obama movement: Why Barack Obama speaks to America's youth.* Lincoln, NE: iUniverse.

Volkan, Vamık D. & Itzkowitz, Norman (1984). *The immortal Atatürk: A psychobiography.* Chicago: University of Chicago Press.

Von Drehle, David (2008, August 21). The five faces of Barack Obama. *Time.*

Wagner, Erica (2009, January 20). Critique of Elizabeth Alexander's presidential poem. *Times Online.* http://www.timesonline.co.uk/tol/news/world/us_and_americas/us_elections/article5555612.ece

Wagner, Heather Lehr (2008). *Barack Obama.* New York: Chelsea House.

Walker, Clarence Earl & Smithers, Gregory D. (2009). *The preacher and the politician: Jeremiah Wright, Barack Obama, and race in America.* Charlottesville: University of Virginia Press.

Wallace-Wells, Benjamin (2007, April 1). Obama's narrator. *The New York Times Magazine.*

Wallace-Wells, Benjamin (2004, November). The great black hope: What's riding on Barack Obama? *Washington Monthly.*

Wallsten, Peter (2007, February 19). Fellow activists say Obama's memoir has too many I's. *Los Angeles Times.*

Walsh, Kenneth T. (2007, August 26). On the streets of Chicago, a candidate comes of age: As a community organizer, Obama was a pragmatic leader. *U.S. News and World Report.*

Walsh, Kenneth T. (2009, February 4). Obama's Daschle "mistake" damages the president: In interviews with several networks, Obama says he made a mistake in choosing Daschle. *U.S. News and World Report.*

Walton, Hanes, Jr., Allen, Josephine A.V., Puckett, Sherman & Deskins, Donald R., Jr. (Eds.) (2009). *Letters to President Obama: Americans share our hopes and dreams.* New York: Skyhorse Publishing.

Wamalwa, Chris (2006, September 2). Envoy hits at Obama over graft remark. *The Standard* (Nairobi).

Wamba, Philippe E. (1999). *Kinship: A family's journey in Africa and America.* New York: Dutton.

Washington, Laura (2007, January 1). Whites may embrace Obama, but do "regular black folks"? *Chicago Sun-Times.*

Watson, Paul (2007, March 15). As a child, Obama crossed a cultural divide in Indonesia. *Los Angeles Times.*

Watson, Robert P. (Ed.) (2009). *Michelle Obama: The report to the first lady.* Hauppauge, NY: Nova Publishers.

Weatherford, Carole Boston (2010a). *Obama: Only in America* (Robert Barrett, Illustrator). New York: Marshall Cavendish.

Weatherford, Carole Boston (2010b). *Michelle Obama: First mom.* New York: Marshall Cavendish.

Weir, Richard (2009, August 30). Funeral mass unites Pols. *Boston Herald.*

Weixel, Nathaniel (2007, November 15). Feingold, Obama go after corporate jet travel. *The Hill.*

Wenner, Jann (2008, July 10–24). A conversation with Barack Obama. *Rolling Stone*, nos. 1056–1057.

Wheeler, Jill C. (2009). *Barack Obama*. Edina, MN: ABDO Publishing.

Wheeler, Jill C. (2010). *Michelle Obama*. Edina, MN: ABDO Publishing.

White, Jesse (Ed.) (2000). *Illinois Blue Book, 2000, Millennium edition*. Springfield: Illinois Secretary of State.

White, Walter F. (1948). *A man called White: The autobiography of Walter White*. New York: Viking Press.

White, Walter F. (1949, August 30). Has science conquered the color line? *Look*. Reprinted in *Negro Digest*, December 1949.

Willis, Deborah & Bernard, Emily (2009). *Michelle Obama: The first lady in photographs*. New York: Norton.

Wills, Christopher (2007, October 24). Obama learned from failed Congress run. *USA Today*.

Wills, Christopher (2008, April 1). Obama's "godfather" an old-school Chicago politician. *Pantagraph.com*. http://www.pantagraph.com/news/article_6e8c6532-9b88-512c-820d-9d18072afe49.html

Wilson, John K. (2008). *Barack Obama: This improbable quest*. Boulder, CO: Paradigm Publishers.

Winnicott, Donald Woods (1953). Transitional objects and transitional phenomena: A study of the first not-me possession. *International Journal of Psycho-Analysis*, 34, 89–97. Reprinted in Winnicott, Donald Woods. (1987). *The child, the family, and the outside world*. Foreword by Marshall H. Klaus. Reading, MA: Addison-Wesley.

Winnicott, Donald Woods (1965). Ego Distortion in Terms of True and False Self. In Winnicott, Donald Woods, *The Maturational Precesses and the Facilitating Environment*. London: The Hogarth Press and the Institute of Psycho-Analysis.

Winnicott, Donald Woods (1971). *Playing and Reality*. London: Tavistock Publications.

Wise, Tim J. (2009). *Between Barack and a hard place: Racism and white denial in the age of Obama*. San Francisco: City Lights Books.

Wolffe, Richard L., Ramirez, Jessica & Bartholet, Jeffery (2008, March 31). When Barry became Barack: It didn't happen overnight. But in college, the young Barry took to being called by his formal name. What this evolution tells us about him. *Newsweek*. http://www.newsweek.com/2008/03/22/when-barry-became-barack.html

Wolffe, Richard L. (2009). *Renegade: The making of a president*. New York: Crown Publishers.

Wright, Jeremiah A., Jr. (1990). The audacity to hope. In Jeremiah Alvesta Wright, Jr., *What makes you so strong? Sermons of joy and strength from Jeremiah A. Wright, Jr.* (Jini Kilgore Ross, Ed.). Valley Forge, PA: Judson Press. (Reprinted from *Preaching Today*, 1990) http://www.preachingtoday.com/sermons/sermons/audacityofhope.html

Wright, Jeremiah A., Jr. (2003, April 13). *Confusing God and government*. Sermon delivered at Trinity United Church of Christ in Chicago. http://www.black past.org/?q=2008-rev-jeremiah-wright-confusing-god-and-government

Wright, Jeremiah Alvesta, Jr. (2008, March 27). *The day of Jerusalem's fall*. Excerpts from a sermon delivered at Trinity United Church of Christ in Chicago on September 16, 2001, transcribed by Kofi Khemet from an audio recording posted by Roland S. Martin. *The Guardian*. http://blakfacts.blogspot.com/2008/03/day-of-jerusalems-fall.html

Ybarra, Michael J. (1990, February 7). Activist in Chicago now heads Harvard Law Review. *Chicago Tribune*.

York, Byron (2008, June 30). What did Obama do as a community organizer? And is it really a qualification to be president? *National Review*.

Young, Andrew (2009, January 26). Barack Obama is a global citizen and an all-American boy. He defies categorization. *Time*. http://205.188.238.181/time/specials/packages/printout/0,29239,1871648_1871684_1871653,00.html

Young, Jeff C. (2009). *Michelle Obama*. Greensboro, NC: Morgan Reynolds.

Younge, Gary (2007, November 13). Obama: Black like me. *The Nation*.

Youngman, Sam & Blake, Aaron (2007, March 14). Obama's crime votes are fodder for rivals. *The Hill*.

Zeleny, Jeff (2005a, December 24). The first time around: Sen. Obama's freshman year. *Chicago Tribune*.

Zeleny, Jeff (2005b, September 12). Judicious Obama turns up volume. *Chicago Tribune*.

Zeleny, Jeff (2005c, June 26). When it comes to race, Obama makes his point—with subtlety. *Chicago Tribune*.

Zeleny, Jeff (2007, October 9). Obama proposes capping greenhouse gas emissions and making polluters pay. *The New York Times*.

Zeleny, Jeff (2008, April 17). Book sales lifted Obamas' income in 2007 to a total of $4.2 million. *The New York Times*.

Žižek, Slavoj (2008, September 2). The audacity of rhetoric. *In These Times*. http://www.inthesetimes.com/article/3862/

Zumbusch, Amelie von (2010a). *Barack Obama: Man of destiny*. New York: PowerKids Press.

Zumbusch, Amelie von (2010b). *First family: The Obamas in the White House*. New York: PowerKids Press.

Zumbusch, Amelie von (2010c). *Michelle Obama: Our first lady*. New York: PowerKids Press.

INDEX

ABOUT THE AUTHOR

DR. AVNER FALK is a U.S.-trained Israeli clinical psychologist. He was an active psychotherapist for three decades, and is now engaged in full-time scholarly activity. He was a senior and supervising clinical psychologist at several mental health centers in Jerusalem as well as a clinical lecturer in psychiatry at the Hebrew University Medical School. He is also an internationally known scholar who has published 10 books and dozens of articles in the interdisciplinary fields of psychohistory, psychobiography, psychogeography, political psychology, and other areas of applied psychoanalysis.